Success in

ELEMENTS OF

BANKING

FIFTH EDITION

Success Studybooks

Accounting and Costing
Accounting and Costing: Problems and Projects
Biology
Book-keeping and Accounts
British History 1760–1914
British History since 1914
Business Calculations
Chemistry
Commerce
Commerce: West African Edition
Communication
Economic Geography
Economics
Economics: West African Edition
Electronics
Elements of Banking
European History 1815–1941
Financial Accounting
Financial Accounting: Questions and Answers
Geography: Human and Regional
Geography: Physical and Mapwork
Information Processing
Insurance
Investment
Law
Management: Personnel
Mathematics
Nutrition
Office Practice
Organic Chemistry
Physics
Principles of Accounting
Principles of Accounting: Answer Book
Statistics
Twentieth Century World Affairs

Success in

ELEMENTS OF BANKING

FIFTH EDITION

David Cox, FCIB, FCCA
Senior Lecturer in Banking
Worcester Technical College

JOHN MURRAY

First published 1979
Reprinted 1981
Second edition 1983
Reprinted 1984, 1985
Third edition 1986
Fourth edition 1988
Fifth edition 1989

Printed and bound in Great Britain by
Richard Clay Ltd, Bungay, Suffolk.

British Library Cataloguing in Publication Data

Cox, David, *1946–*
    Success in elements of banking.—5th ed.—
    (Success studybooks)
    1. Great Britain. Banking
    332.1'0941

ISBN 0-7195-4702-4

Foreword
to Fifth Edition

Banking is a career which has become increasingly attractive to young people in recent years. It is a profession where there are excellent opportunities for promotion and where, from the beginning, employees are given every encouragement to follow part-time courses of study leading to higher levels of professional qualifications.

This book provides a self-contained course designed to give all students a thorough grounding in the main aspects of banking. It covers the historical background of the development of money and banking, and goes on to consider the present-day structure of banking in Britain, and the role of banks and the controls under which they operate. Important bank services are all described in detail, as are the various aspects of bank lending.

Success in Elements of Banking is suitable for The Chartered Institute of Banker's Banking Certificate papers 'The Business of Banking', 'Economics and the Banks' Role in the Economy' and 'Banking Operations I and II' and for its Foundation Course 'Elements of Banking' paper, as well as similar examinations of other Institutes of Bankers and colleges. It is also appropriate for students taking the units 'Elements of Banking 1 and 2' as part of a BTEC National Certificate or Diploma in Business Studies, for those working for professional examinations which contain a banking paper and for those following correspondence courses.

The questions set at the end of each Unit are designed either for self-testing or for use in class. Many are chosen from past papers set by The Institute of Bankers (before it became The Chartered Institute of Bankers in 1987). Teachers and students, particularly those following BTEC and Foundation Courses, will find the Assignments (pp. 366–82) will fully complement their own requirements, and provide valuable guidelines for individual work and research. Sets of multiple-choice questions have been included at intervals throughout the book—these provide a quick and easy method of testing progress. Many teachers now incorporate this type of assessment in the final examination.

For this fifth edition the text has been revised and tables and statistics have been updated. New diagrams and illustrations have been added where appropriate. However, banking is a continually changing subject and students should keep abreast of developments by reading articles in financial and professional newspapers and magazines and, of course, by noting new services introduced by the banks. The last ten years have seen more changes in banking than any other decade in the history of banking; this trend is likely to increase in the next ten years as the financial services revolution gathers momentum and the traditional roles of banks and other financial institutions are merged.

D. C.

Acknowledgments

In writing this book I have been helped by many people, especially those teachers, lecturers and professional bankers who appraised and criticized it at different stages. I am particularly grateful to Eric Glover, Peter Spiro, A. R. Rendel and John Mortimer of The Chartered Institute of Bankers; to Mike Fardon, Pamela and Stephen Green, Peter Gutmann, Leslie Harfield, Bill Harrison, Gerald Klein, Geoffrey Parkinson and Rod Winfield.

My thanks also go to Anne Webster, Bob Davenport and Flair Kennett of the Success Studybooks series, and to Jean Macqueen, Jean Cox and D. E. O. Cox.

The assistance of the following organizations is gratefully acknowledged: Access (the Joint Credit Card Company Limited) for permission to reproduce their Access card (p. 219); the Bank of England for permission to reproduce material taken from the Bank's *Quarterly Bulletin* and to reproduce a photograph of the Bank of England (p. 36) and a tender form (p. 73); Barclays Bank PLC for permission to reproduce photographs of the dealing room of Barclays de Zoete Wedd, London (p. 114), a bank branch interior (p. 147) and a Connect card (p. 174); the Central Statistical Office for permission to quote material from the *Annual Abstract of Statistics*, *Financial Statistics* and *Monthly Digest of Statistics*; the Controller of Her Majesty's Stationery Office for permission to reproduce a Treasury bill (p. 63), which is Crown copyright; the *Financial Times* for permission to quote share prices (p. 118); The Chartered Institute of Bankers for permission to use questions from past examination papers (some set by 'The Institute of Bankers', before its award of a Royal Charter in 1987); Lloyds Bank Plc for permission to reproduce their balance sheet (p. 79), specimen cheques (p. 170), bank giro credit slip (p. 171) and cheque card (p. 216); the London Chamber of Commerce and Industry for permission to use their certificate of origin (p. 251) taken from the Barclays Bank PLC booklet *Documentary Letters of Credit*; Midland Bank plc for permission to reproduce a sterling certificate of deposit (p. 287), their personal loan agreement form (p. 307) and a bill of lading form (p. 253); National Westminster Bank PLC for permission to reproduce their euro-cheque and eurocheque card (p. 218), photographs of their automated teller machines (p. 223) and a travellers' cheque (p. 225); the Simplification of International Trade Procedures Board (SITPRO) for permission to use their invoice (p. 250); the Solicitors' Law Stationery Society plc for permission to reproduce their bill of exchange form (p. 151); the Stock Exchange for permission to reproduce a photograph of the Stock Exchange building, London (p. 71) and a specimen share certificate (p. 115).

Cartoons were kindly provided by *Accountancy* (pp. 17, 52, 80, 112, 142, 187, 193, 210, 221, 226, 243 and 331); the Banking Information Service (p. 11); the *Journal of The Chartered Building Societies Institute* (pp. 102 and 228); and the *Journal of The Institute of Bankers*, now *Banking World* (pp. 4, 138, 144, 164, 202, 230, 235, 247, 310 and 324).

D. C.

Contents

The Business of Banking

1.1 What is a Bank?

If you mention a bank most people in England and Wales will think of the branches of Barclays, Lloyds, Midland and National Westminster—the 'big four' banks—or of the Royal Bank of Scotland, TSB or Girobank; all have branches on every High Street. Such banks are commonly known as either *clearing banks* or *retail banks*. Clearing banks take part in the clearing system through which many thousands of cheques and credits are 'cleared', or sorted, daily (see Unit 11.9); retail banks are those which have extensive branch networks—and also participate in the clearing system. The clearing banks, together with a range of more specialized banks such as merchant banks, foreign banks and savings banks, plus the central bank, the Bank of England, make up the varied structure of British banking. (The Bank of England—which, despite its name, controls all aspects of banking throughout the United Kingdom—and the present-day British banking structure are considered in Units 4 and 5 respectively.)

Banks operating in the United Kingdom must be recognized by the Bank of England (under the Banking Act 1987). Every bank performs three basic functions :

(i) it accepts and safeguards deposits of money from customers;

(ii) it permits money to be withdrawn or transferred from one account to another;

(iii) it lends the surplus of deposited money to suitable customers who wish to borrow.

The word that is common to these functions is *money*, and the development of money is discussed in Unit 2.

1.2 Responsibilities of Banks

A sound banking system depends partly on the control exercised by the central bank and, to a large extent, on trust: that is, the customer's trust that his deposits will be looked after in the best possible way and that when he wishes to withdraw his money, the funds will be available. The banks have a major responsibility to behave like good citizens in business: while profitability remains a major consideration, this must sometimes be set aside in favour of an informed and ethical judgement that takes account of the interests of others. In Britain in the early 1970s, for instance, some banks made errors of judgement in lending too much to certain sectors of the business community, notably in the property market. Several of the smaller banks would have failed if it had not been for assistance organized by the Bank of England, funded mainly by the clearing banks. In 1984, the Bank of England stepped in to rescue a bank that was facing difficulties. More recently, the banks have had problems with their lending to third-world countries, and large amounts have had to be set aside as provisions for bad debts.

Whenever banks lend money they must remember that the source of their funds is customers' deposits, and so it is important that they should lend where there is a minimal risk of non-repayment. They have often been criticized for not lending more freely, but a high risk of loss will frequently deter them from granting an advance even if the highest rates of interest could be charged.

1.3   The Role of the Banks

In Unit 1.1 we saw that the basic functions of any bank are to accept, safeguard and lend the surplus funds of its customers while permitting the withdrawal of funds, or their transfer from one account to another. Nowadays, the banks have come a long way from their origins in the London goldsmiths of the late seventeenth century (see Unit 3.1), and while some specialize in meeting the needs of particular groups of customers, such as companies or small savers, the clearing banks provide a range of services to satisfy the financial needs of all types of customer, from the smallest personal account holder to the largest company. These services can be grouped under the following headings:

   (i) deposits and savings;
   (ii) advances;
  (iii) money transmission;
  (iv) financial and advisory services;
   (v) foreign services.

We shall consider the scope of these services briefly, one by one, though each is dealt with in greater detail later in this book.

(i) **Deposits** are the funds that customers leave in their accounts, whether these are current accounts, which are for 'current' money that is not intended to be saved, or deposit or savings accounts which are for money that will not be required immediately. Customers with a current account are usually issued with a cheque book which enables them to *draw* or write out cheques that instruct the bank to pay cash from the account or to make payments to other people. Deposit and savings account holders do not have the benefits of a cheque book; instead they are paid interest on monies left with the bank.

(ii) **Advances** are the monies lent by a bank, generally in the form of an *overdraft* on a current account, by which the customer draws out more money than he has put into the account. They may also be made by means of a *loan* or *personal loan*. Interest is charged on all advances, the rate varying with the method of granting the advance, the creditworthiness of the customer and the length of time for which the funds are borrowed. Advances represent that part of customers' deposits which the bank considers may safely be lent, while the remainder is retained in the form of cash and other assets.

(iii) **Money transmission** enables customers to make payments without having to carry around large sums of cash, because the cheque is a convenient method of settling a debt. Equally a customer can pay in money at any bank branch for the credit of an account at another branch by completing a simple form known as a *bank giro credit*. He may also instruct his bank to *debit* or deduct amounts from his account to make regular payments to meet recurring debts, such as club subscriptions, life assurance premiums or mortgage repayments, by means of the *standing order* or *direct debit* systems (see Unit 12).

Besides enabling customers and, to some extent, non-customers to transfer funds quickly and easily by means of a piece of paper or electronically, the banks physically move many thousands of pounds worth of notes and coin from branch to branch each day. This is to ensure that branches which regularly pay out more notes and coin than they receive will never be short of cash. For instance, some denominations of coin are in constant demand by shopkeepers, and other coins are needed by private customers for gas and electricity meters. So some branches, particularly those where gas and electricity boards and bus companies pay in, regularly have surpluses of coin needing to be transported to other branches that have a deficit.

(iv) **Financial and advisory services** cover a wide range of facilities that can be tailored to suit the individual needs of the customer. Financial services vary. One is the *cheque guarantee card* for personal customers, which can be used to guarantee or 'back up' a cheque when paying for goods in a shop or drawing cash at branches other than that at which the account is maintained. Another might be a business service such as *factoring*, in which the bank administers a client's sales ledger and enables a company to obtain an advance against debts which are due to it. The banks are always willing to give advice, from suggesting suitable investments to a customer with a few hundred pounds, to advising a private limited company of the best time to 'go public', that is, to have its shares quoted on a stock exchange. These services are discussed more fully in Units 15 and 16.

(v) **Foreign services** of the banks include travellers' cheque and currency services; they also make international payments. All large banks have links with overseas banking groups, so payments of this kind can easily be made. Some banks have linked more formally with a number of overseas banks to form consortia which are able to provide large-scale finance to suit the needs of multinational corporations. Foreign banking services are discussed more fully in Units 12 and 17.

1.4   The Economic Importance of Banks

Britain has a highly developed banking and financial system: over 75 per cent of the adult population have a bank account of some kind. The most popular bank account is the *current account*, and nearly 65 per cent of adults have such an account. The London clearing banks have between them some 11 000 branches, mainly in England and Wales, while in other parts of the United Kingdom branch networks are maintained by the Scottish clearing banks and the Northern Ireland banks. The result is that almost anywhere in Britain it is difficult to be more than a few miles from a bank. A developed banking system permits payments by one person to another to be made safely at reasonable cost both in Britain and overseas. The payments mechanism enables trade and industry to function more efficiently and the role of the banks in financing international trade is a considerable contribution to the economy of Britain.

The banks are important economically because they act as *financial inter-mediaries* between the large number of depositors and those who wish to borrow: in this way they encourage savings by providing the means of attracting and collecting funds through the various types of accounts they offer and their extensive branch network, while at the same time they put such funds to effective use. In June 1988 their total deposits in sterling amounted to £351 920 million, and their sterling advances to customers to £225 003 million,

'No, you tell them the Board has refused the loan, and I'll keep the engine running'

much of this being lent to help finance the commerce and industry that is so important to a trading and manufacturing nation such as Britain. The provision of finance to businesses encourages enterprise and leads to the provision of extra jobs, increased production and less reliance on the import of foreign goods. Lending to personal customers, on the other hand, stimulates demand for goods which again helps to increase production. The banks are able to 'create' money by granting loan or overdraft facilities to a customer to buy goods, since paying for these goods effectively produces new money as soon as the borrower's cheque is paid into the seller's bank account. Thus by allowing an advance, a bank deposit has been created; this process is known as the *credit-creation multiplier* (see Unit 2.10).

During the nineteenth century, London developed into a major financial centre of the world, and today still plays an important part in the provision of world-wide financial services. All major world banks are represented in London and in few other cities is it possible to find such a wealth of expertise. British banking, by providing services overseas and to overseas customers, contributes greatly to the nation's balance of payments (the account which records imports and exports of Britain in money terms). Banking and other financial services provided by the City of London are known as *invisible exports* because they are services rather than tangible goods. Each year banking institutions contribute several billions of pounds to the nation's invisible earnings.

Everybody in Britain is affected by the work of the banks, whether as a personal deposit customer, as a borrower or simply in working for a business that benefits from a bank advance and the expertise of British banking services. It follows that, with such an important role in the economy, there should be adequate supervision and control of the banking system and this is provided by the central bank, the Bank of England, which is considered in detail in Unit 4.

1.5 Electronic Banking

Banks in Britain have always been widespread users of the very latest in technology. Even by the time of the First World War the quill pen and handwritten ledger were being replaced by mechanical accounting machines, although certain types of accounts continued to be handwritten until the introduction of computers. The banks started to use computers in their accounting operations during the 1960s and, by the early 1970s, most branches were 'on-line' to a central computer. The 1970s and 1980s have seen an increasing use of technology, with automation moving from behind the scenes to the 'front of the office' where it involves the customer. Automated teller machines (ATMs)—see Unit 15.5—have become more common, while cashiers are now often provided with their own terminals, linked directly to their bank's computer system.

As we move towards the last decade of the twentieth century we shall see an increasing use of automated systems both for the processing of cheques and other debit items, and for credits. There will be an expansion of the Clearing House Automated Payments System (CHAPS) to provide bank branches throughout Britain with access to a service for the same-day clearance of payments (see Unit 11.9) while for the transfer of funds from one country to another, increasing use will be made of the computer-based network known as SWIFT (the Society for Worldwide Interbank Financial Telecommunication)—see Unit 12.10. The advancement of technology not only enables larger networks such as clearing systems, CHAPS and SWIFT to be constructed, but also facilitates smaller systems based on microcomputers. Branch managers and staff at regional and head offices now have increasing access to customer information—for example, details of customers' names, addresses, accounting transactions and securities held are widely available through microcomputers.

The services offered by automated teller machines are becoming more sophisticated and besides dispensing cash they can handle routine enquiries, statement provision, cheque book ordering and account-to-account transfers. While the so-called 'cashless society' may still be a long way off, retailers' use of electronic funds transfer at point of sale (EFTPOS) terminals is advancing rapidly (see Unit 12.6). The provision of banking services that make use of computer terminals is extending to the offices of business customers and to the homes of personal customers, using telephone lines to link the customers to the banks' computers (see Units 16.3(h) and 15.6).

Banking is undoubtedly an ever-changing subject and, as technology advances, so the banks will use automation to provide an efficient service, as cheaply as possible, to their millions of customers.

1.6   The Financial Services Revolution

While the 1980s have seen dramatic changes in the uses of electronic technology in banking, they have also seen a revolution in the provision of financial services. The increasing—and sometimes bewildering—range of services offered by financial institutions shows no sign of slowing down. Traditional roles are rapidly changing:

banks offer mortgages;
building societies offer banking services;
retailers offer credit cards;
new standards of personal service are offered by smaller banking groups;
banks buy stockbroking firms;
the Stock Exchange roles of stockbroker and stockjobber merge;
the discount market takes on new functions;
new markets emerge, for instance, the London International Financial Futures Exchange.

The pace of change in financial services has never been greater than during the late 1980s. It is certain to continue as, thanks to electronic banking, customers' needs become more and more sophisticated and higher standards of service are required.

1.7 Questions

1. What are the basic functions of any bank?

2. How does a sound banking system contribute to the prosperity of a country?
   (*The Institute of Bankers*)

3. What are the main services provided by the banks?

4. What is meant by 'deposit banking', and in what ways does it contribute to the expansion of trade and industry?
   (*The Institute of Bankers*)

5. The activities of the banking sector impinge on all our lives. Briefly outline these activities and show how they affect us.
   (*The Chartered Institute of Bankers*)

Unit Two
The Development of Money

2.1 A Definition of Money

We saw in Unit 1.1 that *money* is the word common to all the basic functions of a bank. Money can be defined as *anything which passes freely from hand to hand and is generally acceptable in the settlement of a debt.* Although most countries now use a system of banknotes and coins, many different commodities have been used as money by people in various parts of the world and at various times in history: precious metals such as gold and silver, base metals such as iron, beads, stones, seashells and paper, while even cigarettes, soap and chocolate were used in Austria and Germany during and after the Second World War. All of these, at the time of their use as money, passed freely from hand to hand and were generally acceptable in the settlement of a debt.

We are all pleased to receive money as a birthday present and expect to be paid a sum of money at the end of a week's or month's work. This is not because we like the pictures on the banknotes or the colour of the coins: money by itself gives us no benefit—only by spending it can we obtain the things we want. Without some form of money in circulation, the range of goods and services available to us would be considerably reduced and business transactions would be difficult to carry out.

2.2 The Development of the Money System

Although we should find it difficult to manage without money nowadays, people once used to get by without it. The present system, with notes and coins as money, has been arrived at in three distinct stages.

(a) Direct Production
This means obtaining or making all the goods you need entirely by yourself without help from others. This was the way in which people lived in Britain right up to the end of the Old Stone Age around 3000 BC; during this period each man and his family unit were completely independent of others. Everything that was needed had to be made or obtained by the family: if they were hungry, they had to go out and catch food; if they wanted somewhere to live, they had to build it themselves. In our technological society, direct production of all goods is wholly impracticable: think how difficult it would be if you had to make your own transistor radio or your own clothes and shoes.

(b) Indirect Production using Barter as the Medium of Exchange

Indirect production means producing goods for others as well as for yourself. It develops when a man has more than enough goods for his own family and decides to barter or exchange his surplus with someone who has other goods available. For example, a man who is skilled at fishing but poor at catching rabbits can exchange his surplus fish with a man who is a clever rabbit-catcher but an incompetent fisherman. With indirect production goods are exchanged for other goods—an arrangement that was common throughout Britain from the beginning of the New Stone Age (about 3000 BC) until the arrival of the Romans in AD 43.

There are several drawbacks to barter:

(i) **Double coincidence of wants.** This is the problem of finding someone who wants what you have on offer *and* who also has available what you want. The fisherman seeking a change of diet might try to find someone with eggs to offer, but having found such a person he might be disappointed to learn that he isn't anxious to exchange his eggs for fish but instead wants some cooking pots.

(ii) **Exchange rates.** The difficulty here is in fixing the relative values of the two commodities being bartered: for example, how many fish is one rabbit worth?

(iii) **Giving change.** With small items like fish and rabbits, this is not much of a problem. However, imagine a man who, having worked for days making a table, now wants a rabbit for his dinner. He realizes that his table is going to be worth a considerable number of rabbits but, if he only wants one, what will the rabbit-catcher give him for 'change'? It is rather like going into a baker's shop for a loaf of bread with only a £10 note, and finding that the baker can't give you change in the form of money and you have to take the 'change' in extra bread and cakes!

Thus bartering makes it possible for a person to obtain the goods or services that he has not the skill or the time to produce for himself, but it is beset with problems and is a slow and inefficient way of trading.

(c) Indirect Production using Money as a Medium of Exchange

This is the stage of monetary development that we have now reached in Britain and in all other developed countries; in this system money overcomes the problems inherent in barter, and acts as the medium of exchange. In these countries indirect production is carried to a high degree so that people specialize in their own jobs. The economist Adam Smith in his book *The Wealth of Nations*, which was published in 1776, pointed out the benefits of specialization and the division of a production process into separate tasks each performed by a different person. A modern factory is an example of this: as the item being manufactured passes along the production line, each worker in turn adds the parts or performs the tasks that are his contribution to the finished product. This specialization and division of labour is a part of almost everybody's experience, whether or not he works in a factory: bank clerks, doctors, nurses, teachers, secretaries and shop assistants are all specialists in their own particular skills and make their own contributions to trade and society.

In return for doing our specialist jobs, we each receive money at the end of the week or month. Some people are paid in cash, but many of us have our earnings paid direct into our bank accounts: we then withdraw whatever we require in the form of cash or we can write cheques in favour of those to whom we owe money. When we pay for goods and services, money acts as the medium of exchange: just as we are prepared to accept money in exchange for our work, a shopkeeper is prepared to accept it in payment for goods.

2.3   Functions of Money

Whether it is in the form of shells or sovereigns, iron bars or paper banknotes, coins or bank deposits, the functions of money are the same.

(a)   A Medium of Exchange
Money forms the intermediary in a trading transaction. If we want to sell something, we are prepared to accept money from the buyer; if we want to buy, we know that the seller will accept money in payment.

(b)   A Unit of Account
This function of money enables prices to be directly compared. One of the problems of the barter system lies in the agreement of a rate of exchange between commodities: how many fish is one rabbit worth, or how many rabbits should be paid for a cooking pot? When all rates of exchange have a common denominator—money—it is easy to compare the prices of different commodities.

A unit of account also enables us to keep accounting records, such as bank statements, invoices and ledgers, by using money amounts.

(c)   A Store of Value
Money should, ideally, remain reasonably stable in value so that if we save we know that, when we come to spend our savings, we can buy a similar amount of goods as we could have done at the time when we put the savings aside. In times of inflation, money does not perform this function very well. For example, something that could have been bought for £1 in Britain in 1946 would cost £14 in 1989.

For money to be a store of value it is not necessary for it to be valuable in itself; the fact that money does buy, and will buy in the future, a certain quantity of goods means that it fulfils this function. A Bank of England £5 note by itself has little value—it is only a piece of printed paper—but provided there are goods to purchase in the future, it acts as a store of value.

(d) A Standard for Deferred Payments

Money acts as the measure in which deferred or future payments are to be made. For example, a bank loan agreement states that the borrower will repay a certain amount of money each month for a number of months: these deferred payments, to be received by the bank in the future, are stated in terms of money.

2.4 The Qualities of Money

In order to perform the functions of money satisfactorily, the money in use must have certain qualities.

(a) Acceptability

This is the most important quality of money: people must be prepared to accept the money in use. Otherwise it will cease to be regarded as money, and either the barter system will return, or some other acceptable commodity will take over as money.

(b) Cognizability

To assist in acceptability, money should be cognizable—that is, people should recognize it easily as the money in use.

(c) Divisibility

As we said in Unit 2.2, one of the drawbacks of the barter system was the difficulty of giving change. As an aid to acceptability, money should be easily divisible with a range of denominations in issue to ensure that goods of different prices can be purchased with the exact money or that change can easily be given where money of a higher denomination is offered.

(d) Durability
It is a help if the money in circulation is durable—that is, it should last for a reasonable time without deterioration. If dead rabbits were acceptable as money they would soon start to go bad and there wouldn't be much incentive to save. In Britain, banknotes have an average life of about twelve months and coins usually last about twenty years.

(e) Portability
Money should be easy to carry in both large and small amounts. If blocks of granite were used as money, you would find it difficult to carry your life savings with you and such a currency would soon be replaced by something more portable.

(f) Scarcity
To be generally acceptable, the supply of money must be restricted. If money consisted of stones picked up from the ground or shells washed up on the seashore, the supply would be relatively unlimited and people would not be prepared to accept them in exchange for goods. For many years, precious metals such as gold and silver were used to make coins and because such metals were relatively scarce the supply of money could not increase suddenly. Nowadays most coins are tokens that are worth less as metal than as coins, while for larger denominations we use paper banknotes that are intrinsically almost worthless. However, the quality of scarcity is maintained because the money stock is controlled by the government and the central bank of the country. In Britain the Treasury (the Government department concerned with finance) and the Bank of England exercise these controls.

(g) Homogeneity
This means that every coin or note has the same buying power and is identical in all respects to every other coin or note of the same denomination. A coin that was minted ten years ago, when it would have bought more than it can today because of the effects of inflation, nevertheless has the same buying power now as a brand-new coin of the same denomination. Equally one new ten-pence piece buys the same amount of goods and services as any other, and all ten-pence pieces look alike, weigh the same and are just the same size.

2.5   A History of Coins in Britain

In Britain coins can be traced back to the first century BC when iron bars were used as currency in the Midlands and south-west, while at the same time some gold and silver coins imported from Gaul (northern France) were also circulating alongside the iron bars in the south. The first true coins to be minted in Britain were crudely made from copper and tin and were in use during the half-century before the arrival of the Romans. When the Romans arrived in AD 43 they brought with them their own coins, which were usually made of silver, and gradually the iron bars and the old copper and tin coins went out of circulation. During the third century AD the Romans started to mint their own coins in London.

Following the departure of the Romans in AD 410, many people in Britain must have reverted to barter for a time. The minting of coins was restarted during a time of prosperity in the Anglo-Saxon period when the local rulers in each area minted their own silver coins. During the reign of Offa, king of Mercia, in the eighth century, a coinage was introduced based on a pound weight of silver. The Latin words for pound by weight were *libra pondo*, hence our present word 'pound'; from this weight of silver 240 coins were made named 'denarii' after a Roman coin of similar value. Until the end of the thirteenth century the denarius (or penny as it later became known) was virtually the only coin in circulation in Britain. William the Conqueror continued the development of the silver coinage by introducing a new silver standard, known as *sterling silver*, which had 925 parts of pure silver in every 1 000. This standard was to remain in use almost continuously up to 1920.

The Norman kings established the pounds, shillings and pence system which was to remain unchanged until the decimalization of the British currency in 1971. The Normans used the Roman system of accounting with the *libra* (one pound weight of silver) as the major unit of currency. The *libra* was divided into twenty *solidi* (later to become the shilling), and these were further subdivided into twelve *denarii* (pennies). This currency was based on the weight of silver and it was not until the thirteenth and fourteenth centuries that gold coins started to reappear.

Henry VII introduced the gold sovereign in 1489, with a money value of one pound—the first time that a pound coin had been issued. By 1504, he had also introduced the silver shilling, which remains in circulation today as a cupro-nickel five-pence piece. During the reign of Charles II the silver penny was withdrawn and copper coins were introduced (in 1672). One of the problems of gold and silver coins was the ease with which unscrupulous people could 'clip' scraps of the precious metal from their edges, a difficulty that was overcome when Charles II introduced a machine designed by a Frenchman to manufacture coins with milled edges. Even today the British cupro-nickel five- and ten-pence and £1 coins retain the milled edge.

Gold and silver coins circulated in Britain for hundreds of years and silver continued to be used in the coinage until 1947. The silver standard, with the *pound 'sterling'* based on one pound weight of silver, continued until the recoinage of 1816 when the country 'went on to the gold standard', that is, the currency became linked to the price of gold and all banknotes could be exchanged for gold (see Unit 2.7). Since 1947, coins in circulation in Britain have had no precious metal content, and their metal content is worth less than their face value.

The Royal Mint, which is under the control of the Chancellor of the Exchequer, manufactures coins for use in Britain and other countries. The metal is purchased in the market and British coins are sold at face value to the banks, which arrange distribution to their branches. As most coins are token coins the Royal Mint makes a considerable profit each year, and this passes to the Government.

2.6   A History of Banknotes in Britain

The history of the banknote is bound up with the development of the banking system in Britain. Here we are concerned only with the banknote itself; Unit 3 deals in detail with the history of banking systems.

From Roman times onwards, coins were the only form of money in Britain until the second half of the seventeenth century, when London goldsmiths started to hold gold and silver coins for safe-keeping on behalf of their clients. In exchange for these coins they would issue receipts promising to repay the amount deposited on demand. As the goldsmiths were well-known and trusted, their promissory notes soon began to circulate among merchants as a form of currency in the settlement of debts. To encourage this the goldsmiths began issuing their receipts in convenient denominations, such as £10 and £50, and made them payable to bearer rather than to a named individual—this helped to make them more easily transferable. In 1694 the Bank of England was founded and, from the start, had the right to issue notes (see Unit 4).

Outside London there were few goldsmiths, and banking and banknotes were slower to develop. During the eighteenth and early nineteenth centuries, however, wealthy industrialists and merchants in most parts of the country formed a large number of small private banks. Nearly all of these banks issued their own notes which circulated freely in their respective localities.

A series of Acts of Parliament in the nineteenth century gradually established the monopoly of the note issue in England and Wales in the hands of the Bank of England. The most important of these, the Bank Charter Act of 1844, was to extinguish the note issues of the private banks as they went bankrupt or merged with the developing joint-stock banks, which have become the present-day clearing banks. The monopoly of the note issue in England and Wales was not achieved until 1921 when the last private bank with its own note issue (Fox, Fowler & Company of Wellington in Somerset) was absorbed by Lloyds Bank.

A further provision of the 1844 Bank Charter Act gave the Bank of England the authority to make a *fiduciary issue* of banknotes. A fiduciary issue (or *trust issue*) is backed solely by Government securities and not by gold and silver. The Act permitted the Bank of England to make a fiduciary issue of £14 million, with every note issued above this amount being backed pound for pound by gold and silver held in the vaults. The issue was to be increased by two-thirds of the amount of the note issue of any private bank that merged with a joint-stock bank or went bankrupt.

The fiduciary issue has increased greatly over the years, largely as a result of two World Wars and the general inflationary trend. In 1939, at the outbreak of the Second World War, the remaining stock of gold backing the note issue was transferred to pay for imports and since that date there has been no gold backing the note issue; that is, it has all been a fiduciary issue backed entirely by Government securities. From £14 million in 1844, the fiduciary issue had increased to nearly £15 000 million by October 1988. Under the Currency Act 1983, the Treasury has the power to vary the level of the fiduciary issue at its discretion. Nowadays, the amount of notes in circulation depends in practice on public demand: the Treasury and the Bank of England are less concerned with the value of notes in circulation than with controlling the growth of the money stock (see Unit 2.8).

Table 2.1   Notes and coins circulating in Britain (£ million)

Date	Total	Bank of England	Scottish clearing banks	Northern Ireland banks	Estimated coin	Held by banks	Estimated circulation outside banks
December 1978	10 349	9 306	424	49	570	1 458	8 891
December 1982	12 774	11 271	591	89	823	1 586	11 188
May 1985	14 375	12 106	930		1 339	1 934	12 441
May 1987	15 747	12 941	1 103		1 703	2 349	13 398
May 1988	16 651	13 642	1 241		1 768	2 555	14 096

Source: *Monthly Digest of Statistics*, Central Statistical Office

In Scotland, the Bank of England's monopoly of the note issue did not apply, and there were no restrictions at first on the growth of joint-stock banking as there were in England and Wales (see Unit 3.2). Such banks developed early and each issued its own notes. In 1845, an Act of Parliament was passed regulating Scottish note issues: no new note-issuing banks were to be allowed and a fixed fiduciary issue was imposed on the nineteen issuing banks already in existence. Amalgamations have reduced the number of Scottish banks retaining their own note issue, and now only three remain: the Bank of Scotland, the Clydesdale Bank and the Royal Bank of Scotland. Nowadays the note issues of the Scottish banks are comparatively small and, apart from the fiduciary issue, are largely backed by holdings of Bank of England notes. A similar scheme operates in Northern Ireland where a few banks also retain the right to issue their own notes. Table 2.1 compares the currency circulation of Bank of England notes with those issued by the Scottish and Northern Ireland banks.

2.7   The Gold Standard

When Britain went on to the gold standard in 1816, the gold sovereign became the legal standard coin. When countries were on the gold standard the currency was worth a fixed amount of gold, and banknotes could be exchanged for the gold at which they were valued. In Britain the Mint price of gold was fixed at £3. 17s. 10½d. (£3.89) per standard ounce, eleven-twelfths fine (this means a purity of eleven parts of pure gold in every twelve parts of metal).

The convertibility of banknotes into gold continued almost without a break until it was suspended at the outbreak of the First World War in 1914, when gold sovereigns were withdrawn from circulation and replaced by special bank notes issued by the Treasury which circulated alongside Bank of England notes.

The gold standard remained suspended until 1925 when the gold bullion standard was introduced. This was different from the gold standard in that individual banknotes were not convertible, but gold bullion (the metal in the form of bars) was obtainable at the Bank of England in a minimum quantity of a 400-ounce bar at a cost of approximately £1 500, so that the currency was still technically convertible into gold. Naturally, few people took advantage of this arrangement; it was abandoned in 1931 and the currency has been inconvertible ever since. After their withdrawal in 1914, gold coins were never re-introduced for use in Britain.

2.8   The Money Stock

The growth of the fiduciary issue in Britain from £14 million to nearly £15 000 million by October 1988 does not reflect the even bigger increase in the growth of bank deposits. (Bank deposits are also referred to as *financial assets*, because they are financial claims on banks.) We use notes and coins to pay bills and make purchases: these obviously form part of the money stock. We also use cheques to make payments: cheques are not money in themselves but are a claim on the money in a bank account and are often accepted as a means of payment. Therefore, when calculations are made about the size of the stock of money in a country, the balances of bank current accounts are included. A further widening of the calculation of the money stock also includes other items, such as the balances of deposit accounts, that are not generally accepted as money in the narrow sense of being a medium of exchange, because they are subject to a period of notice of withdrawal. These are included because they affect the growth of bank lending and credit creation (see Unit 2.10).

A bewildering number of definitions of the money stock are in use in Britain—official statistics are published for M0, M1, M2, M3, M3c, M4

'It's not so much the money supply that worries me—it's the credit card supply'

and M5. Definitions for M0, M1 and M3 are given below, while M2 is considered in Unit 2.9 (The whole topic of the various methods of measuring the money supply and techniques of monetary policy is dealt with fully in Unit 18.)

(i) M0 ('M nought') consists of notes and coin in circulation with the public, plus banks' till money, plus banks' operational balances with the Bank of England. (Till money is cash held by the banks to meet day-to-day needs; operational balances with the Bank of England are held to cover day-to-day transactions, that is, banks' current accounts with the Bank of England, although banks' cash ratio deposits—see Unit 7.2(*a*)—are excluded.) M0 is referred to as the narrow definition of the money stock.

(ii) M1 consists of notes and coin in circulation with the public, plus sterling sight bank deposits held by the United Kingdom private sector. (*Sight bank deposits* are funds available on demand, such as bank current account balances, and money placed overnight; the *private sector* means individuals, companies and institutions not owned by the state; the *public sector* includes all Government departments and state-owned corporations.)

(iii) M3 is a broad definition of the money stock and consists of

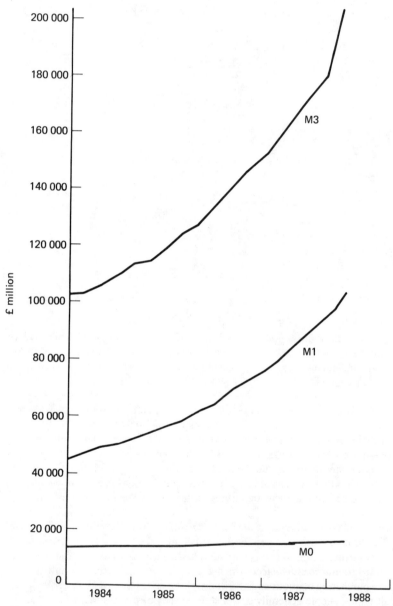

Fig. 2.1   Money stock: amounts outstanding, seasonally adjusted (from data given in the Bank of England Quarterly Bulletin)

notes and coin in circulation with the public together with all sterling bank deposits (including certificates of deposit) held by United Kingdom residents in the private sector. (*Certificates of deposit* are a special type of long-term bank deposit and are discussed in Unit 7.2(g).)

In the definitions of M1 and M3 the deposits considered are confined to those held with institutions included in the United Kingdom monetary sector (fully defined in Unit 4.11, but consisting principally of the banks and other authorized institutions). Sixty per cent of the net value of sterling transit items (cheques and credits passing through the bank clearing system) is deducted. Fig. 2.1 shows the growth of M0, M1 and M3 from 1984 to 1988.

2.9   Near-money

We have seen in Unit 2.8 that M1 consists of notes and coin in circulation with the public plus sterling sight bank deposits held by the United Kingdom private sector. Clearly notes and coin are part of the money supply and, for most purposes, cheques are an acceptable means of payment. However, under certain circumstances, cheques are not as acceptable as notes and coin—try paying for a daily newspaper with a cheque. Nevertheless, a cheque is generally accepted in settlement of a debt and therefore sight deposits can be included as part of the money stock.

Certain types of financial assets function more as a store of value than as a medium of exchange and these are known as *near-money* (or quasi-money). The broad definition of the money stock, M3, includes a type of near-money found in the monetary (banking) sector, that is, deposits subject to notice of withdrawal. Most bank deposits accounts are subject to a minimum notice of withdrawal of seven days but, in practice, cash can usually be withdrawn on demand, although this may result in the holder being subject to a loss of interest for the notice period. Clearly other types of financial assets, such as the balances of accounts held with building societies and the National Savings Bank, can be included under the heading of near-money, as funds can be withdrawn with similar ease. (These types of near money are included in the wider definitions of the money stock, M4 and M5—see Unit 18.2.) Note that all these types of near-money are held more with a view to earning interest (a store of value) than as a medium of exchange; the opposite is true of a bank current account. Near-money has the two characteristics of *liquidity* and the *need for conversion* into 'true' money before it is available for spending.

A further definition of the money stock, M2, is used to include what are called *transactions balances*—that is, balances which are likely to be used in the purchasing of goods and services rather than for investment purposes. For example, people generally consider money in most types of building society account as being immediately available to buy goods, instead of holding it solely for investment purposes. Thus M2 comprises notes and coin in circulation with the public, plus sterling retail deposits held by the United Kingdom private sector with the United Kingdom monetary sector, with building societies and in National Savings Bank ordinary accounts. As with M1 and M3, 60 per cent of the net value of sterling transit items is deducted. The criteria used to identify retail deposits include consideration of the maturity (date of payment), which will be relatively short, the size of deposits (to exclude large 'wholesale' or investment funds) and the type of account (so as to include those accounts from which funds can be transferred to third parties or withdrawn at relatively short notice).

2.10   How the Banks 'Create' Money

In June 1988 notes and coin estimated to be in circulation with the public in Britain totalled £13 840 million, M1 was £101 091 million and M3 was £202 212 million. Thus the money stock definitions of M1 and M3 greatly exceed the value of notes and coin in circulation.

This happens because of the way in which the banks are able to create money in the form of bank deposits. It has been said that every bank loan creates a bank deposit. Whenever overdraft or loan facilities are granted by a bank, the customer will have a reason for wishing to borrow—to buy a new car, perhaps—and will draw a cheque on his or her account to pay for it. The cheque will be paid into another bank account (that of the garage selling the car) thus creating a new deposit and, when it has passed through the clearing system, will take up the facilities granted by the bank. Therefore by granting a loan or an overdraft, a new deposit has been created somewhere in the banking system and the money stock increased.

The banks generally lend between 65 and 75 per cent of their total deposits, the remainder being held in the form of easily realizable assets so that the banks will always have sufficient resources to enable them to repay their depositors. Every loan creates a new deposit, and a proportion of every new deposit may be re-lent to create still further deposits. This process can continue until the total of the new deposits created is several times the amount of the original advance.

An example will show just how this process works. Bank A grants its customer, M, an overdraft of £500 to buy some new furniture. M writes out a cheque and hands it to the seller of the furniture, N, who pays it into his account with bank B. This bank keeps 35 per cent of the deposit as reserves and re-lends the other 65 per cent, £325, to customer O to pay for his holiday. O gives a cheque for this amount to the travel agent P, who pays it into his account with bank C. This bank lends 65 per cent of the deposit, £211, to customer Q, who issues a cheque for this amount, which creates another deposit within the banking system, and so the process goes on (see Fig. 2.2).

The amount by which the banks can create further bank deposits, and thus increase the money stock, is measured by the *credit-creation multiplier*. From Fig. 2.2 it can be calculated that an original advance of £500 has created deposits totalling £1 416. In this example there is, therefore, a multiplier effect of

$$\frac{\text{Total amount of new deposits created}}{\text{Amount of original advance}} = \frac{\text{£1 416}}{\text{£500}} = 2.8 \text{ times}$$

The multiplier is easy to calculate if you know the percentage of deposits retained as reserves and not re-lent. In the example, 35 per cent was retained as reserves. Divide the reserves percentage (35 per cent) into 1 (100 per cent) and the answer, approximately 2.8 times, is the multiplier effect. If banks kept only 10 per cent of deposits as reserves, then the multiplier effect would be 10 times (100 divided by 10), so that our original deposit of £500 could create up to £5 000 of new deposits. If reserves were 50 per cent, then the multiplier effect would be 2 times (100 divided by 50), so the original deposit of £500 could create up to £1 000 of new deposits. It is important to appreciate that the banks' ability to create money can be expanded or restricted by altering the reserves percentages that they maintain. We shall return to this theme in Unit 18.5.

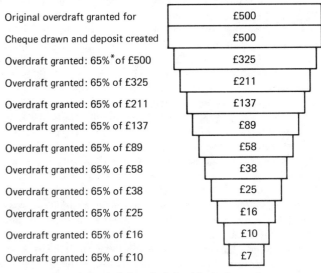

Original overdraft granted for	£500
Cheque drawn and deposit created	£500
Overdraft granted: 65%* of £500	£325
Overdraft granted: 65% of £325	£211
Overdraft granted: 65% of £211	£137
Overdraft granted: 65% of £137	£89
Overdraft granted: 65% of £89	£58
Overdraft granted: 65% of £58	£38
Overdraft granted: 65% of £38	£25
Overdraft granted: 65% of £25	£16
Overdraft granted: 65% of £16	£10
Overdraft granted: 65% of £10	£7

* Assumes that 35% of all deposits is kept in the form of reserves

Fig. 2.2   The credit-creation process

As we have just seen, one of the main limitations to credit creation is the amount of reserves that banks maintain. A further limitation is that of 'leakages' in the flow of money out of the banking system. For example, the public may wish to hold more cash, thus lowering the level of bank deposits;

certain transactions between the Government and the public have the effect of transferring funds from bank accounts of members of the public to the Government's bank account at the Bank of England (see also Unit 18.3).

Of course, a bank manager does not have to wait for deposits to be paid in before loan or overdraft facilities can be granted; but the bank as a whole must consider its total deposits when formulating its lending policy. However, the rate at which banks are able to create deposits depends, to some extent, on the rate at which they are able to increase their lending. The volume of bank lending is determined by the banks themselves, by the demand for advances in the economy and by competition from other lenders.

2.11   The Effect of Inflation on the Functions of Money

Inflation is a general upward movement of prices combined with a corresponding fall in the value of money. In Britain the effect of inflation is measured by using an index number; the one that is most commonly used is the *retail price index* (RPI). This index is based on a 'basket' of goods and services which are regarded as representative of the average person's purchases. Thus money is valued in terms of what goods and services it will buy.

When considering the effect of inflation on the functions of money, it is important to consider the *rate* of inflation. A low rate of inflation has little effect on the functions of money; however, as the rate of inflation rises, it begins to affect the store of value function. Holders of money will seek alternative assets in which to place their wealth. Money will still be used for buying and selling, for paying wages and for settling debts, but holdings of money will be restricted to the minimum necessary to meet the medium of exchange function. Even under conditions of very high inflation money will continue to function as a medium of exchange. (In the 1980s some countries have inflation rates of 400 per cent per annum!) It is only in conditions of hyper-inflation, such as experienced by Germany in the 1920s, that money is likely to be rejected as a medium of exchange.

The unit of account function is also affected by inflation. Nowadays business accounts are often adjusted to allow for the effects of inflation. Assets are revalued at their current cost and the profit and loss account is adjusted to show the effects of inflation.

In order to reduce the consequences of inflation, Governments may introduce various forms of *index-linking*, that is, prices, wages and debts for example are periodically adjusted in line with the rate of inflation. In some countries index-linking has been used extensively but widespread index-linking has not been adopted in Britain. However, the Government has introduced a number of index-linked investments such as index-linked National Savings Certificates and index-linked gilt-edged stocks. A problem with index-linked investments is that since the inflation rate in Britain in the 1980s has fallen faster than the level of interest rates, they have lost their attraction for savers who have been able to obtain better terms on other investments.

2.12   Legal Tender

Legal tender may be defined as the notes and coins which must be accepted by law when offered in payment. In Unit 2.8 we saw how cheques are a claim on the money in a bank account; while they are usually acceptable as a medium of exchange, they are not legal tender and the person being paid can, if he wishes, refuse to accept a cheque in settlement. He is, however, legally bound to accept notes and coins within certain limits: in England and Wales, Bank of England notes and £1 coins are legal tender up to any amount, fifty-pence pieces and twenty-pence coins are legal tender up to £10, five- and ten-pence coins up to £5 and bronze coins up to 20 pence. Scottish and Northern Ireland banknotes are not legal tender anywhere, although in their own areas they enjoy general acceptance. (A quirk of the Currency and Bank Notes Act 1954, is that only banknotes of less than £5 issued by the Bank of England are legal tender in Scotland or Northern Ireland: this means that the largest denomination which is legal tender in these areas is the £1 note or coin.)

2.13   Questions

1. Give a definition of money; describe the main functions of money.

2. What qualities must money possess? Discuss how these qualities are found in today's money.   (*The Chartered Institute of Bankers*)

3. Trace the development ot (i) notes and coin, and (ii) paper money in England and Wales.

4. Define any *two* of the following, giving illustrative examples as appropriate: (*a*) near-money; (*b*) legal tender; (*c*) the fiduciary issue.
                                                      (*The Institute of Bankers*)

5. What are the disadvantages of the barter system?

6. Trace the development of paper money in England and Wales from goldsmiths' receipts to the present-day banknote.   (*The Institute of Bankers*)

7. Whatever comes into use as money must possess certain qualities. Discuss these qualities as found in present-day forms of money.   (*The Institute of Bankers*)

8. What are the main functions of money? What effect does inflation have upon money's ability to perform these functions?   (*The Institute of Bankers*)

9. You are taking part in a training exercise to develop an alternative to notes and coin as a method of buying and selling. You have the following options available to you:

    —5 000 cigarettes.
    —Weekly stock of food for a family of four.
    —Game of Ludo, which contains: 2 dice, 4 sets of 4 coloured counters and a playing board.
    —24 bottles of assorted wines.

    Which option would you choose? Justify your choice.
                                          (*The Chartered Institute of Bankers*)

Multiple-choice Questions—1

Read each question carefully. Choose the *one* answer you think is correct. Answers are given on page 390.

1. A fiduciary issue of banknotes is backed by:

   A gold   **C** gold and Government securities
   B Government securities   **D** nothing at all

2. Which function of money enables prices to be compared directly?

   A store of value   **C** unit of account
   B medium of exchange   **D** standard for deferred payments

3. Homogeneity of notes and coins means:

   A their supply is controlled by the Government
   B they provide a range of different denominations, so enabling change to be given
   C each note or coin has the same buying power as another of the same denomination
   D notes and coins must, by law, be accepted in settlement of a debt

4. Legal tender includes:

   A coins only   **C** notes and coins
   B notes only   **D** notes, coins and cheques

5. Which definition of the money stock consists of notes and coin in circulation with the public, plus banks' till money, plus banks' operational balances with the Bank of England?

   A M0   **C** M2
   B M1   **D** M3

6. Which item is added to M1 to give M3?

   A sterling sight bank deposits
   B sterling time bank deposits and certificates of deposit
   C public sector time bank deposits
   D operational balances held with the Bank of England

7. Money stock definition M2 features *transactions balances*; these include:

   A monies held in a bank current account
   B banks' operational balances with the Bank of England
   C the amount of transit items, that is, cheques and credits in course of clearance
   D certain monies held with building societies and in National Savings Bank ordinary accounts

8. *Near-money* is:

   A bank current account balances
   B Scottish and Northern Ireland banknotes of £5 or more
   C credit created by banks
   D those financial assets which function more as a store of value than as a medium of exchange

9. In a particular economy banks are required to keep 20 per cent of all deposits in the form of reserves; this gives a *credit-creation multiplier* of:

    A five   **C** six
    B one-sixth   **D** one-fifth

10. Which one of the following statements is correct?

    A Britain is on the gold standard
    B Inflation is a general downward movement of prices
    C As the rate of inflation increases it begins to affect the store of value function of money
    D Scottish and Northern Ireland banknotes are legal tender

The Development of Banking in Britain

3.1 Origins

In the days before the London goldsmiths of the seventeenth century began accepting deposits of coin and other valuables (see Unit 2.6), city merchants and other wealthy people kept such items at the Royal Mint, which at that time was situated in the Tower of London. In 1640 King Charles I needed money to pay for his army and, unable to persuade Parliament to vote him the cash he wanted, he seized £200 000 of bullion belonging to the merchants. This, of course, meant that the Mint could no longer be used as a public safe-deposit so the merchants began to search for other places where they could keep their valuables. The goldsmiths, because of their trade, had excellent strongrooms, so they became an obvious choice.

As an acknowledgement for deposits the goldsmiths issued receipts and soon found that their receipts were being passed from one trader to another in the settlement of debts. This saved a trader with a debt to pay from having to go to his goldsmith, present the receipt, draw out the coins required and then hand them over to his creditor, who would immediately deposit them with his own goldsmith: it was much simpler just to transfer the receipt. To help in this, the goldsmiths began to issue receipts in convenient denominations and to make them payable to bearer so that title to the receipt would 'pass by delivery'. Present-day British banknotes are payable to bearer in the same way and whoever is in possession of a note, provided he came by it honestly, has the legal title to it and may pass the title on by *delivering* the note to another person.

The goldsmiths began to concentrate on the banking side of their business and soon found that, at any one time, only a small proportion of the coins they were holding for safe-keeping would be required to meet demands for repayment of their receipts. They began to lend the surplus monies and to charge interest for doing so; other services were developed such as deposit accounts, discounting (or 'cashing') bills of exchange before the date for payment, and dealing in bullion and foreign currencies. By 1677 there were forty-four goldsmith–bankers operating in London.

3.2 Formation of the Bank of England

The Bank of England was founded in 1694 with a capital of £1.2 million by a group of wealthy London merchants and financiers. It was established under royal charter, which gave it *joint-stock* status, a rather quaint phrase implying that its standing was equivalent to that of the present-day limited company. At that time there was no concept of the company; the most usual forms of business unit were the individual and the partnership. When a group of people wished to pool their money in a common venture it was necessary to obtain a special charter from the Crown. The king, William III, was only too pleased to grant a royal charter to the Bank of England, because in return the capital subscribed of £1.2 million was lent to him to finance his war against France. The charter, which was to be periodically renewed, also gave the new bank the right to issue notes, payable on demand, up to the amount of the loan to the king.

The Bank of England Act of 1709 renewed the Bank's charter, and also laid down that, as long as the Bank continued in business, no other corporation or partnership of more than six persons could issue banknotes payable on demand or within six months in England and Wales. This clause gave the Bank an effective monopoly of joint-stock banking which was to last until 1826 (see Unit 3.4).

In 1715, for the first time, the Bank acted as agent for the issue and management of a British Government loan, which we know today as the National Debt, and during the first half of the eighteenth century it became banker to the principal Government departments. Both of these functions are still performed by the Bank today.

The London goldsmith–bankers, together with a number of new firms, continued to issue their own notes until 1770 when they decided to abandon their own issues in favour of Bank of England notes. The withdrawal of their notes brought about a more general use of cheques in London and in 1773, for their mutual convenience, they established the London Bankers' Clearing House to provide a central place where cheques could be exchanged between themselves. As time went by, they opened accounts with the Bank of England, in which they deposited their spare funds: they came to regard these funds as their ultimate reserves and, when necessary, would ask the Bank for loan facilities to help them overcome a financial crisis. This helped to establish the Bank as a 'lender of last resort' (see Unit 4.8).

3.3 Rise of the Private Country Bank

Outside London the business of banking was slower to develop: the goldsmiths did not attempt to open branches in the provincial cities because of the problems of transport and communications in the late seventeenth and early eighteenth centuries. There were also restrictions on the size of banking firms imposed by the 1709 Act (see Unit 3.2). Nor, at this time, did the Bank of England open any branches in the provinces. It was left to the wealthy merchant to found a bank in his own locality. Thus, just as the goldsmiths had done, the merchants added banking to an already established trade and the numbers of country banks grew rapidly, especially in the second half of the eighteenth century (see Table 3.1).

Table 3.1   Numbers of private and clearing banks (excluding the Bank of England and foreign banks) in England and Wales, 1750–1934

Year	Number of private banks (partnerships) outside London	Clearing banks Number of banks	Number of branches
1750	12	—	—
1776	150	—	—
1797	230	—	—
1800	350	—	—
1810	721	—	—
1825	554	—	—
1833	430	50	not known
1844	273	105	486
1884	172	118	1 621
1904	35	65	4 414
1934	nil	11	10 131

Most banks printed their own banknotes and nowadays these old notes are in demand as collectors' items. From 1808, a private bank needed a licence before it could print money, but this cost only £30 per year and the bank was then free to print and issue as many notes as the public could be persuaded to accept, the only restriction being that the value of the minimum-denomination note was to be £1. Some country banks also issued their own coins, but this practice was prohibited by Parliament in 1812. Outside London the cheque did not start to come into general use before the development of the joint-stock banks in the 1830s (see Unit 3.4), and until this time most payments for substantial amounts were made using the notes of the private banks.

A major problem of the private country banks was that, if they wished to issue notes, the 1709 Act restricted their size to a maximum of six partners—in practice many were smaller. This meant that they were unable to set up large branch networks, such as those maintained by the major banks today, and few developed beyond their immediate neighbourhoods. Moreover, there was the additional difficulty that a small local bank was unable to spread its risks: if it operated in an agricultural area, a farming crisis could result in failure of the bank; similarly, in an industrial town, the collapse of one or two large businesses could affect it severely. A further problem was that banking had developed initially as a sideline to other businesses—rather like the present-day sub-post office and stores—and there was often a lack of professional banking expertise and sometimes a conflict of interest in decision-making. Since, apart from the licensing system, there was no central control of the note issue, a bank could issue as many notes as it could put into circulation. With the country on the gold standard from 1816 onwards, anybody holding banknotes could demand to be paid in gold: there only had to be a rumour that the local bank was in difficulties and it would be besieged by crowds of people demanding payment, almost certainly leading to the bank closing its doors and possibly failing.

3.4   Development of the Joint-stock Banks

In 1825 there was a severe financial crisis, resulting in the failure of ninety private banks. This led the Government to pass legislation in 1826 in an attempt to stabilize the banking system. The opening of joint-stock banks, with their own note issue, was to be allowed outside a radius of sixty-five miles (105 km) from London, although they were not to be permitted to set up offices within the area around the capital. In addition, the Government persuaded the Bank of England to establish a number of provincial branches, they were opened as follows:

1826: Gloucester, Manchester, Swansea
1827: Birmingham, Leeds, Exeter, Liverpool, Bristol
1828: Newcastle upon Tyne
1829: Norwich, Hull
1834: Plymouth, Portsmouth

(Today the Bank, with its head office in Threadneedle Street in the City of London, has branches in Birmingham, Bristol, Leeds, Manchester and Newcastle upon Tyne, together with representative offices in Glasgow, Liverpool and the Southampton area.)

For a time the development of a branch network by the Bank of England delayed the establishment of joint-stock banks and the first was opened outside the area covered by the Bank, at Lancaster in 1826, followed shortly by others at Norwich, Bristol and Huddersfield. By 1833 nearly fifty joint-stock banks had been established and, in the same year, the Act of Parliament renewing the Bank of England's charter permitted joint-stock banking within the London area provided that the new banks did not issue notes—a restriction that hastened the development of the cheque as a means of money transfer. The Act also made Bank of England notes legal tender.

The success of the 1826 and 1833 Acts is demonstrated by the rise in the number of joint-stock banks and the simultaneous fall in the number of private country banks shown in Table 3.1. In 1844, following further severe financial crises, the Bank Charter Act was passed; it had three main provisions:

(i) the note-issuing function of the Bank of England was to be separated from the Bank's other activities by forming two departments: the Issue Department and the Banking Department.

(ii) the establishment of a fiduciary issue (see Unit 2.6) of £14 million; beyond this amount, all notes had to be backed pound for pound by gold and silver held by the Bank.

(iii) ultimately to centralize the note issue of England and Wales in the hands of the Bank of England: the Act prohibited banks already issuing their own notes from increasing the number in circulation. As private banks merged with the developing joint-stock banks or went bankrupt, they were to lose their rights of note issue.

By 1844 the number of joint-stock banks had reached 105 and few new banks were established after this date; by this time also, as Table 3.1 shows, the decline of the private banks had set in. The next sixty years saw the virtual extinction of the private bank, a reduction in the number of joint-stock banks as they merged with one another, and the growth of branch networks. The development of large banks with branches throughout the country was helped by an Act of Parliament in 1862 which extended the privilege of limited liability to banking concerns and opened the way to the establishment of large limited company banks as we know them today. In 1882 the Bills of Exchange Act brought together in one statute the law relating to bills of exchange and cheques. It contained specific provision for crossed cheques and gave protection to banks and customers against loss through theft and fraud, so increasing the usefulness of the cheque and giving banks greater scope for developing their current account business. A series of amalgamations between 1890 and 1914 brought most commercial banking into the hands of sixteen banks; a further series of mergers in 1917 and 1918 reduced the numbers to five large clearing banks, each with a nationwide branch network, and a few smaller banks. There were fears that any continuation of this trend would lead to monopolies in commercial banking that would leave little or no choice for the customers. A Treasury Committee was set up to look into the situation, and its report in 1918 suggested that Government approval should be required for any further amalgamations. Though this recommendation was not given the force of law, the banks concerned entered into a general undertaking not to consider further amalgamations without seeking Treasury approval.

In Scotland joint-stock banking developed much faster than in England, because although the Bank of Scotland was originally granted a monopoly of joint-stock banking similar to that of the Bank of England, this privilege was not continued when its charter was renewed in 1716. Thus the first half of the eighteenth century saw the rapid development of the Scottish banking system along the lines that still exist today.

3.5   The Bank of England Develops as a Central Bank

With the development of the joint-stock banks, the importance of the Bank of England as a commercial bank started to decline. As it strengthened its hold over the note issue, there was a fall in the circulation of private banknotes; all the other banks opened accounts with the Bank of England and settled their indebtedness with one another by drawing cheques on these accounts.

The emergence of the discount market as a market for discounting bills of exchange (see Unit 6.4) in the second half of the nineteenth century helped to consolidate the Bank's position as a central bank: in 1890 the Bank announced that it would always in future rediscount approved bills for the discount market at 'bank rate'. This meant that the Bank would act as 'lender of last resort' to the discount market and thus, because of the inter-relationships between this market and the banks, indirectly to the banking system.

During the twentieth century the Bank has steadily strengthened its position as a central bank. Early in the century it took the decision to decline new private business of a kind that would put it in direct competition with the other banks. During the First World War, while the Government was borrowing on a substantial scale to finance the war, the Bank was entrusted with the responsibility of raising many loans. In the Second World War it played a large part in devising and implementing measures to deal with the financial and economic consequences of the war effort, and again had the task of covering the Government's wartime borrowing requirements. Interest rates were kept low and the bank rate, to which at that time all bank overdraft rates were related, was held at 2 per cent for the whole of the war, except for a few months in late 1939 when it stood at 4 per cent. In the immediate post-war period the Bank had the task of restoring the country's financial and economic machinery by means of its monetary policies.

Ever since its foundation in 1694 the Bank had remained a company owned by private stockholders, despite its increasing involvement in the financial and economic affairs of the country. In 1946 the Government felt that so important an institution should be brought under its own control, and in that year the Bank of England Act nationalized the Bank. The private stockholders were compensated by the issue of Government stock and the composition of the Court (or board) of Directors, appointed by the Crown, was widened to include representatives of industry and trade unions (previously it had been composed mainly of bankers). The Act gave the Bank wide powers: if the Bank thought it in the public interest, it could request information from bankers and make recommendations to them which, if authorized by the Treasury, could be turned into directions using the force of law, although in such a case the banker would always first be given the opportunity to make representations and explain his position. However, the Bank has no power to make requests and recommendations with respect to the affairs of any particular customer of a banker. Thus the Act gave the Bank legal powers to control the banking and financial systems; previously the Bank had relied on the voluntary co-operation of bankers, and in practice, even today, much of the control is still carried out on an informal and voluntary basis.

Changes have taken place to bring all banks—and deposit-taking institutions—under the closer jurisdiction of the Bank of England by a system of statutory control. The Banking Act of 1979 brought Britain into line with the banking directive of the European Community (EC). Additionally, the Banking Act set up a Deposit Protection Fund which partly insures those who deposit money with banks and other deposit-taking institutions. To further tighten up the Bank of England's supervisory role, a new Banking Act was passed in 1987 (see pages 43–4).

3.6   Emergence of the 'Big Four'

For nearly fifty years after the general undertaking given in 1918 by the clearing banks to obtain Treasury approval of further amalgamations, there was a period of stability in the British banking structure. The only changes from 1918 until the late 1960s were the absorptions of some of the smaller banks by the larger banks: the system in England and Wales became dominated by the 'big five'—Barclays, Lloyds, Midland, National Provincial and Westminster banks. It was a time of consolidation: branch networks were built up, new services were introduced, and affiliations were developed with banks in Scotland and Northern Ireland.

In 1967 a report on bank charges was published by the National Board for Prices and Incomes, which had been set up by the Government to make recommendations about price increases of goods and services and about wage rises. The report, besides considering bank charges, was critical of the 'wasteful' nature of bank competition, and in particular of the spread of new branches of all five of the major clearing banks. The report contained the historic statement:

> Further amalgamation among the banks, carried through to the appropriate point could permit some rationalization of branch networks. The Bank of England and the Treasury have made it plain to us that they would not obstruct some further amalgamation if the banks were willing to contemplate such a development.

Thus the go-ahead was given for further amalgamations, and within a few months the Westminster Bank and the National Provincial Bank (which already owned Coutts & Co and the District Bank) announced plans for a merger. The proposed merger could have been referred to the Monopolies Commission for investigation to determine whether it would bring about a monopoly and, if so, whether or not it would be detrimental to the public interest; the Government chose not to do this and allowed the merger to take place. The new company became the National Westminster Bank, while Coutts & Co continues to trade under its own name.

Almost at the same time, Barclays, Lloyds and Martins announced plans to merge into one bank: this would have created a huge banking group which would have had 5 500 branches in England and Wales (out of a total of some 12 000 branches at that time for all the clearing banks). The Government referred this proposal to the Monopolies Commission, which rejected the proposed merger of the three banks, but agreed that Martins, the smallest of the three, could be absorbed either by Barclays or Lloyds; shortly after this, Martins was absorbed into Barclays. In their rejection of the amalgamation of all three, the Monopolies Commission was critical of the way in which the clearing banks did not have to disclose their true profits, and of the joint fixing of interest rates. Both of these matters have now been dealt with: by mutual agreement the banks started to disclose true profits from 1969 and the collective agreement on interest rates was abandoned in 1971.

In 1970 some of the smaller clearing banks—Glyn, Mills & Co, Williams Deacon's Bank and the English branches of the National Bank—merged to form Williams and Glyn's Bank. In Scotland too, there were mergers to form three large banking groups: the Bank of Scotland, the Clydesdale Bank and the Royal Bank of Scotland, which forms part of the Royal Bank group. This last group now owns the branches of the former Williams and Glyn's bank and operates in both England and Wales, and Scotland, under the same name.

3.7   Development of the Trustee Savings Bank

Trustee Savings Banks (TSBs) were founded in Scotland in the early nineteenth century to provide non-profit-making savings facilities for working people. At that time the joint-stock and private banks were only interested in wealthy customers and provided no services for the small saver: they required a minimum deposit of £10 to open an account and this was the equivalent of a year's earnings for most workers. The idea was to collect people's savings, pool them and then place them on deposit with a joint-stock bank at a rate of interest. The interest thus earned could be passed back to the savers in proportion to their deposits.

The 1817 Savings Bank Act marked the beginning of a period of development for these banks and provided that savers' funds could be placed in a Government fund called the Fund for the Banks for Savings, where it could earn interest. The fund was guaranteed by the Government (in contrast to the unreliability and frequent failures in the private sector at that time) and the banks were to be managed by unpaid local trustees—hence the name given to the banks—acting on behalf of the National Debt Commissioners who control the debt of the central Government.

Since 1964, TSBs have developed a wide range of banking services far removed from the old 'savings bank' image, beginning with the introduction of current accounts. The changes have been particularly marked as a result of the publication in 1973 of the report of the Committee to Review National Savings which was chaired by Sir Harry Page. The Page Committee Report, as it has become known, recommended that the TSBs should be allowed to develop as a major force in banking in the private sector, and since then the TSBs have made several moves to expand their services. The Central Trustee Savings Bank was established in 1973 to co-ordinate and supervise the activities of the local TSBs and to provide the central organization necessary to enable them to develop away from the savings bank image, and two years later it became a member of the Bankers' Clearing House, so enabling the TSB to clear its own cheques and credits. In 1975 the existing seventy-three local TSBs operating throughout Britain were merged into twenty larger regional units. The 1976 Trustee Savings Bank Act embodied the Page Committee recommendations and permitted TSBs to withdraw their monies from the Fund for the Banks for

Savings and to invest them in the best interests of their depositors. Since the passing of the Act, the development of full banking services has been rapid: in 1977 personal lending was introduced; in 1978 Trustcard, the group's credit card operation, was launched; the following year the bank offered mortgage services; and in 1981 it acquired a finance house, United Dominions Trust. In 1983 further amalgamations of the regional TSBs took place to form major operating groups, such as TSB England and Wales, and TSB Scotland. TSB Group plc issued its shares to the public in 1986 and obtained a Stock Exchange quotation. This completed the task originally envisaged by the Page Committee of transforming the TSBs into a major force in British retail banking.

3.8   Summary

Banking in Britain is dominated by the 'big four' London clearing banks (Barclays, Lloyds, Midland, National Westminster), the TSB, Scottish clearing banks and Northern Ireland banks, which altogether have some 13 500 branches and sub-branches across the country and employ nearly 400 000 staff. During recent years the British banking structure has been enhanced by a range of newer banks: some from abroad, some formed to meet specialist financial needs, and some—particularly Girobank (see Unit 5.2 (iv))—providing important competition in their bid for the personal customer. The present structure of banking in Britain is considered in detail in Unit 5.

3.9   Questions

1. Outline the history and development of the Bank of England.

    (*The Institute of Bankers*)

2. What effect did the report of the National Board for Prices and Incomes on bank charges in 1967 have on the development of British banking?

3. Trace the development of commercial banking in England and Wales from the London goldsmiths of the seventeenth century to the 'big four' London clearing banks of the 1980s.

4. What were the main provisions of the 1844 Bank Charter Act?

5. Outline the development of Trustee Savings Banks from their foundations in Scotland in the early nineteenth century to their present position as a major force in retail banking.

The Bank of England

4.1 What is a Central Bank?

Every country with an established banking system has a central bank which acts as banker to the Government in the widest sense. It liaises with and advises the Government on monetary policy and ensures that the necessary steps are taken to carry it through.

Central banks differ from commercial banks in certain respects:

(i) they do not aim to maximize profits, which is traditionally an objective of a commercial bank owned by shareholders (central banks are normally nationalized institutions);

(ii) those who govern them are much more closely involved with the work of Government departments than are their counterparts in commercial banking;

(iii) they have a supervisory role over the commercial banks which usually has the backing of law;

(iv) they are able to influence the actions of the commercial banks and other financial institutions, particularly with regard to lending;

(v) they control the issue of notes and coin;

(vi) they do not compete for business with the commercial banks, but they usually maintain the Government bank accounts;

(vii) they act as 'lender of last resort' to the banking system;

(viii) they do not provide a full banking service for personal and commercial customers.

In Britain, the central bank is the Bank of England (Fig. 4.1).

4.2 The Weekly Return

The 1844 Bank Charter Act (see Unit 3.4) divided the Bank of England for book-keeping purposes into two principal departments: the Issue Department and the Banking Department. It also specified that the Bank had to issue a *weekly return* showing the assets and liabilities of each department: this is still published today and Table 4.1 shows a modern return.

The liabilities of the Issue Department are notes in circulation and notes held in the Banking Department ready for issue to the other banks as required. As the note issue is now entirely fiduciary (see Unit 2.6) the assets backing it compromise Government and other securities—Government debt in the form

Fig. 4.1   The Bank of England, with Threadneedle Street in the foreground

of stocks, Treasury bills and other advances, together with local authority debt and other securities. (Treasury bills are *promissory notes*, that is, promises to repay, issued by the Treasury, usually for 91 days, to finance Government short-term expenditure.)

The liabilities of the Banking Department are the capital, reserves and deposits of the Bank. The *capital* is the amount subscribed by the original stockholders, together with accumulated interest and reserves; it has been held by the Treasury since the nationalization of the Bank in 1946. *Public deposits* are the balances of the Government accounts maintained at the Bank (see Unit 4.4(*a*)), *special deposits* are those which banks and certain finance houses are required to maintain from time to time with the Bank of England as part of the Government's monetary policy (see Unit 4.9(*b*)) and *banker's deposits* are the cash ratio deposits (see Unit 4.9) and working balances which the clearing banks maintain at the Bank. The balances of the Bank of England's other customers, together with undistributed profits and reserves, are included in *reserves and other accounts*.

The assets of the Banking Department consist mainly of holdings of Government securities—stocks and Treasury bills; included among *advances and other accounts* are loans made to the discount houses (see Unit 6.5) and other customers of the Bank; *premises, equipment and other securities* are miscellaneous other assets. The final item *notes and coin* comprises notes ready for issue to the other banks, as an opposite entry to the liability amount

Table 4.1   Bank of England weekly return for 12 October 1988 (*Figures are rounded to the nearest million by the Bank of England, so individual totals and sub-totals do not always add up.*)

Issue Department

Liabilities	£ million	Assets	£ million
Notes issued:		Government debt	11
In circulation	14 328	Other Government	
In Banking Department	12	securities	10 366
		Other securities	3 963
	14 340		14 340

Banking Department

'Capital'	15	Government securities	618
Public deposits	89	Advances and other accounts	597
Special deposits	—	Premises, equipment and	
Bankers' deposits	1 177	other securities	1 908
Reserves and other accounts	1 854	Notes and coin	12
	3 135		3 135

Source: *Bank of England*

on the Issue Department's return, together with the holding of coin for the Bank's own use.

4.3   The Functions of the Bank of England

The Bank of England's roles are widely varied and far-reaching in their significance.

  (i) It acts as banker to:
      the Government,
      the banks and other financial institutions,
      some overseas central banks and international financial organizations,
      a few private sector customers, and
      its own staff.
 (ii) It is the note-issuing authority in England and Wales.
(iii) It serves as registrar of Government and other stocks.
 (iv) It manages the Exchange Equalization Account.
  (v) It acts as lender of last resort to the discount houses.

(vi) It carries out the Government's monetary policy.

(vii) It supervises the banking institutions of the United Kingdom.

These functions, which are discussed one by one on the next few pages, are shared between a number of specialized areas working under the general control of the Court of Directors (Fig. 4.2).

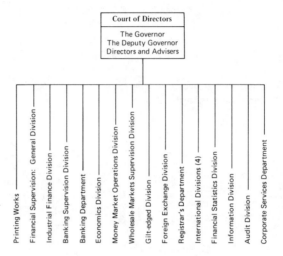

Fig. 4.2   Organization of the Bank of England

4.4   The Bank of England as a Banker

(a) Banker to the Government

Although the Government maintains a large number of small accounts with the commercial banks, its main accounts are kept with the Bank of England. The Exchequer account ultimately receives all Government revenues, in the form of taxes and other income, and all Government expenditure originates from it. Other accounts are those of the National Loans Fund, the National Debt Commissioners and various dividend accounts that enable the Bank to pay interest on the Government stocks for which it acts as registrar.

While the Bank was originally founded to make a loan to the Government, this is not a major part of its work nowadays. The only direct lending is of a very short-term nature, usually overnight. However, the Bank arranges all the Government's borrowing—short-term through the issue of Treasury bills and longer-term through the issue of Government stocks. It advises the Government on terms and the state of the market, and provides other services as well (see Unit 4.6).

(b) Banker to the Banks and other Financial Institutions

The Bank acts as banker to the commercial banks, the discount houses, accepting houses and a large number of the overseas banks operating in

London. The clearing banks, and most other banks, are required to hold an amount equal to 0.45 per cent of their eligible liabilities (see Unit 7.6) in non-interest earning balances, known as cash ratio deposits, at the Bank of England. In addition they maintain other, working, accounts, or *operational balances*, from which they settle the daily cheque clearing and other inter-bank indebtedness. These latter accounts are also drawn upon when new banknotes and coins are required and they are increased when surplus or damaged notes and coins are paid in.

(c) Banker to Overseas Central Banks and International Financial Organizations

Accounts for a number of overseas central banks, principally of countries of the British Commonwealth, are maintained by the Bank of England together with those of such bodies as the International Monetary Fund, the World Bank and the Bank for International Settlements.

(d) Banker to Private Sector Customers and its Staff

Although the Bank ceased to compete for business with the commercial banks in the early years of this century, it still maintains some private sector accounts for companies and individuals that have close associations with the Bank. These accounts are said to give the Bank practical experience of commercial banking. Recently the Bank suggested that it would like to increase its range of private sector customers by taking on new business. It also maintains accounts for the members of its own staff.

4.5   The Note-issuing Authority

The Bank of England, as Unit 2.6 explained, has the monopoly of the note issue in England and Wales. Nowadays it is a major task to withdraw worn and soiled notes, which are sent to the Bank from other banks throughout the country for destruction, and to print new notes. Each working day at the Bank's printing works, millions of old notes are burnt in the furnaces which power the heating system—certainly the most expensive heating system in the country! Millions of notes are printed each day and, in terms of staff, this is the Bank's biggest undertaking.

4.6   Registrar of Government Stocks

In 1715, just twenty-one years after its foundation, the Bank acted for the first time as an agent for the issue and management of a Government loan (see Unit 3.2). This function continues today and a glance at the *Financial Times* in the closing prices section headed 'British Funds' will indicate some of the stocks currently managed by the Bank—Exchequer and Treasury stocks. The Bank arranges to issue the stock to cover the Government's longer-term borrowing requirements and then fulfils the role of a company registrar, attending to recording the transfer of stocks from one holder to another and to the payment of dividends and interest at the right time and, when a stock is due for repayment, sending cheques to the stockholders.

In addition to dealing with British Government stocks, the Bank acts as a registrar for stocks issued by the nationalized industries, some local authorities, public boards and Commonwealth Governments.

4.7   Management of the Exchange Equalization Account

The Bank manages, on behalf of the Treasury, the Exchange Equalization Account, which holds Britain's official reserves of gold, foreign exchange and Special Drawing Rights on the International Monetary Fund. It is through this account that the Bank sometimes intervenes on the foreign exchange market—where currencies are bought and sold—to prevent undue fluctuations in the exchange value of sterling against other currencies.

4.8   Lender of Last Resort

Most central banks act as 'lender of last resort', so that if there is a general shortage of funds, the central bank is always prepared to lend. In Britain, the Bank of England is a direct lender of last resort to the discount houses (see Unit 6) and, as these act as an intermediary between the central bank and other banks, last-resort lending is available indirectly to the banks. While the Bank is prepared to act in this way, it does so on its own terms, often charging a higher rate of interest than that prevailing on the money markets and requiring lending to be backed by securities on which there will be no possibility of loss. By taking these precautions, the Bank ensures that, while it is prepared to make funds available, they will only be requested 'as a last resort' after every other possible source has been approached.

In 1988 the Bank of England announced that it was prepared to extend the range of parties to which it would act as a lender of last resort. The new parties could include specially established subsidiary companies of banks.

4.9   The Government's Monetary Policy

All central banks liaise with and advise their Governments on monetary policy (see Unit 18.4) and act as the link between the Government and the banks and other financial institutions in carrying out that policy. In Britain, the Treasury and the Bank of England—collectively referred to as *the authorities*—are concerned with *monetary control*, that is, controlling the growth of the money stock and the ability of the banks and other financial institutions to create credit.

At present there are four ways in which the Bank of England is able to carry out the Government's monetary policy in controlling bank lending. These methods of monetary control are:

(a) Directives

The Bank of England gives instructions telling the banks the action they are required to take to implement the Government's policy on bank advances; for instance they might be told to lend to manufacturing industry, but not to property companies.

(b) Special Deposits

These are a call on most institutions within the monetary sector to deposit an amount equal to a certain percentage of their eligible liabilities (basically their deposits; the term is explained fully in Unit 7.6) with the Bank of England. This has the effect of taking money out of the banking system, which means banks must restrict or reduce their lending in order to maintain adequate reserves. A repayment of special deposits puts money back into the banking system and will have the effect of expanding lending.

(c) Interest Rate Policy

In theory low interest rates create a demand for bank loans while high interest rates have the effect of reducing the demand for loans. In practice the vast majority of companies are 'locked in' to bank loans and overdrafts and have to pay whatever rates are being charged at the time. The Bank of England has considerable influence over the general level of interest rates.

(d) Open-market Operations

Open-market operations are the buying and selling of Government stocks by the Bank of England in order to increase or restrict bank lending. For example, when the Bank of England buys stocks on the market, it makes payment to the individuals and institutions from whom it has purchased them. When the payment cheques are banked, additional deposits are made in the banking system, that is, there has been a flow of funds from the central bank to the commercial banks. With these additional funds the banks are able to create more money by increasing their lending, as we have seen in Unit 2.10. The reverse happens when the Bank of England sells Government stocks and funds flow from the commercial banks into the Government's bank account. This withdrawal of funds from the banking system reduces the ability of the banks to create credit.

Each of these four methods of controlling bank lending is considered more fully in Unit 18.5.

It is appropriate to consider briefly at this stage the way in which the Bank of

England has exercised monetary control over the banking system during the past two or three decades. Broadly this divides into three main periods:

(i) pre-1971
(ii) 1971–1981: *Competition and Credit Control*
(iii) 1981 to date: *Monetary Control*

Before the 1971 *Competition and Credit Control* measures were introduced, the clearing banks had to comply with a cash ratio and a liquid assets ratio, which required them to hold a minimum percentage of cash and a minimum percentage of liquid assets, in relation to their deposits. During this period before 1971 an 8 per cent cash ratio was required, with a further 20 per cent in the form of liquid assets, giving a liquidity ratio of 28 per cent.

The 1971 measures, entitled *Competition and Credit Control*, required the adoption of a *reserve asset ratio* for all banks (not just the clearing banks). This stipulated that the banks had to hold minimum amounts of specified reserve assets as a ratio of eligible liabilities. Reserve assets comprised such items as working balances at the Bank of England, Treasury bills, money at call with the London money market and certain Government stocks. Eligible liabilities broadly comprise current, deposit and other account balances—the main liabilities of a bank (a full list of eligible liabilities is given in Unit 7.6). The reserve asset ratio was originally set at $12\frac{1}{2}$ per cent for banks and 10 per cent for finance houses.

In 1981 the reserve asset ratio was abolished with the introduction of new measures called *Monetary Control*. The measures called for the 'monetary sector' (see Unit 4.11) to keep 0.45 per cent of their eligible liabilities in non-interest earning balances ('cash ratio' deposits) at the Bank of England. In addition, most of the larger banks are expected to keep a certain percentage of their eligible liabilities with the London money market. In 1982 the Bank of England introduced a new method for measuring bank liquidity. This is based on the principle of matching assets to liabilities in order of repayment, for example, deposits repayable at sight and near-sight are matched with cash and other assets capable of being turned into cash almost immediately.

4.10   Supervision of Banking Institutions

As the central bank in Britain, the Bank of England has the task of supervising the other banks that operate in the country. This *prudential control*, as it is generally known, of the banking system is designed to ensure that financial institutions are soundly and honestly run and that they are able to meet their commitments at all times.

The Bank of England has certain powers conferred on it by the Bank of England Act 1946, but in addition to this the European Community required Britain to introduce a new basic banking law as part of moves towards standardizing Community controls. This led to the Banking Act 1979, of which one of the main provisions was the establishment of a Deposit Protection Fund (see below).

Following the collapse of a recognized bank in 1984 and its subsequent rescue by the Bank of England, a review of the Bank's supervision procedures was carried out. After this, most of the provisions of the 1979 Act were repealed (with the main exception of those relating to the Deposit Protection Fund), and the Banking Act 1987 was passed.

The Banking Act 1987

This Act contains the following main provisions:

(i) all deposit-taking institutions must be authorized to do so by the Bank of England;

(ii) the use of the word 'bank' is restricted to those institutions which have a paid-up capital of at least £5 million;

(iii) any person or company planning to take control of a UK-incorporated authorized institution must notify the Bank of England in advance, and the Bank may object to such a takeover (this gives the Bank of England the right to veto unwanted or undesirable takeovers);

(iv) authorized institutions are required to notify the Bank of England of any loans to a single customer that are greater than 10 per cent of the bank's capital, and to give advance notice of any loan that would exceed 25 per cent of the bank's capital;

(v) the auditors of an authorized institution are required to disclose relevant information to the Bank of England;

(vi) the Bank of England has the power to require information for the purposes of bank supervision from a wide range of people and institutions;

(vii) the setting up of a Board of Banking Supervision within the Bank of England, to oversee the implementation of the Act and give advice on supervisory matters to the Governor of the Bank of England.

Before an institution is authorized to accept deposits, the Bank of England will carry out an investigation to ensure that:

(i) the institution's directors, controllers and managers are fit and proper persons to hold their positions;

(ii) the business is conducted prudently, particularly with regard to adequate capital, liquidity, provisions for bad and doubtful debts, accounting records, and internal controls;

(iii) the business is carried on with integrity;

(iv) the institution has net assets of not less than £1 million.

The Banking Act 1987 gives the Bank of England considerable supervisory powers, which are so essential as we move into the 1990s and increased financial sophistication.

Deposit Protection Fund

This was first established by the Banking Act 1979, and continues under the 1987 Act. The Deposit Protection Fund consists of a central pool to which all authorized institutions contribute. The pool is used to repay 75 per cent of the 'protected deposits' of the depositors of any failed institution. At present there is a limit of £20000 on the amount of the protected deposits of each depositor, so the maximum which can be paid to each depositor per institution is currently £15000. Therefore depositors bear some loss, but not all, if the worst happens and an institution is unable to meet its obligations. The pool is formed by levies drawn from each authorized institution on the basis of the size of its deposit base. In addition, the authorities have the right to make a further call on each institution to produce a larger fund.

4.11   The Monetary Sector

The United Kingdom monetary sector includes:

(i) all authorized institutions (authorized by the Bank of England);
(ii) those banks in the Channel Islands and the Isle of Man which opt to join the cash ratio scheme (see Unit 4.4(b));
(iii) the Banking Department of the Bank of England.

4.12   Questions

1. Outline the functions normally carried out by a central bank.
   (The Institute of Bankers)

2. Outline the ways in which the Bank of England exercises control over bank lending.

3. Describe the main functions of the Bank of England.

4. In most countries, a central authority has responsibility for licensing banks and for regulating banking activities, quite apart from the administration of credit controls. What institution usually has this responsibility and by what means would it seek to exercise effective supervision and regulation of the banking system?
   (The Institute of Bankers)

5. Outline the ways in which the Bank of England supervises banking institutions in Britain.

6. Briefly outline the main functions of the Bank of England. How are commercial banks affected by the operations of the Bank of England when it carries out these functions?
   (The Chartered Institute of Bankers)

Multiple-choice Questions—2

Read each question carefully. Choose the *one* answer you think is correct. Answers are given on page 390.

1. Which one of the following present-day functions of the Bank of England stems from the Bank Charter Act 1844?

    A banker to the Government
    B sole note-issuing authority in England and Wales
    C 'lender of last resort'
    D supervision of banking institutions

2. The Bank Charter Act 1844 divided the Bank of England into two departments:

    A the Issue Department and the Banking Department
    B the Foreign Department and the Banking Department
    C the Issue Department and the Cheque Clearing Department
    D the Domestic Department and the Foreign Department

3. The following is a balance sheet for one of the departments of the Bank of England:

	£m		£m
Notes in circulation	12 540	x	3 704
Notes in Banking Department	25	y	8 861
	12 565		12 565

    x and y are respectively:

    A capital; advances
    B public deposits; bankers' deposits
    C notes and coin; advances
    D Government securities; other securities

4. Which one of the following is a function of the Bank of England?

    A setting the interest rate on mortgages
    B controlling the rate of inflation
    C arranging the issue of shares for companies
    D acting as a registrar for Government stocks

5. To whom is the Bank of England a direct 'lender of last resort'?

    A retail banks
    B discount houses
    C merchant banks
    D building societies

6. The main objective of the Exchange Equalization Account is to:

    A prevent undue fluctuation in the exchange value of sterling against other currencies
    B ensure that notes and coin continue to be acceptable as a medium of exchange
    C control the rate of inflation
    D permit the exchange of payments between banks

7. In the United Kingdom the monetary authorities are:

    A   the Chancellor of the Exchequer and the Treasury
    B   the Treasury and the Bank of England
    C   the Bank of England and the clearing banks
    D   the Bank of England, the Treasury and the clearing banks

8. Open-market operations are the buying and selling of:

    A   company shares on the Stock Exchange by the Bank of England
    B   Government securities by the Bank of England
    C   Government securities by the retail banks
    D   foreign currency by the Bank of England

9. Special deposits are:

    A   amounts deposited by the banks with the Bank of England to enable clearing
        imbalances to be settled
    B   deposits made by the banks with the Bank of England in order to earn high
        rates of interest
    C   deposits made by banks on the instructions of the Bank of England
    D   deposits set on one side by banks in order to meet possible bad debts

10. The definition 'monetary sector' includes:

    A   banks and the Banking Department of the Bank of England
    B   banks and building societies
    C   building societies and insurance companies
    D   building societies, insurance companies and the Banking Department of the
        Bank of England

Unit Five
The British Banking Structure

5.1 Introduction

Although the 'big four' High Street banks—Barclays, Lloyds, Midland and National Westminster—together with the TSB are by far the best known of the British banks, they are only a part of today's banking structure. Fig. 5.1 classifies the whole range of banks under appropriate headings. However, in recent years the distinctions between the various types of banks have become blurred as a result of the diversification of services and the acquisition of interests in other banks and financial institutions. For example, until a few years ago, the term *clearing banks* was used to describe the handful of banks, including the big four, that owned the London Bankers' Clearing House. With the widening of clearing facilities (see Unit 11.9), which allows other banks and financial institutions access to them, the term nowadays strictly includes a wider range of banks; however, it is still commonly used when referring to the large High Street banks. In recent years, the term *retail banks* has also come into use (see Unit 5.2).

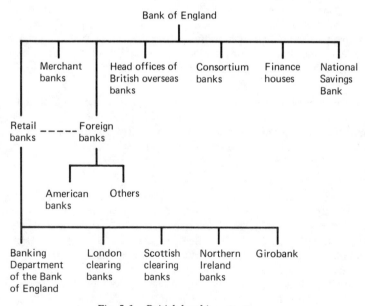

Fig. 5.1   British banking structure

The entire United Kingdom banking structure is, of course, supervised by the central bank, the Bank of England, which exercises prudential and monetary controls.

5.2   Retail Banks

Retail banks comprise the London clearing banks, the Scottish clearing banks, the Northern Ireland banks, Girobank and the Banking Department of the Bank of England. They are called retail banks because they have extensive branch networks in Britain, and/or are the main participants in the clearing system. They offer a wide range of services to their many thousands of personal and business customers through their large branch networks, and by participating in the clearing system they enable the payments mechanism to operate by exchanging cheques and credits between other banks. It should be noted that other banks, particularly some of the American banks, are rapidly developing a retail banking service to rival that of the more 'traditional' High Street banks.

(i) **The London clearing banks** comprise the big four—Barclays, Lloyds, Midland and National Westminster—together with TSB and a number of other, smaller banks. All these banks offer a wide range of similar services, which are considered later in this book.

The TSB (Trustee Savings Bank) completed the transition from small savings bank to a major force in retail banking in Britain with the public issue of shares in 1986—see Unit 3.7. TSB Group plc is the holding company for a number of subsidiaries (Fig. 5.2). The Trustee Savings Bank is able to offer to its personal and small business customers almost identical services to those offered by the major banks.

(ii) **The Scottish clearing banks** are three in number: the Bank of Scotland, the Clydesdale Bank and the Royal Bank of Scotland (which also has a large number of branches in England and Wales), each of which retains the right of note issue. These banks perform similar functions in Scotland to those of the London clearing banks.

(iii) **The Northern Ireland banks** provide similar services in their own areas of operation to those of the London and Scottish clearing banks. There are four member banks of the Northern Ireland Bankers' Association: the Northern Bank, the Ulster Bank, the Allied Irish Banks and the Bank of Ireland. The first two have their head offices in Northern Ireland, retain the right to issue their own notes and operate branch structures both in Northern Ireland (which is of course a part of the United Kingdom) and in the Republic of Ireland, outside the United Kingdom. The last-named two banks have their head offices and main branch structures in the Republic

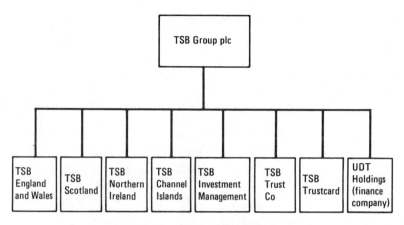

Fig. 5.2   Organization of the TSB Group plc

of Ireland, issue their own notes and maintain a number of branches in Northern Ireland.

Banks operating in Northern Ireland come under the control of the United Kingdom authorities just as do the London and Scottish clearing banks, although some exceptions in control are allowed because of the fact that they operate both in Northern Ireland and the Republic of Ireland.

(iv) **Girobank** was established in 1968 as a subsidiary of the Post Office. It provides a simple, cheap and efficient banking service. In summer 1988 the Government announced that Girobank was to be privatized and sought bids from interested parties. At the time of writing a new owner has not been announced.

Girobank enables certain bills, such as those for electricity, gas and telephone, to be paid by both account holders and non-account holders at any of nearly 20 000 post offices. When a Girobank account holder wishes to pay another account holder he fills in the appropriate form and posts it, using the special envelope supplied, to Girobank's Computer Centre at Bootle in Merseyside, where all accounting transfers are effected. As all the accounts are maintained in one place there is no clearing system to delay payment, and the transaction is carried out immediately upon receipt of the transfer form. Payments to people who do not have a Girobank account may be made by Girocheque which can be paid direct into a bank account; alternatively an open Girocheque without a crossing (see Unit 11.8) may be cashed at a post office after authentication at the Girobank Centre. Cash may be withdrawn by the account holder at certain post offices nominated by him, or at any post office if he has a Girobank guarantee card (which operates in a similar way to a cheque card). In either case the amount that may be withdrawn is restricted, but larger amounts may be drawn in cash if prior arrangements are made. At present the bank makes no charges for operating personal accounts provided that they remain in credit.

Other services include standing orders and direct debits, hire purchase facilities arranged through a finance house, overdrafts and loans (including mortgages), deposit accounts and the supply of travellers' cheques and foreign money. Links with European giro organizations enable British account holders to cash Girocheques at 80 000 post offices abroad. Services introduced for personal customers include bridging loans (a short-term loan used during house purchase to 'plug' the gap which occurs between paying for the new house and receiving the sale proceeds of the old one; see Unit 21.10(a)), budget accounts (a method of spreading the cost of bills more evenly over the year; see Unit 14.9), a credit card (see Unit 15.4) and automated teller machines (see Unit 15.5). Bridging loans, overdrafts and the cheque guarantee card are normally only available to those who have their salary paid directly into their Girobank account.

Customer balances total about £1 501 million (1987), with 30 000 business account holders—for example local authorities, Government departments, nationalized industries, mail-order firms, High Street chain stores—and some 2·5 million personal account holders. Girobank, like any bank, maintains some of its assets in the form of notes and coin, and balances at the Bank of England. It lends some of its funds to the discount market 'at call' (that is, the money is repayable on demand); the remainder of its assets are largely invested in the public sector in local authority loans, bills and bonds and British Government securities.

(v) **The Banking Department of the Bank of England** is classified as a retail bank. Its functions have already been discussed in Unit 4.3.

5.3   Merchant Banks

It is difficult to define the work of a merchant bank briefly: but in essence they are financial institutions providing specialist services which generally include the acceptance of bills of exchange, corporate finance, portfolio management and other banking services. There are perhaps some 100 institutions in Britain that call themselves merchant banks. Most are members of the British Merchant Banking and Securities Houses Association (BMBA).

Several of the present-day merchant banks started in business during the late eighteenth and early nineteenth centuries. Their origins are similar to those of the private country banks in that their founders were merchants, but they traded overseas rather than in Britain. As world trade expanded during the nineteentn century these merchants grew in reputation and soon found themselves being asked to lend their name to lesser-known traders by *accepting* bills of exchange (see Unit 11.3). By accepting a bill they guaranteed that the holder of the bill would receive full value at the date of payment; this *acceptance* business continues today. A bill of exchange that has been accepted by a reputable bank can be discounted or sold before maturity—the due date of payment—at *finer* or lower rates of discount than a commercial bill which bears only the acceptance of a trader.

In the nineteenth century, 'the bill on London' became the main instrument of payment for all goods and produce moving internationally. A bill drawn on a London accepting house or bank was often the preferred means of international payment, despite being almost invariably expressed in sterling. Meanwhile the merchant bankers also helped to increase the volume of international trade by developing the documentary *letter of credit* (see Unit 17.7). This was opened by the bank at the request of the buyer of the goods and authorized the seller to draw his bill of exchange on the merchant bank, with an undertaking that, provided the bill was accompanied by specified shipping and other documents relating to the goods, the merchant bank would accept it. The seller of the goods was satisfied because he knew he would be drawing a bill of exchange on a reputable merchant bank and could therefore sell the bill to someone else and thus receive its present value in cash immediately. The buyer was satisfied because, subject to arrangement with the merchant bank, he was receiving a period of credit. The merchant banker was satisfied because he could charge a commission for the use of his name. By thus specializing in the financing of international trade, the merchant banks were able to build up a store of information on traders throughout the world which further enhanced their expertise in international finance.

As their overseas business developed, the merchant banks began to be recognized as bankers and consultants not only by traders and overseas private customers, but also by overseas local and central governments. Many countries sought their advice in raising loans, and as a result London became the major world financial centre for the issue of foreign government bonds. This business flourished throughout the second half of the nineteenth century and early twentieth century, coming to an abrupt halt with the outbreak of the First World War in 1914.

After the war ended in 1918, the merchant banks attempted to restore their business to that of the pre-1914 world. Not only were they hampered by exchange control regulations which restricted the movement of money around the world; the clearing banks and the foreign and London-based overseas banks also moved into the market for overseas trade, as their competitors. A shrinkage of world trade in the early 1930s hit the merchant banks hard, and sterling declined as a world currency.

In the 1930s the merchant banks accordingly began to look for other areas of business; in particular, their role in the share issue function developed (see below). Also the late 1920s and early 1930s saw the founding of a number of investment trusts, and the merchant banks became involved in the management of their investments.

Since the end of the Second World War, merchant banks have considerably expanded their range of services and most are now active in the field of *corporate finance*, that is, providing companies with financial expertise. They assist their company customers to find suitable sources of finance often by arranging to sell or *issue* the company's shares to members of the public (see Unit 6.12 (*b*)) and obtain a stock exchange quotation for the shares—hence the name *issuing houses* for the banks involved. Such a task may last for several

'One day, young man, you could be wearing this suit!'

years from the first contact between company and bank to the date of 'going public', and requires considerable financial skill. They also have to liaise with the Council of the Stock Exchange, from whom permission has to be sought before a share may be 'quoted'.

Merchant banks also advise and assist companies in other aspects of corporate finance ranging from making a rights issue, under the terms of which existing shareholders are offered additional shares at an attractive price, to advice on merging with or taking over another company. Some banks act as company registrars, as the Bank of England acts as the registrar of Government stocks.

Besides the two main areas of acceptance of bills and corporate finance the merchant banks are specialists in the investment of clients' funds—*portfolio management*—on behalf of pension funds, investment trusts, unit trusts and private individuals. Pension funds collect contributions from people during their working lives and pay them a pension when they have retired; investment and unit trusts bring together sums of money from thousands of individual savers and invest the funds on their behalf. All these require expert investment management, and this can be provided by the merchant banks (see also Units 8.11 and 8.12).

They also offer banking services such as current, deposit and fixed-term deposit accounts, mainly for the company customer. In recent years some have developed factoring (a sales ledger accounting service which may include the granting of an advance against the debts owed to the company), leasing (the 'renting' of machinery and other assets), hire purchase (instalment finance for capital equipment) and insurance broking (see Unit 16). The merchant banks differ from the clearing banks principally in that they have few, if any, branches and are mainly 'wholesale' bankers accepting large sums on deposit, chiefly for fixed terms, from financial institutions, companies and individuals. When they lend it is usually to companies and for medium or long periods of time. Unlike the clearing banks, they may purchase shares in a company customer and play a direct part in its management.

Since the early 1960s, the merchant banks have become involved in dealings on the developing international money or eurocurrency market and the international capital or eurobond market. (Note that euromarkets are not restricted to Europe but are often world-wide—see Unit 19.9. The prefix 'euro-' can also apply to other things such as cheques and again does not imply that they can only be used in Europe.) In both these markets, merchant banks act for United Kingdom and foreign companies and state enterprises to assist in the raising of medium- and long-term finance in a range of currencies.

During the last two decades the major clearing banks have all developed an interest in merchant banking and each has either bought its way into an established merchant bank or set up a new one. Many of the corporate services of the clearing banks described in Unit 16 are offered through their merchant banking subsidiary.

5.4 Foreign Banks

Nearly 500 different foreign banks now operate in Britain, together employing nearly 60 000 staff. Most banks are situated in London, although some are beginning to establish branch networks. During the nineteenth century the merchant banks helped to establish London as the principal financial centre of the world and ever since the 1860s, banks from other countries have established themselves here, with the largest number arriving during the last twenty years. Most initially set up a representative office which does not transact normal banking business but provides a business contact service; later, as business develops, a branch providing a full banking service will be established.

The reasons for wishing to be represented in Britain are:

(i) to develop trade between Britain and the overseas country;

(ii) to provide financial services to businessmen from the overseas country while visiting Britain;

(iii) to provide a banking service to immigrants and foreign nationals from the overseas country, living and working in Britain;

(iv) to act as international bankers in a major world financial centre on behalf of businesses from the overseas country.

The foreign banks are dominated by some sixty American banks, most of them having arrived since 1965—there are now more American banks in London than there are in New York. They are particularly attracted to Britain because London is the centre of the market in eurocurrencies, of which the eurodollar is the most important (this is a market in lending and borrowing currencies outside their country of origin and is considered in detail in Unit 19.9). They are also here because of the development of North Sea oil and the increasing inter-country investment that is taking place between Britain and America. London also has a unique attraction to foreign banks with its 'time' advantage: it is open for business at some point in the day when both New York and Tokyo (and all intervening points of the globe) are also open.

Some American banks have established branch networks and are competing directly with the clearing banks by offering services aimed particularly at the personal customer; at the same time access to the clearing house has been granted to some American banks. A number of ethnic banks, such as Allied Irish Banks, Bank of Cyprus, Bank of Baroda and the State Bank of India, have set up domestic branches in competition with the big banks in districts where people from their own countries have settled in Britain.

5.5   Head Offices of British Overseas Banks

Just as overseas banks have established representative offices and branches in the United Kingdom, so British banks have been established overseas. The major development overseas took place at the height of the British Empire's power during the second half of the nineteenth century. Instead of setting up one branch in each capital city, 'retail' branch banking structures, modelled on those operating in Britain, were developed in the countries of the Empire, particularly in Africa, the Middle and Far East. Since 1945, as these countries have gained their independence, so more control of the banking system has been taken by their new leaders. Some banks have been nationalized, while others have been obliged to establish separate companies in the overseas country with the resultant problems of remitting profits back to Britain. The last twenty years have seen an escalation in the costs of administering a scattered retail branch network and it has not been unknown for the London office of such a bank to make higher profits than all of the overseas branches of the bank put together.

Four major British banking groups with large overseas branch networks still remain:

Barclays Bank has branches or subsidiary companies in Africa, the Caribbean, and more recently, California and New York;

Lloyds Bank has a large branch network in South America (formerly belonging to the Bank of London and South America) and, more recently, branches in a few towns and cities in Europe;

Grindlays Bank (owned by the Australia and New Zealand Banking Group) has branches in India, Pakistan and Africa;

Standard Chartered Bank has branches throughout Africa and the Far East.

With the changes in branch structures as a result of independence or altered politics in host countries, the British overseas banks have sought new areas of profitable business and their London offices have become active in the London money markets, particularly the eurocurrency and certificate of deposit markets (see Unit 19). Some British banks have developed interests in retail banking in North America.

5.6   Consortium Banks

As the name suggests, a consortium bank is formed by a group of other banks, usually from several different countries. The Bank of England defines it as a bank which is *owned by other banks but in which no one bank has a direct shareholding of more than 50 per cent and in which at least one shareholder is an overseas bank*. The first consortium bank to be formed was Midland and International Banks in 1964, the shareholders being the Midland Bank, Toronto–Dominion Bank, Standard Chartered Bank and the Commercial Bank of Australia. There are now just over twenty such banks operating in London.

These banks are formed in order to be able to put together large loan 'packages' to meet the financial requirements of large multinational companies for long periods of time. They are also able to arrange *syndicated loans*: this means sharing out large loans among syndicates of banks. The bank that is organizing the loan, called the *lead bank*, contacts up to fifty other banks inviting them to participate.

Consortium banks obtain their funds partly from the parent banks, but mainly from the eurocurrency markets.

5.7   Finance Houses

The idea behind the services of a finance house or hire-purchase company is that items are purchased on an instalment basis: the goods are supplied after payment of a deposit and the balance outstanding, together with interest, is paid by means of agreed instalments. In Britain, hire-purchase companies date back to the second half of the nineteenth century when they were established to finance the purchase of railway wagons for colliery companies—the word *wagon* still features in the names of some of the companies operating today. With the coming of the motor car in the early twentieth century, the companies turned their attention to financing the purchase of vehicles and during the period between the two World Wars widened their interests to include other consumer goods such as furniture, carpets and radios. During the 1960s and 1970s all the major banks established an interest in finance houses and the facilities they offer now include company services such as industrial hire purchase, factoring and leasing (see Unit 16).

Some of the finance houses developed the concept of the 'money shop': these are outlets situated in shopping centres and, in contrast to a lot of the imposing buildings of the banks, look like normal retail shops. Their hours of business are linked to shopping hours rather than the more limited banking hours, and their aim is to provide, in relatively informal surroundings, a range of services including the provision of hire-purchase 'packages' for a wide range of consumer purchases, acceptance of deposits, a current account service and other banking activities. The money shops owned by subsidiaries of the clearing banks also provide a cheque encashment service, backed by a cheque card, for personal customers of the parent bank. (The money shop concept has also been taken up by the major retail banks as the way forward for their own branches which deal mainly with personal customers.)

Finance houses obtain their funds by borrowing from banks and other financial institutions, and by accepting deposits from industrial and commercial companies and private individuals. As deposit-taking institutions, finance houses are closely supervised by the Bank of England.

The authorities are able to exercise control over the amount of credit granted under hire-purchase agreements by specifying a minimum deposit and a maximum repayment period. Most personal hire-purchase contracts are for the purchase of 'consumer durables' such as cars, washing machines, carpets, furniture or television sets; when the authorities wish to expand credit and make such items more readily available, they reduce the minimum deposit and extend the maximum repayment period. If, on the other hand, they wish to restrict credit and reduce sales of these items—perhaps to enable more to be exported or, more probably, to reduce the number of goods being imported—minimum deposits will be increased and maximum repayment periods will be reduced.

5.8 National Savings Bank

This bank was established under the name of the Post Office Savings Bank by an Act of Parliament in 1861. It was re-named in 1969 when it was separated from the Post Office and came under the control of the Government's Department of National Savings. As its original name suggests, it is operated through post offices and has the advantage of almost 20 000 post office 'branches' with far longer opening hours than banks. It is the largest organization of its kind in the world, with some 21 million active accounts.

Depositors' funds are lodged with the National Debt Commissioners and are invested in Government securities; thus the funds are guaranteed by the Government. There are two types of account: the *ordinary* and the *investment accounts*. The ordinary account carries a tax concession in that the first £70 of interest (£140 for a joint account) earned each year is free of all United Kingdom income tax. NSB accounts are discussed more fully in Unit 8.5.

5.9 Questions

1. Outline the types of bank that make up the present-day British banking structure.

2. In what broad respects does the role of a clearing bank differ from that of: (*a*) a merchant bank; (*b*) a building society?

    (*The Institute of Bankers*)

3. Trace the development of merchant banks and outline their present-day functions.

4. Distinguish between a central bank and a commercial bank. Why is there sometimes a conflict of interest between these two types of bank?

    (*The Chartered Institute of Bankers*)

Unit Six
Money Markets and Capital Markets

6.1 Financial Intermediation

The financial system in Britain consists of a number of different types of institutions of which the banks are one group of special significance. Any institution which provides a service of coming between lenders and borrowers is known as a *financial intermediary*. To understand the role of financial intermediaries, it is important to appreciate that in an economy, at any one time, there are:

(i) those who have a financial surplus, such as savers, who will dispose of these funds by lending them to others;

(ii) those who have a financial deficiency and need to borrow funds.

In a developed financial system the role of the financial intermediary is important in accepting deposits from those who have a financial surplus and then onlending these funds to those with a financial deficit. It is, of course, possible for those with a surplus to lend their funds directly to those with a financial deficit and, to some extent, this does occur. However, it is much more often the case that financial intermediaries, such as banks, building societies or insurance companies, are involved in the transaction. In this way, instead of a direct relationship between the lender and borrower of funds, there are two *financial claims:*

(i) the lender of the funds has a financial claim on the financial intermediary, and

(ii) the financial intermediary has a financial claim on the borrower of the funds.

The process of financial intermediation (Fig. 6.1) also solves problems which would arise if lenders and borrowers dealt directly with one another.

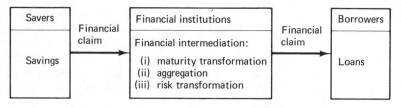

Fig. 6.1   Financial intermediation

These problems include *maturity transformation, aggregation* and *risk transformation*. We will now consider each of these briefly.

Frequently lenders wish to *lend short*, which means having their money available at relatively short notice. However, borrowers often wish to *borrow long*, that is for a lengthy period of time. A good example of this is seen in building societies where the depositors (lenders) want ready access to their funds, while the borrowers wish to borrow funds for perhaps twenty or more years. The building society as a financial intermediary is able to meet the needs of both lenders and borrowers by maturity transformation which is the process of converting the short-term funds of lenders into long-term loans for borrowers.

Savers may have small amounts of money which they wish to lend, while borrowers may require a large loan. The two requirements are reconciled by a process of aggregation, whereby a financial intermediary collects together a large number of relatively small amounts in order to be able to meet the demand for large sums of money.

When a lender directly lends to one borrower, the lender takes an 'all or nothing' risk—the loan may be repaid satisfactorily, or it may become bad and the lender will lose the full amount of his loan. By pooling risks the financial intermediary avoids this situation: while most loans will be good, a few will still go bad, but the impact of the few losses is spread over a greater number of satisfactory loans.

In Britain, banks are one type of financial intermediary and, later in this book, we shall consider more fully the forms in which they take deposits, and the forms in which they lend (see Unit 21). At the same time we must consider the functions of and inter-relationships between the other financial institutions operating in Britain's money and capital markets.

6.2   Money Markets and Capital Markets

Financial intermediaries who come between lenders and borrowers are the participants in the money and capital markets of Britain. A distinction can be made between the following:

   (i) short-term money markets;
  (ii) loan and savings markets;
 (iii) capital markets.

In spite of the above distinction, many of the participants in one of these markets do tend to overlap into others; for example, banks are active in the loan and savings markets and, at the same time, carry out dealings in the short-term money markets. Money markets can be further divided between 'retail' and 'wholesale'; retail markets deal in comparatively small amounts of money, while wholesale markets deal in wholesale sums of money—perhaps a minimum of £50 000.

The main participants in the three markets are:

(i) *short-term money market*—banks, discount houses, accepting houses and the Bank of England (see Units 6.6 and 6.7 for a discussion of the role of discount houses and accepting houses);

(ii) *loan and savings markets*—banks, building societies and insurance companies (see Units 6.9 and 6.10 for a discussion of building societies and insurance companies);

(iii) *capital markets*—the Stock Exchange (see Unit 6.12); finance corporations (see Unit 6.13).

6.3   Short-term Money Markets

As noted above, a money market—and the London money market in particular—provides the intermediation between those who wish to lend money and those who wish to borrow. Other markets, such as the Stock Exchange, have a fixed 'market place' where business is transacted; but the London money market is not centred in any one building. It operates by means of the telephone and personal meetings between those who deal in money.

Until the mid-1950s there was only one type of short-term money market in London—the *discount market*; this remains the primary short-term money market in Britain and its activities are fairly closely controlled by the Bank of England. During the late 1950s and 1960s a number of specialized *parallel* or *secondary markets* developed. These are fully discussed in Unit 19 and include six markets that deal in sterling and two in other currencies—see Fig. 6.2.

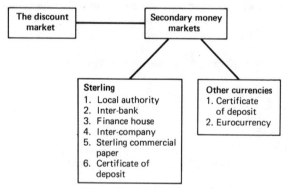

Fig. 6.2   The London money market

6.4   Development of the Discount Market

This market consists of the discount houses which form the London Discount Market Association (LDMA), together with certain firms carrying on a similar type of business and known as *discount brokers*. The origins of the market go back to bill broking in the late eighteenth and early nineteenth centuries: in those days the cheque had not come into general use, and debts between traders in Britain were often settled by means of a *bill of exchange* (see Unit 11). A trader taking an accepted bill from another trader would have to hold the bill until the due date for payment, often three months ahead. If he needed the money sooner, he could sell the bill to a bill broker at face value, less an amount of discount. At first the bill brokers only acted as intermediaries and re-sold or re-discounted these bills to the many small banks then in existence, who had surplus funds available for short-term investment. During the 1820s and 1830s the bill brokers began to act on their own account by holding some of the bills they had discounted, using as finance their own capital and funds borrowed from the banks on a short-term basis—hence the name *discount houses*. A major reason for this development was the building up of larger banking groups with branch networks; if certain branches accumulated surplus cash, this was employed by transferring it to branches that were short of funds, rather than by purchasing bills from brokers. These larger banks instead preferred to lend to the developing discount houses and soon found that they could lend spare funds to the houses for very short periods of time—often overnight. They could call in this money very quickly when they needed it and thus were able to keep a smaller proportion of their deposits in the form of cash, which paid no interest. The banks liked this arrangement because they could put their liquid funds to better use; the discount houses were pleased because they could use the short-term loans to develop their business.

During the second half of the nineteenth century the importance of the inland bill as a means of settlement between traders declined as the use of the cheque increased. At the same time Britain was developing rapidly as a trading nation and a bill of exchange was the accepted method of settling international trading debts, with London as the major centre for much of world trade. The discount houses began to involve themselves in discounting these foreign bills also. Nowadays the practice established in the nineteenth century continues; these houses still take the surplus short-term funds of the banking system and convert them into longer-term money that can be used not only by traders but also by the Government and industry.

6.5   Liabilities and Assets of the Discount Market

Table 6.1 shows the sources of borrowed funds—the *liabilities* of the market. It shows that most funds are obtained from the United Kingdom monetary sector. Much of it is lent on a short-term basis—on 30 June 1988, £9 570 million or 91 per cent of the sterling funds, was borrowed overnight—and the discount houses have to bear in mind that much of this money could quickly be recalled. When money is in short supply and the banks start to call in the funds lent to the discount market, there could be difficulties for the discount houses were it not that the Bank of England acts as their lender of last resort.

The Bank of England can help the market in two ways. Firstly, it can force

Table 6.1   The discount market: sources of borrowed funds (30 June 1988)
(*Figures are rounded to the nearest million by the Bank of England, so individual totals and sub-totals do not always add up.*)

	£ million	£ million
Sterling		
Bank of England	124	
Other UK monetary sector	7 576	
Other UK	2 757	
Overseas	41	10 497
Other currencies		
UK monetary sector	114	
Other UK	144	
Overseas	16	274
Total		10 772

Source: *Bank of England Quarterly Bulletin*

the discount houses, if they have searched elsewhere for funds unsuccessfully, 'into the Bank'. This means that they have to borrow from the Bank at interest rates which are generally higher than market rates. Security for the loan would be provided by Treasury bills and 'parcels' of eligible bank bills (see below) made up into convenient bundles of £50 000 each. Such assistance, while enabling the discount houses to balance their books, means that they make a loss on the business covered by the advance from the Bank—they must pay higher rates of interest on the advance than they can receive on their assets. As discount houses work on narrow margins between borrowing and lending rates, a small increase in their borrowing rates can mean the difference between profit and loss on a transaction. Thus they will only borrow from the Bank if no other financial institution has funds to lend and, because of the importance of the market in affecting other short-term interest rates, the effect of borrowing from the Bank is to increase general market rates.

Secondly, if the Bank does not wish to see interest rates rising, it helps the market by buying Treasury bills from the discount houses and when these are paid for, money will be put into the market without forcing up interest rates. Since 1980 the Bank of England has begun to place more emphasis on open-market operations, and less on last resort lending.

Table 6.2 shows the *assets* of the market, the major items being Treasury bills, other bills (mainly commercial bills), certificates of deposit and British Government stocks.

Table 6.2   The discount market: assets (30 June 1988)

	£ million	£ million
Sterling		
Cash deposits with the Bank of England	12	
Treasury bills	77	
Other bills	3 952	
Certificates of deposit	4 486	
Other funds lent	1 887	
British Government stocks	24	
Local authority investments	—	
Other investments	318	
Other sterling assets	65	10 823
Other currencies		
Certificates of deposit	24	
Bills	36	
Other	206	266
Total		11 087

Source: *Bank of England Quarterly Bulletin*

Fig. 6.3   A Treasury bill (shown at less than actual size)

Treasury bills (Fig. 6.3 is an example) are issued weekly to cover Government short-term debt and to 'tune' the money supply by taking up any surplus funds. They are issued either as *tender* or as *tap bills*, the latter being made available direct to Government departments and certain overseas monetary authorities with surplus funds to invest, while the tender issue is bought mainly by the discount houses, discount brokers and banks. The amount of bills offered each week varies with Government borrowing requirements and the constraints to be placed on the growth of the money supply by the authorities. Since 1971, the members of the London Discount Market Association have agreed to underwrite the Treasury bill issue on a collective but competitive basis. Thus the Government knows that the full amount of the issue will always be taken up; in return, the Bank is always prepared to act as lender of last resort to the market. Treasury bills are issued with a life of ninety-one days after which they are repaid at face value. Each potential buyer tenders for an amount of bills—the minimum tender is £50 000—and as the bills carry no interest, offers to buy at a price below the nominal or face value; for example, an offer might be made at £98.50 for each £100 of face value, representing an annual rate of discount of approximately 6 per cent. The Bank issues the bills to those with the highest tenders, that is, with the smallest rate of discount.

Bills of exchange are still used in inland and international trade to settle indebtedness between businesses or as a means of short-term finance; most involve an element of credit, since they are repayable at some time in the future, commonly after three months. A trader holding a bill on which another trader promises to pay in the future may, if he wishes to receive his money before the maturity date, sell the bill at a discount to a discount house. In order to make a bill saleable at a finer (or smaller) rate of discount—that is, at a higher price—it may be *accepted* by an accepting house or a bank and then becomes known as a *bank bill* or *bank paper*. A commission is charged by the house or bank for this service of lending its 'good name' to the bill and guaranteeing payment of the bill to the holder. The quality of the bank acceptance leads to a distinction among bank bills—they can be either *eligible* or *non-eligible* for rediscount at the Bank of England. Eligible bills are those that bear the acceptance of a large bank—British or foreign; those that are non-eligible have been accepted by smaller banks. This distinction becomes important when the discount houses wish to borrow from the Bank of England—parcels of eligible bank bills are acceptable as security, but other bills are not.

Since the 1960s there has been a considerable revival in the use of the bill of exchange in Britain, less as a means of settling inter-firm indebtedness than as a way of providing businesses with temporary finance. Finance houses and merchant banks, in particular, lend money to companies against the security of a bill of exchange under which the firm agrees to repay at a named future date. *Bill finance*, as this is called, charges interest rates that are usually competitive with other short-term rates, particularly with those paid on overdrafts.

The *local authority securities* held by the discount market consist of stocks, bonds and bills issued by British local authorities to finance their expenditure. The distinction between the three lies in the time period to maturity: *stocks* are usually the longest-dated and are issued only by larger authorities; negotiable *bonds* are issued by more authorities, having periods to maturity ranging from a few days to one year; while some local authorities have the legal powers to borrow by issuing *revenue bills* which are similar to Treasury bills and normally have a life of ninety-one days. Revenue bills are sought after by the discount houses because they, like certain bank bills, are eligible for rediscount at the Bank of England. This involvement in local authority securities has helped to give the discount houses a role in the local authority money market (see Unit 19.2).

The discount market holds a proportion of its assets in the form of *certificates of deposit*. A certificate of deposit is simply a certificate issued by a bank or other financial institution acknowledging that a sum of money—in sterling, dollars or other currency—has been deposited with it for a fixed period of time or at a pre-determined rate of interest. The certificates are negotiable and payable to bearer which means that the title to them can pass freely from one person to another by delivery of the certificate. Thus they are ideal for the discount houses to trade in or to hold as an asset. Like the market in local authority securities, the certificate of deposit market (which is considered more fully in Unit 19.6) has provided a new area of development for the discount houses.

British Government stocks—the longer-term debt of the Government—are also held as assets by the discount market. Most Government stocks have a maturity date (when payment becomes due) and the discount market usually holds those that will mature within five years.

The Bank of England maintains close control over the operation of the discount market. Under the present *Monetary Control* measures, which were introduced in 1981, the discount houses are defined as being part of the monetary sector. They are required to hold 0.45 per cent of their eligible liabilities (see Unit 7.6) in non-interest earning balances with the Bank of England.

In addition, the Bank of England operates rules governing the trading activities of the discount houses. These rules restrict the relationship between their capital and the maximum amount of assets they may hold. Furthermore, the type of assets held—whether of long-term or short-term, high risk or low risk—is tightly controlled by the Bank of England.

6.6   The Role of the Discount Houses

No other major financial centre has discount houses. What, then, is their importance in the London money market?

(i) The discount houses are very useful to the Bank of England because it knows that the weekly Treasury bill tender will always be covered by the market, thus ensuring that the Government short-term borrowing requirement will be taken up. Treasury bills also provide a way for the Bank to exercise fine tuning over the total amount of the money supply: by increasing or decreasing the amount of the tender, money can be taken out of the banking system or put into it, through the intermediary of the discount houses.

(ii) The rate of discount at the weekly Treasury bill tender is a good indicator of short-term interest rates.

(iii) The market is also useful to the Bank in that it makes good use of the short-term funds of the banking system and invests these funds in substantial amounts of public debt that would otherwise have to be financed less conveniently and more expensively.

(iv) To the banks that lend to the market, it is a useful place for short-term funds to earn a satisfactory rate of interest instead of lying idle.

(v) In addition, as mentioned earlier, the discount houses provide a useful source of short-term funds to the company sector by holding commercial bills.

In 1988 the Bank of England announced that it was extending the range of parties with whom it is willing to enter into a money market dealing relationship and hence to whom it will act as a lender of last resort. The new parties will, like the discount houses, participate in the weekly Treasury bill tender. Such new firms will be separate entities (that is, not a department of a retail bank), although they may be separate companies established by banks.

6.7   Accepting Houses

The accepting houses are members of the British Merchant Banking and Securities Houses Association (BMBA). Their business is concerned with accepting bills of exchange—for a commission. By accepting a bill (see Unit 11.3) they lend their name to a bill, and accept responsibility for it—that is, the holder of a bill duly accepted by them has the guarantee that the bill will be paid on the due date. The original holder may hold the bill until maturity or, alternatively, the bill can be sold at a fine rate of discount. Bills accepted by a member of BMBA are eligible for rediscount at the Bank of England: thus they are very suitable assets to be held by the discount market. In their role as merchant banks, accepting houses are involved in many other functions such as corporate finance, portfolio management, leasing and factoring.

6.8   Loan and Savings Markets

These markets are generally at the 'retail end' of the money markets, which means that they accept relatively small deposits from a large number of depositors and lend direct to a lesser, but still considerable, number of borrowers. Financial institutions which can be included in the loan and savings markets are banks, building societies and insurance companies. However, as noted in Unit 6.2, some institutions are also active in other money markets. (The topic of savings and investment is fully considered in Unit 8.)

6.9   Building Societies

Building societies are in theory non-profit-making organizations. They are specialist institutions that attract deposits from the personal saver market and then lend to borrowers who use the money primarily for the purpose of house purchase. Building societies are owned by their depositors who have share accounts and by those who are borrowers of the society. Unlike the shares of companies quoted on the Stock Exchange, the depositors with share accounts can withdraw their share or increase it at will, subject only to the society's regulations.

With branch networks, longer opening hours, a range of savings accounts, and the provision of other financial services, the building societies are the banks' biggest competitors in the personal savings market. Many savers compare the interest paid by building societies and the banks: any advantage of one over the other is quickly noticed and funds are soon transferred across. Within the building society movement there is intense competition on interest rates and services.

There are currently some 130 different building societies operating in Britain: they range from local societies with a few branches to the largest societies with branch networks all over the country. Most belong to the Building Societies Association (BSA), which imposes certain conditions on its members with regard to the maintenance of minimum ratios of reserves to total assets, and restricts the acceptance of very large deposits. In addition the BSA advises member societies on interest rates to be allowed to investors and charged to borrowers; however, in recent years there has been much competition among societies in respect of these rates. Building societies are supervised by the Building Societies Commission; each society is required to make an annual return to the Commission so that its financial perform- ance can be monitored.

Most societies offer a range of accounts which usually include a share account, deposit account, regular savings account, a term share account and high-interest accounts. These are considered in more detail in Unit 8.4. On the lending side, societies grant mortgages—with variable interest rates —for the purchase of a house for terms of up to approximately twenty-five years. There are two different repayment schemes. With a repayment mortgage, borrowers make monthly repayments which cover the interest and repayment of the principal. In the early years of such a mortgage most of the repayment amount meets the interest; in later years, towards the end of the mortgage period, an increasing part of the payment covers repayment of the principal. An alternative method of repayment is based on an endowment life assurance policy (see Unit 8.9); here the borrower takes out an endowment assurance policy to cover the amount of the mortgage. Monthly repayments throughout the period of the mortgage meet the interest payments on the loan, while the life assurance premium is paid monthly. The lump sum payable on maturity of the assurance policy is used to repay the loan.

In recent years building societies have expanded their interests and besides accepting deposits from the public and using funds to grant mortgages they have become involved in the parallel money markets both as investors and borrowers. They are particularly active in the certificate of deposit market (see Unit 19.6) and the eurobond market (see Unit 19.9).

During the last few years some building societies have widened the range of financial services they offer. A number of societies offer cheque book accounts and pay interest on credit balances, and supply travellers' cheques and foreign currency as well as discount and credit cards. In addition, cards have been introduced to enable the withdrawal of cash and other transactions from automated teller machines located at society branches, in large shops and, in some cases, machines outside post offices (which can also be operated by Girobank customers).

In 1986 a Building Societies Act was passed which gives the societies scope to expand their services considerably. While the primary role continues to be the provision of facilities for small savers and for house purchase, they are permitted to offer banking, insurance and stockbroking services. On the deposits side, the Act requires that at least 80 per cent of funds should be raised from personal savings, with a limit of 20 per cent on funds raised through the money markets and other sources. With lending, a minimum of 90 per cent of loans consist of first mortgages of residential property; the remaining 10 per cent can be split between other forms of secured and unsecured lending (increasing to 25 per cent by 1993).

The services which can be offered by societies have been expanded by the Act to include:

(i) a fuller range of personal banking and money transmission services;
(ii) property services such as estate agency and conveyancing;
(iii) agency roles for insurance broking;
(iv) the sale of stocks and shares; and
(v) the giving of investment advice.

Some of the larger societies will also be allowed to open branches, invest and collect savings throughout Europe. Participation in the Investment Protection Board—a method of protecting investors in building societies—is now compulsory. This provides for 90 per cent minimum cover for share account holders and 100 per cent cover for deposit account holders, against the first £20 000 balances held by each investor. An ombudsman has been appointed to consider the public's complaints, in the same way as the banking ombudsman (see Unit 13.2). The Act allows societies to become limited companies, offering their shares to the public.

The changes have had the effect of aligning building societies more closely with banks. This, together with the already increased competition between societies and the future possibilities for diversification, has removed protection from the less efficient societies and accelerated the merger process. In this way it would seem likely that, within a few years, the building society movement will be dominated by a handful of large societies, each with a nationwide branch network.

6.10 Insurance Companies

The main function of an insurance company is to provide financial compensation to those who suffer loss as a result of certain events. The insurance company pools the premiums paid by those who are insured and pays out against claims. Any insurance carries with it an element of risk—the event insured against may or may not happen or, if it is certain to happen, the timing is unknown. It is the job of an *actuary* employed by the insurance company to assess, using statistics, the chances of the event insured against occurring, and from this to calculate the premium payable by the insured.

Insurance companies divide their work into two main areas—*general* and *long-term*. General insurance covers risks ranging from fire and theft to loss of profits and also includes such things as motor insurance and accident insurance. Long-term insurance is concerned mainly with life assurance and pension policies. Notice the term *assurance*, implying that the event covered by the policy is certain, or assured, to happen: a person with a life assurance policy will either reach a certain age or die before reaching that age. Contrast this with *insurance*: the law requires us to take out third-party liability insurance before we drive a car or ride a motor-cycle on the roads—we hope that we will never have to make a claim on the policy but we insure against the possibility.

Both insurance and assurance are services offered by the banks to their customers and, because of the variety of facilities available, plenty of opportunities arise for selling policies to customers. Here the bank is acting as an *insurance broker*, that is, a 'go between' who brings together the insurance company, who issues or underwrites the policy, and the buyer, the customer requiring insurance services. Life assurance and pension policies are discussed more fully in Units 8.9 and 8.11, while other insurance services are dealt with in Unit 15.12.

As insurance companies collect premiums from their policyholders, so they have funds available for investment. Indeed, with life assurance and pension policies, insurance companies may be receiving premiums for a period of between thirty and forty years, sometimes longer, before payment has to be made to the policyholders. So insurance companies are major 'institutional' investors and hold a wide spread of short-, medium- and long-term assets. Short-term assets include cash, balances with banks, certificates of deposit and local authority bills; medium-term assets include Government securities, local authority loans, shares and debentures in British and overseas companies, and unit trusts; long-term assets include mortgages, loans and investments in land and property. With a number of the longer-term policies, such as life policy and pension policies, the insurance company is often prepared to make a loan to the policyholder against the value of the policy.

6.11 Capital Markets

Businesses, in the form of public limited companies (see Unit 13.5) require long-term or permanent capital in order to finance their activities, or to undertake expansion schemes. In a similar way Government, both central and local, needs large quantities of funds in order to be able to provide and expand services such as education, health-care and defence. As the amount of money required by both companies and Government is so large, they will seek to raise money from members of the public—companies will offer loan capital and share capital, while the Government will offer Government stocks. In each case the public are being asked to lend money or take a share in a business, in return for which they will either receive interest on the amount lent or a share of the profits made.

Once a company or the Government has collected funds from the public, it is not possible to repay each individual lender and investor as and when they require. This is because the money has been used and may well now exist in the form of machinery or buildings, for instance. If there was no method of obtaining early repayment, lenders and investors would be unwilling to subscribe their funds. The Stock Exchange solves this problem by providing a market for the buying and selling of existing shares and loans.

In addition to the Stock Exchange, there is an international capital market consisting of the eurobond market which is discussed in Unit 19.9.

6.12 The Stock Exchange

The Stock Exchange (Fig. 6.4) provides a secondary market for shares and other public limited company securities (such as loans) and for Government stocks. Securities listed on the Stock Exchange have the benefit of liquidity and marketability and are thus more attractive to investors than those in companies which are not listed. However, to become listed and to remain

Fig. 6.4   The Stock Exchange building, London

listed companies must sign a *listing agreement* with the Stock Exchange. This agreement requires listed companies to provide information in their annual accounts further to that required by the Companies Acts. The Stock Exchange will not consider granting a listing for a company with a total market value of below £500 000 and at least 25 per cent of the shares must be made available to the public. As the cost involved is substantial, it is usually larger companies who seek a listing.

(a) The Unlisted Securities Market (USM)

The Stock Exchange has established an *Unlisted Securities Market* (*USM*) for smaller, growing, companies. This offers many of the benefits of listing. A smaller company expecting to grow and to come to the Stock Exchange would usually start in the USM, possibly with a view to seeking a listing at a later date. The requirements for the USM are less onerous than for listed companies and costs are considerably lower. There is no minimum size for a company seeking entry to the USM, although it must be registered as a public limited company (see Unit 13.5). Companies are required to offer only a minimum of 10 per cent of their share capital to the public but in addition they must provide considerable financial detail to potential shareholders covering the past three years. A company entering the USM must sign a *general undertaking*, which is a commitment to follow a set of rules of future behaviour and imposes certain obligations concerning the disclosure of information to investors.

(b) Issuing Shares to the Public

A number of merchant banks act as *issuing houses*, in conjunction with stockbrokers, to issue a company's shares (see Unit 5.3). A new issue of shares arises when a company seeks a listing for the first time or when a company that is already listed seeks to raise additional capital. New issues take place in six ways.

(i) **Introduction.** This method is used where a company has shares in issue which are already traded but outside the Stock Exchange. A listing for the company's shares is granted and they can then be traded on the Stock Exchange. This method does not introduce new money into the company.

(ii) **Placing.** In a placing an issuing house or stockbroker purchases a company's shares and offers them to selected clients.

(iii) **Prospectus issue.** Here the company itself offers its shares direct to the public for subscription. The main disadvantage of this method is that the company cannot be certain that the total number of shares will be applied for, and it may be left with a number of unsold shares. This method has largely been superseded by the offer for sale.

(iv) **Offer for sale.** This is the most common method of bringing new companies to the stock market: the company sells its shares to an issuing house, which then offers the shares to the public at a fixed price. Most offers for sale are underwritten—that is, the issuing house arranges with a number of institutions, such as insurance companies, pension funds and banks, for shares to be taken up if they are unsold. The underwriting institutions receive a commission for providing this 'insurance'. If an offer for sale is *oversubscribed*—applications are received for more shares than are being offered—the issuing house scales down the applications and the smaller applications are often subject to a ballot.

(v) **Tender.** A tender issue is exactly like an offer for sale, except that the price of the shares is not fixed in advance. Instead, applicants state on a tender form (Fig. 6.5) the number of shares they are applying for and the price they are prepared to pay; a minimum tender price is usually stated. All the shares are allotted at the same price to those who tendered at or above this price. An

TENDER FORM

This form must be lodged at the Bank of England, New Issues (B), Watling Street, London, EC4M 9AA not later than 10.00 A.M. ON THURSDAY, 21ST FEBRUARY 1985, or at any of the Branches of the Bank of England or at the Glasgow Agency of the Bank of England (25 St. Vincent Place, Glasgow, G1 2EB) not later than 3.30 P.M. ON WEDNESDAY, 20TH FEBRUARY 1985.

ISSUE BY TENDER OF £400,000,000

$2\frac{1}{2}$ per cent Index-Linked Treasury Stock, 2013

TO THE GOVERNOR AND COMPANY OF THE BANK OF ENGLAND

I/We tender in accordance with the terms of the prospectus dated 15th February 1985 as follows:—

Amount of above-mentioned Stock tendered for, being a minimum of £100 and in a multiple as follows:—

Amount of Stock tendered for	Multiple
£100—£1,000	£100
£1,000—£3,000	£500
£3,000—£10,000	£1,000
£10,000—£50,000	£5,000
£50,000 or greater	£25,000

1. NOMINAL AMOUNT OF STOCK

£

Sum enclosed, being the amount required for payment in full, i.e. the price tendered for every £100 of the NOMINAL amount of Stock tendered for (shown in Box 1 above):—

2. AMOUNT OF PAYMENT (a)

£

The price tendered per £100 Stock, being a multiple of 25p (tenders lodged without a price being stated will be rejected):—

3. TENDER PRICE (b)

£ : p

I/We request that any letter of allotment in respect of Stock allotted to me/us be sent by post at my/our risk to me/us at the address shown below.

Please pin top left corner of cheque here

_____February 1985

SIGNATURE......................
of, or on behalf of, tenderer

PLEASE USE BLOCK LETTERS

MR/MRS MISS	FORENAME(S) IN FULL	SURNAME

FULL POSTAL ADDRESS:—		
POST-TOWN	COUNTY	POSTCODE

a A separate cheque must accompany each tender. Cheques should be made payable to "Bank of England" and crossed "New Issues". Cheques must be drawn on a bank in, and be payable in, the United Kingdom, the Channel Islands or the Isle of Man.

b Each tender must be for one amount and at one price which is a multiple of 25p.

Fig. 6.5 A tender form

advantage of issuing shares by tender is that difficulties are avoided over fixing the issue price, particularly in periods when stock market prices are continually changing.

(vi) **Rights issue.** When additional capital is required (perhaps to finance a new project) a company's total number of shares may be increased by means of a rights issue. This gives existing shareholders the 'right' to buy more shares—on a pro-rata basis to their existing holdings—below the market price. Shareholders who do not wish to take up their entitlement can often sell their right to others. The rights issue is an inexpensive way of raising additional capital because no costly advertising to the general public is needed, and existing shareholders will usually be prepared to take up the issue because of their interest in the company.

The purchase of stocks and shares as investments is considered fully in Unit 8.12.

6.13   Finance Corporations

The Stock Exchange provides a major source of long-term funds for large public limited companies, while banks traditionally provide short-term finance for smaller businesses. There has often been criticism that new firms and new industries, together with small- to medium-sized companies, have no capital market which provides them with longer-term finance. *Finance corporations* are companies formed to meet the financial requirements of such businesses. Such corporations are able to provide capital both in the form of loans and equity (ordinary share) finance, together with a range of other financial services.

Investors in Industry plc (known as '3i') is perhaps the most important finance corporation. Its origins go back to 1945 when British industry needed considerable financial assistance. It is owned by the London and Scottish clearing banks and the Bank of England.

3i provides long-term capital, ranging from a few thousand pounds to tens of millions of pounds, to companies of all types and sizes at every stage of their development—from start-up and expansion, through to acquisition and diversification, management buyout or flotation on The Stock Exchange. Loans are granted on repayment terms of between five and twenty years; interest rates may be fixed, variable, or a combination of both. Equity capital, in the form of minority shareholdings, is also provided.

3i also supports small, high-growth businesses, particularly those in the field of new technology.

Equity Capital for Industry Ltd (*ECI*) was established in 1976 to provide equity capital for companies with growth potential that could not readily raise capital from traditional sources. ECI is owned by a consortium of financial institutions and provides finance to companies of between £250 000 and £4 million.

Agricultural Mortgage Corporation PLC (*AMC*) was formed in 1928 to provide finance for the purchase of farm land and buildings, for capital improvements or for working capital. AMC is owned by the London and Scottish clearing banks and the Bank of England. Long-term loans are offered at fixed or variable rates, with the farm property itself used as security.

6.14   Interlinking the Money Markets

We have seen in this Unit how the money markets in Britain divide into three main categories:

(i) short-term money market (including the parallel markets);
(ii) loan and savings markets;
(iii) capital markets.

However, as we have seen in Unit 6.2, it is impossible to 'pigeon-hole' participants into one market rather than another. For example, banks are very active in both the short-term and the loan and savings markets, and also have a part to play in the capital markets through their investments in Government securities. Fig. 6.6 (p. 76) shows, in simplified form, the main participants and their relationships within the short-term money market.

6.15   Questions

1. What are the main sources and uses of funds of the discount houses?

2. What functions are performed by the discount houses?

3. Few major financial centres have discount houses. Why has London?

4. Explain the inter-relationships between the Bank of England, the discount houses and the commercial banks.

5. Distinguish between: (*a*) Treasury bills; (*b*) trade bills; and (*c*) bank bills.

6. Describe the functions of the main participants in the loan and savings market.

7. Compare the main functions of banks and building societies. How do they differ, and how far do they compete directly with one another?

8. By what methods can the shares of a public limited company be issued to the public?

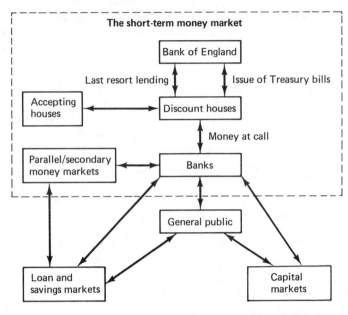

Fig. 6.6   The main participants in the short-term money market; links with other money markets

Multiple-choice Questions—3

Read each question carefully. Choose the *one* answer you think is correct. Answers are given on page 390.

1. A merchant bank is principally concerned with:

    A the operation of 'money shops'   **C** corporate finance
    B hire-purchase   **D** loans for house purchase

2. A consortium bank is:

    A a group of other banks, usually from different countries
    B another name for a major clearing bank
    C the main bank in a country, which usually holds the Government's bank account
    D the representative body of the Committee of London and Scottish Banks

3. Certificates of deposit are issued mainly by:

    A the Treasury   **C** local authorities
    B banks   **D** the Bank of England

4. An eligible bank bill:

    A is accepted by a large bank
    B is repayable in 91 days' time
    C is issued by the Treasury to cover Government short-term debt
    D is issued by banks to cover short-term borrowing from the Bank of England

5. The main reason for the issue of Treasury bills is:

    A to meet the requirements of Government short-term debt
    B to provide the discount houses with working capital
    C to meet the requirements of Government long-term debt
    D to cover the issue of banknotes by the Bank of England

6. The primary short-term money market in London is:

    A the Bankers' Clearing House   **C** the eurocurrency market
    B the Stock Exchange   **D** the discount market

7. Institutions at the 'retail end' of the money market comprise:

    A discount houses and the Bank of England
    B discount houses and the parallel money markets
    C banks, discount houses and the Bank of England
    D banks, building societies and insurance companies

8. The main source of borrowed funds of a discount house is:

    A the Stock Exchange   **C** the Government
    B banks   **D** the Bank of England

9. The Stock Exchange provides a market in:

    A certain Government stocks and company shares
    B the shares of all companies
    C certificates of deposit
    D discounting bills of exchange

10. An offer for sale of shares takes place when:

    A a company's shares are sold to an issuing house, which then offers them to selected clients
    B a company's shares are sold to an issuing house, which then offers them to the public
    C a company offers its shares direct to the public
    D a company, whose shares are already traded outside the Stock Exchange is granted a listing on the Stock Exchange

A Bank's Balance Sheet

7.1 Introduction

It is important to be familiar with the make-up of a bank balance sheet, and you will find it helpful to study the annual Report and Accounts of one of the major retail banks; these are generally readily available from branches and head office from late March onwards, and cover the preceding financial year which usually runs from 1 January to 31 December. As an example of a bank's balance sheet, that of Lloyds Bank Plc at 31 December 1987 is given in Fig. 7.1. This balance sheet is presented in *vertical format*, rather than the *horizontal format* which you may be familiar with from your studies in accountancy. The horizontal format shows the assets of a company on the left and the liabilities on the right whereas the vertical format lists the company's liabilities beneath the assets. Either format is acceptable but the vertical format is favoured by many companies because it shows the assets used by the business, and then the way in which they are financed. The information making up the balance sheet is the same for both formats—it is only the style of presentation that is different.

The assets of a bank comprise:

(*a*) cash and balances at the Bank of England;
(*b*) cheques in course of collection;
(*c*) money at call and short notice;
(*d*) Treasury bills;
(*e*) other bills;
(*f*) other market loans;
(*g*) certificates of deposit;
(*h*) special deposits (when required to be held);
(*i*) investments;
(*j*) advances to customers;
(*k*) investments in subsidiaries and associated companies;
(*l*) premises and equipment.

The liabilities are:

(*a*) issued share capital;
(*b*) reserves;
(*c*) loan capital;
(*d*) current, deposit and other accounts;
(*e*) other liabilities.

Lloyds Bank Plc
Balance sheet at 31 December 1987

Assets employed:	£ million
Cash and short-term funds	3 738
Cheques in course of collection	822
Investments	791
Advances and other accounts	25 706
Balances with subsidiaries	4 578
	35 635
Investments in subsidiaries	1 229
Trade investments	174
Premises and equipment	1 099
	38 137

Financed by:	
Liabilities:	
Current, deposit and other accounts	31 264
Balances with subsidiaries	3 076
Current and deferred taxation	(97)
Dividend	70
	34 313
Dated loan capital	452
Undated loan capital	981
Share capital and reserves:	
Issued share capital	809
Reserves	1 582
	2 391
	38 137

Fig. 7.1   A bank's balance sheet

Published bank balance sheets do not usually show the breakdown of assets
and liabilities in full detail: a number of items are often grouped together
under a cumulative heading.

We shall now consider each of the items that appear on a bank's balance

'Well, we haven't made any profit, but the report may win an Arts Council award'

sheet, and discuss the information that can be derived from the figures presented in it.

7.2   Assets of a Bank

When listing the assets on a balance sheet, most companies begin with those assets that would take the longest time to turn into cash (usually factory premises), followed by those that would take the next longest time, and so on until the very last asset, cash itself. The idea behind this used to be to impress upon a person looking at the balance sheet the strength of the company in its *fixed assets*, as the first items under the assets heading on the balance sheet are called—normally factory premises, machinery, motor vehicles and so on. A bank, on the other hand, prefers to show the readers of its balance sheet its liquid position, that is, that it holds sufficient cash and other liquid assets to be able to repay its depositors. Ever since the days of the country banks, therefore, bank balance sheets have always listed their assets starting with cash, followed by other liquid assets and finishing with fixed assets.

(*a*) Cash and Balances at the Bank of England
Cash represents the amount of notes and coin held by bank branches and head

offices to meet demands for withdrawals by customers. Although under earlier arrangements for control of the banks a minimum percentage of cash to deposits was required, nowadays the banks maintain only sufficient notes and coin to meet demand.

Balances at the Bank of England comprise, in the main, two items. Firstly, under the 1981 *Monetary Control* arrangements, the Bank of England requires all institutions in the monetary sector with eligible liabilities of £10 million or more to keep 0.45 per cent of their eligible liabilities in non-interest earning balances at the Bank of England, that is, as a cash ratio deposit. Secondly there is the operational balance held at the Bank through which the daily cheque clearing and other inter-bank indebtedness is settled. In addition to these two balances, the Bank of England may make a call for special deposits (see (*h*) below).

(*b*) Cheques in Course of Collection

Any cheques paid into a bank that are drawn on other banks and branches need to be 'cleared' through the clearing system, which takes three to four days (see Unit 11.9); a cheque paid in at the branch on which it is drawn is debited to the drawer's account on the same business day. Most cheques, however, have to be cleared, and the asset on a bank's balance sheet represents the claim that the bank has on other banks for items in course of collection. On the balance sheet of Lloyds Bank Plc in Fig. 7.1 this item is £822 million and is the total of all cheques drawn on other banks that have been paid into Lloyds Bank branches for the credit of accounts and which still remain in the clearing system. During the few days following the date of the balance sheet, these items would pass through the Bankers' Clearing House and payment would be received by Lloyds from the banks on which they were drawn. As cheques are constantly being paid into accounts at banks other than that on which they are drawn, at any moment there are always cheques in course of collection.

(*c*) Money at Call and Short Notice

This asset consists of funds lent mainly to the discount houses; they are secured by the deposit of Treasury bills, certain commercial bills and short-dated Government stocks. It is either lent *at call*—that is, it can be called in immediately—or at short notice for periods of up to fourteen days. The rates of interest earned by the banks on this asset vary with the length of the loan and availability of funds in the market. An overnight loan usually earns a lower rate of interest than one for a week; when funds are in plentiful supply on the money markets the rates are lower than when there is a shortage.

After cash, this is the most liquid asset on a bank's balance sheet, and would be called in if the bank was short of funds.

(*d*) Treasury Bills

These provide a safe short-term investment for part of a bank's assets and also earn a reasonable return. Being issued weekly and having a life of ninety-one days they give a 'quick turn-round' from cash back to cash again and can normally be bought and sold through the discount market at any stage in their life. Clearing banks do not buy Treasury bills when first issued; instead they normally hold them when they have been acquired 'second-hand'.

(e) Other Bills

These are bank bills, trade or commercial bills and local authority bills which the bank has either discounted for its customers or purchased in the market to hold as assets until maturity. Bank bills are bills of exchange that bear the acceptance of a bank and, depending upon the quality of the acceptance, these may be either eligible or non-eligible for re-discount at the Bank of England (see Unit 6.5). Trade or commercial bills are those that have been accepted by a business; local authority bills are issued, of course, by certain local authorities as a means of short-term finance. The return on this asset varies depending upon the type of bill held: 'eligible' bank bills, often known as 'fine' bank bills, are considered undoubted and command the 'finest' rates, giving the lowest return; other bank bills, local authority bills and trade or commercial bills bearing the acceptance of a first-class company follow at somewhat higher rates; other trade and commercial bills have the largest rates of discounts and therefore the highest return, but they will carry the greatest risk of non-payment.

(f) Other Market Loans

The banks, besides lending substantially to the discount market, also make other loans on the secondary money markets (see Unit 19) such as the inter-bank, local authority and inter-company markets. Such loans are for differing time periods; most are short-term, but some may be for up to five years.

(g) Certificates of Deposit

These are issued by banks to customers who are prepared to deposit funds for a fixed period of time at fixed interest rates (see Units 6.5, 19.6 and 19.8). Certificates issued by banks in exchange for a deposit received would form a part of the liabilities on the balance sheet in the 'other accounts' section. However, banks also hold certificates issued by other banks as investments and these feature on the assets side of the balance sheet. The rates of interest earned on certificates held vary according to the period remaining to maturity: for those approaching repayment date, rates are close to bank base rate; for those with longer periods to run, rates are higher.

(h) Special Deposits

These are sums of money that all banks may be required to deposit with the Bank of England (see Unit 4.9(b)). While these are held by the Bank of England they cannot be used by the banks, so that they have the effect of reducing the amount that can be lent to customers. Interest is usually paid on these deposits at rates that are linked to the weekly Treasury bill rate, but at certain times when the Bank wishes to penalize the banking system severely, no interest is paid at all.

(*i*) Investments (Other than Trade Investments)

A study of the notes forming part of the annual Report and Accounts of a bank will show the make-up of these assets. The majority of investments are either British Government stocks or stocks guaranteed by the Government—*gilt-edged* securities. Most of these have fixed repayment dates and a bank's investments will aim to give a good spread of repayments over the next five or six years. From the security point of view, they are first-class assets to hold, as the British Government, whatever we may think of it, is unlikely to default on its debts. Interest earned is usually well above the bank's base rate, particularly that on the medium-dated stocks, and if these investments have to be realized, they can be readily sold on the Stock Exchange.

(*j*) Advances to Customers

This is the largest asset on a bank's balance sheet and includes all forms of bank lending; as we saw in Unit 1.1, a basic function of any bank is to lend the surplus funds deposited with it. The balance sheet of Lloyds in Fig. 7.1 shows that its advances and other accounts were at that date £25 706 million, or 82 per cent of current, deposit and other accounts of £31 264 million. Loans and overdrafts are technically repayable on demand, except for amounts lent for a specific period of time, such as medium-term and personal loans. In practice few advances could be repaid immediately and some lending is 'solid', showing little, if any, reduction from year to year. Thus advances, although shown in the current assets section of the balance sheet, are the most illiquid of these assets. The rates of interest charged on loans and overdrafts reflect this illiquidity and also the greater risk of bad debts. Rates (except for those charged to very large companies, which are now often linked directly to money market rates) are generally linked to a bank's base rate: larger companies whose rates are linked to base rate will probably pay lower effective rates (say 1 or 2 per cent above base rate) than small businesses and private customers, who will often pay 3 or 4 per cent above base rate; the difference could reflect a different degree of risk and/or a lesser degree of lending priority. Most interest on advances is calculated on the daily balance outstanding on the account, but that charged on certain types of accounts, particularly personal loans (see Unit 14.8), is calculated on the amount of the original loan for the period of the loan even though regular repayments are reducing the original amount. This means that the 'true' rate of interest is higher than the 'nominal' rate. Unit 9 deals with the topic of interest rates in greater detail.

Table 7.1 shows the amounts lent by banks in the United Kingdom at 31 May 1988 to different categories of borrowers. These amounts will vary somewhat with the time of year; advances to agriculture, for instance, reduce in the autumn as payments are received for crops and increase in the spring when the farmers' expenses often exceed their income. Similarly Bank of England qualitative directives which tell the banks which customers are to receive priority (see Unit 4.9(*a*)) vary the amounts lent to different categories of borrower; thus the Bank can discover whether its directives are being carried

Table 7.1   UK monetary sector: analysis of bank lending in sterling and foreign currencies to United Kingdom residents at 31 May 1988 (*Figures are rounded to the nearest million by the Bank of England, so individual totals and sub-totals do not always add up.*)

	£ million	£ million
Manufacturing industry		
Extractive industries and mineral products	1 971	
Metal manufacturing	1 189	
Chemical industry	2 216	
Mechanical engineering	2 318	
Electrical engineering	3 799	
Motor vehicles	1 358	
Other transport equipment	1 518	
Other engineering and metal goods	2 189	
Food, drink and tobacco	6 937	
Textiles, leather, clothing and footwear	2 348	
Other manufacturing	8 013	
		33 856
Agriculture, forestry and fishing		6 240
Energy and water supply		
Oil and extraction of natural gas	3 144	
Other energy industries and water	808	
		3 952
Construction		8 843
Garages, distribution, hotels and catering		
Retail motor trades	2 883	
Other retail distribution	9 384	
Wholesale distribution	11 433	
Hotels and catering	6 320	
		30 020
Transport and communications		4 557
Financial		
Building societies	7 003	
Investment and unit trusts	6 613	
Insurance companies and pension funds	3 139	
Leasing companies	9 911	
Securities dealers, stockbrokers, jobbers, etc.	14 272	
Other financial	31 767	
		72 705

	£ million	£ million
Business and other services		
Central and local government services	1 421	
Property companies	16 661	
Business and other services	20 152	
		38 234
Persons		
Bridging finance for house purchase	1 538	
Other house purchase	38 183	
Other	30 695	
		70 416
		268 823
TOTAL		
of which:		
Sterling	222 313	
Foreign currencies	46 510	
	268 823	

Source: *Bank of England Quarterly Bulletin*

out by inspecting the regular classification of advances that it calls for from the other banks.

(k) Investments in Subsidiaries and Associates

These are the investments in subsidiary and associated companies and trade investments that the bank has made in order to diversify its activities: a note in the annual Report and Accounts will give a list of these. *Subsidiaries* are companies that are controlled by the parent bank; they may include such companies as the bank's finance company, merchant bank, Scottish and/or Northern Ireland bank, insurance services company, stock exchange firm and so forth. *Associated companies* are those in which the bank does not have a controlling interest, but holds around 20 per cent or more of the share capital on a long-term basis, and participates in management. There are some associated companies in which all the major clearing banks participate, such as BACS Ltd (formed to process computer tapes which contain the details of bankers' orders and direct debits) and The Joint Credit Card Company Ltd (which operates the 'Access' card scheme on behalf of member banks). There are also the major banks' associated companies such as their consortium and overseas banking interests. *Trade investments* are those in which the bank has a smaller holding than 20 per cent of the share capital, and are used to give a bank access to specialist companies or to provide an opening overseas for a British bank. For example, some banks have a holding in Investors in Industry plc (which provides finance for industrial firms that, for various reasons, cannot obtain funds direct from their own banks) and the Agricultural Mortgage Corporation PLC (which provides specialist long-term mortgages for the purchase of farms—the type of lending that, because of the time period, would not be acceptable to a commercial bank). Unit 6.13 gives more detail on these two companies.

(*l*) Premises and Equipment
This represents the investment made by the bank in branch and other premises, and in assets such as vehicles, computers and other equipment.

7.3   Liabilities of a Bank

(*a*) Issued Share Capital
This is represented by a large number of shares held by individuals, institutional investors and companies. Most shares issued by banks are *ordinary shares*, with a nominal value of £1 each, but some have also issued *preference shares* (see Unit 13.5(*b*)).

(*b*) Reserves
There are two types of reserves:

   (i) capital reserves;
   (ii) revenue reserves.

(i) **Capital reserves** come about when assets of the bank or company are revalued, as when branch bank premises that were purchased some years ago are revalued to bring them into line with current property valuations: the premises would be shown at the increased value on the assets side of the balance sheet, while on the liabilities side the amount of the increase would be placed to a capital reserve account called *revaluation reserve*. Another type of capital reserve arises when shares are issued to the public at a higher price than the nominal value: the amount of the issue price in excess of the nominal value is placed to a *share premium account*.

(ii) **Revenue reserves** are the profits earned over the years that have not been distributed to shareholders and that have been set aside to meet possible future requirements.

The important distinction between a capital reserve and a revenue reserve is that the latter can be distributed to the shareholders as a dividend (subject to the business having sufficient cash to pay the dividend), whereas the former cannot be distributed in this way; instead it may be used to give bonus issues of shares.

For many years banks were permitted to make transfers to hidden reserves which were not disclosed in the published balance sheet. The fact that banks were known to have substantial hidden reserves may have led to increased confidence in the British banking system. During the 1960s, however, there was pressure from the press and public for a disclosure of true profits, and matters came to a head in 1968, when the Monopolies Commission report into the merger of Barclays, Lloyds and Martins banks (see Unit 3.6) criticized the veil of secrecy drawn around bank profits and urged disclosure of the true figure. The banks finally agreed to this commencing with their financial years ending 31 December 1969.

(c) Loan Capital

Most of the major banks have loan capital of different types in issue. The loan capital (or stock) may be dated or undated. With *dated* loan capital the funds are lent to the bank for a set time period, and a date for re-payment is given. Some banks have made bond issues on the overseas capital markets; the Report and Accounts will give full details of loan capital in issue, usually as a note. It will often be found that the loan stock or capital is described as *subordinated*: this is a type of stock rarely issued by companies other than banks. In the event of the bank's winding up, the holders of this stock would be paid only after the depositors had been repaid in full; in a company winding up, on the other hand, the normal loan stockholders will often be paid in full before the general creditors. A bank's depositors are in fact its creditors, although they are a special class of creditors needing increased rights.

Most major British banks also issue a type of *undated* loan capital called *perpetual floating rate notes*. Interest on these is paid at a variable rate linked to rates on the inter-bank money market (see Unit 19.3). A feature of this type of capital is that while loan interest is paid to holders, if the bank should go into liquidation the notes rank as preference shares and would be repaid before ordinary shareholders. The notes count as part of the capital of the bank when calculating the free capital ratio (see Unit 7.7).

(d) Current, Deposit and Other Accounts

These form the largest liability on a bank's balance sheet. They are a liability because the customers—personal and business customers as well as other banks—have paid money into their accounts and the bank is liable to repay that money; the depositors, whatever type of account they have, are creditors of the bank and thus have credit balances. In modern banking, deposits may take the form of several different types of account (see Unit 14) besides the traditional current and deposit accounts, although these still form the 'bread and butter' of any bank's balance sheet.

(e) **Other Liabilities**

This section includes any amounts due to subsidiary companies, provisions for taxation on profits due to the Inland Revenue, proposed dividends to shareholders, and other general creditors of the bank to whom amounts are owing at the balance sheet date.

7.4   A Bank's Sources and Uses of Funds

We have already seen in Unit 6.1 that banks act as *financial intermediaries*, accepting deposits from customers and lending a major part of this accumulated 'pool' of money to other customers. Thus the largest liability on a bank's balance sheet is the amount due to its account holders who have deposited money with the bank; the largest asset is the amount due from customers who are borrowing from the bank.

A bank's main source of funds—its liabilities—comes from its depositors but capital is also contributed by the bank's shareholders, and from retained profits. The funds—assets—are used mainly for lending to customers but, at the same time, substantial amounts are kept in the form of cash, short-term funds and investments.

7.5   Liquidity versus Profitability

Many a small private country bank in the mid-nineteenth century went out of business as a result of difficult trading conditions in the district in which it operated. If a rumour began that a bank was having difficulty in making repayments to its customers, no matter how ill-founded it might be, there would soon be a queue of people wanting to withdraw their deposits. This could escalate into a 'run on the bank', which would most probably result in the bank having to close its doors and go out of business. Even in the 1970s and 1980s, there have been banks in Britain unable to meet repayments: in late 1973 and early 1974 several secondary banks faced financial difficulties after becoming over-involved in lending to property speculators, and had to be helped out by means of a rescue operation, known as the 'lifeboat', organized by the Bank of England and largely financed by the major banks. Partly as a result of this, the Banking Act of 1979 was passed in order to improve the Bank of England's ability to supervise banking institutions, while the Banking Act 1987 broadens the Bank's influence further. The 1979 Act also led to the setting up of the Deposit Protection Fund.

It is vitally important for banks to maintain sufficient cash and near-liquid funds that could be used to repay depositors. However, the problem of maintaining assets in the form of cash or near-liquid funds is that the quicker an asset can be turned into cash, the lower the rate of interest it earns. Assets that take longer to turn into cash command higher rates of interest, and the highest rates are charged for the most illiquid of a bank's assets, advances to

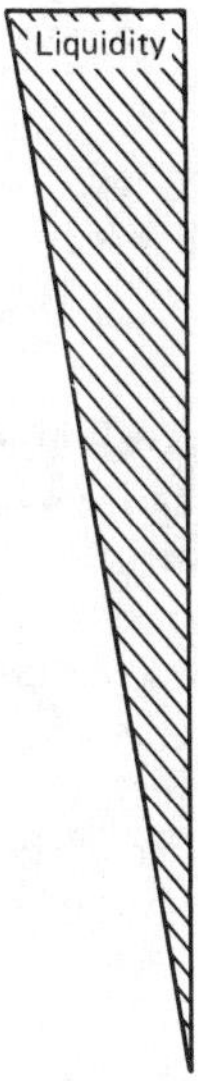

Asset	Period of loan	Borrower	Approx. per cent yield*
Cash	–	–	Nil
Money at call and short notice	1-14 days	Mainly discount houses	10-11
Bills discounted	Average about 1½ months (some mature regularly)	Government, businesses, local authorities	11½ (Treasury bills) 12 (other bills)
Other market loans	Up to 12 months or longer on exceptions	Banks, local authorities	11½-12½
Investments	Up to 5-6 years (spread of repayments)	Government and local authorities	9½-11
Advances	Technically overdrafts are repayable on demand (but see Unit 7.2); loans may be for a fixed term	Private persons and industry	14-17

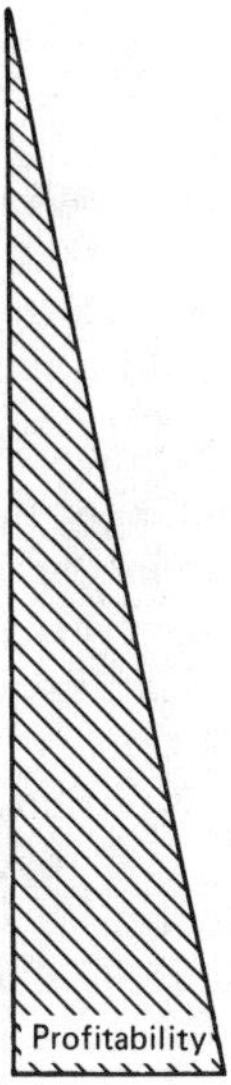

Liquidity (top-left) ... *Profitability* (bottom-right)

*Approximate rates at October 1988 (bank base rates 12%)

Fig. 7.2   Liquidity versus profitability

customers. Thus a bank has to strike a balance between good liquidity and its reducing effect on profits, and high profitability with the consequent worsening of the liquidity position. Fig. 7.2 highlights the problems of liquidity versus profitability—you can find the current rates in the *Financial Times*.

7.6   Eligible Liabilities

The *Competition and Credit Control* measures of 1971 introduced the term 'eligible liabilities'. A bank's eligible liabilities comprise:

(i) sterling deposits, of an original maturity of two years or under, from United Kingdom residents (other than banks) and from overseas residents (other than overseas offices), and all funds due to customers or third parties which are temporarily held on suspense accounts (other than credits in course of transmission);

(ii) all sterling deposits—of whatever term—from banks in the United Kingdom, less any sterling claims on such banks;

(iii) all sterling certificates of deposit issued—of whatever term—less any holdings of such certificates;

(iv) the bank's net deposit liability, if any, in sterling to its overseas offices;

(v) the bank's net liability, if any, in currencies other than sterling; less

(vi) 60 per cent of the net value of transit items in the bank's balance sheet.

(The *Monetary Control* measures introduced in August 1981 amended the calculation of an institution's eligible liabilities by allowing 'offsets' in respect of:

(*a*) funds lent to the other institutions in the monetary sector; and

(*b*) money placed at call with money brokers and gilt-edged jobbers on the Stock Exchange and secured on gilt-edged stocks, Treasury bills, local authority bills and bills accepted by 'eligible' banks.)

Put more simply, eligible liabilities consist of all the sterling deposits of the banking system that are repayable within two years—current and deposit accounts and so forth, plus the net balances of deposits from other banks (whenever they are repayable), plus the net amount deposited in respect of certificates of deposit, plus net deposits in foreign currencies. Deducted from this total is 60 per cent of net transit items to allow for credits in course of transmission (a liability) and cheques in course of collection (an asset). The 60 per cent figure applies because 'transit' items affect overdrawn or loan accounts as well as credit accounts and this is thought to be a fair estimate of the proportion concerning credit accounts.

Under the *Competition and Credit Control* measures, which were in operation from 1971 until 1981, the banks were required to maintain a certain percentage of their eligible liabilities in the form of eligible reserve assets. This was known as the *reserve asset ratio*, and for most of the period of *Competition and Credit Control* the figure was 12½ per cent. The eligible reserve assets broadly comprised balances at the Bank of England, Treasury bills, money at call with the London money market, certain Government and nationalized industries' stocks, and certain local authority and commercial bills eligible for rediscount at the Bank of England. The reserve asset ratio was abolished by the 1981 *Monetary Control* measures.

7.7   Bank Balance Sheet Ratios

Although we have considered the problems of liquidity versus profitability in Unit 7.5, a number of balance sheet ratios can be used to assess a bank's balance sheet. These include:

(i) free capital ratio;
(ii) cash and balances at the Bank of England to deposits;
(iii) liquid assets to deposits;
(iv) capital base.

(*a*) Free Capital Ratio

$$\text{Free capital ratio} = \frac{\text{Shareholders' funds and loan capital less fixed assets}}{\text{Deposits}}$$

This ratio is used by the Bank of England to judge the capital adequacy of banks. Free capital, that is capital minus fixed assets, is compared with deposits. The Bank of England does not work to any specific minimum level of free capital to deposits, instead using the ratio as an indicator of capital adequacy. Clearly the ratio will vary from one institution to another because of the different size and scope of operations of the individual institutions making up the monetary sector. However, a free capital ratio of between 5 and 6 per cent would probably be considered to be adequate.

(b) Cash and Balances at the Bank of England to Deposits

Cash and balances at the Bank of England to deposits =

$$\frac{\text{Cash and balances at the Bank of England}}{\text{Deposits}}$$

This compares the funds that are either cash itself (notes and coin) or closest to cash (the operational balances held at the Bank of England) with deposits. As a measure it is a cash ratio and, as no guidelines are now laid down, it can be used to make comparisons from one accounting return to the next, or between banks. On 30 June 1988 notes and coin and operational balances at the Bank of England held by United Kingdom retail banks amounted to just under 2 per cent of their total sterling deposits (this figure would be somewhat different for banks such as merchant banks which were involved less in retail banking and more in specialist types of banking).

(c) Liquid Assets to Deposits

$$\text{Liquid assets to deposits} = \frac{\text{Liquid assets}}{\text{Deposits}}$$

The liquid assets of a bank are those assets that are cash itself, together with other assets which can be readily turned into cash either by selling the assets or calling in short-term loans. A bank's liquid assets comprise:

(i) notes and coin;
(ii) operational balances with the Bank of England;
(iii) market loans, including
   (a) money at call and short notice deposited with the London Discount Market Association;
   (b) other sums lent to institutions in the United Kingdom monetary sector;
   (c) certificates of deposit, issued by institutions in the United Kingdom monetary sector;
   (d) certain loans to United Kingdom local authorities.
(iv) bills, including
   (a) Treasury bills;
   (b) eligible local authority bills;

(c) eligible bank bills;
(d) other bills.

On 30 June 1988 liquid assets held by the United Kingdom retail banks amounted to 24 per cent of their total sterling deposits.

(d) Capital Base

(i) Capital base $= \dfrac{\text{Shareholders' funds}}{\text{Assets}}$

(ii) Capital base $= \dfrac{\text{Shareholders' funds and loan capital}}{\text{Assets}}$

These ratios compare the capital of the bank (which can be expressed in the two ways shown) with the bank's total assets. The calculations, when expressed as a percentage, are used to make comparisons between two or three years' accounts for the same bank, or between different banks.

After the reserve assets ratio was scrapped in 1981, the Bank of England issued a paper in 1982 entitled, *The Measurement of Liquidity*. The Bank now approaches the measurement of bank liquidity by means of a potential cash flow approach. This means that an individual bank's liabilities and assets are placed on a 'maturity ladder': for example, the first rung on the ladder—the first maturity band—compares sight and near-sight liabilities (current and deposit accounts) with cash and assets capable of generating cash immediately. In this way, longer-term liabilities are linked, on the ladder, with longer-term assets. This technique reflects the considerable changes that have taken place during recent years to the structure of bank balance sheets: on the one hand an increasing proportion of deposits (liabilities) are placed for fixed terms instead of at sight; on the other hand, an increasing amount of lending (assets) is for the medium- and longer-term (for example home loan mortgages), rather than overdrafts which are technically repayable on demand. Using this maturity ladder technique, the Bank of England is provided with a framework for discussions with individual banks about the need for liquidity, taking into account the bank's particular circumstances. The Bank of England also concerns itself with the balance sheets (and other aspects) of the other companies within the banking group—finance company, trust company and so on. While these usually operate separately from the bank itself, they come under the supervision of the Bank of England.

Table 7.2   Retail banks: assets and liabilities at 30 June 1988
(Figures are rounded to the nearest million by the Bank of England, so individual totals and sub-totals do not always add up.)

	£ million	£ million		£ million	£ million
Liabilities			**Assets**		
Notes issued		1 221	*Sterling assets*		
			Notes and coin		2 280
Sterling deposits			Balances with Bank of England		
UK monetary sector	20 774		(including cash ratio deposits)		857
Other UK	129 084				
Overseas	18 426				
Certificates of deposit	12 368		Market loans:		
		180 652	Secured money with LDMA*	5 031	
			Other UK monetary sector	21 321	
Other currency deposits			UK monetary sector certificates		
UK monetary sector	6 920		of deposit	4 343	
Other UK	6 665		UK local authorities	953	
Overseas	28 483		Overseas	4 868	36 516
Certificates of deposit	4 545	46 613			
			Bills:		
Capital and other			Treasury bills	52	
liabilities		42 863	Eligible local authority bills	476	
			Eligible bank bills	6 951	
			Other	368	
					7 847
			Advances:		
			UK	131 257	
			Overseas	4 698	
					135 955
			Banking Department (of Bank of		
			England) lending to central		
			Government		626
			Investments:		
			British Government stocks	5 185	
			Other	4 490	9 675
			Other currency assets		58 167
			Sterling and other currencies		
			Miscellaneous assets		19 425
		271 348			271 348

* London Discount Market Association

Source: *Bank of England Quarterly Bulletin*

7.8   Sterling and Other Currency Deposits

In Unit 5 we discussed the wide range of banks operating in Britain today, from the clearing (or retail) banks to overseas banks from most countries of the world. In this Unit we have looked particularly at a major retail bank's balance sheet, but the other banks also have comparable assets and liabilities. The main difference between the banks lies in the proportions in which they hold their assets and liabilities. Table 7.2 shows the assets and liabilities of retail banks at 30 June 1988. It can be seen from this that their sterling deposits

Table 7.3   Banks in the United Kingdom: assets and liabilities at 30 June 1988
(*Figures are rounded to the nearest million, so individual totals and sub-totals do not always add up.*)

	£ million		£ million	£ million
Liabilities		**Assets**		
		Sterling assets		
Notes outstanding	1 221	Notes and coin		2 317
Sterling deposits	351 920	Balances with Bank of England:		
		Special and cash ratio deposits	996	
Currency deposits	571 492	Other	310	
				1 306
Items in suspense and				
transmission	17 423	Market loans:		
Capital and other funds	58 989	LDMA*	7 664	
		Other	113 636	
				121 300
		Bills		9 257
		Advances	225 003	
		Banking Department (of Bank of England) lending to central Government	626	
		Investments	21 430	
		Miscellaneous	23 201	
				270 260
				404 435
		Foreign currency assets		
		Market loans	419 154	
		Advances	126 510	
		Bills	3 065	
		Investments	37 739	
		Miscellaneous	10 141	
				596 609
	1 001 045			1 001 045

* London Discount Market Association
Source: *Bank of England Quarterly Bulletin*

totalled £180 652 million, while their other currency deposits totalled £46 613 million; thus sterling dominates the deposits of these banks. On the assets side of their balance sheets, a similar position results when sterling assets are compared with other currency assets.

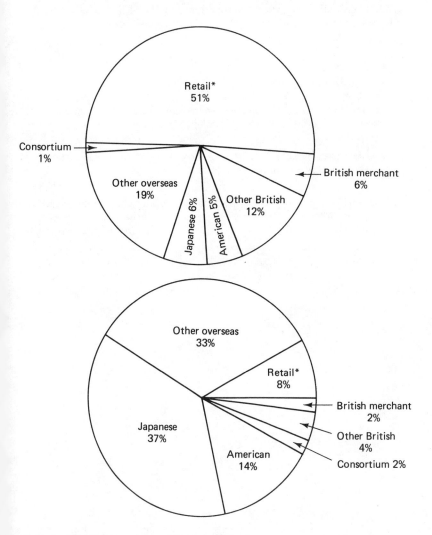

*Includes Banking Department of Bank of England

Fig. 7.3   Banks in the United Kingdom: (a) sterling deposits and (b) other currency deposits 30 June 1988 (from data given in the Bank of England Quarterly Bulletin)

Table 7.3 shows the assets and liabilities at 30 June 1988 of *all* banks operating in the United Kingdom. The surprising fact to emerge is that currency deposits exceed sterling deposits by nearly two to one; likewise with currency assets. Table 7.3 also shows that a very high proportion of currency assets are in the form of market loans and reflect the importance of London as a major centre in the eurocurrency market. Fig. 7.3 illustrates the relative importance of sterling and other currency deposits to the different types of banks.

7.9   Questions

1. Describe the main assets that appear in a retail bank's balance sheet, indicating their special characteristics and their relationships to banking business.

    (*The Institute of Bankers*)

2. Why does a bank need liquidity? How does a bank provide for liquidity in the use it makes of the deposits entrusted to it?

    (*The Institute of Bankers*)

3. The whole business of banking depends upon maintaining the confidence of depositors. What steps does a banker take to safeguard depositors' interests?

    (*The Institute of Bankers*)

4. What is meant by the term 'liquidity'? Identify the liquid assets held by banks. Explain why and how the assets side of a bank's balance sheet is affected by a conflict between profitability and liquidity.

    (*The Chartered Institute of Bankers*)

Unit Eight
Savings and Investment

8.1 Why Save?

Saving may be defined as *not spending income on consumption*. Therefore that part of our after-tax income that we have not spent on consumption or expenditure on goods and services is saved.

Why do we save? There are two main reasons: we may save for a specific purpose, such as to pay for a holiday or a motor-cycle, or we may save for an unspecific purpose, such as 'for a rainy day' or to have something to fall back on in the event of some unexpected expense occurring in the future.

To save for either of these reasons would involve refraining from spending a part of our income and putting it on one side. We could put it in a jug on the mantelpiece or, more sensibly, into a bank or building society account or some other form of savings scheme: the length of time before the savings are likely to be needed determines the most suitable place for them.

The definition includes another form of saving that does not involve the task of transferring money into an account and can be called 'unconscious' saving because it takes a form that most people would not acknowledge as saving: examples of this kind of saving are payment of premiums on a life assurance policy and the repayment of a mortgage on a house. In each of these, money from present after-tax income is not being spent on consumption but is being put aside for the future. At some stage the life assurance company will pay out a lump sum of money on their policy and the mortgage will be repaid, the cash value of the house representing savings.

While most saving is voluntary—each individual takes his own decision to save—some saving is compulsory, such as National Insurance, which pays for sickness and other benefits, and contributions to pension funds.

In Britain the three main sectors of the economy, the general public, businesses and the Government, all 'save': for example, companies may not distribute all of their profits to the shareholders, but will retain them, or plough them back into the business; similarly, the Government may have a surplus of income over expenditure, and there are many other organizations and institutions that have surplus funds. Each of the three sectors uses savings to make investments. Investment, in economic terms, is the use of savings to provide the finance required:

   (i) for businesses to buy new premises, machinery, and to raise the funds to finance increased manufacturing capacity;

   (ii) for the public sector to carry out public works, such as building new or reconstructed houses, roads, schools, hospitals and sewers;

(iii) for individuals to buy new, or improve existing, houses.

Thus investment increases a country's productive capacity, and raises the standard of living. It is through a range of savings media that small amounts of personal savings are collected and the amounts pooled to provide the finance for investment projects.

Table 8.1 shows the extent of savings and investment in the United Kingdom and also the net savings or investment for each sector. You will note that the companies are net savers, while the personal and public sectors are net investors.

Table 8.1   United Kingdom savings and investment (1987)

	Personal sector £m	Public sector* £m	Industrial and commercial companies £m
Savings	14 824	5 572	45 540
Investment	(22 048)	(10 723)	(34 525)
Net surplus (deficit)	(7 224)	(5 151)	11 015

* Central Government, local authorities and public corporations
Source: *Bank of England Quarterly Bulletin*

The retail banks with their nationwide network of branches are able to provide a first-class money transfer service in which they have few competitors: they also offer various savings and investment facilities to their customers, but in this area they meet competition from a whole range of institutions offering numerous schemes with a bewildering array of differing interest rates and conditions. The objective of this Unit is to consider the range of savings and investment facilities provided by banks and other financial intermediaries. As rates of interest offered to savers are subject to fluctuations, none are quoted in the text, but Table 8.3 (see p. 122) gives those of the major savings institutions at the time of writing. A column of the table has been left blank for you to enter the current rates.

8.2   Retail Banks

The clearing or retail banks directly offer the following savings and investment facilities:

(i) deposit and/or savings accounts;
(ii) fixed-term deposits; and
(iii) their own unit trusts.

Indirectly they offer the facilities of their associated finance houses (see Unit 8.3) and act as agents in the provision of most of the savings and investment schemes mentioned in this Unit.

(a) Deposit and/or Savings Accounts

The operation of these accounts is fully considered in Units 14.3 and 14.4. They are ideal places in which to keep savings that are temporarily not needed. The money is readily available: normally seven days' notice of withdrawal is required, but in practice it is usually possible to make withdrawals without prior notice. Interest is calculated on a day-to-day basis and is usually credited to the account twice a year, often in June and December. It is paid *net*, after deduction of *composite rate tax* (CRT), for personal customers. However, for limited companies, clubs, charities and overseas residents, interest is paid in full without deduction of tax. It should be pointed out that both banks and building societies pay interest on deposit and other accounts net. There is no further basic rate income tax to pay on the interest received—the bank or building society accounts directly to the Inland Revenue in respect of the composite rate tax. The level of CRT is set each year by the Government and is at a rate less than that of basic rate income tax. The rate takes into account the fact that not all depositors pay income tax and thus is an estimate of the balance between non-taxpayers and those who pay basic rates. Higher rate taxpayers are required to account to the Inland Revenue only for the difference between higher rate and the basic rate. CRT deducted cannot be reclaimed, even by non-taxpayers. Thus for a non-taxpayer, such as a person living only on a State pension, neither banks nor building societies are the best places to keep too large an amount of savings. However, personal customers, resident in Britain, can obtain interest gross if they place deposits with an 'offshore' bank, for example the subsidiary company of a major bank based in the Channel Islands or the Isle of Man. The tax rules in such centres are applied in a different way than in mainland Britain.

In recent years a range of special accounts has been introduced by most banks which allows interest on credit balances and also provides cheque book facilities (although the use of cheques may be restricted in certain ways). There are also accounts paying interest on credit balances which also permit overdrafts—see Unit 14.5.

(b) Fixed-term Deposits

Where a customer has from about £500 to invest, all banks can offer improved interest rates if the sum of money can be deposited for a set period of time, ranging from a few days to up to five years. The rate of interest will either be fixed for the term or be variable, linked to market interest rates. A fixed rate depends on the time period and how the bank views the trends in interest rates in the future: usually the longer the time, the higher the rate of interest. The customer benefits in that the interest rate is fixed for the period or, where variable rates apply, they will be higher than that paid on deposit accounts. Against this, however, none of the funds can be withdrawn before the end of the term. Interest on these deposits is paid net to personal customers (gross to certain others—see (a) above), usually twice a year.

(c) Unit Trusts

These provide a way for a saver to invest in shares and gilt-edged securities indirectly: units may be bought or sold easily by dealing direct with those who run the trust—the unit trust managers—without the need to go through stockbrokers. Most people do not have sufficient time, experience or capital to be able to invest directly in stock exchange securities; a unit trust solves this problem by collecting together a pool of money subscribed by a large number of individual savers and then buying and selling securities with this money, using the expertise of professional investment managers. In return for his funds, the individual saver receives either a certificate or a statement, showing that he holds a certain number of units in the trust. The income of the trust consists of dividends and interest on the investments paid by the companies and, after deduction of certain management expenses, this is divided between the investors on the basis of the number of units held by each, and either distribution cheques are sent to them or the income is used to buy more units on their behalf.

The value of units in a trust varies with the changes in value of the securities purchased by the investment managers, and prices at which units may be bought (offer price) and sold (bid price) appear in most daily newspapers. While such transactions can be carried out by dealing direct with the unit trust, any bank is able to make purchases or sales for its customers. An investment in a unit trust should always be regarded as long-term because of the changes which may take place in the value of the securities owned by the trust as a result of fluctuating stock exchange prices; such changes will, of course, affect the value of the units.

There are at present a large number of different unit trusts—some connected with banks, others with insurance companies, and a number with professional savings companies. Most unit trusts state clearly their investment strategies. The first is whether the unit trust is to be a *general fund*, which invests in a variety of shares of industrial and commercial companies, or a *specialist fund*, which will concentrate its investments into specialist shares such as those of small companies, overseas companies and markets, groups of shares such as those of financial or oil companies, or gilt-edged securities. The second strategy is whether to invest for *capital growth* (that is, so that the value of the units will increase over a period of time) or for *income* (by concentrating its investments into shares which are likely to pay high dividends so that large distributions can be made to unitholders).

While an intending investor can buy units of certain trusts from the bank, he can buy others direct from insurance companies and the professional savings companies. There is a variety of purchase schemes such as *straight purchase* (a sum of money is paid and a certain number of units received), *regular instalments* (monthly or other regular payments are made to the trust managers to be applied in the purchase of units) and *share exchange schemes* (an exchange of units for shares already held). There are some savings schemes linked with life assurance which are offered by a number of trusts, including those operated by the banks. The terms and conditions vary, particularly with the age of the unitholder: details are readily available from banks, unit trust managers and life assurance companies.

In law a unit trust is constituted by a trust deed made between the managers and the trustee, who must be independent of each other. The *trustee* of the fund—usually a bank or an insurance company—safeguards the interests of the purchasers of units who are beneficiaries of the trust fund, controls the issue of units, maintains a register of holders and generally watches over the management of the trust. The *managers* are the promoters of the unit trust, having the task of persuading the investing public to entrust its money to them for managing, and are responsible for investment policy and the day-to-day management of the fund, and for making a market in the units. They aim to make a profit out of promoting the trust from the charges they are entitled to levy for their services. The trustee will not interfere with the day-to-day management of the trust unless the actions of the managers are in conflict with the interests of unitholders.

8.3   Finance Houses

Most banks have a finance house as a subsidiary or associated company and there are a number of houses not connected with a bank. All of these offer, among other facilities, hire purchase to personal and business customers. Most accept deposits from members of the public as a source of a part of their funds and pay interest at rates that vary with the amount of money and the time period. Where larger amounts, commonly more than £1 000, can be deposited for fixed terms of between one and three years, higher rates of interest can usually be obtained. Interest on accounts is paid net, that is, after deduction of income tax at the basic rate. Depending on the type of deposit, notice of withdrawal will vary between one month and twelve months.

8.4   Building Societies

The role of building societies as financial intermediaries and the part they play in the loan and savings market have already been discussed in Unit 6.9. As noted there, building societies are the main competitors of banks for the retail savings market. Most societies offer a range of accounts which will usually include a share account, a deposit account, a regular savings account, a term share account and high-interest accounts for larger sums of money. The terms of these accounts—minimum deposit, notice of withdrawal required, maximum 'on demand' withdrawal account, and so on—vary from one society to

'It's something of a needle match between the bank manager and the building society manager'

another; it would be useful for you to obtain some leaflets from different societies and make a comparison between them. As with banks, interest on building society accounts is paid net (after deduction of composite rate tax—see Unit 8.2(*a*)).

(*a*) Share Account

This is the commonest type of building society account. The account holder is deemed to be a member of the society and holds shares, but unlike shares of companies quoted on the Stock Exchange, he may withdraw his share or increase it at will, subject only to the society's regulations. Interest is calculated on a day-to-day basis and is normally paid twice a year, and most societies give the investor the option of either having his interest credited to his account or receiving it by cheque. Withdrawals can be made either in cash or by cheque, subject to any limitations imposed by the society.

(*b*) Deposit Account

The deposit account offers the same facilities as a share account but with even greater security: a depositor only lends his money to the society whereas a share account holder has a share in the society. In the unlikely event of a society meeting financial difficulties, the depositor would be repaid in full before the share account holders. The additional security is recognized by the payment of a slightly lower rate of interest on deposit accounts than on share accounts.

(c) Regular Savings Account

This account is for people who wish to save a part of their income regularly. The saver agrees to make monthly payments into the account of, usually, between £1 and £200 (£400 for a joint account)—the amount can be altered, subject to the maximum and minimum limits, if financial circumstances should change. The time period for saving is not fixed and limited withdrawals are permitted; alternatively, the account may be closed when the funds are required. Interest rates are higher than for share and deposit accounts.

(d) Term Share and High-interest Accounts

Building societies offer higher rates of interest if funds can be deposited for a fixed period of time, rather like the fixed-term deposits of the banks. Unlike the bank deposit rates, however, the interest rates are subject to fluctuation but are usually 2 to 3 per cent above those offered on share accounts, depending on the length of the period for which the funds are deposited; but minimum deposits are much lower than those required by the banks and may be as low as £500, although this varies from one society to another.

Societies also offer high-interest accounts where the rate of interest paid by the society alters according to the balance held in the account. For example, with balances below £500 the rate will be at a certain level, with balances of £500 and above but below, say, £1 000 a slightly higher rate will be paid (on the entire sum deposited), an even higher rate will be paid on balances of between £1 000 and £5 000, and so on. There are often restrictions on this type of account, such as ninety days' notice of withdrawals being required or, if immediate withdrawals are permitted, there is a loss of interest in lieu of notice.

Perhaps the biggest benefit that the building societies can and do offer is their ability to give special consideration to their investors for a mortgage. Some societies have devised special accounts for first-time home buyers whereby they will guarantee a mortgage after a set period of regular savings, subject to certain conditions. However, not all investors are interested in obtaining a mortgage and building societies offer a safe, convenient place to keep savings with a range of accounts to suit most requirements, but, as noted in Unit 8.2(a), building societies generally are not a good investment medium for the non-taxpayer to keep all or most of his or her savings.

8.5   National Savings Bank

This public sector bank has already been discussed briefly in Unit 5.

The National Savings Bank, which is run by the Government's Department for National Savings, offers two accounts for savers—the ordinary account and the investment account.

Ordinary accounts may be opened by anyone aged seven or over, clubs and societies, and any amount from £1 may be deposited up to a maximum balance of £10 000. Interest is calculated on a monthly basis from the first day of each month. It is credited to the account on 31 December each year and is paid gross of tax. A tax concession applies in that the first £70 of interest (£140 for a joint account) is free of all United Kingdom income tax. A depositor may withdraw up to £100 cash on demand at any savings bank post office but the pass book may be retained for checking at Savings Bank Headquarters. Larger amounts may be withdrawn in cash or by crossed warrant (which is similar to a cheque) by completing a notice of withdrawal form, but it takes a few days for the transaction to be authorized. A limited range of free banking services is also available with this account:

(i) *Paybill*: this service allows customers to pay bills that would normally be payable at a post office, by debit to the account. Such bills include electricity, rates, vehicle road fund licence and television licence. It is also possible to make payment to other organizations who have Girobank accounts, although a small charge may be made.

(ii) *Standing orders*: regular payments by standing order can be made provided the frequency is not more than once a month.

Ordinary accounts have a two-tier interest rate structure: a higher rate of interest is paid on accounts which retain a certain minimum balance (currently £500) for a complete month.

Investment accounts are intended for longer-term savings. The interest rate is higher than that on ordinary accounts; it is calculated on a daily basis but is paid gross of tax with no tax concessions. Accounts may be opened on similar terms to the ordinary account. The minimum deposit is £5 and the maximum balance is £100 000. One month's notice of withdrawal is required and this is effected by completing a withdrawal form, the payment being made either in cash at a named savings bank post office or by crossed warrant.

8.6   National Savings

The Department for National Savings offers a variety of savings facilities, besides the National Savings Bank. These include National Savings Certificates, Yearly Plan Certificates, Premium Savings Bonds, Income Bonds and Capital Bonds; all may be bought at most banks and all savings bank post offices. Certain Government stocks and bonds may be bought through the Department at low rates of commission (see Unit 8.7).

(a) National Savings Certificates
These were first issued in 1916 and there have been several subsequent issues. At present there are two types of National Savings Certificate available: *fixed interest* certificates which are a longer-term investment with a guaranteed tax-free return and *index-linked* certificates which are a tax-free investment with full protection against inflation and an extra return as well. Both types of units may be purchased by almost anyone.

With the fixed interest certificates units are purchased (each unit of the current issue costs £25 and a purchaser may hold up to 40 units, or a maximum of 440 units if the proceeds from earlier certificates are reinvested) and they increase in value over the term of the issue—a five-year term from date of purchase for the current issue. Repayment of units can be effected at any time but usually units increase in value most towards the end of the term of the issue. After the end of the term units continue to increase in value but more slowly. The interest, which is paid only when certificates are cashed, is free of all United Kingdom income tax and capital gains tax.

The index-linked issue is designed to protect the buying power of savings. Certificates do not have a set growth rate but, instead, increase at a guaranteed differential above the rate of inflation: this rate is measured using the United Kingdom retail price index (RPI), comparing the change in the index between the month of purchase and the month of sale of the certificates. The certificates must have been held for at least one year before this calculation may be made, only the purchase price being repaid on certificates encashed during the first year. The differential over the inflation rate is guaranteed to be paid, and increases the longer the certificates are held over their five-year term. Repayments are free of all United Kingdom income tax and capital gains tax. Currently the maximum that can be invested is £5 000.

(b) Yearly Plan Certificates
This scheme is designed as a regular savings plan, linked to a guaranteed rate of interest. Investors agree to put in between £20 and £200 a month for a period of one year. After twelve payments have been made the investor receives a Yearly Plan Certificate which is then held for a further four years. The guaranteed rate of interest is fixed at the commencement of the plan, and will continue at this rate throughout the five years when the certificate is encashed

and the savings, plus accumulated interest, are repaid. However, a lower rate of interest is paid if the plan is maintained by the investor for less than two years. The interest paid is tax free. After the first Yearly Plan Certificate has been received, savers may continue making monthly payments to buy further certificates.

(c) Premium Savings Bonds

These provide a popular method of combining a form of 'saving' with the possibility of winning a large prize. They may be held only by individuals, not by clubs or societies, and may not be bought by anyone below the age of 16, although they may be purchased on a child's behalf by a parent or guardian. Bonds may be bought in multiples of five £1 units, the minimum purchase being £10, and the maximum holding by one person is 10 000 units. When it has been held for three clear calendar months each bond is eligible for inclusion in the draw for prizes. The prize fund is formed by calculating one month's interest at the rate of 6.5 per cent per year on the bonds eligible for the draw. Each month there is a top prize of £250 000, followed by other monthly prizes of £10 000, £5 000, £1 000, £500, £100 and £50. Additionally, each week there is a subsidiary draw for one prize of £100 000, one of £50 000 and one of £25 000. The numbers of the winning bonds are selected by an electronic device nicknamed ERNIE ('Electronic Random Number Indicator Equipment') and each £1 unit can only win one prize in each draw for which it is eligible. If, by chance, more than one prize should be won by the same £1 unit, it will be allotted the highest prize for which it is drawn. All prizes are free of all United Kingdom income tax and capital gains tax and bondholders are notified by post of any winnings. Bonds are easy to encash, the funds being received within a few days of completion of an encashment form.

(d) Income Bonds

The aim of these bonds is to provide regular income from capital. The bonds offer income paid monthly either direct to a bank account or National Savings Bank account, or by warrant. A minimum of £2 000 may currently be invested, then multiples of £1 000, to a maximum of £100 000. Interest rates are variable but are designed to be competitive; the interest, which is calculated on a day-to-day basis, is paid gross but is subject to tax. Either three or six months' notice must be given for repayment. When three months' notice is given no interest will be paid during the period of notice; when six months' notice is given interest is paid in full: different interest rules apply in the year of purchase. The bonds can be held for a guaranteed initial period of ten years from the first interest date after purchase. Almost anyone can buy Income Bonds—they may be bought on behalf of children under seven although, under such circumstances, the bond is not normally repayable until the child reaches seven and interest is normally credited to a National Savings Bank account in the child's name.

(*e*) **Capital Bonds**

These bonds are designed to be held for five years, with a minimum investment of £100 but no upper limit to the size of the investor's holding. The rate of interest increases in fixed steps over the five-year term. Interest and capital are paid on redemption. Interest is paid gross, but is liable to taxation: Capital Bonds are therefore attractive investments for non-taxpayers not requiring a regular income.

8.7   Government Stocks and Bonds

While a wide range of Government borrowing in the form of stocks and bonds is quoted on the Stock Exchange, some are also listed on the National Savings Stock Register and may be bought and sold through savings bank post offices without having to use a stockbroker. This makes them very easy to buy and sell and low rates of commission are charged. There are currently between forty and fifty different stocks and bonds in which transactions may be effected in this way: these range from $2\frac{1}{2}$ per cent Consols and $3\frac{1}{2}$ per cent War Stock, both with no fixed date for repayment, to $7\frac{3}{4}$ per cent Treasury Stock to be repaid between the years 2012 and 2015. All are bought and sold on the Stock Exchange by the National Debt Commissioners at the price ruling at the time of the transaction. As with any other quoted stocks, the buying and selling prices fluctuate and they should, therefore, be regarded as a longer-term investment, to be held for at least one year.

To make a purchase, an investment application form is completed and sent with a cheque or other payment to cover the estimated cost to the Bonds and Stock Office of the Department for National Savings—any over-payment would be returned. Like other stocks and shares (see Unit 8.12), an investor receives a certificate showing the description and amount of the stock or bonds registered in his name. To sell, a sale application form is completed and sent with the certificate to the Bonds and Stock Office. Using this system it is possible to buy up to £10 000 cash value of any particular stock or bond on any one day, but there is no limit to the total amount that may be held, nor to the amount that may be sold on any one day. Interest is paid half-yearly (quarterly for certain stocks) by the Bank of England, without deduction of income tax (although it is taxable): this applies only to those stocks on the National Savings Stock Register. There is no capital gains tax on British Government securities.

8.8   Local Authorities

For the saver who is prepared to deposit his money for a number of years, local authorities provide a safe investment at fixed rates of interest. In return for his deposit, the saver receives a bond issued by the authority. Rates of interest, which is usually paid twice a year, vary with the amount of money and the period of the deposit: generally, the larger the amount and the longer the period, the higher is the interest rate. The minimum amount accepted by most authorities is £500 (often more), and the time period ranges from one to ten years. As the money is deposited for a fixed period of time it is extremely difficult to withdraw it before the due date of repayment, although nearly all local authorities make an exception in the case of the death of the investor.

Most local authorities accept loans from members of the public and some advertise their rates and terms in newspapers.

Another form of local authority borrowing is carried out by the issue of one-year bonds, known as *yearlings*, which are quoted on the Stock Exchange and may be purchased by private individuals.

8.9   Life Assurance

Every life assurance salesman will tell you what a good form of saving for the future it is to take out one of his company's policies. While this may be true, some assurance companies have a better record than others and it pays to compare the terms offered by several companies.

The primary objective of most life assurance policies is to give protection to dependent relatives from the payment of the first premium by promising to pay out a sum of money in the event of the death of the assured. (Notice the term *assurance*, implying that the event covered by the policy is certain or assured to happen. The difference between *assurance* and *insurance* is fully explained in Unit 6.10). The secondary objective is, in the case of certain policies, to provide a long-term method of saving.

Life assurance policies are sold by insurance brokers and banks, who usually deal with a range of assurance companies and earn a commission on sales, and also by company agents who only deal with their own company's policies and are paid a salary plus commission on sales.

The main types of policy are endowment, whole-life and term assurance. With all policies the amount of the premium paid depends on the *term* of the policy (the time period before the 'assured' event happens), the age of the life assured, the state of his or her health, the sum assured and whether the policy is with or without profits (see below).

An endowment policy provides life assurance for an agreed term of years for a fixed amount of money, known as the *sum assured*, and pays out at the end of the term or on death, whichever occurs first. It provides a way of saving for retirement while at the same time giving protection to dependent relatives in the event of the early death of the life assured. The term of assurance can be arranged to suit the needs of the individual. A young man of twenty considering such a policy would probably take one out for a forty-year term, to mature when he is sixty. This would give financial protection to any dependants he might have in the future and would provide him with a lump sum of money at or near retirement age. An endowment policy with a shorter term—perhaps ten years—might be taken out by a middle-aged or older man.

Endowment policies can be used as a means of financing house purchase. A mortgage is obtained, and at the same time an endowment policy is taken out for a sum that will repay the amount of the mortgage. During the period of the mortgage, the borrower pays only the interest and none of the capital sum; at the same time he pays the premiums on the endowment policy. At the end of the period, the endowment policy matures and the capital sum of the mortgage is paid off with the proceeds. In the event of the assured's death before the end of the period, the proceeds of the policy would always be sufficient to repay the amount of the mortgage. This method is particularly beneficial when a 'with-profits' endowment policy (see below) is used.

Whole-life assurance differs from endowment assurance in that the assurance company pays the benefits only upon the death of the life assured, whenever it may occur. The premiums are usually paid for the whole of a person's life, although some policies specify that premiums shall only be paid up to a certain age, after which the policy will remain in force without payment of further premiums.

Term assurance is similar to a whole-life policy in that it pays the benefits only on the death of the life assured, but differs in that the period of the assurance is restricted to a specified term: thus the assurance company only pays out if the assured person dies before the end of the term. Premiums are payable only for the term of the policy. A particular attraction of this type of assurance is the large sum which can be assured for relatively low premiums. Thus it is a form of short-term assurance which can be used to give protection to dependent relatives at a much lower cost than an endowment or whole-life policy. It is an attractive policy for a man with a wife and young children who wants to provide a substantial sum of money for them in the event of his early death. If the assured survives the term of the policy he receives no benefits. There are variations on this type of policy: one of these, instead of paying a lump sum on the death of the assured, provides regular payments to the assured's wife for a certain number of years; another provides a mortgage protection policy, which will cover the amount of a mortgage in the event of the early death of the mortgagor.

All endowment and whole-life policies can be taken out *with profits* or *without profits*. By investing the premiums paid by policyholders in stocks, shares and other investments the assurance company earns profits. The policyholders can share in these profits by taking out a 'with profits' policy—the premiums for this will be higher than an equivalent 'without profits' policy. The share of the profits or *bonus* is added to the original sum assured and the increased amount is paid out either upon maturity of the policy or upon the death of the assured, depending on the type of policy. During inflationary times, it is sensible to take out a 'with profits' policy as the profits earned will help the sum assured to go some way towards retaining its purchasing power, although there is no guarantee that it will do so.

Many companies offer life assurance linked to the purchase of unit trusts. Under this type of scheme a percentage of the premiums paid by the assured is invested in a named unit trust, and the balance is used to provide term assurance. At the end of the agreed term the policyholder receives either the sale proceeds of the units purchased by him over the period or the units themselves, which may be held as long as he wishes; in the event of the life assured's death within the term, the dependants would receive either the value of the units bought up to the date of death or a guaranteed sum of money, whichever is the greater. The advantage of such a scheme is that if the value of the units rises during the term of the policy, there could be a substantial increase in the sum paid when it matures. The disadvantage is that the value of the units might fall, although schemes may guarantee a minimum payment upon maturity. Schemes of this type are offered by banks, building societies and unit trusts as well as by assurance companies; advertisements appear in most Sunday newspapers.

Besides being good methods of long-term saving, most endowment and whole-life policies may be used as security for a bank loan or overdraft (see Unit 21.6).

8.10   Annuities

There comes a time in most people's lives, usually at retirement, when they can no longer save and have to start using their accumulated savings to supplement any pension they may receive. The problem at this stage is to know how much of the savings can be used each year to see them through to the end of their lives: a person may live to a 'ripe old age' or may die within a few months, so that the savings may have to last over a considerable number of years or only for a little while. Life assurance and certain specialist companies help to resolve this problem by selling *annuities* which, in return for a lump sum of a person's savings, will provide him with a guaranteed income until his death, the company taking over the 'risk' that he will live to a considerable age.

There are different annuity schemes including *reversionary annuities* where payment is made to a person during his lifetime, with continuance in full on his death to his widow until her death. Some annuities are *immediate*, starting to pay a regular income from the date of purchase; others are *deferred*, commencing at some future specified date, and offering an opportunity for a saver to prepare for retirement by paying regular premiums while he is still in work, up to the date of the start of the annuity. *Temporary annuities* can be arranged for a fixed period of time, such as five or ten years; upon payment of the lump sum of money, the annuity will be paid for the period.

Rates charged for annuities vary with the type required and with the age, health and sex of the saver. The amount paid under an annuity may be quoted per £100 of capital invested; alternatively, the capital cost of a specified amount of income each year may be quoted by the company. For income tax purposes, payments under an annuity are regarded partly as capital and partly as income.

8.11 Pension Funds

Many large employers operate pension funds on behalf of their employees. In most schemes the employee contributes an amount of money each week or month and the firm also makes a contribution. Both of these represent saving: the employee is deferring some part of his present income until retirement, while the employer is similarly saving on behalf of the employee. Pension funds have considerable investment resources at the disposal of their trustees and are often managed by professional advisers such as insurance companies and specialist bank departments; their funds may be invested in stocks and shares, in property and sometimes even in works of art. When an employee reaches retirement age he or she starts to receive the benefits of the fund based on the contributions made to it.

Pension funds and personal pension plans for certain individuals are approved by the Inland Revenue and contributions to such funds are allowable for tax relief. The funds are free from United Kingdom taxes provided that the benefits obtained from contributions do not exceed certain limits.

8.12 Stocks and Shares

A *stock exchange* is a market place for 'second-hand' stocks and shares issued by public limited companies, public bodies and governments: those who have stocks or shares to sell are put in touch with those who wish to buy. The stocks and shares are 'second-hand' because the company or institution issued them to the public when it wanted to raise funds and it receives no further benefit as they now change hands: the only effect is that one shareholder or stockholder is substituted for another. *Stock* is always stated in nominal terms—for instance, £50 of 3½ per cent War Loan—and is usually issued by the Government and other public bodies; *shares*, which are usually issued by limited companies, are stated by the number—for example, 20 shares in

Midland Bank plc. (Shares and limited companies are considered more fully in Unit 13.5.)

Purchasing units in a unit trust is a way of investing in stocks and shares indirectly; but many people like to invest directly on the Stock Exchange, buying and selling the shares of their choice. It is often thought that to invest in stocks and shares one must have a lot of money and know a stockbroker; neither is true. A hundred pounds or so can be invested just as easily as ten thousand and a bank will always buy or sell stocks and shares on the instructions of a customer, using its own broker. It should be said that a Stock Exchange investment is usually a long-term venture and is not the place for money that may be needed urgently, and also that, while shares can go up in value, sometimes quite dramatically, they can fall in value equally dramatically. This is one of the best reasons for investing in a unit trust; a fall in the value of one or two investments is likely to be evened out by the other shares making up the unit trust's *portfolio*, or selection, of shares. Unit trusts can be readily bought and sold in small quantities; for investors with a little more money, there are *investment trust* companies that operate in a similar way—they pool the resources of their investors and purchase a portfolio of stocks and shares. Investment trusts have their shares quoted on the Stock Exchange and so have to be bought or sold through a stockbroker.

The problem with both unit and investment trusts is that though the investor is able to ascertain the general aims of the trust managers, he has no personal say in the purchase or sale of specific shares. Many people prefer to make their own investment decisions and, while a basic understanding of the techniques

'If I'd had a fortune I'd have lost it all'

and procedures is required, it is not difficult to find sources of information. The *Financial Times* is the leading daily financial newspaper, and most stockbrokers, professional advisers and some banks also subscribe to the highly specialized *Stock Exchange Daily Official List*. These two newspapers are usually somewhat complex for the private investor, who is better advised to read the financial pages of the Sunday newspapers where certain shares are 'tipped' by financial journalists. It is worth remembering that shares recommended in this way will be 'marked up' on the Stock Exchange when it opens for business because of the expected increase in demand, and will cost more than the price quoted in the paper. There are also *investors' letters* available on subscription that claim to make recommendations of shares to buy or sell, but because of their cost these letters are often not appropriate for the small investor. Stock exchange firms' *opinions* on particular shares: these are usually well written and worth taking note of, but they are time-consuming to produce and the stock market price of the share can alter during their preparation. It is also usually possible to obtain a brief opinion over the telephone. Banks do not give advice on individual shares but will always obtain an opinion from a stock exchange firm on behalf of a customer.

When a person has decided which stocks or shares he wants to buy, he gives the necessary instructions to a stock exchange firm either directly, or indirectly through his bank. (Most banks—and other financial intermediaries—wholly or partly own a stock exchange firm.) If a person is buying shares, he states the number of shares he requires; if stock, the nominal value of the stock. Alternatively, he may ask the firm to invest a certain amount of money—that is, to buy as many shares or as much stock as the money will buy. If there are likely to be sudden fluctuations in the price of the stocks or shares he wants, he may give the firm a limit above which it may not purchase without reference back to the investor; any limit, however, should be chosen with care in order not to handicap the firm—the price of a share quoted in a newspaper may well be the *middle price*, which is a price midway between the buying price and the selling price (see Unit 8.14). Once instructions have been received from a client, the firm will attempt to buy the number of shares required. Most stock exchange firms are able to act as broker/dealers and can contact directly the broker/dealers who make a market (*market-makers*) in the particular shares they want to purchase. Fig. 8.1 shows the dealing room of a large broker/dealer in London. The market-makers perform the function of jobbers, each specializing in the shares of certain types of company, such as banks, or insurance, engineering, shipping or oil companies and will always buy or sell shares of the companies in which they specialize. They sell shares at a higher price than that for which they bought them, the difference being their *turn* or profit. If demand for the shares of a particular company is strong then both the buying price and the selling price will be increased or marked up; if sellers exceed buyers the price will be marked down. Most broker/-dealers buy or sell shares over the telephone, with current prices shown by market-makers on a monitor screen, using the *stock exchange automated*

Fig. 8.1   The dealing room of a broker/dealer

quotations system (SEAQ). The deal is completed with settlement carried out by computer. Thus the 'single capacity' of separate stockbrokers and stockjobbers which existed until 1986 has largely been merged into 'dual capacity' broker/dealers, some of whom act as market-makers (the jobbing function) in particular shares.

A recent development intended to make investment easier has been the opening of a number of *share shops*, where shares may be bought and sold. The main aim of these shops is to make it easier for the public to make stock market investments in a very informal atmosphere. Other services offered may include the acceptance of deposits, the changing of foreign currencies and the provision of tax and investment advice. A number of share shops are operated by leading stockbrokers.

The client who buys shares receives a *contract note* from the broker which advises the number of shares purchased, the price, details of commission and expenses and a *settlement date*. The Stock Exchange year is divided into a number of *accounts*, usually of two weeks' duration, and the settlement day, when all transactions of the account are settled and payments between brokers are made and received, falls just over a week after the end of each account. Contract notes should always be kept by investors because they are the evidence the tax authorities require to determine whether there is any liability to capital gains tax.

The shares belong to the investor from the date of the contract note but it will be some time before he receives the share certificate (Fig. 8.2). In any

No. of Certificate	Transfer No (s)		Date of Registration	No. of Shares
103640	7399		13DEC83	1614

ORDINARY SHARES
Worldfoods plc
(Incorporated in England under the Companies Act, 1948–1980)

This is to Certify that DEREK WEST GRIFFIN HOUSE 4 OXTED ROAD KENLEY SURREY

HUNDREDS OF THOUSANDS	TENS OF THOUSANDS	THOUSANDS	HUNDREDS	TENS	UNITS
			ONE	SIX	ONE	FOUR

is/are the Registered Holder(s) of

ORDINARY SHARES of twenty-five pence each, fully paid, in **WORLDFOODS plc**, subject to the Memorandum and Articles of Association of the Company.

Given under the Common Seal of the Company

Note: No transfer of any of the Ordinary Shares comprised in this Certificate will be registered until this Certificate has been lodged with the Registrars

Fig. 8.2   A share certificate

transaction there are two brokers involved, one selling and one buying. The selling broker asks his client, who is disposing of the shares, to sign a special form called a *stock transfer form* and to return this to him with the certificate for the shares that have been sold. The signed stock transfer form and this share certificate are passed to the buyer's broker who, after inserting the name and address of his client, sends them both to the registrar of the company whose shares have changed hands. The company registrar, using the stock transfer form, withdraws the old share certificate, deletes the name of the original holder from the records and issues a new certificate in the name of the purchaser, recording his name and address in the register of shareholders. The new owner of the shares will normally receive dividends at least once a year (commonly twice), as his share of the company's distributed profits, will be sent the directors' report and accounts after the end of the company's financial year and is entitled to vote at the company's annual general meeting and certain other meetings of the shareholders. He is not entitled to participate in the day-to-day running of the company, this being the responsibility of the chairman and board of directors who are voted into office by the shareholders at the annual general meeting. The purchase or sale of shares in a company or of stock in a Government loan does not affect the total number of shares or the total amount of stock in issue; all that has happened is that one stockholder or shareholder is removed from the records and another one put in his place.

On the United Kingdom Stock Exchange trading takes place in many thousands of different company shares and Government and other stocks; but the total of these is only increased by fresh companies coming 'to the market' or by new stocks and shares being issued. This happens when a private company has reached a large enough size to become a public limited company (see Unit 13.5) and makes arrangements with an issuing house for its shares to be placed before the public in the form of a *new issue*, a procedure that may be carried out in several different ways (see Unit 6.12). One method is the placing of an advertisement or prospectus in financial newspapers inviting the public and financial institutions such as insurance companies, unit trusts and investment trusts—the *institutional investors*—to subscribe to the capital of the company. By law, the prospectus must contain certain information about the issue and the company. If sufficient subscriptions are received permission will be sought from the Stock Exchange Council for the shares to be quoted and dealt in on the Stock Exchange, and once this permission has been granted trading in the shares of the company may begin.

The total of stocks and shares may also be increased when a company already quoted on the Stock Exchange wishes to raise extra money, perhaps to finance a new project. This is usually done by means of a *rights issue* which gives shareholders the 'right' to buy more shares, often at an especially good price, in proportion to their existing holdings. Sometimes a *scrip* or *bonus issue* is made to shareholders—this is a book-keeping entry that gives a shareholder a number of extra free shares in proportion to the number he already holds. This is done when profits have been retained in the business rather than being distributed to shareholders as extra dividends, and also where the assets of the company, particularly land, have increased in value over the years. It may then be felt appropriate to increase the share capital of the company to reflect this enhanced value and these benefits are passed on to the shareholders. It may seem like 'something for nothing' but the shareholders are unlikely to be much better off because when a bonus issue is made, the stock market price of each share usually falls in direct proportion to the number of extra shares issued. Unless the rate of dividend is increased the shareholder's income will not change, because the company's total dividend will remain the same, though it will be spread over a greater number of shares.

8.13   Investor Protection

During the first half of the 1980s, much consideration was given to reviewing the protection required by investors and to discussing the need for statutory control of dealers. In 1985 the Government published a white paper entitled *Financial Services in the United Kingdom* and, as a result of this paper, the Financial Services Act was passed in 1986.

The Act establishes a system for regulating the conduct of investment business, with the principal aim of promoting confidence among investors. The main points of the Act are:

(i) investment business is defined as dealing, arranging deals, managing and advising on any investment product (but bank deposits are excluded);

(ii) all firms engaging in investment business are required to be authorized to do so;

(iii) the power of authorization is given to a special agency—the Securities and Investments Board (SIB)—or to a number of Self-Regulatory Organizations (SROs) recognized by SIB.

The SIB acts as an overall city watchdog, but various SROs cover particular aspects of the investment business. Examples of SROs include:

(i) FIMBRA (the Financial Intermediaries, Managers and Brokers Regulatory Association), which deals with firms of independent intermediaries who provide investment advice;

(ii) LAUTRO (the Life Assurance and Unit Trust Regulatory Organization) which is responsible for insurance companies and the marketing of unit trusts.

SROs establish their own rules, and members must abide by these. The SIB has to be satisfied that the rules of the SRO give adequate protection to investors. SROs, for their part, require their members to satisfy a 'fit and proper' test involving:

(i) proof of adequate financial resources;

(ii) compliance with rules covering the way that investment business is conducted;

(iii) participation in arrangements to deal with complaints and compensation.

Compensation is payable to investors who lose money when authorized investment firms go into default.

Bank staff who give investment advice to customers must be careful to ensure that they do so within the terms of the Financial Services Act 1986.

8.14   Understanding the Financial Press

Information in the *Financial Times* about stocks and shares is classified under broad headings, such as 'Banks, hire purchase and leasing', 'Industrials' and 'Mining'. Table 8.2 shows how the newspaper presents the details of the shares of the major banks: information about most other stocks and shares is set out similarly.

High and low. As the heading suggests, this column gives the highest and lowest prices, in pence, reached by the company's shares during the period in question—in this case from 1 January 1988 to 19 September 1988.

Table 8.2   The presentation of share prices

| 1988 | | | | | Tuesday 20 September 1988 | | | |
High	Low	Stock	Price	+ or −	Dividend net	Cover	Yield gross	P/E
463	302	Barclays £1	394	+2	19.93	3.5	6.7	5.6
317	238	Lloyds £1	293	+6	13.2	4.6	6.0	4.6
448	370	Midland £1	415	+1	20.1	3.0	6.5	5.6
605	522	Nat West £1	541	+3	24.0	5.0	5.9	4.5
380	297	Royal Bank of Scotland	342	. . .	12.7	4.3	5.0	6.2
117½	96	TSB	98½	. . .	4.7	3.2	6.5	6.6

Banks, hire purchase and leasing

Source: *Financial Times*

Stock. This gives the name of the company whose stocks or shares are quoted. The *nominal value*—the face value, as opposed to the market value—of the shares may also be stated; this is £1 in the case of the first four banks. In the *Financial Times*, if the nominal value is not stated, it is 25p—for example, the Royal Bank of Scotland. This amount is the commonest nominal value of all shares. As there is no indication otherwise, they are all 'ordinary' shares (see Unit 13.5(*b*)).

Price. The price, quoted in pence, is the *middle price*—midway between the buying and selling price—at the time that the exchange closed on the previous day. This is not necessarily the price that will be found ruling when the exchange opens the next morning, for there may have been 'after hours trading' following the closing of the exchange. Although the nominal values of the shares of some banks are the same, it does not follow that the different market prices reflect in any way the relative strength or weakness of a particular bank—many other factors are involved.

Sometimes 'xd' is marked against a company's shares to indicate that dealings take place *ex-dividend*. This means that the company is shortly to pay a dividend, so that buyers of shares cannot be recorded on the shareholders' register in time to receive the dividend, and it will therefore be paid to the seller who will be entitled to keep it. The opposite of this is 'cd' or *cum dividend*, where the buyer is entitled to receive the dividend; should he not be registered in time so that the payment is sent to the seller, the amount of the net dividend has to be handed over to the buyer.

+ or −. This gives the change in the share price in pence from the previous closing price.

Dividend net. This indicates the dividend paid (in pence per share) to the shareholders in respect of the last financial year. For example, for each £1 ordinary share held in Barclays Bank, the holder would have received dividends of almost 20p (£0.20) from the profits earned by the bank in the previous financial year. It is a net dividend and there is no further liability on the part of the shareholder for basic rate taxation because of the special way in which companies pay tax on their profits as assessed by the Inland Revenue: this tax is known as *corporation tax*. If required, the *gross dividend* may be found by making the following calculation:

$$\text{Gross dividend} = \frac{100}{100 - \text{basic rate tax \%}} \times \text{dividend received (£)}$$

Using the Barclays Bank figures, and allowing for basic rate taxation at 25 per cent:

$$\text{Gross dividend} = \frac{£1}{£0.75} \times £0.20 = £0.267$$

For shares with a nominal value of £1, this is equal to a 26.7 per cent dividend. On the advice sent to the shareholder with the dividend warrant or cheque, it would be shown as 'dividend payable £0.20, tax credit £0.067'. The *tax credit* is payable by the company to the Inland Revenue and represents a part payment of corporation tax: shareholders who pay little or no tax may be able to claim relief or payment to them of the amount of the tax credit.

Most shareholders own more than one share in the company and they would, of course, receive only one dividend warrant for all their shares.

Cover. Cover states the number of times the net profit earned—the profit after payment of all expenses and tax—for potential distribution to the ordinary shareholders covers the amount required for the gross dividend. Thus, while Barclays Bank paid a gross dividend of £0.267 on each £1 ordinary share, this amount was covered 3.5 times by profits available for distribution. Cover therefore gives an indication of the profitability of the company and shows that profits are being retained to increase the value of the business: the bank may well pay higher dividends in the future.

Yield gross. This translates into terms of the share's market price the dividend that the company paid in the previous year: it shows the amount of gross income that can be expected if £100 is invested. Supposing that I ask my stockbroker to invest £100 in National Westminster Bank ordinary shares and he is able to obtain them at £5.41 each (see Table 8.2), I would then become the owner of about eighteen shares (£100 ÷ £5.41). If the bank paid the same dividend this year as last, the gross earnings of the shares would amount to approximately £5.76 made up as follows: £4.32 net dividend on eighteen shares at £0.24 per share (paid to me) plus £1.44 tax credit (paid to Inland Revenue by the company as a part of the corporation tax due. (Gross dividend = (100 ÷ 75) × £4.32 = £5.76.) The difference between £5.76 and the gross yield of £5.90 indicated in Table 8.2 arises because of the rounding of figures.

When investing £100 in shares with a nominal value of £1 the gross dividend is also the gross yield in percentage terms. However, it may be calculated for any shares as follows:

$$\text{Gross yield} = \frac{\text{Gross dividend} \times 100}{\text{Market price}}$$

Gross yield enables the shares of one company to be compared with those of another and comparison can also be made with interest rates payable by other investments.

P/E. The price/earnings ratio, or P/E ratio as it is usually called, denotes how many years' purchase of the latest earnings per share (after allowing for corporation tax) is represented by the current share price: put simply, this is calculated by dividing the market price by the earnings per share. Thus a share with a current stock market price of £1.50 and earnings per share of 15p, will have a P/E ratio of 10; a share with a price of £2 and earnings of 25p, will have a P/E ratio of 8. Thus it will take ten and eight years respectively for the annual earnings per share to equal the current market prices. It follows that the lower the price/earnings ratio, the sooner the current market price of the shares will be 'purchased' by earnings; the higher the ratio, the longer this will take. Thus the P/E ratio provides an indicator of the 'earning power' of different shares and comparison may be made between companies in the same sector. (It is not always possible to calculate the P/E ratio from the other information given in financial newspapers: this is because the calculation of a company's earnings adjusts the profit by certain taxation items and extraordinary profits or losses.)

You will find it useful to have a look at the share prices in a newspaper such as the *Financial Times*, perhaps comparing the major banks with some of the other quoted banks and hire-purchase companies. Look at the cover, gross yield and price/earnings ratios too, and contrast them with shares listed in other sections.

8.15   Choosing an Investment

The range of investments available to a saver is extensive and, to some, bewildering. The answers to the following questions should be considered before making an investment decision:

(i) How much money have I available for investment?
(ii) How long before I shall need the money?
(iii) Shall I need a part of the savings in an emergency?
(iv) Do I pay basic rate income tax and will I continue to do so in the future?
(v) How safe will my savings be?

If the amount of money to be saved is fairly small—perhaps less than

£500—the choice of investments is restricted, since certain facilities are only available for minimum amounts; for bank fixed-term deposits the minimum is about £500 and building society term share accounts start at about £100. Usually, the larger the sum to be invested, the higher is the rate of interest. The period of time for which the money can be left is very important: generally the longer the period, the higher are the rates, although the actual rates obtained will depend on the borrower's view of the likely long-term trends in interest rates. Similarly, the longer the period of notice of withdrawal, the higher are the rates. Where money is deposited for a long period of time, emergency withdrawal facilities are usually very restricted or even non-existent: this reflects the view that a borrower who pays high rates of interest should be entitled to the full use of the money for the whole period.

The present and future tax position of the saver needs to be considered: if there is no liability to basic rate income tax the saver, for the sake of simplicity, would be better with an investment where the interest is paid gross of tax, such as Government stocks and bonds on the National Savings Stock Register or a National Savings Bank investment account. In particular, a non-taxpayer should avoid putting too much in a bank or building society because interest is paid 'net' of tax and it is not possible to reclaim tax that has already been paid.

As far as security of savings is concerned, most large institutions are completely safe. There should be no worries about leaving money with the large banks and their associated finance companies, the National Savings Bank, any of the National Savings securities and Government stocks and bonds, building societies, local authorities and large insurance companies. Care should be exercised with smaller institutions advertising attractive rates of interest with short notice of withdrawal, though these may simply be perfectly sound organizations that do not have the backing of a major institution. Before investing in one of these, it is wise to make inquiries, to see a copy of the balance sheet and to ask advice—from the bank manager!

Where an investment in stocks and shares is being considered, it is wise for a beginner to purchase units in a unit trust or shares in an investment trust: direct dealings in stocks and shares are for those with more financial expertise who are, if necessary, prepared to lose some of their money. A stock exchange investment, whether made directly or indirectly, should always be considered only on a long-term basis.

Table 8.3 compares the interest rates available at the time of writing from the major savings and investment institutions, with a column left blank for you to fill in the rates at the time of reading.

All savings and investment represent a part of the 'money-go-round': the banks pool the savings of their millions of account holders and lend to commercial and industrial firms as well as to agricultural and personal customers; the building societies attract savings and channel them towards helping people to buy houses by granting mortgages; the issue of shares channels investors' funds into meeting the long-term capital requirements of industry and the Stock Exchange provides a market in shares; the purchase of Government stocks and bonds and National Savings securities helps to finance

Table 8.3   Interest rates paid by major savings institutions, October 1988
(the final column has been left blank for the reader to complete)

	Percentage return		Percentage return	
	Gross	Net of tax at 25%	Gross	Net of tax at 25%
Bank deposit account	7.00	5.25		
Bank 6 months deposit	12.00	9.00		
National Savings Bank:				
Ordinary account*	5.00	3.75		
Investment account	10.00	7.50		
National Savings Certificates				
(thirty-fourth issue)	10.00†	7.50†		
National Savings Income Bonds	10.75	8.06		
National Savings Capital Bonds	—‡	—‡		
National Savings Yearly Plan	10.00†	7.50†		
Building societies:				
Share account	7.33	5.50		
High-interest account	12.67	9.50		

* The first £70 of interest is free of all United Kingdom income tax. Interest rate quoted only applies on deposits that remain at over £500 for a complete month
† Assumes National Savings Certificates and Yearly Plan Certificates are held for five years to maturity
‡ Capital Bonds available from 1989

a part of central Government debt, and investments in local authorities help to assist their financing. Assurance and insurance companies are also a part of this 'money-go-round': they pool the premiums and annuities paid to them and invest this in many different ways until some part of the pool is needed to pay a claim on a policy; principally they put their investment funds into shares and Government stocks. So the savings of many millions of individuals, when combined or pooled, help to keep the industry of a country turning by indirectly providing the finance that is essential to keep businesses up to date with new machinery and processes.

8.16   Questions

1. What savings and investment facilities do the retail banks offer to the personal saver?

2. Describe the savings facilities offered by the Department of National Savings.

3. What are the main functions of a stock exchange? Of what benefits are these functions to Government and industry?

(The Institute of Bankers)

4. Distinguish between endowment, whole-life and term assurance policies.

5. Mrs Brown, a customer of the bank where you work, is aged 60 and has recently been widowed. She has £15 000 available from her late husband's estate and asks your advice as to suitable investments for this money. Advise her.

6. Describe the administration and operation of a unit trust. Outline the attractions of this type of investment to small savers.

(The Institute of Bankers)

7. A Mr Smith has written to the branch asking advice on the investment of an unspecified amount of money. His account has only been open a short while and, whilst satisfactory, gives no clue as to his needs. Draft a brief letter to Mr Smith, offering to meet him, in which you outline the basic information you will need to consider in order to assess his needs.

(The Chartered Institute of Bankers)

8. Mrs Brown has called at the enquiry counter and told you that she has inherited £5 000 worth of equities [ordinary shares]. She is concerned that the money is presently invested in only two companies and has been advised that unit trusts would spread the risk. Mrs Brown is most interested in a general fund giving a balance of income and capital growth. From your knowledge of her financial affairs you believe that this is sensible, but Mrs Brown is worried about the cost of selling her recently inherited shares and confused about the significance of the 'bid' and 'offer' prices for unit trusts shown in the morning newspaper.

Mrs Brown asks for guidance, as she has no idea how to acquire a suitable unit trust. In short paragraphs, outline your response to Mrs Brown, setting out the explanations she requires.

(The Chartered Institute of Bankers)

Multiple-choice Questions—4

Read each question carefully. Choose the *one* answer you think is correct. Answers are given on page 390.

1. The main asset on a bank balance sheet is:

A	loans and overdrafts	C	capital and reserves
B	deposits	D	cash

2. The main liability on a bank balance sheet is:

A	loans and overdrafts	C	deposits
B	capital and reserves	D	loan stock

3. Which one of the following *cannot* be included in a bank's eligible liabilities?

   A foreign currency deposits
   B sterling deposits from United Kingdom banks
   C sterling certificates of deposit
   D sterling deposits of an original maturity of more than two years

4. The free capital ratio compares shareholders' funds and loan capital, less fixed assets, with:

   A advances
   B deposits

   C liquid assets
   D cash and balances at the Bank of England

5. Which one of the following is not subject to any taxation?

   A bank deposit accounts
   B building society share accounts

   C National Savings Bank investment accounts
   D National Savings Certificates

6. Which one of the following can be bought or sold on the Stock Exchange?

   A unit trust units
   B investment trust shares

   C building society shares
   D National Savings Capital Bonds

7. An endowment life policy:

   A pays a lump sum either at the end of a specified time or on the prior death of the assured
   B pays a lump sum only if the assured dies during the period of assurance
   C always shares in the profits of the insurance company
   D provides an inflation-proof savings medium

8. A bonus issue of shares:

   A introduces additional cash into the company
   B increases the share capital of the company
   C will not affect the stock market prices of the shares
   D is another name for a rights issue

9. The £1 ordinary shares of ABC plc have a market price of £2; the most recent dividend paid was 20p per share. The dividend and yield percentages are respectively:

   A 20% and 10%
   B 20% and 40%

   C 10% and 20%
   D both 10%

10. A widowed lady aged 60 asks your advice on suitable investments for the sum of £20000. She tells you that she doesn't pay any income tax, but requires a good return on her money; also, she doesn't anticipate needing to withdraw any of the funds in a hurry. Broadly, in which should she invest the money?

    A Government securities on the National Savings Stock Register
    B bank deposit account
    C building society account
    D Premium Savings Bonds

Unit Nine
Interest Rates

9.1   The Meaning and Role of the Rate of Interest

In Unit 1.1 we saw that two of the basic functions of a bank are to accept deposits from customers, and to lend surplus funds to customers who wish to borrow. On the balance sheet of a bank (see Unit 7) the largest asset is 'advances to customers', while the largest liability is 'current, deposit and other accounts'. Despite the wide range of banking services offered to customers, it is clear that a bank's main business is to act as a financial intermediary, paying a rate of interest on customers' deposits and charging a rate of interest on funds lent to customers.

A rate of interest represents a price, that is, the charge required by the lender for temporarily losing the use of his or her money to another. A borrower will view a rate of interest as the charge that has to be paid to acquire the temporary use of another person's money. Inevitably, there is a conflict of interest: the lender seeks the highest rate possible, while the borrower will look for the lowest rate. Thus the rate of interest, like other prices, is largely determined by supply and demand. Of course, there is no compulsion for a person who has surplus funds to earn a rate of interest on them—money that is placed 'under the mattress' will earn no interest, because it is not being put to use by a borrower.

There are several economic theories that can be used to explain interest rates. We will consider here the traditional *loanable funds theory*, although later on in your banking or economics studies you will certainly consider other theories in some detail.

The loanable funds theory considers that a rate of interest is reached by the operation of the mechanisms of supply and demand. The supply of funds comes mainly from peoples' savings and the amount of funds they are prepared to supply will vary with the price (rate of interest) that they are offered. Thus, if rates of interest are very low most people will decide that it is not worth lending out their savings—they will prefer to keep them in liquid form and available for spending if required. As interest rates rise, so the amount of savings that people are prepared to lend will increase, and the supply of funds becomes greater. This is illustrated in Fig. 9.1 by the supply curve sloping upwards to the right.

Those who wish to borrow funds regard a rate of interest as a cost and so the lower that cost, the greater the demand; as rates of interest increase, so the demand for borrowing falls. We can see the reason for this from the point of view of industry. For example, a project, such as the purchase of a new

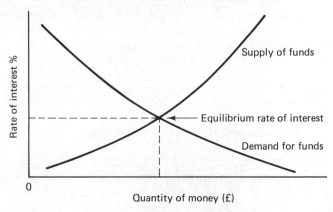

Fig. 9.1   The loanable funds theory

machine or other asset, is worth while at lower rates of interest but becomes increasingly less worth while as rates increase. You can see in Fig. 9.1 that the demand curve slopes downwards to the right. The point where this curve crosses the supply curve is, in theory, the equilibrium rate of interest (the rate at which the supply of funds is equal to the demand for funds). Of course, many factors affect interest rates and some of these are considered in Unit 9.2.

The loanable funds theory of interest can be seen in practice whenever there is a change in bank lending rates. Look for the comments of the leaders of industry—an increase in interest rates will be described as adding a cost to business and making fewer new projects viable; on the other hand a fall in interest rates will be welcomed as reducing the burdens on industry and increasing the possibility of new projects going ahead.

9.2   Factors which Influence Interest Rates

The loanable funds theory is an oversimplification of a complex matter. Any change in conditions of demand or supply of funds will affect interest rates. For example, an increase in savings will result in a greater supply of money being available which, if not balanced by an increase in the demand for funds, will move the supply curve to the right and establish lower rates of interest. Conversely, an increase in the demand for funds which is not matched by a similar increase in the supply, will move the demand curve to the right and will establish a higher rate of interest.

The following four factors influence interest rates:

(i) **Supply of, and demand for, funds.** As explained above, an increase in the supply of funds and/or demand for funds will alter rates of interest.

(ii) **Risk premium.** There are two components within any rate of interest—

firstly there is the reward paid to the lender for forgoing the use of his or her money and secondly there is a part that covers the risk factor of not being repaid. Where money is lent without any risk whatsoever, the rate of interest is known as *pure interest*. The returns paid on Government stocks are an example of this rate; there is no likelihood of the Government failing to repay. As the risk of non-repayment increases, so higher rates of interest are charged by the lender. In this way different and increasing rates apply to bank lending depending on the circumstances of the loan—is the borrower providing security or is the loan unsecured? is it a personal or a business loan?—and the same applies to rates charged by credit card companies, hire-purchase and other finance companies.

(iii) **Amount and time period.** The amount and period of the loan are also reflected in the rate of interest. Thus a bank or a building society may charge borrowers a higher rate of interest for amounts borrowed above a certain sum. Equally a bank customer who is placing funds on deposit may receive a higher rate of interest for larger amounts; similarly, the time period of the loan is often linked to higher rates.

(iv) **Inflation factors.** At times when inflation rates are high, lenders often expect a higher rate of interest in order to compensate them for the expected loss in the real value of their capital. How far lenders are able to achieve this objective is open to debate although it is certainly true that when inflation was running at high levels in Britain in the late 1970s and early 1980s, interest rates were running at equally high levels.

The problem of inflation can be quantified in the following way. If inflation is running at 10 per cent per annum and you place £100 in a deposit account then, at the end of the year, the real value of your capital has fallen to:

$$£100 \times \frac{100}{110} = £90.9$$

An interest rate of 10 per cent per annum will maintain the real value of your capital intact:

$$(£100 + £10 \text{ interest}) \times \frac{100}{110} = £100$$

An interest rate of 12 per cent per annum will provide some measure of compensation for the loss of use of your capital for the year:

$$(£100 + £12 \text{ interest}) \times \frac{100}{110} = £101.82$$

Of course, we have assumed here that interest is credited only once a year, and at the end of the year. The majority of bank and building society accounts pay interest half-yearly, or sometimes monthly or quarterly. The effect of such regular interest payments is for the saver to earn 'interest on interest'. However, as we have seen in Unit 8, most interest paid to depositors is subject to income tax, and this also needs to be taken into account.

9.3   Nominal and True Rates of Interest

As noted in Unit 9.2, where interest is paid to depositors at half-yearly or more frequent intervals, there is a compounding effect of 'interest on interest'. This means that if interest is credited to the capital sum half-way through a year, the capital sum plus this interest will then earn further interest which is credited at the end of the year. As an example, let us assume that you have placed £100 in a deposit account where it will earn interest at the rate of 10 per cent per annum, with interest being credited half-yearly. The interest and capital amounts will be:

1 Jan.	Placed in deposit account	£100

30 Jun. Interest for half-year credited

$$£100 \times \frac{10}{100} \times \frac{6 \text{ months}}{12 \text{ months}} \qquad = \quad £5$$

31 Dec. Interest for half-year credited   £105

$$£105 \times \frac{10}{100} \times \frac{6 \text{ months}}{12 \text{ months}} \qquad = \quad £5.25$$

31 Dec. Balance at year-end   £110.25

Thus, although interest was at a *nominal rate* of 10 per cent per annum, if the half-year's interest is reinvested, the *true rate* (or *compounded annual rate*) is 10¼ per cent. If interest is credited quarterly, or monthly, this has the effect of making the compounded annual rate higher still. The effect is the same for a bank customer who is borrowing—where interest is debited half-yearly or quarterly, the true rate will be higher than the nominal rate.

A further aspect of real rates of interest is the disclosure of *annual percentage rates* (of charge) abbreviated to *APR*. Under the Consumer Credit Act of 1974 many lenders are required to disclose both the nominal and the true rates of interest charged to borrowers. You may have seen APR quoted on literature about personal loans or on price tags in shops where goods are sold on credit. In such cases there is often a considerable difference between the nominal rate and the true rate, because the amount of interest is based on the capital sum originally borrowed, rather than, as with overdrafts, on the amount of the loan outstanding on a daily basis. For example, on a loan of £1 000 over three years at a nominal rate of 10 per cent per annum, the total interest payable is £300 (£1 000 × 10% × 3). Because repayments reduce the balance outstanding, this works out at an annual percentage rate of around 20 per cent. You can also see an APR quoted on credit card statements.

9.4   Gross Interest, Net Interest and Gross Equivalent Interest

As we saw in Unit 8.2(a), banks, building societies and other financial institutions pay interest to personal customers *net* of composite rate tax (CRT). Certain other customers such as limited companies, clubs, charities and overseas residents receive their interest *gross*.

Composite rate tax is deducted at a rate below that of basic rate income tax, in order to reflect the average basic tax rate paid by depositors. As most children and many pensioners do not pay tax this means that, assuming a basic rate tax of 25 per cent, the average CRT contribution—allowing for the non-taxpayers—is, say, 22 per cent. The differences between depositors' basic tax rates mean that banks, building societies and other financial institutions involve themselves in quoting three (sometimes four) basic terms for each type of account when they describe rates of interest available to depositors.

Gross 10 per cent p.a. This rate is of interest to those customers—limited companies and so on (see above)—who are paid interest gross.

Net 7.8 per cent p.a. This shows the rate that will be received by personal customers after deduction of composite rate tax (assumed, for the purposes of this calculation, to be deducted at a rate of 22 per cent). All personal customers will receive 7.8 per cent on their deposits on which they will not suffer any further basic rate income tax.

Gross equivalent 10.4 per cent p.a. The difference between the gross and net rates quoted so far is the deduction of composite rate tax at 22 per cent. However, a basic rate taxpayer pays 25 per cent and thus 'gains' a benefit from the application of CRT. The gross equivalent rate shows what the interest rate is worth to a basic rate taxpayer by converting the net rate into a gross rate for a basic rate (25 per cent in this example) taxpayer:

$$7.8 \text{ per cent} \times \frac{100}{75} = \underline{\underline{10.4 \text{ per cent}}}$$

The fourth term quoted is *compounded annual rate* (see Unit 9.3). A rate of 10 per cent per annum paid half-yearly becomes 10.25 per cent. The net and gross equivalent rates also have their own compounded annual rates!

The increasing sophistication of some depositors means that they want as much information as possible in order to help them to make comparisons between the rates offered by banks, building societies and other financial institutions. However, this information which helps those customers with some knowledge of financial affairs, can often only confuse those who know very little of such matters.

9.5   Fixed and Fluctuating Interest Rates

Most bank interest rates allowed to depositors and charged to borrowers are fluctuating rates—the rate is liable to alteration either upwards or downwards—with little or no notice. Some interest rates, notably those allowed on some longer-term deposits (see Unit 9.6(b)) and charged on personal loan accounts (see Unit 9.6(c)) are fixed.

A fixed rate of interest has the advantage that the depositor and borrower know in advance the amount of interest that will be allowed or charged. However, there is the disadvantage to the bank customers of being 'locked in' to a certain interest rate for a set period of time and, whatever happens to other interest rates, their rate will not alter. Thus the depositor who placed monies with the bank at fixed rates when the general level of rates was low, will be at a disadvantage if rates increase. On the other hand, the borrower who took out a fixed rate loan at a time of low rates will benefit if rates rise. The reverse is also true, of course. Fluctuating rates have the benefit of following the general level of rates so that both depositor and borrower are receiving and are charged the current rates.

9.6   Bank Interest Rates

(a) Base Rate

A bank's base rate is an important interest rate for most borrowing customers. It is to this rate that all small and most large overdrafts are linked. A base rate represents the rate that a bank must charge its borrowers in order to meet most of the costs of running the bank, while attracting sufficient deposits. Base rate will always be very close to short-term money market rates and, therefore, will be subject to fairly frequent changes. If, for example, a bank's base rate was below money market rates, a customer could borrow from a bank and lend these funds to the money market, thus making a profit on the deal.

Most borrowing customers pay a margin over base rate to meet the interest rate charged on loans and overdrafts. The amount of this margin will vary largely according to the degree of risk perceived by the bank, and to some extent on the amount borrowed and the time period of the loan, together with the security, if any is offered. Therefore a large company customer of undoubted financial integrity will be able to borrow at rates down to as low as one per cent over base rate. (Such a rate is known as a *blue-chip rate*, taken from the Stock Market terminology, where a blue-chip company is one that is first class.) Other borrowers will pay higher rates of between 2 and 4 per cent over base rate, with any security offered being taken into account when fixing the rate. For unauthorized overdrafts, such as a personal customer anticipating receipt of his or her salary or personal and business customers exceeding an agreed overdraft limit, very high rates over base rate are charged, frequently at 10 to 15 per cent over base rate. Some customers may also be subject to structured interest rates: that is, one rate will be charged up to a certain overdraft amount, while another rate, usually higher, will be charged for advances above this amount and up to the agreed limit.

Interest is calculated on the amount borrowed on a daily basis and usually charged to the account quarterly, but sometimes half-yearly. In this way, bank borrowing is a relatively inexpensive form of finance because the customer is only charged for the amount borrowed. However, where borrowing facilities are granted, a bank will often make a special charge for arranging them and committing the bank's money, whether the facilities are used or not—this is known as an *arrangement fee*.

(b) Deposit Rate
The current rate of interest allowed on deposit accounts is displayed in all bank branches. The rate is not directly linked to base rate, but changes will always follow the trend of base rate. Deposit rate is usually some 2–3 per cent below base rate and, clearly, the difference between deposit rate and rates for borrowers represents one source of gross profit for the bank, out of which must be paid the bank's operating expenses.

In addition to the rate paid on deposits, most banks operate savings accounts with their own structure for rates of interest. Also, most banks accept larger sums of money for fixed terms at either fixed or fluctuating rates of interest.

(c) Personal Loan Rates
We have already seen earlier in this Unit that the interest charged on personal loans is usually fixed for the period of the loan and also that the interest rate quoted is a flat rate although the lender is obliged by law to state in writing the annual percentage rate. The APR charged on personal loans will always, at any one time, be considerably higher than that charged on comparable over-drafts, and will be approaching the rates charged by hire-purchase companies.

(d) House Purchase Loan Rates
The rate charged by banks on loans for house purchase is one that varies with the general level of interest rates. However, the banks have made an attempt with this rate to try to avoid the frequent changes that their other major rates (base rate and deposit rate) are subject to. Rates charged are very close to those made by building societies (who are, of course, the banks' major competitors in this market).

(e) London Inter-bank Offered Rate (LIBOR)
Interest rates charged to the larger company customers by banks are often related to rates on the inter-bank wholesale money market (see Unit 19.3), where the rates are linked to LIBOR rather than to a bank's base rate. The reason for this different 'starting point' in calculating borrowing rates for

company customers is that LIBOR is a more accurate indicator of the cost of money to the banks. This is because of the way in which interest rates on the inter-bank market are determined by the balance between supply and demand. For example, when demand for advances is rising strongly and banks are under pressure, the competition between them for scarce funds will quickly drive up rates on the inter-bank market. Large borrowings are usually charged to bank customers at a rate linked to LIBOR because a bank which needs funds in excess of its customers' deposits has to pay the London inter-bank offered rate to obtain them.

9.7   Changes in Interest Rates

In Britain short-term interest rates are partly determined by the Bank of England as a result of its day-to-day interventions in the money market. As we have already seen in Unit 4.8, in making funds available to the discount houses, the Bank can control the rates on marginal funds loaned to the banking system. The rates of interest it charges to the market signals the direction in which the Bank wishes rates to move. If, for example, the Bank of England raises the rate of discount on its purchases of commercial bills, then the discount market will, in their turn, raise the rate of discount on the short-term securities in which they deal. Thus interest rates on commercial bills, Treasury bills, certificates of deposit and other financial instruments will all tend to rise.

Meanwhile the banks who supply funds to the discount market will raise the rates they charge on this money. The effect of this will spread to the secondary or wholesale money markets (see Unit 19). If the rise in interest rates is expected to persist banks will find that they are having to offer higher rates of interest on certificates of deposit and, where they are borrowing on the inter-bank market, having to pay higher rates. This will put pressure on the banks to increase their base rates in order to maintain a sufficient margin between the cost of borrowed funds and the return on funds employed. An increase in base rates will, while increasing the earnings on advances, cause a rise in the rate paid on deposits.

A rise in base rate, if sustained, will cause a flow of funds into the banks out of accounts with building societies and the National Savings Bank. In order to stem this flow, building societies and the National Savings authorities will increase the returns they offer to depositors and savers. Building societies will also have to increase the rate they charge on mortgages to cover the additional cost of funds.

Thus, a change in short-term rates of interest will have a 'rippling' effect through a number of rates of interest. It will also have some effect on longer-term rates of interest, although these will be affected by other factors such as the rate of inflation and exchange rates with other currencies. Nowadays, longer-term interest rates are particularly affected by changes in rates in other international financial centres. For example, interest rates are often influenced world-wide by developments in the United States economy.

A change in the general level of interest rates has a major effect upon the economy of a country as a whole. High rates of interest will slow down demand for bank loans and overdrafts. At the same time, economic activity will be reduced and the public will be less inclined to buy capital goods such as cars, televisions, carpets and new houses; this reduces demand from manufacturing industry who, in their turn, will postpone investment in new machinery and buildings, thus having a direct effect upon employment prospects. Lower levels of interest rates will, by and large, have an opposite effect. However, it is obviously not just interest rates which have an influence on the economy of a country and many other factors must be considered—exchange rates with other currencies, the price of oil and other raw materials, and the standard of living for example.

9.8   Questions

1. Explain with the aid of diagrams the *loanable funds theory* of the rate of interest.

2. What factors influence interest rates?

3. Explain the difference between nominal interest rates and true interest rates.

4. What are the advantages and disadvantages of a fixed rate of interest to (i) lenders; and (ii) borrowers?

5. Distinguish between: (i) a bank's base rate; (ii) LIBOR; (iii) deposit rate; and (iv) a bank's personal loan rate.

Unit Ten
Organizational Structure of a Clearing Bank

10.1 Head Office and Regional Offices

All the major clearing banks have broadly similar organizational structures, with a head office in the City of London and regional offices situated in various parts of the country, each controlling a number of branches. Fig. 10.1 indicates, in simplified form, the type of structure adopted by the banks with specialist services—foreign, executor and trustee, corporate finance and so on—available to head office, regional offices and branches. With a total of nearly 13 500 branches and 400 000 staff between them, the organizational structure of the major banks is, of necessity, somewhat complex.

Fig. 10.2 shows the management structure, again simplified, of a major clearing bank. The *shareholders* are the owners of the bank and their elected representatives, the *chairman* and *board of directors*, control general policy and approve certain very large applications for loan and overdraft facilities. Most members of the board of directors do not work full-time for the bank; they usually come from families that have had connections with the bank for many years, and are often people who have distinguished careers in industry, the civil service or the armed forces. The *chief general manager*, the highest position a full-time employee can reach, is usually a member of the board of directors as is one or more of his deputies, the *assistant chief general managers*. After the chief general manager and his deputies come the *general managers*,

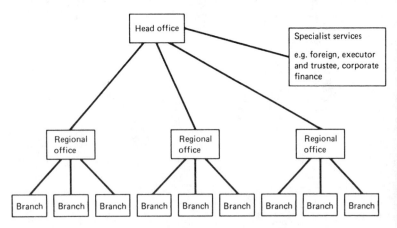

Fig. 10.1 Structure of a clearing bank

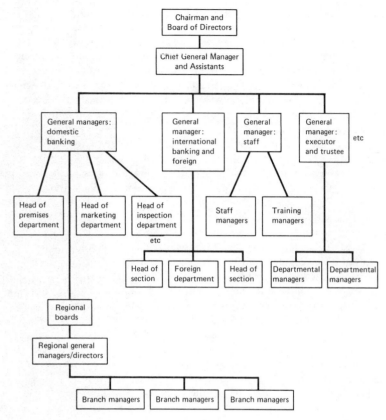

Fig. 10.2   Management structure of a clearing bank

each of whom normally has a responsibility for a specific function in the bank. A group of general managers has responsibility for domestic banking (that is, banking in Britain), and a smaller number may be responsible for overseas banking. Individual general managers take charge of such areas as corporate services (covering all aspects of services for company customers; see Unit 16), executor and trustee department (dealing with wills and trusts; see Unit 15.13) and those areas concerned with the efficient running of the bank such as staff, training, administration and management services.

The organization continues 'down the line' from the general managers. Domestic banking, for example, delegates authority to regional offices and it is here that the management structure of the regions differs from bank to bank. To consider one instance: Midland has its eighteen regional head offices under the control of a *regional director*, supported by assistants. Lloyds, on the other hand, has fifteen regional boards each with a chairman and up to six or seven regional directors who, like members of the main board of directors, are not usually full-time employees of the bank but are people who have distinguished careers in fields other than banking and who are well known locally; each regional board also has a full-time *regional general manager*. The other banks have also developed regional structures; this decentralization establishes a local identity for the bank and to some extent helps to dispel the idea that all decisions are taken at a large impersonal head office in London. The regional offices exercise considerable power over the branches in their areas: most applications for loan and overdraft facilities, or for their renewal, that are too large for a branch manager to approve on his own can be sanctioned by the regional office without reference to head office; only requests for very large advances will be above the limit of the regional office and require the approval of head office and possibly the main board of directors. Regional offices are also able to report to head office about the state of local industry and commerce, and each has a responsibility to ensure that Bank of England directives are adhered to in their area. After the regional directors and managers come the *branch managers*—the highest-ranking member of the bank's staff that most customers will meet; Unit 10.2 considers the people involved in the organization of a 'typical' branch.

A more recent structural development of banking is to group a number of support (or satellite) branches within a locality under the control of the manager of the key (or main) branch—see Fig. 10.3. Each support branch provides basic banking facilities while the more specialist services are available through the key branch—this topic is discussed more fully in Unit 10.3.

Other divisions of the bank besides domestic banking are often also organized on a regional basis: a specialist foreign branch and an office of the executor and trustee department often serve each region.

The more specialist divisions of the bank which do not warrant regional representation, such as corporate services, have a structure that ranges

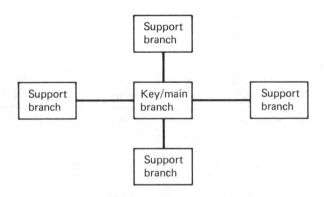

Fig. 10.3   Structure of key and support branches

downward from the general manager responsible for the service, involving specialist managers or heads of departments. The services of these divisions are available to both regional offices and branches to enable them to provide specialist advice to customers, and are fully discussed in Units 15 and 16. Additionally, every major bank includes departments that provide specialist services to assist in the smooth running of its organization or to promote its image and services generally. We will discuss these one by one.

(a) Staff Department/Personnel

This is concerned with recruitment, transfer from branch to branch of staff to ensure that they gain a variety of experience at branches of different sizes, training, welfare and the consideration of suitable staff for promotion. Members of this department regularly interview staff so that career prospects, problems and difficulties can be identified.

(b) Training Department

The training department works closely with the staff or personnel department, and has overall responsibility for the training of every member of the bank's staff. Training courses take a variety of forms such as:

   (i) in-house videos and study packs: used by the trainee at the branch at which he or she is based;
   (ii) a visiting instructor: an experienced member of the bank's staff who comes to an individual branch to train particular staff in specific tasks;
   (iii) attendance at a regional training centre or large central training branch.

The first training course is designed as an induction course for new entrants and covers the basic book-keeping routines of branch operations. As a member of staff progresses in the bank he or she will learn how to be a terminal operator (using the computer terminals installed in branches through which accounting information is fed into the central computer), a cashier, a foreign clerk and a security clerk (the duties of these staff members are discussed in Unit 10.2). More advanced courses for staff being considered for appointment to branch accountant, and management development courses for branch accountants, assistant managers and managers are usually run at regular intervals at large country houses that have been bought by each bank and converted into management training centres.

(c) Inspection Department

With so many branches involved, it is essential to ensure that each carries out the day-to-day banking operations in a uniform manner in accordance with the instructions from head office. It is the job of the inspection department to visit branches and to help or advise staff on correct practice. The inspectors are also available to managers in any emergency which needs the attention of bank investigators from outside the branch, such as a large discrepancy of cash.

'*I had a touch of sciatica last night. That usually means the inspectors are coming*'

(*d*) Marketing Department

Nowadays the banks are increasingly using marketing techniques to sell their services (see Unit 15.1). Marketing involves undertaking research to find out what services the customer wants, planning new services and advertising in all its forms—in newspapers and magazines, on television, with posters and through leaflets displayed in the branches and mailed to customers. The department is also concerned with training managers and staff to sell new services—this is particularly important because unless staff fully understand a new (or existing) service and can point out its advantages to customers, the service will be undersold.

Working closely with the marketing department, and perhaps a part of it, are staff dealing with public relations, concerned with the 'public image' of the bank. This department is particularly involved with releases to the media—press, radio and television—concerning developments within the bank, and with commenting on banking topics in the news.

Other departments providing specialist services within the bank include the *premises department*, involved in all aspects of acquisition, maintenance and sale of bank premises, the *computer department*, which organizes computer operations, the *organization and methods department*, which studies the work of branches and makes recommendations as to methods of doing certain tasks that are more efficient or otherwise improved, and the *bullion department*, which arranges the distribution and collection of banknotes and coin throughout the branch network.

During the last twenty years, the major banks in Britain acquired and formed companies providing highly specialized services. These subsidiaries, associated companies and trade investments, together with the parent bank, together make up the banking group and, although they may be separate in legal, management and name terms from the main bank, the services they provide are available to its customers. They are involved in areas such as hire purchase, factoring, insurance and merchant bank services, and are considered more fully in Units 15 and 16. The clearing banks differ from each other in the ways in which they fit these specialized areas into their structure, however: one bank may provide a service through the parent company, while another may provide the same service through a subsidiary or associated company. As far as the customer is concerned this difference does not matter, but it is of interest to the banking student as representing a different organizational structure.

10.2   Branch Organization and Staff

This section gives an indication of the work carried out by each member of staff within a branch. Terminology will vary from one bank to another and the size of the branch will be reflected in the degree of specialization possible. In a small branch the securities clerk will almost certainly deal with foreign work and will probably also carry out the duties of a manager's assistant, as well as being required to act as a relief cashier if necessary! Fig. 10.4 illustrates the staff structure and main responsibilities in a medium-sized branch.

(a) The Manager
In the eyes of the local community, the manager is the bank and it is his duty to sell the services and develop the business of his branch. In this task he has overall responsibility for his customers but can, as we have seen, call in specialists from the various divisions and departments of the bank and can always look to his regional director for advice and guidance. A manager will have spent many years in the bank, usually having started as a junior straight from school and worked his way up through the various different banking tasks—all good preparation for the day when he takes charge of his 'own' branch. While at present most managers are men, all bank jobs are open to women and there are increasing numbers of female managers, assistant

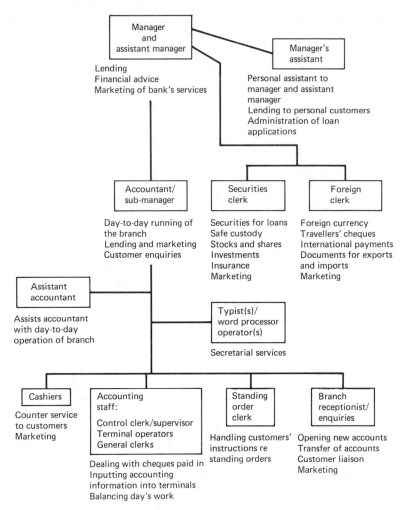

Fig. 10.4   Staff structure and main responsibilities in a medium-sized branch (job titles will vary from bank to bank; the structure will vary with size of branch)

managers and accountants. (However, for the sake of simplicity, we shall continue to refer to individual staff as 'he'.)

The manager does not spend all his time lending money; while many of his visitors wish to see him for this purpose, many call to seek advice on a wide range of financial and personal problems. It follows, therefore, that the ideal manager must be good at lending the bank's money (and getting it back safely!), well versed in all aspects of finance, a good listener and able to get on well with people from all walks of life. The manager doesn't spend all the time at his desk—part of his job is to get to know local people by visiting them in shops, factories and on the farm.

Depending on the size of the branch and his experience as a manager, he is given a limit up to which he can lend without reference to his regional office. This ensures that, for ordinary day-to-day lending, the manager can make up his mind quickly and not keep the customer waiting for days for a decision by somebody else further up the hierarchy, who doesn't personally know him. The lending limit usually applies to the maximum amount that the manager may lend to an individual customer and may be higher if the advance is secured; when requests are made for advances above his limit the manager must send full details of the request to his regional office for sanction. The regional office also has a lending limit, although a much higher one than that of most branch managers, and only requests for the very largest loans and overdrafts are required to be submitted to head office for the approval of the board of directors. All advances are approved for a fixed period which will not normally exceed twelve months, except in the case of medium-term loans (see Unit 16.2(b)). At the end of the period the manager reviews the advance with his customer, and where appropriate renews, or requests his regional office to renew, the facility for a further period. Thus much of the manager's time is spent in reviewing existing lending.

The manager has overall responsibility for the staff of his branch and for ensuring that it is run in accordance with head office instructions. In larger branches he has one or more *assistant managers* or *manager's assistants* to help him in certain areas of the work.

(b) The Accountant

This is the person who is responsible for the day-to-day organization and administration of the branch so that the bank's business is run efficiently and correctly. Depending on which bank he works for, he may be called *sub-manager*, *administration manager* or *accountant*. As the last title suggests, he is particularly concerned with the smooth running of the accounting side of the branch and handles enquiries from customers about their accounts and from people who wish to open new accounts. During an average day he meets a good many customers at the enquiry counter, on a less formal basis than can the manager in his office. He is also usually involved in lending and often deals with requests for loans and overdrafts from personal rather than business customers. Besides these tasks his main responsibilities are to ensure the smooth and efficient running of the branch, that staff are trained within the branch in different aspects of the bank's work and that appropriate returns and other information are sent to head office at the right time and correctly completed. In his work he may be helped by one or more *assistant accountants*.

The accountant, like most staff, has usually worked for the bank since leaving school and has spent periods at several branches doing different tasks. During this time he will have attended appropriate courses at the bank's training branches. In his present job he will already be preparing for his next promotion—perhaps as manager of a small branch, or accountant or assistant

'I need the jacket to accommodate a pocket calculator, a pocket bleeper and a pocket dictating machine'

manager at a larger branch—by deputizing for the manager or assistant manager during holiday or sickness periods.

The manager, assistant manager, manager's assistant, accountant and his assistants are often known as *appointed officers*; this indicates that they have reached a certain level of responsibility in their careers and are appointed by head office to run the branch at their different work levels.

(c) The Security Clerk
He is concerned to see that, when the manager accepts security for an advance (see Unit 21), the necessary formalities are carried out to ensure that the securities are held by the bank in a correct manner to cover the advance. He is also concerned with buying and selling stocks and shares and other investments for the bank's customers, with taking deeds, documents and other valuables into safe custody for those who wish to leave them in the bank's safe and with giving advice about a wide range of bank services.

Special training courses help to prepare for this job and promising young men and women who are making good progress in The Chartered Institute of Bankers' examinations will be chosen to attend. A sound level of legal knowledge, banking practice and financial awareness are required to understand the implications of this job which, in smaller branches, may also incorporate the work of the foreign clerk. In very large branches the security clerk may be an 'appointed officer' and in many branches, because of his contact by letter with customers, solicitors and stockbrokers, the security clerk often has authority to sign 'for manager'.

The security clerk works closely with the manager in dealing with securities and in preparing the 'application for advance' forms that are needed when a customer wishes to borrow an amount above the manager's limit and reference has to be made to the regional office. Administratively, the security clerk is directly under the control of the accountant, and, in holiday and sickness periods, may 'move up' and deputize for him or his assistant. This is all good training for his next promotion which may be as assistant accountant at a large branch or accountant at a small branch.

(d) The Foreign Clerk

Most larger bank branches employ a clerk who deals specifically with foreign work. During the peak holiday periods the foreign clerk spends a lot of his time making up *travel orders* consisting of travellers' cheques and foreign currency (see Unit 15.7) for customers going abroad, and handling unused foreign currency brought back to the bank after holidays are over. The foreign clerk must therefore be fully conversant with rates of exchange for currencies and with the advantages and disadvantages of different types of travel facilities.

Travel orders are only one part of a foreign clerk's duties, however: nearly every branch has at least one business customer who deals with either exporting or importing and the bank is almost always involved in settlements with his overseas customers. To handle this work requires a good working knowledge of the receipts and payment processes, the documents involved and how to deal with any discrepancies. Business customers also seek advice and information about exporting or importing and the foreign clerk is expected to know most of the answers. (Exporting and importing are dealt with fully in Unit 17.)

Like all bank staff, the foreign clerk will have spent some years learning the basic routines of banking and then will have been specially selected and trained for his present job. He may choose to continue to specialize in foreign work and his next promotion might be transfer to a regional foreign branch; alternatively he may wish to remain in normal branch banking and seek promotion to assistant accountant at a large branch or accountant at a small one.

(e) The Cashiers

These are the people who meet the bank's customers more than any other members of the staff. The branch is usually judged in its locality by the efficiency, pleasantness, helpfulness and courtesy given by the cashiers to customers. The banks have realized the importance of the cashier as the main link with the customers and place great emphasis on this aspect in the training course for cashiers.

In large branches the cashiers spend the whole of the day at the counter and deal with all aspects of paying in and drawing out by branch customers and total strangers. At the same time, besides being courteous and efficient, the cashier has to bear in mind many other things such as endorsements on cheques (when necessary), stopped cheques, lost or stolen cheque and credit cards, and the list of customers (one hopes, a short one) for whom cheques should not be cashed without reference to the manager or accountant. The bank's internal regulations, especially those concerning the control of cash, should also be adhered to, and at the end of the day the cashier must balance his till against the total cash he has received and paid out. In a smaller branch, besides counter duties, cashiers are involved in dealing with general enquiries, cheque books, statements, standing orders, travellers' cheques and foreign money, although in a large branch most of these matters are handled by an *enquiry clerk* who passes the customers on to the appropriate specialist staff.

It is not unusual for a cashier to be relatively new to the bank, perhaps having spent twelve months as a junior clerk and then going on a cashiers' course at the bank's training branch. During a period of counter duties, a cashier may have the opportunity of gaining further experience of the bank's procedures by spending time as the *first cashier*, responsible to the accountant for the counter. The ambitious cashier looks for opportunities to progress to security clerk and will spend his time working hard at The Chartered Institute of Bankers' examinations (see Unit 23.3) and finding out as much as possible about work concerned with securities.

(f) The Accounting Staff

These are the people who carry out the accounting functions of the branch; they work directly under the supervision of the accountant. The *control clerk* is responsible for controlling and balancing the work of the branch each day and

for making appropriate book-keeping entries. The *terminal operator* uses a terminal unit situated in the branch and connected, usually by telephone line, direct to the bank's computer centre, to feed in information concerning customers' accounts—credits received and cash, cheques and standing orders drawn on the account. He should also be looking out for irregularities on cheques such as 'stops' or cheques not signed in accordance with the mandate held by the bank. The *remittance clerks* are concerned with credits paid to the cashiers: they sort credits and cheques paid in by customers into different banks and, at the end of the day, balance the totals of these with the total credits paid in. The credits that have been paid in for other branches and other banks, together with the cheques drawn on other branches and other banks, are then sent off to head office where they are handled by the bank's clearing department and those drawn on other banks passed through the clearing house (see Unit 11.9).

A young person joining the bank is likely to start as a remittance clerk. In small branches the junior clerk is also expected to deal with outgoing post, answer the telephone, handle requests for statements and other enquiries at the enquiry counter and make coffee in the morning and tea in the afternoon!

In medium-sized or large branches there are also *secretaries* who make appointments for customers to see the manager and assistant manager, type outgoing correspondence from all departments of the bank and are concerned in keeping the non-accounting records of customers up to date. In smaller branches there may well be no typist and it is not unknown for managers to have to do their own typing.

In this Unit, the broad areas of staff work and responsibility have been discussed with reference to the ways in which they fit into the working of a branch. But of course different banks are organized in different ways, and there are often variations even between branches of the same bank. You should compare carefully the organization of the bank you know best with the description given above, and make notes of differences of which you are aware.

10.3   Recent Changes in the Organization of Branch Banking

The 1980s have seen considerable changes in the organization of branch banking in Britain. Many sub-branches—that is, a branch staffed directly from another branch, perhaps only by a cashier and guard and often with very restricted opening hours—have been closed in an effort to reduce the high costs of operating the branch network. Some branches have been downgraded from a 'full-manager' branch to 'sub-manager' status. The sub-manager in charge of the branch has only limited lending powers but these are sufficient to meet the needs of most personal and small-business customers. For bigger lending propositions the sub-manager may well have to call in a more senior manager from the nearby larger branch under whose control he falls.

A further extension of the sub-manager principle is the grouping of a number of smaller (support) branches in a fairly close area either under the control of a larger (key) branch (see Fig. 10.3) or a local area office. Each of the support branches within the area is staffed with the intention of providing only the basic banking services of paying-in, drawing out and a limited range of personal services; each is run by a 'clerk-in-charge' who may also have very limited lending powers. None of the specialist personal and business services of the bank are available from these support branches unless a prior appointment is made for the customer to meet a specialist from the key branch. Under such a system, all the lending managers and other specialists such as the foreign business clerk and the securities clerk work from the key branch. The customer must attend the main branch to discuss loans and to make use of the specialist personal and business services; alternatively, as indicated above, the lending manager or other specialist will attend a support branch by appointment. Certainly such a system has several virtues: a branch manager no longer has to know 'a little about everything' and can instead specialize in certain aspects of banking; costs can be reduced with the concentration of specialist functions in a key branch instead of being offered in every branch; a higher standard of professional management should be available from the specialist team and decision-making about lending propositions should be faster. Balanced against this is the lack of convenience for the customer: a visit to the key branch must be made for all but the non-specialist services or an appointment must be made to meet the lending manager from the key branch at the support branch. It is no longer possible to 'drop in for a chat' with the bank manager—the 'general practitioner' has been replaced by the specialist. At the same time the relationship between bank manager and bank customer is weakened—most customers nowadays have never met their bank manager and have no need to since often either a large overdraft or a lot of money are prerequisites to meeting the manager!

Increasing competition from other financial intermediaries (particularly building societies and smaller banks) has forced the major retail banks in Britain to introduce changes into the banking system to make it more attractive to the personal customer. New services have been introduced in the 1980s. The Saturday opening of banks—a service withdrawn in 1969—has returned. There is even Sunday opening in certain areas. Nowadays, however, Saturday hours are more flexible; and some banks are open for longer than others while others are not open at all. Thus a branch in a busy shopping centre may be open for Saturday morning and part of the afternoon, while a branch on a factory estate where no one works on a Saturday will not be open. In addition certain branches have been identified as having mainly personal, rather than business, customers and have been entirely redesigned to provide a comfortable environment for the private customer. The public area of such branches has been extended: there is plenty of seating, the cashiers' security screens have been removed (Fig. 10.5) and a number of staff work in the public area as enquiry clerks or personal account officers and no appointment is necessary to see them. One or more automated teller machines (ATMs) (see

Fig. 10.5   Interior of a modern bank branch

Unit 15.5) are often installed in the public area of such branches, so that cash withdrawals and other transactions can be undertaken speedily and efficiently. Some branches have been replaced entirely by ATMs and the use of an ATM card or credit card will open a door which then gives access to a number of machines. At other branches, a separate ATM area—called a *card-access lobby*—has been constructed and customers gain access to the machine through a door opened by their ATM card or credit card.

Until the end of the 1970s, the major retail banks did not lay great stress on being attractive to personal customers. However, the increasingly competitive environment of the 1980s has already produced major improvements in the quality of the service offered to personal customers, while that offered to the business customer has become more sophisticated and professional. As we move towards the 1990s, such standards can only improve.

10.4 Branch Computer Systems

Branch banking is now almost totally reliant on computer systems for the handling of all basic book-keeping transactions. All branch staff are able to operate terminals within the branch for the purpose of inputting information and making enquiries. Besides the main system linked by telephone line to the bank's central computer, an increasing number of branches use a local computer system. This holds information such as branch records of correspondence with customers, interview notes and details of securities held on behalf of customers. It is also used as a word-processing system for preparing letters, and for producing management information, such as cash budgets on behalf of customers.

While computers in banking started in the 'back office', they have spread in

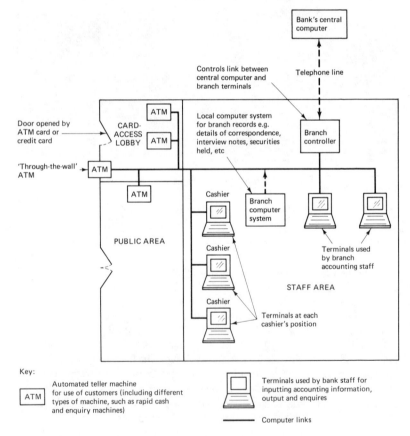

Fig. 10.6   Layout of computer systems within a medium-sized branch

recent years to the public side of the branch, in the form of ATMs, card-access lobbies and enquiry terminals; all of which are operated by the customers. With developments in EFTPOS (electronic funds transfer at point of sale—see Unit 12.6), electronic banking is moving away from the branch into retail outlets, and into home banking (see Unit 15.6).

Fig. 10.6 gives an indication of the basic computer systems to be found in a medium-sized branch.

10.5   Questions

1. Describe the main divisions of responsibilities of the general managers of a major clearing bank, indicating the areas with which each is concerned.

2. Detail the organizational structure of the branch where you work. Who is responsible for the different aspects of the work of the branch?

3. Draw up a job specification for the person in charge of the securities department of a medium-sized branch.

Bills of Exchange and Cheques: an Introduction

11.1 An Introduction to Negotiable Instruments

Cheques are familiar to most people and are commonly used to settle debts. *Bills of exchange* are not so well known but are used extensively in the settlement of overseas trade: they may be payable on demand or may be worded so as to make the payment due at some future date, thus giving the purchaser of goods a period of credit.

Cheques, unless crossed 'not negotiable' (see Unit 11.8), and bills of exchange are examples of *negotiable instruments*, as are banknotes, Treasury bills, certificates of deposit and certain other documents. The characteristics of a negotiable instrument are:

  (i) the document must be transferable by delivery, or by endorsement and delivery;

  (ii) the legal title passes to the person who takes it in good faith and for value and without notice of any defect in the title of the transferor;

  (iii) the legal holder for the time being can sue in his own name;

  (iv) notice of transfer need not be given to the party/parties liable on the instrument;

  (v) the title passes free from equities or counter-claims between previous parties of which the transferee has no notice.

A banknote is payable to bearer and thus, unlike most cheques, needs no endorsement to transfer the title. How do you know that one of the banknotes in your wallet or handbag has not at some time been stolen? As banknotes are negotiable instruments and provided you acquire them 'in good faith and for value' (that means that you had no idea they had been stolen and you either earned them, received them as a present or were given them in change) you have no need to worry—your title to them is 'good'. Most cheques and bills of exchange are *payable to order*—take a look at one of your own cheques and you will see the words 'or order' already printed—and require endorsement and delivery to transfer the title: the exception to this rule are those that are *payable to bearer* when, like bank notes, the title passes by delivery.

In this Unit we are mainly concerned with bills of exchange and cheques: as bills developed before cheques came into general use, we will consider them first.

11.2 Bills of Exchange: a Definition

The Bills of Exchange Act 1882, which remains an important piece of legislation for bankers, gives the definition as:

> an unconditional order in writing addressed by one person to another, signed by the person giving it, requiring the person to whom it is addressed to pay on demand, or at a fixed or determinable future time, a sum certain in money to or to the order of a specified person or bearer.

This definition sounds complex, but using the specimen bill of exchange shown in Fig. 11.1 we can examine its elements one by one, and see how it has been built up.

'An unconditional order.' There are no conditions stipulated that must be carried out before payment; the bill simply says 'pay'. A *conditional order* is a document ordering payment subject to the fulfilment of some condition, for example 'Pay *AB* the sum of £100 on condition that the receipt below is duly signed and dated'.

'In writing.' The bill must be in writing, whether typewritten or in ink, print or pencil. The writing may be on paper, parchment or cardboard—in a famous case it was even on the side of a cow!

'Addressed by one person to another.' It is addressed by Smith, Jones & Co Ltd to Singh & Co.

'Signed by the person giving it.' It is signed by the directors on behalf of Smith, Jones & Co Ltd.

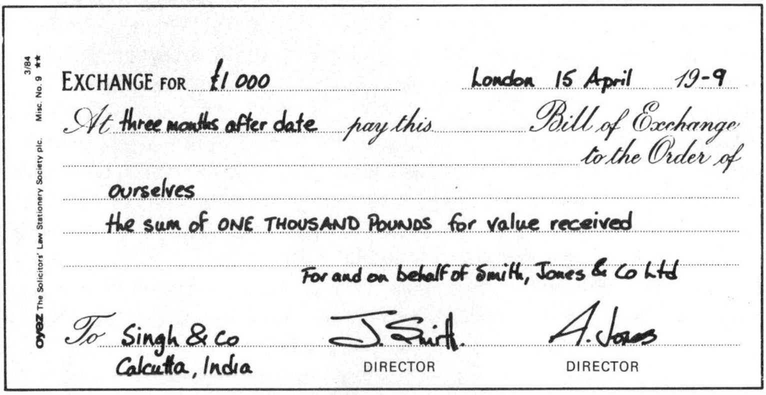

EXCHANGE FOR £1 000 London 15 April 19-9

At three months after date pay this Bill of Exchange to the Order of

ourselves

the sum of ONE THOUSAND POUNDS for value received

For and on behalf of Smith, Jones & Co Ltd

To Singh & Co
Calcutta, India

J Smith DIRECTOR A. Jones DIRECTOR

oyez The Solicitors' Law Stationery Society plc. Misc. No. 9 ** 3/84

Fig. 11.1 A specimen bill of exchange

'Requiring the person to whom it is addressed to pay.' It is addressed to Singh &
Co and they are the people required to pay.

'To pay on demand or at a fixed or determinable future time.' This bill is not
payable on demand, nor is it payable at a fixed future time, since it does not say
'pay on 15 July 19-9; instead it is payable at a determinable future time—three
months after date—and is therefore determined to be payable on 15 July 19-9.

'A sum certain in money.' The exact money amount, £1 000, is clearly stated.

'To or to the order of a specified person or bearer.' This bill is not a bearer bill,
which would say 'pay . . . to the Order of Bearer'; instead it says 'pay . . . to the
Order of Ourselves', the 'ourselves' being Smith, Jones & Co Ltd; the words
'to the Order of Ourselves' allow Smith, Jones & Co Ltd to transfer their
interest in the bill to another person by endorsement (see Unit 11.4).

The words 'value received' are often added to the wording of a bill to establish
'valuable consideration' which is normally one of the essentials of a valid
contract.

11.3 Parties to a Bill

There are initially three parties to a bill: drawer, drawee and payee. The
drawer is the person who has drawn the bill; the *drawee* is the person on whom
it is drawn and who has to make payment; the *payee* is the person to whom the
money is to be paid. On the bill shown in Fig. 11.1, the drawer is Smith, Jones
& Co Ltd, the drawee is Singh and Co and the payee is also Smith, Jones & Co
Ltd: in this example, therefore, Smith Jones & Co Ltd is both the drawer and
payee. It sometimes happens that there are three different parties to a bill at
the start: if Smith, Jones & Co Ltd owed £1 000 to W. Harris who was prepared
to accept the money direct from Singh & Co in settlement of the debt due to
him, then the bill would be drawn to read 'three months after date pay to W.
Harris or his order the sum of one thousand pounds', and Harris would be the
payee.
    Where a bill is payable at a time in the future it is known as a *term
bill*—because it is drawn for a certain term—and must be sent to the drawee
for *acceptance*. This is done by the drawee 'accepting' his liability by signing his
name on the bill and agreeing to pay the bill at maturity. The bill shown in Fig.
11.1 would be sent to Singh & Co for their acceptance and, when this was done,
they would be known as the *acceptors*. If the bill had been payable at sight—a
sight bill—there would be no need to obtain the acceptance of Singh & Co
because they would be expected to pay immediately on 'sight' of the bill; if the
bill had been payable three months after sight, the bill would need to be
presented for acceptance and the acceptance dated, in order to determine the
date of payment.

There are two major types of acceptance: a general acceptance and a qualified acceptance. A *general acceptance* confirms that the drawee is in agreement with the terms of the bill as drawn. A *qualified acceptance*, however, has the effect of varying the terms of the bill as drawn; for example, there may be a partial acceptance of the amount: a bill drawn for £1 000 may be accepted for £900 only. If the holder takes a qualified acceptance he generally loses his right of recourse against previous parties to the bill (see Unit 11.5).

11.4 Endorsement of a Bill

The bill shown in Fig. 11.1 is an example of an *order bill* in that it contains the words 'pay to the order of ourselves'. This means that such a bill may be transferred to another person on the 'orders of' the payee by endorsement and delivery—handing over—of the bill to the other person: this transfer of title is called *negotiation*. More precisely, a bill is payable to order when:

(i) it is expressed to be payable to order; *or*

(ii) it is payable to the order of a particular person; *or*

(iii) it is payable to a particular person and does not contain words prohibiting transfer.

For example, a bill payable to 'J. Smith or order' is obviously an order bill; a bill payable to 'J. Smith' is also an order bill because it does not contain words prohibiting transfer; but a bill payable to 'J. Smith only' is not an order bill and may not be transferred to another person.

When an order bill is transferred to another person by endorsement and delivery, a number of different types of endorsement are possible, and these also apply to cheques.

(i) A *blank endorsement* specifies no endorsee (that is, no person in whose favour it is endorsed) and therefore the bill or cheque becomes payable to bearer. For the bill in Fig. 11.1 a blank endorsement would appear on the reverse as:

> for and on behalf of Smith, Jones & Co Ltd
> J. Smith   A. Jones (signed)
> Directors

(ii) A *special endorsement* specifies the endorsee:

> Pay D. Williams or order
> for and on behalf of Smith, Jones & Co Ltd
> J. Smith   A. Jones (signed)
> Directors

Notice that the words 'or order' could be omitted and the bill would still be an order bill. A blank endorsement may be converted by any holder into a special endorsement by adding the words 'pay ....', naming the person to whom it is to be payable.

(iii) A *restrictive endorsement* prevents further endorsement of the bill:

Pay D. Williams only
for and on behalf of Smith, Jones & Co Ltd
J. Smith   A. Jones (signed)
Directors

11.5   Negotiation of a Bill

Under the terms of the Bills of Exchange Act, every person who has signed a bill guarantees to a subsequent holder that it will be paid on the due date. Thus the holder of a bill that is not paid on the due date (see Unit 11.6) may sue any or all previous parties to the bill. Therefore a bill that carries the acceptance of a reputable person known to be of first-class financial standing is considered better than a bill carrying the acceptance of an unknown trader. This recalls the origins of the merchant banks among the wealthy merchants who, for a fee, began to lend their name to bills by accepting them for less well-known merchants (see Unit 5.3). They continue to accept bills on behalf of their customers—hence the name *acceptance houses* for the banks most involved in this business—and such bills command a finer rate of discount than other trade bills.

A holder of an accepted bill of exchange can:

(i) sell the bill for face value less discount to his own bank or a discount house; *or*

(ii) negotiate the bill by asking his bank for a loan against the bill and request the bank to collect the proceeds upon maturity; *or*

(iii) hold the bill until maturity if he does not need the money urgently.

11.6   Discharge and Dishonour of a Bill

Normally a bill will be paid by the acceptor upon presentation on the due date; the legal obligations on the bill are then said to be *discharged*. There are other circumstances in which a bill may be discharged:

(i) where the acceptor of the bill is or becomes the holder of the bill at or after maturity—that is, he becomes the owner of the bill on which he is liable;

(ii) where material alteration has been made to the bill—such as a change of the date or the amount payable—without the assent of all parties liable on the bill, then all parties liable prior to the alteration will be discharged, but not those liable by negotiation after alteration;

(iii) where the holder renounces his rights and makes a written cancellation on the bill itself, that is, he makes it clear in writing that he will not make a claim on the acceptor for the amount of the bill;

(iv) where the bill becomes *statute-barred* under the provisions of the

Limitation Acts; this means that no bill is enforceable in law after six years from the date when the cause of action first happened, subject to certain complex rules regarding the revival of a statute-barred debt.

Most bills are correctly accepted when presented for acceptance and paid when presented for payment. Sometimes acceptance is refused and the bill is then said to be *dishonoured by non-acceptance*; similarly a failure by the acceptor to pay on the due date leads to *dishonour by non-payment*. It is important for the person presenting a bill which is dishonoured to take the correct legal steps. For foreign bills (generally drawn in this country and payable abroad) these steps are known as *noting* and *protest*.

A bill is *noted* in order to secure official evidence that it has been dishonoured. The holder of the bill that is to be noted applies to a legal official called a *notary public* whose job it is to attest deeds and documents to confirm their authenticity. The notary public re-presents the bill for acceptance or payment, whichever is required, and if the drawer (or acceptor) still refuses to accept (or pay) the bill, the bill is noted. The noting is a minute made by the notary public which contains the date of presentment, the notary's charges, a reference to the notary's register and his initials. This noting is a preparatory step to a formal document called a *protest* which bears the seal of the notary public and attests that the bill has been dishonoured. A protest is accepted in the courts of most countries as evidence that the bill has been dishonoured.

Where a dishonoured bill has to be protested and no notary public is available at the place of dishonour, any householder or substantial resident may in the presence of two witnesses, give a certificate, signed by them, attesting the dishonour of the bill, and the certificate will operate as if it were a formal protest of the bill. This is known as a *householder's protest*.

These legal procedures are necessary to establish the liability of previous parties to the bill.

11.7   Definition and Development of Cheques

The Bills of Exchange Act defines a cheque as a *bill of exchange, drawn on a banker, payable on demand*.

The parties to a cheque are the same as for a bill: drawer, drawee, and payee. The *drawer* is the person who has signed the cheque, the *drawee* is the bank on which the cheque is drawn and the *payee* is the person to whom the cheque is payable and who is to receive the benefit. The drawee bank is also the *paying bank*, while the bank at which the payee pays in a cheque is known as the *collecting bank*. A cheque does not need to be accepted prior to payment as it is payable on demand. Cheques differ from bills of exchange in that notice of dishonour by non-payment is rarely needed in order to claim against the drawer of a cheque. This is because non-payment is almost always due to lack of funds or because the cheque has been 'stopped' by the drawer: both of these are valid excuses for not giving notice to the drawer. Where the holder is concerned, mere return of the cheque is deemed to be sufficient notice of dishonour, but in practice an answer is always written on the cheque (see Unit 11.10). The steps known as noting and protest are not necessary in order to preserve the right of recourse against the drawer or endorser of an inland bill. Most cheques in Britain fit the definition of an inland bill—they are drawn and payable within the British Isles—and therefore these legal steps do not apply.

Cheques came into general use in Britain with the emergence of the joint-stock banks in the second quarter of the nineteenth century. The Bills of Exchange Act brought cheques within the general scope of all the provisions of the Act applicable to bills payable on demand. In particular the Act contains specific provisions relating to crossed cheques which give valuable protection against loss through theft and fraud (see Unit 11.8). Under section 60 of the Act, banks are protected when they pay in good faith and in the ordinary course of business a cheque bearing a forged endorsement, and will not be liable to the customer for the amount, provided it is an order cheque payable on demand and drawn on the bank (see also Unit 20.6). The Act, with its protection for both bank and customer, also brought together—or *codified*— previous law relating to crossings on cheques, and gave banks considerable scope for developing current account business.

The other major legislation concerning cheques is the Cheques Act 1957, which removed the requirement that payees should endorse cheques before paying them in to their bank account, with the exception of a few specific cases. The Act also provides that an unendorsed cheque, if it appears to have been paid by the drawer's bank, should be evidence of receipt by the payee of the amount of the cheque. This explains why, when bills are paid by cheque, receipts are only issued on request; in the event of any dispute over payment, the paid cheque can be obtained from the drawer's bank as proof of payment.

11.8   Crossings on Cheques

Unlike a bill of exchange, a cheque may be *crossed* by drawing two parallel lines across its face.

This ensures that the cheque cannot be cashed at a bank but must be paid in for the credit of an account. Thus crossed cheques provide a safer means of payment than open cheques which can easily be cashed at the drawee bank. A thief who has stolen crossed cheques is forced to pass them through a bank account, most probably by asking shops or pubs to cash them for him and pass them through their accounts, and this may lead to him being traced by the police. The only exception to the rule on not cashing crossed cheques is, of course, when the account holder or 'his known agent'—his wife or a firm's wages clerk, perhaps—wishes to draw cash. Most cheques issued by banks nowadays already carry a pre-printed crossing but under certain circumstances open cheques may be useful to a customer who wants another person to be able to draw cash from the bank on his behalf.

There are two main types of crossings: general and special. A *general*

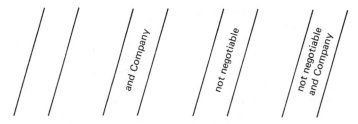

Fig. 11.2   Crossed cheques: general crossings

crossing is described by the Bills of Exchange Act as being two parallel lines across the face of a cheque, with or without the words 'and company' (or any abbreviation) and with or without the words 'not negotiable'. Fig. 11.2 shows some examples of general crossings as described in the Act.

The effect of all these crossings is that the cheque must be paid into a bank account: the words 'and company' have no legal significance and date back to the days of private banks when it was usual for the payee of a cheque, when paying it in for the credit of his account, to add his bank's name which would end in 'and company'; thus the words were pre-printed on cheques as a service to payees. 'Not negotiable' as a crossing is considered below.

A cheque is *specially crossed* when, *with or without the addition of two parallel lines*, it bears across its face the addition of a banker's name: the cheque is then said to be crossed specially to that banker. Fig. 11.3 illustrates some examples of special crossings.

The effect of a special crossing is that the cheques can only be paid into an account with the specified bank and, if indicated on the crossing, the specified branch. All banks cross cheques paid in by customers specially to themselves by means of a rubber stamp which bears the name and address of the branch, together with its sorting code number, so that if the cheques were lost in transit to the drawee bank, they would be useless to anyone and could not again be paid into a bank account. The identification of the collecting bank also helps when cheques are returned unpaid by the drawee bank (see Unit 11.10).

As most cheques are negotiable instruments—unless they bear the words

Fig. 11.3   Crossed cheques: special crossings (note: parallel lines are not a legal requirement of a special crossing)

'not negotiable'—it is possible to obtain a good title even though the transferor's title was faulty or non-existent. Suppose that a thief steals a cheque which has conveniently already been endorsed in blank by the payee, and negotiates the cheque to an innocent shopkeeper who agrees to cash it in exchange for goods. Under such circumstances, the transferee (the shopkeeper) has a right to the value represented by the cheque and all previous parties would be liable. Thus the drawer of a stolen cheque may still find himself liable for the amount of it even though he may have placed a 'stop' on it. The way to avoid such possible liability is to cross cheques 'not negotiable': this does not mean, as is often mistakenly thought, that the cheque cannot be transferred from one person to another, but that a person taking such a cheque shall not have and shall not be capable of giving a better title to the cheque than that of his transferor. This means that a break in the 'good title' remains broken and an innocent transferee cannot acquire any better rights than those of the person from whom he received it. To be absolutely certain that you will not be liable for the amount of your cheques in the event of their being stolen, you should always cross them 'not negotiable'. Nowadays most cheques are paid into the account of the payee without transfer and there is little risk; but where cheques are customarily passed from one person to another there is always the chance that a negotiable cheque could, after being stolen, be passed to an innocent person—known as a *holder in due course*—who could recover the value of the cheque from any previous party. A holder in due course (see Unit 20.3)—who could be our innocent shopkeeper, for instance—is a person who has taken a bill or cheque in good faith, complete and regular on the face of it (that is, with nothing apparently wrong with it), for value, before it is overdue, and without notice of any defect in the title of his predecessor or of the dishonouring of the bill.

The crossing 'account payee' has no statutory significance: it is not mentioned in the Bills of Exchange Act or the Cheques Act. However, by custom, when a cheque crossed in this way is paid in for the credit of an account, the bank accepting it—the *collecting bank*—looks to see if it is being credited to the account of the payee. If it is not, the collecting bank is *put on enquiry* and should take steps to find out why it is being paid into another account. If it does not obtain a satisfactory explanation, the collecting bank may be liable for *conversion* (allowing a cheque intended to be of benefit to one person to be converted to the benefit of another).

Sometimes when a person is buying goods by mail order, he does not know the exact cost of the purchase and sends a signed and dated cheque to the supplier requesting him to complete the amount in words and figures. The danger is that the signed cheque could be made out for a much larger amount than that intended, and one way around this is for the drawer to cross the cheque 'not to exceed £—'. While this crossing has no statutory significance, the paying banker will observe his customer's wishes when the cheque is presented for payment and will return it where the amount exceeds the limitation of the crossing. A signed cheque or bill of exchange made out in this way is known as an *inchoate (incomplete) instrument*.

11.9   The Clearing System

This is the means whereby banks exchange cheques drawn on each other. During the course of a day's business a bank has many cheques paid in by its customers that are drawn on other branches and banks and the total of those on other banks appears on the bank's balance sheet as an asset. Most of these have to pass through the Bankers' Clearing House where they are exchanged so that each bank receives the cheques drawn on its own branches. To settle differences in amounts, one bank will pay another by drawing a cheque on its account at the Bank of England. Prior to the establishment of the clearing house, clerks used to go round the banks, handing over cheques and receiving payments. To ease their task, the clearing house was started in 1773 in a London coffee house where the clerks would meet to exchange cheques and reach a settlement (and, of course, have a cup of coffee). From simple beginnings, the business of the clearing house has expanded enormously and now handles several million cheques each working day.

How a Cheque is Cleared
The process of clearing a cheque is perhaps most easily studied by monitoring the route followed by an imaginary example.

(i) On Monday morning Smith, a customer of Midland Bank, Worcester, pays into his account a cheque for £10, drawn on the account of Williams at Lloyds Bank, Gloucester. The remittance clerk at Midland, Worcester lists the cheque and includes it in the daily total of cheques drawn on Lloyds Bank. It is sent off to Midland's head office at the end of the day along with all the other cheques drawn on branches and banks other than Midland, Worcester.

(ii) On Tuesday morning the cheques from the Worcester branch are received at Midland's clearing department at head office along with cheques from all the other Midland branches. All the cheques drawn on Lloyds are placed together and a summary is made to arrive at the total amount. Cheques drawn on the other clearing banks are dealt with in the same way.

(iii) Clerks from Midland take the cheques and listings to the clearing house where they are handed over to representatives of each of the other clearing banks, who also have cheques to hand over.

(iv) The clerks of the various banks, now with bundles of their own cheques, return to their head offices. Thus the £10 cheque arrives at the clearing department of Lloyds Bank along with the others received in the exchange that day. All the cheques are sorted according to the different Lloyds branches on which they are drawn, and their details fed into the bank's computer so that the customers' accounts can be debited next day. The cheques themselves are then posted off to the various branches, the one for £10 being included in the bundle for Gloucester branch.

(v) On Wednesday morning, Gloucester branch receives the cheque clearing from head office. Cheques that are in order are automatically debited

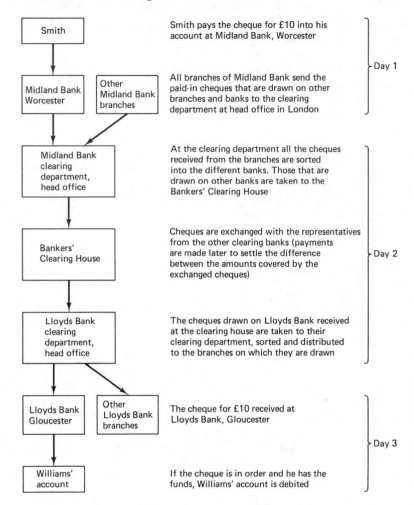

Fig. 11.4   Clearing a cheque

to the drawers' accounts, including the £10 on Williams' account, by the bank's computer.

The above, which is illustrated in Fig. 11.4, is a simplification of the clearing procedures: a high degree of automation has been introduced, involving cheque-sorting and listing equipment and the banks' computer systems. In the example, clearing has taken three days; this assumes that there have been no delays and normally represents the fastest time in which a cheque can be cleared. Not all cheques pass through the clearing house: in particular, those that are paid in at other branches of the bank on which they are drawn (such as a cheque drawn on Midland Bank, Gloucester being paid in for the credit of an account at Midland Bank, Worcester) only travel as far as the bank's head office, where they are sorted into branch order and dispatched to the branches on which they are drawn: this is known as the *inter-branch* clearing.

It should also be mentioned that sometimes a 'same branch' clearance may occur. This happens where the drawer and the payee of the cheque both bank at the same branch—this could be quite common in smaller towns. Once the payee has deposited the cheque, provided the cheque is technically correct (see Unit 11.10) and the drawer has sufficient funds or an overdraft arranged, he may draw cash or cheques against the deposit.

Inter-bank clearing operations are under the control of three operating companies each of which deals with different aspects of the clearing:

(i) paper bulk clearing, covering the general and credit clearings (Cheque and Credit Clearing Company Ltd);

(ii) the high-value same-day clearing, covering the Clearing House Automated Payments System (CHAPS) and the Town clearing (CHAPS & Town Clearing Company Ltd);

(iii) the electronic bulk clearing (Bankers' Automated Clearing Services— BACS) of direct debits, standing orders and so on (BACS Ltd).

Membership of each operating company is available, subject to certain restrictions, to those financial organizations that make use of a particular clearing system. For example, a number of building societies are members of Cheque and Credit Clearing Company Ltd and of BACS Ltd.

All three operating companies are under the overall control of the Association for Payment Clearing Services (APACS). A fourth company covers EFTPOS (electronic funds transfer at point of sale—see Unit 12.6) transactions (EFT–POS Administration Ltd).

General clearing. Most of the cheques handled by the clearing house pass through the general clearing by the procedures as outlined above.

Credit clearing. Since 1960 a clearing system similar to the general clearing has operated for credit transfers—or bank giro credits—for the credit of accounts at branches and banks other than the one at which they are paid in. Like cheques, credits may be inter-branch or inter-bank, and both kinds are sent to the clearing department at head office by each branch of the bank. There they are sorted, and inter-branch items are dispatched to the different branches; the inter-bank items are amalgamated and taken to the clearing house where, like cheques, they are handed over to the representatives of the other banks. In recent years credits have been standardized so that they can be read by computers and sorted electronically in a similar way to cheques.

Clearing House Automated Payments System (CHAPS). CHAPS was introduced in 1984 and is a sophisticated inter-bank settlement system, operated by computers. Each bank participating in the system is able to transmit payments to other banks for receipt on the same day. The payments cannot be revoked once they are accepted into the system and, therefore, the funds are guaranteed and can be drawn upon immediately by the beneficiary. The system is available for payments anywhere in Britain. While at present its use is limited to remittances of £10 000 and over, it is likely that this limit will be reduced as the system becomes more widely used.

The larger company customers of banks are also able to link themselves into the system through a computer terminal in their own offices and are able to initiate payments and to be advised of incoming transfers.

Town clearing. A fast clearing service operates for bank branches in the City of London that are within walking distance of the clearing house in Lombard Street; such branches can easily be identified because the cheques they issue have the letter 'T' after the national sorting code number, which is printed in the top right-hand corner of the cheque. The Town clearing operates for cheques of £10 000 and over that are drawn on and have been paid into one of the branches participating in the clearing: all other cheques pass through either the general clearing or the inter-branch clearing. The clearing is also used for bills of exchange accepted payable by or on a Town clearing branch, bankers' payments and bankers' drafts.

The Town clearing exists to serve the banks, insurance companies, shipping companies, the Stock Exchange and other financial institutions operating in the City of London. As these concerns continually deal in large amounts of money they need a speedy system for clearing cheques and this is what the Town clearing offers: a cheque can be paid in for the credit of an account just before the banks close for business in the afternoon, and it is possible to find out later that day if it is cleared.

It is likely that in the future CHAPS will take over many of the payments that would have previously passed through the Town clearing system.

BACS Ltd (Bankers' Automated Clearing Services). With the increasing use of computers in banking, a special clearing system has been developed to make possible the transfer of funds from one bank account to another by putting details of transfers to be made on to magnetic tapes that can be 'read' by a computer. To facilitate the use of this system and in an attempt to cut down the volume of paperwork required daily to effect transfers, the banks make use of BACS Ltd, which has its computer centre at Edgware in Middlesex. The system is used by the banks and some of their large customers who prepare magnetic tapes containing details of transactions to be made. The tapes are than handed or sent to BACS or the data can be transmitted direct to BACS over the telephone, using the BACSTEL service. At BAACS the information is read by a computer and the entries are electronically sorted into the various banks and branches for which they are intended. The entries are then transferred to other magnetic tapes, one for each bank, which are then passed to the appropriate bank. The tapes are then run into each bank's own computer system and the transfers involved are effected automatically, each branch receiving a print-out of the details of the transfers concerning its own accounts. This clearing system can be used for both bank giro credits and direct debits (see Units 12.3 and 12.4).

A number of building societies are members of BACS Ltd.

The daily settlement. This is the means by which the exchanges of cheques and credits between banks is balanced. It is effected at the end of each working day and settles the clearing of the previous day. Each clearing bank prepares a summary of the balances due to be received from other banks and due to be paid to other banks as a result of the various credit and debit items that have passed through the clearing house. The summary is totalled and a balance worked out which is the net amount due to be received (or paid) in respect of the transactions. This balance is settled either by making a payment out of, or receiving a credit into, that bank's account at the Bank of England. Each clearing bank follows the same procedure, so that the total settlement cheques received by the clearing house equal the total settlement payment that it makes.

Other clearings. We have already mentioned the *inter-branch clearing* which does not pass through the clearing house but is dealt with at the clearing department of each bank. A large number of banks are not members of the Bankers' Clearing House: some of these have an agency arrangement whereby one of the clearing banks allows their cheques to be cleared through them. Other cheques drawn on merchant banks, Government departments and the Post Office do not pass through the clearing house but, instead, are dealt with by the *walks clearing*. This operates by branches sending such cheques to their clearing department at head office where they are sorted into the different banks and payment offices. The cheques are then taken by messenger— 'walked'—to the banks and offices where they are payable and exchanged for a banker's payment or a cheque drawn on a clearing bank.

A *dollar clearing* exists for cheques drawn in dollars on a United Kingdom account and paid into another United Kingdom bank account. The American and other banks participating in this clearing do so through a clearing bank acting as their agent.

If a customer wishes to know quickly if a cheque has been cleared he or she can ask the bank to arrange a *special presentation*: the bank then sends the cheque direct to the drawee bank and telephones next day to find out if it is cleared. A fee is normally charged for this service, but it does enable a customer to discover the fate of a cheque within twenty-four hours, instead of waiting for it to pass through the clearing system.

A further system of special presentation can be used on a local basis within the same town. On request, a cheque paid in which is drawn on a bank in the same town or city centre can be 'walked' round to the bank. It is presented for payment and, if paid, is exchanged for a bankers' payment (similar to a bank draft, but a method of payment between banks). In this way a same-day clearance is possible for cheques paid in and drawn on nearby banks.

'Our branch is beautifully situated—two hundred miles from the head office computer'

Truncation

The 1980s and 1990s are certain to see considerable changes in the operations of the clearing system. Truncation, which is already used extensively inter-branch, will be extended on an inter-bank basis. Truncation is the process whereby the flow of paper is stopped as it enters the banking system and moved no further than the branch of deposit or encashment. Using document reader machines, information from both cheques and credits can be 'captured' and passed through computer systems to debit and credit the appropriate accounts almost immediately. Truncation is already widely used in a number of European countries and it has been found that the costs of cheque-processing have been halved.

11.10　Payment of Cheques

Every working day, each branch bank receives from its head office an in-clearing of cheques drawn on that branch which have been paid in for the credit of accounts at other banks and branches. Its task now is to ensure that each cheque is technically correct and that the branch has the authority to debit the customer's account. It must ensure that the customer has not countermanded or 'stopped' payment of the cheque, that the customer has sufficient funds in his account to meet the cheque or that sufficient overdraft facilities have been arranged, that the cheque is signed and the drawer's signature is genuine, agreeing with the specimen held by the branch, and that the cheque is signed in accordance with the bank's authority (for example, a joint account with husband and wife may require the bank to pay only cheques bearing both signatures). Even if all these are in order, the following technical errors might still cause non-payment:

(i) the value of the cheque given in words is different from that stated in figures;

(ii) the cheque is out of date (usually this means it is dated to suggest that it was written six months or more ago);

(iii) the cheque is *postdated*, that is, dated at some time in the future;

(iv) no payee's name is entered on the cheque;

(v) alterations made to the cheque have not been initialled or signed by the drawer of the cheque as being correct;

(vi) the cheque has been mutilated in some way, perhaps torn completely in half, and there is no banker's confirmation that the mutilation was accidental;

(vii) drawer's signature does not appear on the cheque;

(viii) the cheque is crossed by two bankers, without an indemnity being given by one of them to the paying banker.

Note: Cheques drawn under a cheque card agreement must be paid provided that the conditions of use of the cheque card have been complied with (see Unit 15.2).

Ideally, every cheque should be inspected by the paying bank before the drawer's account is debited. However, with the costs that this would incur and the huge volume of cheques presented each day, most banks physically inspect only those cheques above a certain amount—the base level varies from £50 or £100, up to £1 000. Some banks will check the drawer's signature at an intermediate level, and most will carry out a full verification on a sample basis. Nevertheless, whether cheques are inspected or not, the legal responsibility rests with the bank and, if a cheque is paid in error, the bank will be liable.

The death of a customer cancels a bank's authority to pay his cheques, as do certain other legal circumstances such as notice of his mental incapacity or bankruptcy. Cheques that are not to be paid are returned on the day of receipt by the drawee bank direct to the collecting bank—this is where the special crossing applied by rubber stamp to all cheques paid in helps to identify the bank and branch to which a cheque must be returned. A special form for unpaid cheques is used to adjust the book-keeping entries between the two banks. When an unpaid cheque is received back at the collecting bank, the payee's account will be debited (having been previously credited when the cheque was paid in) and the cheque posted back to him. It is then up to the payee to contact the drawer of the cheque and, if it has been returned because of technical errors, to ask him to correct them. If the cheque has been returned because the drawer has insufficient funds on his account, the payee will certainly have questions to ask.

It is particularly important that a collecting bank receiving back an unpaid cheque, forwarded for collection on behalf of the customer, must give the customer notice of dishonour. As we have said, this is usually done by returning the cheque to the customer with a covering letter. Sometimes the bank will re-present the cheque for payment—for instance, where the bank confirms an irregular endorsement—but must nevertheless send notice of dishonour to the customer. Failure to do so could mean that in the event of the cheque being dishonoured a second time, perhaps for a different reason, the customer could refuse to have his account debited on the grounds that he did not receive notice of dishonour the first time and assumed the cheque was paid. From the point of view of both the collecting bank and the paying bank, therefore, the procedure for non-payment is important in order to retain the liability of the customer for the cheque.

11.11   Bills of Exchange and Cheques: Further Aspects

As bills of exchange and cheques are so fundamental to the transfer of funds we need to consider more fully the rights and duties of the various parties to each instrument in more detail. Also, it is necessary to look further at the position of a bank, which may be collecting or paying such instruments. Further aspects of bills of exchange and cheques are dealt with in Unit 20.

11.12   Questions

1. Define a bill of exchange. How may a bill be used in settlement of a debt?

2. What are the characteristics of a negotiable instrument? Explain by reference to cheques the terms 'negotiable' and 'not negotiable'.

3. You have just opened a current account for Mrs Williams; she asks if she should use crossed or open cheques. Advise her.

4. *A*, the drawer of a crossed order cheque, sends it through the post to *B*, the payee, who also has a bank account. Trace the course of the cheque until it is finally paid.
    (*The Institute of Bankers*)

5. What is the significance of a crossing on an order cheque? Is this affected in any way if the words 'not negotiable' are included?
    (*The Institute of Bankers*)

6. (a) What is the practical effect of crossing a cheque?
    (b) Explain the types of crossing that appear on cheques.
    (c) What is the effect of adding the words 'account payee' to a crossed cheque?
    (*The Chartered Institute of Bankers*)

7. What advice would you give to a cashier in the following situation?
        An open cheque for £250, drawn by your customer J. Bloggs and payable to C. Farnsbarnes, has been presented for payment in cash. The cashier tells you that the cheque was endorsed C. Farnsbarnes in her presence, but she feels nervous about cashing it as the presenter is unknown to her.
    (*The Chartered Institute of Bankers*)

Multiple-choice Questions—5

Read each question carefully. Choose the *one* answer you think is correct. Answers are given on page 390.

1. A rise in interest rates will cause:

   A an increase in borrowing and a slowing-down of credit creation
   B a decrease in borrowing and an increase in credit creation
   C an increase in borrowing and an increase in credit creation
   D a decrease in borrowing and a decrease in credit creation

2. Which borrowing is sometimes linked to LIBOR (London Inter-bank Offered Rate)?

   A loans and overdrafts of companies   **C** personal loans
   B unauthorized overdrafts   **D** house purchase loans

3. The drawee of a cheque is:

   A the person who is to receive payment
   B the bank that has to make payment
   C the last person to endorse the cheque
   D the person whose bank account will be debited

4. Title in an order cheque passes by:

   A endorsement   **C** endorsement and delivery
   B delivery   **D** endorsement, delivery and payment

5. A special crossing consists of:

   A the words 'not negotiable'
   B two parallel lines
   C the name of a banker
   D the words 'not negotiable', written between two parallel lines

6. The crossing 'not negotiable' on a cheque payable to 'J. Smith or order':

   A means that the cheque is transferable
   B means that the cheque is not transferable
   C means that a collecting bank is put on enquiry, if the cheque is paid in for the credit of an account other than that of the named payee
   D has no significance to an innocent party who takes a stolen cheque in good faith and for value

7. A cheque crossed 'account payee':

   A can only be accepted for the account of the named payee
   B can be accepted for the credit of an account other than that of the named payee provided the collecting bank makes enquiries
   C prevents negotiation of the cheque and, therefore, has the same effect as a 'not negotiable' crossing
   D is an example of a special crossing

8. A cheque payable to H. Sanderson is endorsed by her 'pay S. Green only'. What type of endorsement is this?

   A blank   **C** restrictive
   B general   **D** special

9. A large company wishes to pay its employees' wages direct into their bank accounts: it also needs to make a guaranteed payment of £20 000 to another firm as quickly as possible. Respectively, which clearing methods are most likely to be used for these transactions?

   A general clearing; BACS (Bankers' Automated Clearing Services)
   B CHAPS (Clearing House Automated Payments System); general clearing
   C BACS; CHAPS
   D BACS; credit clearing

10. A cheque dated seven months ago is:

    A a post-dated cheque   **C** legal tender
    B an out-of-date cheque   **D** not negotiable

Unit Twelve
Methods of Payment through the Banking System

12.1   Introduction

There are various ways of making a payment through the banking system and those appropriate for inland payments within Britain differ from those used for overseas payments. In this Unit we shall consider the following:

Inland:
cheques;
bank giro credits and standing orders;
direct debits;
credit cards;
EFTPOS (electronic funds transfer at point of sale);
bankers' drafts;
telephone and computer transfers.

Overseas:
cheques and credit cards;
international money transfers;
bankers' drafts.

12.2   Inland Payments: Cheques

Cheques are well known to most people and represent a convenient method of making payments—although, of course, they are not legal tender and creditors may refuse to accept them (see Unit 2.12). Specimen cheques are shown in Fig. 12.1.

When writing out a cheque, care should always be exercised to ensure that all details are completed: the date, name of payee, amount in words and figures and the drawer's signature. Cheques should always be written in ink and no room should be left for fraudulent additions, any blank spaces being ruled through. Where an open cheque book is in use, cheques should be crossed, preferably 'not negotiable', whenever they are to be sent through the post. If any corrections or changes are made to the cheque by the drawer he should, besides signing the cheque in the normal way, also place his signature against the alterations. Naturally, sufficient funds should be available in the drawer's account to meet cheques when they are presented for payment and cheques drawn should be technically correct.

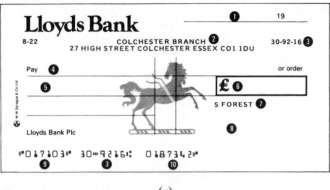

(a)

(1) Date
(2) Name of the account-holding branch
(3) The sorting code number of Lloyds Bank, Colchester
(4) Payee's name—the person to whom the cheque is payable
(5) The amount in words
(6) The amount in figures
(7) The name of the account
(8) Signature
(9) The cheque number
(10) The account number
The numbers along the bottom of the cheque are written in specially designed characters ('E13B') that can be read by cheque-sorting and listing machines.

(b)

Fig. 12.1   Specimen cheques: (a) blank, (b) completed

In order to increase the acceptability of cheques, the clearing banks issue *cheque cards* to suitable customers. This plastic 'card' acts as a guarantee that the drawer's cheque will be paid up to a maximum (at the time of writing) of £50 in any one transaction (see also Unit 15.2) and has been particularly useful in persuading retailers to accept cheques from strangers in payment for goods. A cheque card can also be used with a cheque book to draw cash at any branch of the major British banks, although a charge is usually made for this service when encashment is made at a different bank from the customer's own, for example if a customer of the Midland cashed a cheque at Barclays.

12.3   Inland Payments: Bank Giro Credits

Bank giro credits—or *credit transfers*, as they are often called—enable a person to pay money into someone else's bank account, whether he has an account of his own or not. For example, if Smith owes Jones £10 and Jones has an account with National Barllands Bank, Worcester, Smith can go into that bank and make out a credit for Jones's account and pay the £10 in cash; alternatively he can go into any other bank branch and pay the cash in, together with a credit made out in the favour of Jones's account at National Barllands, Worcester. In the second case the credit would be passed through the credit clearing system to arrive at Jones's bank two working days after being paid in, subject to any delays. Equally, Jones can use a bank giro credit when he wishes to pay money into his own account at National Barllands Bank, Worcester at another branch of National Barllands or at some other bank. Fig. 12.2 shows a specimen bank giro credit slip.

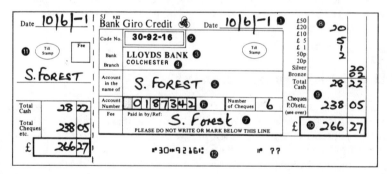

Fig. 12.2   A specimen bank giro credit slip

(1) Date
(2) Sorting code number of the account-holding branch
(3) Name of the account-holding bank
(4) Name of the account-holding branch
(5) The name of the account
(6) Account number of payee
(7) Signature of person paying money in
(8) Breakdown of cash paid in
(9) Amounts of cheques paid in
(10) Total of the credit to the account (cash and cheques)
(11) Counterfoil (record of what has been paid in)
(12) Magnetic ink symbols to enable automatic processing by computer

The bank giro credit system is particularly useful for paying accounts such as gas, electricity, telephone and rates, and often the bills for these services have a credit form pre-printed on them. Hire-purchase companies, home shopping clubs and building societies often issue their customers with books of bank giro credit forms. Employers can use the system for paying wages and salaries: a credit slip is made out for each employee with the details of the name and number of the account to be credited, the bank and branch where it is maintained and the money amount, and these slips, together with a summary slip detailing all the payments, are handed to the bank with one cheque payable to the bank for the total amount. This method of making wage and salary payments has the obvious advantage of not requiring large quantities of cash to be withdrawn on pay day, with the attendant security problems, but the system cannot operate unless each employee has a bank account and agrees to be paid in this way. Many companies, instead of making out a voucher for each payment, prepare computer tapes containing details of all the payments to be made and these are passed through BACS (see Unit 11.9).

The banks use the system themselves for making *standing order* or *bankers' order* payments. If a customer has regular payments to make for fixed amounts—for a mortgage, for instance, or for insurance premiums or club subscriptions—he can give the bank instructions to make payments on his behalf. The bank will automatically do this by debiting his account and putting the payment details on a computer tape and passing this through BACS.

12.4   Inland Payments: Direct Debits

Standing orders, just mentioned, are a convenient method of making regular payments for fixed amounts. Direct debits are also used for regular payments but they differ from standing orders in two ways. Firstly, they can be used for either fixed or variable amounts and/or where the time intervals between payments vary. Secondly, it is the beneficiary of the payment who prepares the voucher or computer tape that acts as a debit to the payer's account and is passed through the clearing system in the same way as a cheque; this contrasts with the standing order system where the payer's bank prepares a credit which is passed through the credit clearing system to the bank and branch of the beneficiary. Under the direct debit system there are safeguards to prevent irregular use of the system:

(i) only organizations approved by the banks are allowed to operate it;

(ii) direct debits must be made strictly within the terms of the instructions signed by the customer;

(iii) where the bank customer's instructions permit the payment of variable amounts (*variable amount direct debits*, often abbreviated to *VADD*), the organization concerned has to inform the customer in advance of the amount and date of the payment;

(iv) each organization operating the system has to give the banks an indemnity in case of mistakes: the banks will reimburse a customer if a debit which does not conform to the instructions held is charged to his account.

The system is particularly useful for insurance companies, building societies, hire-purchase companies and indeed for any organization which receives large numbers of payments. It operates rather like the bank giro credit system for wages and salaries in reverse: the beneficiary prepares the direct debit forms or computer tape and takes them to his bank together with a credit for the total amount. The debits are distributed through the clearing system to the banks and branches to which they are addressed and the payers' accounts are debited; in the meantime, the credit is applied to the account of the beneficiary. The great savings for the beneficiary are in administration: checking large numbers of standing order payments received into the account is much more laborious than initiating direct debits, and the payments are made without the delays involved in waiting to receive credits through the clearing system. Moreover, any direct debits which cannot be paid are returned quickly and the follow-up steps can be instituted promptly.

12.5   Inland Payments: Credit Cards

Credit cards (see also Unit 15.4) are issued by banks, building societies, retail groups and other organizations. They provide a means of obtaining goods and services immediately but paying for them later. Each cardholder is given a credit limit on his credit card account, which is entirely separate from his normal bank account and, for bank-issued cards, is maintained at his bank's credit card department. Payment for goods and services can only be made by this method at premises having the special machine for preparing sales vouchers to record the transaction, and retail outlets usually display the signs of the credit cards they are prepared to accept.

To pay for goods, the card is handed to the retailer, who places it in the special machine together with a sales voucher: when the machine is operated the embossed characters on the card, which detail the name and number of the account, are recorded on the sales voucher, together with the retailer's name and address. Transactions of a higher value than the retailer normally undertakes need a telephone authorization to the credit card company to enable the retailer to check that the card presented can be accepted. The details and amount of the sale are entered on the voucher and signed for by the purchaser; after comparing this signature with that on the card and being satisfied with its authenticity, the retailer gives a copy of the voucher to the purchaser and hands back the card. The retailer sends his part of the sales voucher to the credit card company through a local branch bank, and receives payment accordingly.

Credit cards can also be passed through EFTPOS (electronic funds transfer at point of sale) terminals installed in retail outlets—see Unit 12.6. The terminals authorize the credit card transaction with the credit cardholder entering his or her personal identification number (PIN) in confirmation. The credit card account is debited automatically and the funds transferred to the retailer's account immediately.

Each month a cardholder is sent a statement detailing his purchases and he has the option of either paying the full balance of the account or paying a certain minimum amount and carrying forward the remaining balance to next month. Cardholders are charged interest on outstanding balances and retailers are required to allow the credit card company a rate of discount on all card sales—this varies from one trade to another, and averages between 2 and 4 per cent. The card can also be used to draw cash at bank branches and correspondent banks displaying the relevant credit card sign.

The present extensive use of credit cards means that the Government may control their use at times when it wishes to restrict credit, as it does with hire-purchase facilities: it may impose minimum monthly repayment amounts and restrict the use of the card's cash withdrawal facilities.

12.6　Inland Payments: EFTPOS and Debit Cards

Electronic funds transfer at point of sale (EFTPOS) is a step towards the 'cashless society', where there would be no need to carry around large sums of money and only small change would be needed. It is a system which allows a retail outlet to debit the bank or credit card account of the purchaser at the point of sale and, at the same time, to credit the retailer's bank account.

Fig. 12.3　A debit card

Besides the need to carry less cash, the system reduces the need for paper vouchers such as cheques and credit card slips.

The system is operated by the customer in the retail outlet selecting a purchase and presenting his or her plastic card at the checkout. The card is then inserted into a special terminal and the total amount of the purchase is entered into the computer-linked checkout till. At the same time the customer keys in his or her personal identification number (PIN) on a keyboard. Both the number of the card which is read by the terminal and the number keyed in by the customer are transmitted via the computer link to a central computer where they are checked as belonging to one another. The purchase amount is checked against the funds in the customer's bank account or available credit in a credit card account. If everything is in order, the customer's account is debited and the retailer's account is credited with the appropriate amount.

The cards used in the EFTPOS system are either the banks' debit cards (of which 'Connect' and 'Switch' are examples)—see Fig. 12.3—credit cards or other acceptable cards such as building society or in-store cards. The latest generation of cards, known as *smart cards*, incorporates a microchip which stores information about the cardholder and his or her account.

12.7   Inland Payments: Bankers' Drafts

A bankers' draft is a payment instruction, similar to a cheque, drawn by a branch bank on its head office: it is issued on request to a customer who has to make a guaranteed payment, that is, in circumstances where the payee wishes to be absolutely certain that the cheque will be paid upon presentation. After cash, the next best thing is a bankers' draft, which avoids the necessity of having to carry sums of money to effect a payment. An example of the use of a bankers' draft is in buying a house, when the seller's solicitors want to be certain of payment—they cannot afford the risk of a 'bouncing' cheque—and they will usually only hand over the deeds of the property against receipt of a draft.

Naturally, before issuing a draft the bank checks to see that the customer has sufficient funds in his account to pay for it, his account is then debited and a credit passed to head office to meet the draft when it is presented for payment.

12.8   Inland Payments: Telephone and Computer Transfers

Urgent transfers of funds can be made within the banking system either by telephone or by computer, which is more likely nowadays. Both of these allow for the same-day transfer of cleared funds and are especially useful to solicitors effecting settlements for the transfer of property, and to any company which needs to move funds between businesses. Telephone transfers need verification by means of a codeword or number and are usually passed via the head office(s) of the bank(s) concerned. If it is a computer transfer the

Clearing House Automated Payments System (CHAPS) is used—see Unit 11.9. Whichever method is adopted, funds are cleared and the recipient can draw upon them immediately.

12.9   Overseas Payments: Cheques and Credit Cards

It is not a satisfactory payment method to use a normal cheque when buying goods abroad or to settle with an overseas supplier for goods imported. One of the problems concerns the exchange control regulations imposed by a number of countries, since a cheque used in this way must be officially stamped to confirm that exchange control approval for the payment has been granted. Also, the cheque would normally have to be drawn in the home currency and this might not suit the overseas supplier who would have to ask the bank to collect the proceeds on his behalf—this would cost money in bank charges and he would have to wait some time before receiving the proceeds.

Both cheque and credit cards can be used abroad to obtain cash from banks. Eurocheques, backed by a eurocheque card (see Unit 15.2), can be used to obtain goods and services while visiting any European country, and can also be used at selected banks outside Europe, the cheques being written out in the currency of the country being visited. Credit cards can also be used as a means of payment at overseas outlets of the card company and its associated companies.

12.10   Overseas Payments: International Money Transfers

A customer may instruct his bank to make an international money transfer (IMT) to a person abroad. The customer has his account debited in sterling and the beneficiary receives the sterling equivalent in his own currency, either paid in cash or credited to his bank account. All charges are normally debited to the sender's account but can, if required, be deducted from the amount received by the beneficiary. An IMT is carried out either by using a *mail transfer* or by using the SWIFT network (see below). Where a payment has to be made more quickly, an express international money transfer (EIMT) is made either by means of a *telegraphic* or *cable transfer*, or through SWIFT.

SWIFT (the Society for Worldwide Interbank Financial Telecommunication) is an international communications network formed by some 2 600 banks from about 60 countries to speed up the transfer of international money transfers and other messages between themselves. It does this by making use of the computer systems of participating banks. Thus when a customer wishes to make an international payment by mail transfer his bank, if a participant in SWIFT, sends a 'SWIFT message'; transfers and messages previously sent by telegraph or cable will become 'urgent SWIFT messages'. As a safeguard, wherever funds are sent by urgent SWIFT message or telegraphic transfer, some form of coding is included which is checked by the recipient bank to prove the authenticity of the instruction.

The actual transfer of funds is effected by the bank in Britain contacting a convenient bank in the overseas country. All the major banks have their *correspondent banks* overseas with whom they maintain currency accounts, and similarly the correspondent banks maintain sterling accounts in this country. These accounts are known as *nostro* and *vostro accounts*—the Latin words for 'our' and 'your' respectively.

Nostro accounts (our account with you). From the point of view of a United Kingdom bank, its nostro accounts are those currency accounts which are maintained in its name in the books of banks overseas. For example, if Midland Bank has an account maintained in United States dollars with the Bank of America, San Francisco, then this is a nostro account for Midland Bank.

Vostro accounts (your account with us). Again, from the point of view of a United Kingdom bank, its vostro accounts are those sterling accounts in the names of overseas banks that are maintained with it. For example, if Bank of America maintains a sterling account with Midland Bank, London, then this is a vostro account for Midland Bank.

Notice that nostro and vostro accounts can be looked at *the other way round*. Consider the accounts mentioned above from the point of view of Bank of America: its nostro account is its sterling balance maintained with Midland Bank, London; while its vostro account is the dollar account maintained with it in the name of Midland Bank.

The method of transferring funds is simple but we must be careful to distinguish between payments made in the home currency and those made in a foreign currency. We will consider an example of each:

(a) Payment in the Home Currency
A customer of a United Kingdom bank wishes to remit sterling to an overseas beneficiary in, for example, Toronto, Canada. The procedure is as follows:

(i) the customer completes a bank application form stating the beneficiary and the method of remittance to be used—telegraphic or mail transfer, or bank draft;

(ii) the bank selects an appropriate Toronto correspondent bank and then debits its United Kingdom customer with the amount and credits the (sterling) vostro account of the correspondent bank;

(iii) the remittance is then made and the beneficiary receives, or his bank account is credited with, the Canadian dollar equivalent of the sterling amount; and

(iv) to complete the book-keeping, the Toronto bank debits, with the sterling amount, a record account it maintains in its books which 'mirrors' its sterling account in London.

(If the beneficiary in Canada had operated a foreign currency account designated in sterling, then clearly this could have been credited with the sterling amount, rather than converting it into Canadian dollars. In other respects the transactions would have been the same.)

(b) Payment in a Foreign Currency

If a customer of a United Kingdom bank wishes to pay an amount of currency other than sterling, for example United States dollars, to a beneficiary in, say, New York the procedure is as follows:

(i) the customer completes the bank application form, as in (a)(i) above;

(ii) the bank debits its customer with the sterling equivalent of the dollars or, if the customer operates a foreign currency account designated in dollars, debits that account;

(iii) the United Kingdom bank credits the dollar amount to the account in its books which mirrors the dollar account maintained with its New York correspondent;

(iv) the remittance is then made and the New York bank debits the United Kingdom bank's nostro account and credits the beneficiary with the dollar amount.

It is important that you understand the operation of nostro and vostro accounts, because they are used for most international money transfers. The concept of the *mirror account* can appear difficult to follow: it always has an exact opposite balance to that of the appropriate nostro account, that is, if the nostro account of a United Kingdom bank held in America has a *credit* balance of US $10 000, then the mirror—or record—account maintained in the United Kingdom will have an equal but opposite *debit* balance of US $10 000. A mirror account also has a column which records transactions on the nostro account in terms of the home currency.

It is easier to understand the operation of nostro, vostro and mirror accounts by studying a few transactions passed through the accounts of the home bank and the overseas correspondent bank.

(c) Examples of Nostro, Vostro and Mirror Accounts in Operation

(i) Midland Bank, London, maintains an account designated in sterling on behalf of the Bank of America, San Francisco. The balance of this account is currently £20 000 and the rate of exchange is £1 = US $1.40. (To Midland Bank this is a vostro account.)

(a) A customer of Midland Bank wishes to pay £1 000 to a supplier in San Francisco by mail transfer. The action taken by each bank is:

Midland Bank
1. Debit customer with £1 000.
2. Credit vostro account of Bank of America with £1 000.

Bank of America
1. Debit mirror account with £1 000.
2. Credit customer with US $1 400.

(*b*) A customer of Bank of America wishes to pay £250 to a supplier in London by mail transfer. The action taken by each bank is:

Bank of America
1. Debit customer with US $350.
2. Credit mirror account with £250.

Midland Bank
1. Debit vostro account of Bank of America with £250.
2. Credit customer with £250.

The ledger entries appear as follows:

MIDLAND BANK

Dr.	**Account of Bank of America**		*Cr.*
	£		£
Customer (*b*)	250	Balance b/d	20 000
Balance c/d	20 750	Customer (*a*)	1 000
	———		———
	21 000		21 000
	═══		═══
		Balance b/d	20 750

Customer (*a*)

	£		£
Bank of America	1 000		

Customer (*b*)

	£		£
		Bank of America	250

BANK OF AMERICA

Dr.	**Mirror of account with Midland Bank**				*Cr.*
	$	£		$	£
Balance b/d	28 000	20 000	Customer (*b*)	350	250
Customer (*a*)	1 400	1 000	Balance c/d	29 050	20 750
	———	———		———	———
	29 400	21 000		29 400	21 000
	═══	═══		═══	═══
Balance b/d	29 050	20 750			

The balance brought down on the mirror account is US $29 050 which, at a rate of US $1.40, equals £20 750.

(ii) Midland Bank, London, maintains a United States dollar account with Bank of America, San Francisco (to Midland Bank this is a nostro account). The balance of this account is currently US $14 000 and the rate of exchange is £1 = US $1.40.

(*a*) A customer of Midland Bank wishes to pay US $1 400 to a supplier in San Francisco by mail transfer. The action taken by each bank is:

Midland Bank
1. Debit customer with £1 000;
2. Credit mirror account with US $1 400;

Bank of America
1. Debit nostro account of Midland Bank with US $1 400;
2. Credit customer with US $1 400.

(*b*) A customer of Bank of America wishes to pay US $700 to a supplier in London by mail transfer. The action taken by each bank is:

Bank of America
1. Debit customer with US $700;
2. Credit nostro account of Midland Bank with US $700.

Midland Bank
1. Debit mirror account with US $700;
2. Credit customer with £500.

The ledger entries appear as follows (excluding entries on customers' accounts):

BANK OF AMERICA

Dr.	Account of Midland Bank		Cr.
	$		$
Customer (*a*)	1 400	Balance b/d	14 000
Balance c/d	13 300	Customer (*b*)	700
	14 700		14 700
		Balance b/d	13 300

MIDLAND BANK

Dr.	Mirror of account with Bank of America			Cr.	
	£	$		£	$
Balance b/d	10 000	14 000	Customer (*a*)	1 000	1 400
Customer (*b*)	500	700	Balance c/d	9 500	13 300
	10 500	14 700		10 500	14 700
Balance b/d	9 500	13 300			

Note: A bank will not allow a balance to build up in its overseas currency (nostro) account. Its dealers will buy currency from the market and sell currency to the market (at market selling and buying rates respectively) in order to keep the balance as low as possible.

12.11   Overseas Payments: Bankers' Drafts

A banker's draft used to pay an overseas debt is similar to the draft used as an inland payment method, but instead of being drawn by a branch bank on head office, it is drawn by the overseas department of a British bank on one of its correspondent bank accounts. An overseas draft is usually available in a wide range of foreign currencies. A customer requesting a draft has his account debited in sterling and, within a few minutes, is handed the draft to send direct to the beneficiary. The transfer of funds from bank to bank is effected in the same way as described in Unit 12.10.

12.12   Questions

1. List the various methods of making payments within the United Kingdom through the banking system. Describe the main features of two of the methods listed which are most likely to be used for the payment of insurance premiums.

    (The Institute of Bankers)

2. Compare and contrast direct debits and standing orders as methods of payment.

3. You live in Britain and are planning to go on holiday to France and rent a cottage. The owner of the cottage, who lives in France, requires a deposit of 250 French francs. What method of payment, using the banking system, would be the most suitable? Why would the other methods be inappropriate?

4. A 'high tech' firm employing 500 staff wishes to pay its staff monthly into a bank account rather than by cash as at present. What methods of payment are open to it and what advantages are there both for firm and employee in using such methods?

    (The Chartered Institute of Bankers)

Multiple-choice Questions—6

Read each question carefully. Choose the *one* answer you think is correct. Answers are given on page 390.

1. Direct debits are:

   A originated by the payer's bank and sent through the clearing system to the beneficiary's bank
   B originated by the beneficiary's bank and sent through the clearing system to the payer's bank
   C used for fixed amounts only and for regular payment dates
   D originated by the beneficiary, passed to his/her bank and sent through the clearing system to the payer's bank

2. A customer makes regular payments (i) to his building society share account, and (ii) for the premium on a life policy. Which methods of payments will, most probably, be used?

   A both by standing order   C both by direct debit
   B (i) standing order;   D (i) direct debit;
       (ii) direct debit   (ii) standing order

3. A company wishing to pay the salaries of its employees direct into their bank accounts will use:

   A direct debits   C bank giro credits
   B standing orders   D cheques

4. A credit card such as Access (but not Barclaycard) will:

   A guarantee cheques
   B enable the holder to buy goods on credit
   C enable the holder to cash cheques at any bank
   D enable the holder to buy goods, up to certain amounts, on credit from certain persons

5. You are selling your car for £1 500 to a person you do not know. Which method of settlement would you prefer?

   A bank draft   C credit card
   B personal cheque   D personal cheque, backed by
                                          a cheque card

6. A bank customer wishes to send some money abroad urgently. Which method would be used?

   A international money transfer
   B bank draft, sent by air mail
   C express international money transfer
   D personal cheque, sent by air mail

7. International payments and other messages are often sent through an international computer network called:

   A CHAPS   C BACS
   B SWIFT   D EIMT

8. National Barllands Bank, London, has a United States dollar account with the Bank of America; at the same time it maintains a sterling account for a Swiss bank, Credit Suisse. Respectively, to National Barllands, these accounts are:

A   vostro; nostro   C   nostro; mirror
B   mirror; vostro   D   nostro; vostro

9. Your bank has to remit sterling to a beneficiary in Germany on behalf of one of your customers. Which book-keeping transactions are correct?

A   debit customer;   credit vostro   (United Kingdom bank)
    debit mirror;   credit beneficiary   (German bank)
B   debit customer;   credit mirror   (United Kingdom bank)
    debit nostro;   credit beneficiary   (German bank)
C   debit customer;   credit nostro   (United Kingdom bank)
    debit mirror;   credit beneficiary   (German bank)
D   debit customer;   credit vostro   (United Kingdom bank)
    debit nostro;   credit beneficiary   (German bank)

10. If the above transaction had been for the remittance of an amount of Deutschmarks, which would have been correct, from the United Kingdom bank's viewpoint?

A   B   C   D

Unit Thirteen
Who are the Customers?

13.1 Legal Relationships

A customer of a bank is someone who either:

  (i) has a current or deposit account, or some similar relationship; or
  (ii) has entered into a contract to open an account.

In the bank/customer relationship, duration is not a consideration.

In this Unit we shall consider the larger groups of different customers and, where these operate within a specialist legal framework, briefly consider this from the bank's point of view.

Legally speaking, the banker/customer relationships that can exist are:

debtor and creditor (or vice versa);
principal and agent;
bailor and bailee;
mortgagor and mortgagee;
relationships defined by the rules of banking practice.

The basic legal relationship is that of *debtor* (bank) and *creditor* (customer) respectively, although the roles are, of course, reversed when the customer is overdrawn. In the case of *Joachimson* v. *Swiss Bank Corporation* (1921), it was laid down that the bank undertakes to receive money for its customer's account, and that money so received is not held in trust for the customer but borrowed from him with a promise to repay it or any part of it during banking hours at the branch of the bank at which the account is kept, against the customer's written order addressed to the bank at that branch. Thus the general rules of the law of contract apply, in that both bank and customer are required to carry out certain courses of action and a failure to do so may result in a breach of contract and could result in a legal action by one party against the other.

The relationship between the two parties is that of *principal and agent* when a bank is acting as its customer's agent by collecting cheques for him.

The *bailor/bailee* relationship is established when a bank (the bailee) takes charge of the valuables of a customer (the bailor) for safe custody; the bank is then bound to take reasonable care of its customer's property (see Unit 15.10).

The *mortgagor/mortgagee* relationship applies when a bank (the mortgagee) takes a mortgage over securities when granting an advance to a customer (the mortgagor)—see Unit 21.4.

The *rules of banking practice* that have developed over the years are generally enforced by courts of law; for instance, a bank that failed to follow the practice of taking references or other suitable procedures when opening a current account would be held to be negligent.

13.2   Personal Customers

These form by far the largest group of customers in terms of numbers. Most receive wages or a salary at the end of each week or month which is often paid direct into the bank account by the employer; others are retired, receiving a State pension and perhaps a pension from a former employer; another group are students who may be in receipt of a grant cheque each term. The formalities required for an individual to open an account in his own name are minimal and while each bank has its own regulations, all require the same basic information: the person's name, address and occupation and a specimen signature. If it is a current account that is being opened (see Unit 14.2), the names and addresses of two *referees* are often required, although a reference from the current employer is usually satisfactory. A reference may also be required when a deposit account (see Unit 14.3) is opened with a cheque. Some banks have dispensed with the need to supply references and use the technique of *credit scoring* to decide whether or not to open an account for the potential customer.

Credit Scoring

Credit scoring is defined as 'the measurement of the statistical probability that credit will be repaid'. The technique involves awarding points to answers given to questions listed on an application form. Questions cover such areas as:

  (i) marital status and dependants;
 (ii) age;
(iii) number of years at present address;
 (iv) nature of property occupied—whether it is owned or rented;
  (v) occupation;
 (vi) length of time with employer;
(vii) previous credit experience.

Each question will carry a maximum possible score which will be higher for important questions such as occupation and lower for questions such as age and marital status. The score awarded to each answer will vary: for example, if the question asks for the number of years at present address, ten points might be awarded for each year, up to a maximum of, say, 100. In the same way certain occupations will be awarded higher marks than others. When a final score is known the controller relates the total to the guidelines. For instance if the system is being used to check whether or not a person should have a bank account and the score is above a certain number this means that the account can be opened and a cheque book issued; if the score is below this number but above another, lower, number this means that the account may be opened, but no cheque book is to be issued.

The technique of credit scoring can be used for all routine applications where some exercise of judgement would formerly have been needed. It is commonly in use for opening current accounts, issuing cheque cards and credit cards, and for personal loan applications.

It is quite usual for a bank to carry out other checks before opening an account. For example, a search may be made against the potential customer's name through a *credit reference agency*. This will reveal (*a*) whether the address given is correct, (*b*) whether or not the potential customer is on the Register of Voters, and (*c*) if any County Court judgements have been made against the would-be customer.

Importance of Procedures when Opening an Account

The question of taking references, or of using credit scoring and search techniques, is a very important one. Firstly the bank wishes to confirm that the new customer is reputable; secondly, the bank must follow the correct procedures for opening an account in order to avoid liability for conversion, on the grounds of negligence, if any stolen cheques should be paid in by the new customer. Under such circumstances the defence a bank could employ is that its staff acted in good faith and without negligence in accordance with section 4 of the Cheques Act 1957. In a past case, negligence has been attributed to a collecting bank where it has failed to attend to all the necessary formalities in opening an account for a customer who, later, converted cheques and used the bank to collect the proceeds. Negligence has been held to include, among other things, failure to obtain references or to follow up references when opening an account, and failure to obtain the name of a customer's employer— see also Unit 20.6. Thus the procedures for opening accounts should be strictly adhered to: legal cases on this subject include *Lloyds Bank Ltd* v. *E. B. Savory & Co* (1933) and *Marfani & Co Ltd* v. *Midland Bank Ltd* (1968).

Nowadays a husband and wife often open a *joint account*. The details required are the same as for an account in a sole name but the bank also needs to know who is going to sign cheques and other withdrawals from the account. The customers are asked to complete a *joint account mandate* which usually gives the bank the authority to pay on the signature of either account holder. If required, the mandate can be worded so that the signatures of both account holders are required. The mandate also establishes *joint and several liability* for any monies owing to the bank: this means that the parties are jointly liable for indebtedness and are also liable for the full amount as individuals. For example, suppose that Mr and Mrs Brown have a joint account with an overdraft of £1 000. Should the bank need to take legal action to recover this amount, it can proceed against both of them jointly *and* as individuals. Thus Mrs Brown cannot, by paying £500, discharge her liability because it is joint and several, and if her husband fails to pay anything her liability is £1 000.

Under the terms of the Consumer Credit Act 1974, each party to a joint account is entitled to an identical copy of the bank statement of their account. The requirement may be dispensed with if the customer signs a 'dispensing notice'.

Opening a bank account for a *minor* (a person under eighteen years of age) poses no problems as long as the account remains in credit. The important point to note is that a minor has a limited contractual capacity and can only be held liable for contracts for 'necessaries' such as food, clothing and accommodation. However, under the Minors' Contracts Act 1987, a young person can, after attaining the age of majority, ratify contracts entered into which would otherwise have been unenforceable against him or her.

From a bank's point of view, lending to a minor should be undertaken with care; such lending will be valid only if for necessaries. If lending does take place, the bank will usually take a *guarantee* from an adult as security. Under the Minors' Contracts Act 1987 such a guarantee will be enforceable even if the young person is not liable in law for the debt.

The issuing of a cheque card to minors can create similar problems over the enforceability of any debt incurred as a result of misuse of the card. The bank could then either recover the card and close the account, or it could seek a guarantee from an adult. However, in practice, cheque cards are usually issued at the discretion of the branch manager to sons and daughters of satisfactory existing account-holders.

The Banking Ombudsman
Since 1986 personal customers have been able to take complaints about their bank to a *banking ombudsman*. The decision to appoint an ombudsman came out of a recommendation by the National Consumer Council in a special report on banking services in 1983. The National Consumer Council found that although customers were generally satisfied with the service provided by their

'I want to make this withdrawal from my husband's half of our joint account'

banks many saw the need for an independent body to resolve disputes. The role of the ombudsman is totally independent, although the banks pay for the scheme—the costs being shared by the banks in relation to the size of their personal business. All recognized banks can join the scheme and all major retail banks are participating in it.

The ombudsman deals only with complaints from personal customers: business customers must seek redress through the courts if they have an unresolved complaint against a bank. This option is also open to those personal customers who, having consulted the ombudsman, disagree with the decision. To reduce the number of complaints referred to the ombudsman, the banks require that their own internal procedures are exhausted before the matter is taken further.

The ombudsman can deal with complaints on any of the banks' personal services to customers ranging from problems with cheque and credit cards to the banks' position as executor or trustee. The ombudsman is empowered to make awards of up to £100 000 to aggrieved customers.

13.3   Business Customers: Sole Traders

Sole traders are people who are in business on their own: they run shops, small factories, farms, garages and so forth. The businesses are generally small because the owner, being in business by himself, usually has limited funds—or capital—with which to start and profits are often small and, after the owner has taken his share as drawings, are ploughed back into the business.

Why do people set up in business on their own? There are several reasons:

(i) The owner has independence—he can run the business as he thinks fit without consulting anyone else.

(ii) In a small business with few, if any, employees, personal service and supervision by the owner are available at all times—the customers are not dealing with a large, impersonal organization and receive good service; employees can be personally supervised and there is generally little wastage of resources in the business.

(iii) The business is easy to establish legally. It may either operate under the owner's name, or use a trading name, such as 'Southtown Grocers'. A bank would record the account of a sole trader using a trading name such as 'J. Smith, trading as Southtown Grocers' in its records.

The disadvantages of a sole-trader business are:

(i) The owner has unlimited liability for the debts of the business. This means that if the firm should become insolvent, the owner's personal assets may be used to pay its creditors.

(ii) Expansion is limited because it can only be achieved by the owner ploughing back profits to increase his stake in the business or by borrowing, usually from a bank.

(iii) The owner usually has to work long hours and it may be difficult for him to find time to take holidays. If he should fall sick the work of the business will at best slow down, and at worst stop altogether.

Opening a bank account for a sole-trader business follows the same procedures as for a private individual. If the business is using a trading name, the bank will wish to see some evidence of the trading name, such as headed notepaper or business cards, before accepting for the account any cheques payable to that name.

The bank is often the only source of finance used by sole-trader businesses, and a lot of the branch manager's time is spent in attending to the needs of this category of customer. Some businesses, such as farmers or toy manufacturers, need finance or extra finance at certain times of the year because their trade has a seasonal nature; others, like grocers and garage proprietors, have a steady all-the-year-round trade and may require finance throughout the year. While there is no legal requirement for a sole trader to produce a set of accounts at the end of his financial year, it is usual for these to be prepared in order that the profit (or loss) shown by the accounts may be used by the Inland Revenue to assess liability to tax. If the bank is lending, the manager will wish to see these year-end accounts and balance sheet so that he can tell how profitable the business has been and can assess any risk to the bank advance.

13.4 Business Customers: Partnerships

A partnership is defined by the Partnership Act 1890 as *the relation which subsists between persons carrying on a business in common with a view of profit.*

The partnership is in many respects very similar to the sole trader as a business unit, but is often larger because, as there is more than one owner, there is likely to be more capital. A partnership may be formed to set up a new business or it may be the logical growth of a sole trader firm taking in partners to increase the capital. Besides the types of business mentioned in Unit 13.3 for sole traders, partnerships are often formed by professional people such as doctors, dentists, accountants and solicitors.

Why form a partnership?

(i) There is the possibility of increased capital because there are more owners to subscribe capital and also (it is to be hoped) larger profits to plough back into the business.

(ii) Individual partners may be able to specialize in areas of work that interest them.

(iii) With more people running the business, there is cover for sickness and holidays.

There may, however, be problems:

(i) As there is more than one owner, decisions may take longer because each partner may need to be consulted.

(ii) There may be disagreements among the partners.

(iii) The death of one partner may adversely affect the business because his capital may need to be withdrawn to pay the beneficiaries of his estate.

As with the sole trader, the names of the individual partners, or a trading name, may be used. Also, like the sole trader, each partner is fully liable for the debts of the firm. Legally, a partnership may be created orally, by conduct or in writing; however, it is sensible for partners to draw up a written deed of partnership which sets out their rights and duties. If there is no deed of partnership, the Partnership Act applies; among other things, this Act states that profits and losses are to be shared equally among the partners, even where one partner has contributed a greater proportion of capital. The Act also restricts the number of partners: the minimum is two and the normal maximum is twenty, although this may be exceeded by partnerships of certain professional people.

From the banking point of view, the usual formalities for opening an account are followed. Instructions are needed as to who is to sign cheques and standing order and direct debit authorities on the account and a mandate is taken to determine this, which is signed by all partners and which establishes the joint and several liability of each partner for any monies lent to the partnership. If a trading name is being used by the partnership, evidence, such as headed notepaper, needs to be seen before cheques can be accepted in that name. A problem could arise when the partnership wishes to arrange a loan or overdraft, in that any one partner is presumed in law to have authority to enter into contracts on behalf of the partnership in the ordinary course of its business—any one partner in a firm of builders, for instance, could arrange to obtain building supplies on credit and the business would be liable to pay. A bank advance, however, is likely to be outside the ordinary course of business and therefore would need the authorization of all partners. As a partnership may have up to twenty (or sometimes more) partners, it might prove impracticable to get them all to come to the bank; therefore the banks usually insert a clause in the mandate which says that an act carried out by any partner in connection with the bank account is deemed to be for carrying out the ordinary course of business. This means that one partner can arrange an advance for which all partners will be jointly and severally liable.

When one partner retires from a partnership which is to continue in business, he or she remains liable for partnership debts incurred before retirement. A partner can also be liable for debts incurred *after* retirement if he or she does not carry out the correct procedures of firstly advising customers in writing, and secondly advertising his retirement in the *Gazette* (which is an official publication for this and other notices). From a banking point of view, a change in partners will require the completion of new mandates and, where appropriate, new security forms. If the partnership bank account is in credit, the account may be continued, although it would be necessary to seek confirmation from the remaining partners for any cheques signed by the retiring partner and presented for payment after retirement. If the partnership bank account is in debit and the bank wishes to retain the liability of the retiring partner, it must be *stopped* and a new account opened in the name of the continuing partnership. By doing this, the retiring partner's liability for the debt is established: the same procedure should be followed on the death, mental incapacity or bankruptcy of a partner. The reason for stopping an overdrawn account is to prevent the operation of the *Rule in Clayton's Case* (1816).

The Rule in Clayton's Case states that payments made into a bank account extinguish the debit items in the order in which they occur. For example:

Partnership bank account

	Debits	Credits	Balance
1 Jan. Balance			£2 000 overdraft
10 Jan. Cheques paid in		£3 000	£1 000 credit
12 Jan. Cheques drawn	£3 000		£2 000 overdraft

If one partner announced his intention to retire on 1 January and the bank account was *not* stopped, his liability to the bank at that date would be extinguished by the credit on 10 January. The overdraft created on 12 January would, in such circumstances, be the liability of the remaining partners. Thus it is important that, on the retirement, death, mental incapacity or bankruptcy of a partner, an overdrawn bank account should be stopped if the bank wishes to establish the liability of the partner in question. All future transactions of the remaining partners are then passed through a new account; only in this way can the outgoing partner's liability be established.

13.5   Business Customers: Limited Companies

The logical step for a partnership growing in size is the formation of a *limited company*. There are two types of limited company: private (of which there are some 900 000 in Britain) and public (of which there are about 5 500). The important advantage that both types of companies have over sole traders and partnerships is that of *limited liability*. This means that the owners of a limited company—the shareholders—are liable only for the amount of their share capital: this is their 'limit' and their personal assets cannot be taken to pay the debts of the company. The limited company has a separate legal entity and anyone taking legal action would normally take it against the company and not the individual shareholders; this contrasts with sole traders and partnerships where legal action would be taken against the individual or partners forming the business. All limited companies are controlled specifically by the Companies Act 1985 (which consolidates a number of previous Companies Acts). Under the terms of this Act all companies are required to file their annual accounts and directors' report with the Registrar of Companies, where they are available for public inspection.

A public company is a company limited by shares:

(i) the memorandum (see below) of which states that it is to be a public company;

(ii) which has been registered as such;

(iii) the name of which ends with the words 'public limited company' (or its Welsh equivalent) or with the letters 'plc';

(iv) which has not less than two members;

(v) which has a minimum issued share capital of £50 000.

All other companies not meeting the above requirements are private companies. Public companies alone may raise money for capital from the public and, as a consequence, are usually considerably larger than most private companies.

Private companies are often formed by partnerships seeking limited liability or by a group of friends pooling their savings to provide a service or manufacture a product for which they think there is a demand. The private limited companies' scope for capital raising, although restricted by their inability to advertise shares for sale, is considerably greater than that of sole traders and partnerships because there may be more shareholders, and there is the advantage of limited liability. The shareholders in a limited company have no right to a say in the day-to-day affairs of the business but instead elect a board of directors for this purpose; where a partnership has been converted into a private limited company, it is likely that all the general partners of the former partnership (those who took an active part in running it) will form the board of directors and will, therefore, continue to have a say in the affairs of the company.

A public limited company is normally the largest form of business unit in the private sector; its shares are often quoted on a stock exchange. Most present-day public companies were once private, having at some stage 'gone public' with the aid of a merchant bank. The big advantage of forming a public company is that advertisements may be placed in financial newspapers inviting the public to apply for shares: a *prospectus*, as this advertisement is called, gives details of the company's past trading record and estimates of future earnings, together with other information required by law. Prospectuses can be seen from time to time in newspapers; sometimes a clearing bank is involved in the issue and copies of the prospectus are then sent to branches to be made available to interested customers. Not all public companies are quoted on the Stock Exchange: if a company wishes its shares to be quoted, it must apply to the Stock Exchange Council and then undergo a thorough investigation to ensure that it fulfils the strict requirements of the Council. If the company is found to be satisfactory, the Council will agree to grant a quotation of its shares.

(a) Forming a Limited Company

As a limited company has a separate legal personality, there are a number of steps that must be taken in its formation. The bank where the company wishes to open an account will want to see copies of the two controlling documents: the Memorandum of Association and the Articles of Association.

The *Memorandum of Association* is a document signed by the first members of the company setting out its constitution and powers. It governs the relationship of the company with the outside world and contains six main clauses:

(i) the name of the company ending with the words 'public limited company' (or its Welsh equivalent) in the case of public companies limited by shares, or with the word 'limited' (or its Welsh equivalent) in the case of private companies limited by shares. (The memorandum of a public company will state that it is to be a public limited company.)

(ii) a statement as to whether the registered office of the company is to be in England, Wales or Scotland;

(iii) a description of the objects of the company, that is, the purposes which the company is to pursue;

(iv) a statement as to whether or not the liability of the members is limited (there are a few unlimited companies in existence; see Unit 13.5(*c*));

(v) details of the capital structure of the company;

(vi) the *association clause*, which is an undertaking signed by the founder members of the company that they wish to form a company and agree to purchase the number of shares stated against their name.

The *Articles of Association* are regulations for the internal management of the company. They define the method of appointment and duties of the

'I changed my name by deed poll to "Bank"'

directors and secretary, the directors' borrowing powers, the provisions as to notice of general meetings and procedure to be followed at such meetings, details of the issue, transfer and forfeiture of shares, voting rights of shareholders, and provision as to audits, accounts and so on.

Registration of a company is effected by depositing the Memorandum and Articles of Association with the Registrar of Companies. A 'model' set of articles is given in a Statutory Instrument, and if a company does not deposit its own set of articles with the Registrar, these model articles apply. They also apply to those companies which do have their own set of articles, but where the articles are silent on a particular point. There are certain other legal formalities to be observed before the Registrar will issue a *Certificate of Incorporation*—a document that has been described as the company's 'birth certificate'. A private company may commence trading upon the granting of the Certificate of Incorporation, but a public company has to raise its capital from the public and observe certain other legal formalities before the Registrar will issue a *Trading Certificate* enabling it to start in business.

(b) Types of Shares Issued by Limited Companies
Paragraph (*a*) above mentioned that one clause of the Memorandum of Association states the proposed share capital of the company and its division into shares of fixed amount. This is known as the *authorized share capital*, and contrasts with the amount that the company has issued. You will recognize the distinction between the two if you study a company balance sheet, which normally shows both the authorized and issued capital; for instance, the authorized share capital of Lloyds Bank Plc at 31 December 1986 was 700 million shares of £1 each, of which just over 536 million had been issued and were fully paid. The issued capital can never exceed the authorized: if a company which has issued the full extent of its authorized capital wishes to

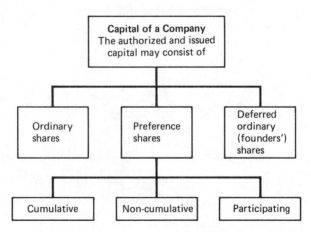

Fig. 13.1   Types of share

make an increase it must first pass the appropriate resolution at a meeting of the shareholders.

The authorized and issued share capitals are divided into a number of classes or types of share which usually include ordinary shares, perhaps preference shares and, more rarely, certain other classes (Fig. 13.1). An example of a share certificate is shown in Fig. 8.2 (see p. 115). Each share has a *nominal* or *face value* which is entered in the accounts and is commonly 25p or £1, although shares may be issued with nominal values of 5p, 10p or 50p. Thus a company with an authorized capital of £100 000 might state in its Memorandum of Association that this is divided up into:

100 000 ordinary shares of 50p each	£50 000
50 000 seven per cent preference shares of £1 each	£50 000
	£100 000

The nominal value of the shares often bears little relationship to their true value. The way to assess the value of shares in a public limited company is to look at their price in the *Financial Times* or *Stock Exchange Daily Official List*. As shares of a private company are not quoted on a stock exchange and, moreover, are subject to restrictions on their transfer, it is more difficult to value them. One way is to obtain a copy of the company's latest balance sheet and then calculate the value of net assets (assets less liabilities) belonging to each share, based on the 'book' values shown in the balance sheet; or calculate the value of net assets if the company had to be sold—the 'break-up' basis; another way is to consider the earnings of the company and to multiply this by a certain number, based on the ratio between earnings and price paid for other companies in the same type of business that have recently been sold (see also price/earnings ratio, Unit 8.14). Other methods exist but, like these, are at best only estimates.

Ordinary or *equity shares* are the most commonly issued class of shares, and they take a share of the profits available for distribution after allowance has been made for all expenses of the business, including loan interest and corporation tax. When the company makes good profits, it will be able to pay high dividends to the ordinary shareholders (subject to any Government restrictions); when poor profits or losses are made, these shareholders will receive a small or no dividend. Companies rarely pay out all their profits in the form of dividends, however; most retain some in the form of revenue reserves. These can be used to enable a dividend to be paid in a year when the company makes little or no profit, always assuming that the company has sufficient cash to make the payment. In the event of a company winding up (going out of business), the ordinary shareholders will be the last to receive any repayment of capital on their shares. They therefore carry the main risks of the company; but the concept of limited liability nevertheless means that the maximum a shareholder can lose on fully paid shares is the amount paid for them, or any amount which remains unpaid in the case of partly paid shares.

Preference shares have a fixed rate of dividend—7 per cent, for example—

which, as their name suggests, is paid in preference to the ordinary shareholders; but it is only paid if the company makes profits. In the event of winding up the company, the preference will usually also extend to the repayment of capital before the ordinary shareholders. There are two main classes of preference shares: *non-cumulative* and *cumulative*. If insufficient profits are made during a certain year to pay the preference dividend and the shares are designated as non-cumulative, then there is no provision for payment of 'lost' dividends in future years. This contrasts with cumulative shares (all preference shares are cumulative unless otherwise stated): if the dividend on these is not paid in one year, it accumulates so that past dividends will always be paid provided that the company makes sufficient profits in the future. A *participating preference share* is a further variation. With this class of share, the fixed rate of dividend is paid first and then, if the ordinary shareholders are paid more than a specified percentage, extra dividends are paid; thus in a profitable year when large dividends are paid to ordinary shareholders, the preference shareholders will also participate in the company's increased prosperity.

Deferred ordinary shares or *founders' shares* are now very rare but are sometimes issued to the original founders or promoters of the company. These shares usually receive their dividend only after the ordinary shareholders have been paid up to a certain maximum; any remaining profits are then distributed to the owners of the deferred ordinary shares. In a highly profitable company the holders of these shares could earn the highest rates of dividend.

The Companies Act permits a company under certain circumstances to issue *redeemable ordinary and preference shares*. These shares meet the requirements of a company that is in need of temporary capital but is unwilling to issue shares that cannot be redeemed once the need for additional capital has passed. When redeemable shares are repaid, certain steps are taken to protect the interests of creditors. The Act requires that, when the shares are paid off, the amount so paid is replaced by a new issue of shares, either ordinary or preference. The new issue will protect the interests of the creditors of the company because any cash going out of the company to repay the redeemable ordinary or preference shareholders is immediately replaced by the receipts from the new issue of shares.

This method of redeeming shares permitted by the Companies Act may not appeal to a lot of companies: there may be little point in replacing redeemable shares with shares that cannot be redeemed. An alternative procedure is allowed by the Act: the company may capitalize some of the distributable profits (the balance on profit and loss account, or general reserve, for example)—in other words, 'freeze' some of the distributable profits and make sure they can never be distributed to shareholders. This can be done by taking part of the profit and loss account balance, or, perhaps, general reserve and transferring it to a capital reserve account (which cannot be used to pay dividends); the Act insists that this be called a *Capital Redemption Reserve*. This protects the creditors because, while the company has not received any cash, it ensures that a certain amount of the existing or future cash balance will never be paid to shareholders and has therefore conserved cash that might otherwise have been paid out. It is also possible for a company to repay its redeemable shares partly from the proceeds of a new issue of shares and partly by a transfer of distributable profits to the Capital Redemption Reserve. The main thing is that each of these methods of redemption prevents the company from repaying such shares to the detriment of its creditors. Redeemable preference shares might well be replaced with ordinary shares (whether redeemable or not) to replace payment of a fixed rate of dividend with payments linked more closely to profit.

In addition to money provided by shareholders, who are the owners of the company, further funds can be obtained by borrowing in the form of *debentures*. These are a form of loan capital earning interest that must be paid whether the company makes profits or not, just like other business expenses. (Debenture-holders may be contrasted with shareholders who receive dividends appropriated from profits and who, in a bad year, might not receive anything.) Some public company debentures are quoted on the Stock Exchange and these usually represent a good safe investment particularly as, in the event of the winding up of the company, debenture-holders would be repaid before the shareholders. Debentures are either 'secured' or 'naked': *secured* debentures are backed by assets such as deeds of property that, in the event of winding up, could be sold and used to repay the debenture-holders before the other creditors; *naked* debentures do not have this backing.

(c) Other Types of Company

So far, we have been concerned with companies limited by shares, this being the most usual form of company operating in Britain. There are two other types of company for which a bank may be asked to open an account, however: companies limited by guarantee and unlimited companies, both of which may be either private or public.

Companies limited by guarantee are usually non-profit-making organizations such as professional societies, educational bodies or the larger sports clubs and societies. Each member of such a company guarantees to contribute a specific amount of money in the event of winding up, but no more. The name of such a company will end with the words 'limited by guarantee'.

Unlimited companies are those in which the liability of members to pay the company's debts is unlimited. As you can imagine, such companies are rare in the business world, where one of the benefits of forming a company is to limit liability. A slight advantage for an unlimited company is that, if it can meet certain conditions, it need not file accounts and directors' reports with the Registrar of Companies. Such companies are usually formed only for charitable non-profit-making purposes.

(d) The Bank and the Limited Company Customer

When a bank opens an account for a limited company customer, it needs to see the Certificate of Incorporation and, in the case of a public company, the Trading Certificate. The bank usually asks to have copies of the Memorandum and Articles of Association as well, together with a copy of the resolution passed by the company authorizing the opening of the bank account. The bank also needs a mandate giving specimens of the signatures of those who will sign the company's cheques.

As a company is a separate legal entity, any loans are made to the company and not to the shareholders. All trading companies have an implied authority to borrow money and to give security, subject to any limitation imposed in the Memorandum of Association. One of the dangers of lending to a company is that the amount lent may exceed this limit. All lending beyond this amount would be known as *ultra vires*—beyond the powers of the company—and this phrase is used to describe any act not permitted by a company's Memorandum. Where there is an *ultra vires* loan to a company the lender, if he is aware that the loan is outside the powers of the company, may only:

   (i) enforce any collateral guarantee given;
  (ii) obtain a 'tracing order' to follow the money through into assets;
 (iii) take the place of any creditor who may have been paid using the *ultra vires* loan.

Thus there is the danger that a bank could lose money if it makes an *ultra vires* loan to a company. However a lender, such as a bank, acting in good faith and unaware that a loan is outside the company's powers, is protected by section 35 of the Companies Act 1985, and would be able to recover the amount of the advance. However, it is considered by leading authorities that a bank would not successfully be able to plead this section because it invariably has a copy of the Memorandum of Association in its files and therefore is deemed in law to be aware of any limitations on the company's borrowing. This problem can be alleviated to some extent by requesting a certificate from the company secretary stating that the proposed advance is within the powers of the company (and also within the powers of the directors, although this latter point is not so serious).

The separate legal personality of a company causes a problem when a bank wishes to take security. As the company cannot sign the bank's charge forms, an equivalent process has to be carried out by affixing the seal of the company to the documents, or *under hand* where officials of the company are authorized to sign on its behalf. In either case, any charge that has been created must be registered with the Registrar of Companies within twenty-one days of its creation. The bank's internal regulations will detail the procedure for registering such a charge.

The directors must present to the company's shareholders the annual accounts and directors' report within a stipulated period of time after the end of the financial year. The Companies Act requires that, for all types of company, these should be audited by independent auditors, who must be members of certain accountancy bodies, and that certain minimum information should be contained in the accounts. The bank should each year obtain copies of the reports and accounts of companies to which it is lending.

13.6   Other Customers

So far in this Unit we have considered the most common types of personal and business accounts; a few specialist accounts should also be mentioned.

(a)   Clubs and Societies

Most branches have accounts of small clubs and societies such as social clubs, sports clubs or church societies. These accounts usually deal with small sums of money, the income comprising mainly subscriptions and the expenditure being outgoings in connection with running the club or society. The bank account will be opened in the name of the club and a mandate will be taken giving details of who is to sign, with their specimen signatures. The mandate usually includes a clause confirming that a resolution to open an account has been approved by a committee meeting. Unincorporated clubs and societies cannot be sued for a debt, nor can any member of the committee; if the bank is to lend on the account, therefore, it is usual for someone connected with the society to assume personal responsibility for the overdraft. This is customarily done by the bank taking a guarantee from that person to secure the account.

(b)   Executors and Administrators

Most branches have a few accounts of executors or administrators. When someone dies, his will should appoint certain persons to deal with his estate by collecting all monies due to the estate and making distributions to the beneficiaries of the will: these people are called *executors*. Where no valid will is left—that is, the person dies *intestate*—or where the executors named in a will are unwilling or unable to act, relatives are usually appointed as *administrators* to deal with the estate. There are certain distinctions between executors and administrators in the way in which they handle the estate of the deceased; but both may need to borrow money to pay capital tansfer tax. This tax is based on the value of a person's estate at death and also takes into account certain transfers of money and assets made by the deceased during his lifetime. Some transfers, both on a person's death and during his lifetime, are exempt from the tax and, with smaller estates, no tax will be paid. If capital transfer tax is payable, this must be attended to before the executors can obtain a document called a grant of *probate* which is their legal authority to deal with the estate of the deceased; administrators obtain a grant of *letters of administration*. Wills and intestacy are discussed further in Unit 15.13.

(c)   Trustees

Executors or administrators hold their appointments for the relatively short time it takes to collect together the assets of a deceased person, pay any tax that may be due and distribute the estate to the beneficiaries. A person who looks after another person's property for a long period of time is known as a *trustee*, and most branches have trustee accounts. A common example of a trust is where a sum of money is left in a parent's will to be invested and held 'in trust' for the children until they reach a certain age, often eighteen years: here the trustee's responsibilities are to invest the funds (the choice of investments is often limited by law to those having 'trustee' status—that is, the authorized investments to which trustees are confined by the Trustee Act 1925 and the Trustee Investment Act 1961), to receive interest and to pay the money to the children in accordance with the terms of the trust. Another type of trustee takes charge when a person goes bankrupt; he has the task of selling the assets of the bankrupt and then using the money to settle his debts.

(d) Liquidators and Receivers

We saw in Unit 13.5(a) that the Certificate of Incorporation can be regarded as a company's birth certificate. When a company 'dies' or is wound up, the final formalities are carried out by a *liquidator*. The liquidator is appointed by the Court in a compulsory winding up, or by the members of the company in a voluntary winding up where a declaration of solvency of the company is made, and by the creditors in a creditors' winding up where a declaration of solvency cannot be made. The task of a liquidator, as the name suggests, is to gather together all the assets of the company, realize them and distribute the proceeds among those entitled to receive a share.

The work of a *receiver* is often associated with that of a liquidator, and in a company liquidation they may be the same person. A receiver is frequently appointed by the Court to manage the business of the company until such time as it may be liquidated; this is because a business will often sell for more if it can be kept working normally until a buyer is found who will take it as a going concern, rather than if it ceases trading and all the assets are sold at an auction. A receiver carries out other duties: he may be appointed by the Court to attend to the assets of a mentally disordered person, to deal with the dissolution of a partnership, to receive rents and profits of property in the administration of an estate or to act as an interim receiver of a debtor's estate.

(e) Solicitors

Most bank branches have a solicitor as a customer, and for their business solicitors usually maintain at least two accounts. One of these is always designated *clients' account*, and this contains funds received by the solicitor on his clients' behalf that will be paid to them at a later date; this account should never be overdrawn. The other account is usually designated *office account* and is concerned with the day-to-day expenses of running the business.

(f) Churches

The operation of church bank accounts varies with the type of church. Church of England accounts are headed 'Parochial Church Council of . . . . . . Parish'. Parochial Church Councils (PCC) have corporate status, that is, they have a separate legal existence from their members. The bank's mandate to operate such an account must incorporate a certified copy of the PCC's resolution authorizing the person appointed as treasurer to sign cheques. The mandate must be signed by the chairman and two other members of the PCC.

For Roman Catholic churches a bank account is opened on the authority of the diocesan Bishop. It is held in the names of two or three priests, with one usually being authorized to sign.

Accounts for other churches, such as the Methodists, are held in the name of 'Trustees of . . . . . . Church'. The bank's mandate incorporates a resolution with regard to opening or continuing the account and authorizing signatories to cheques.

(g) Local Authorities

A bank account for a local authority is operated with a mandate which incorporates the authority's resolution to open or continue a bank account. The mandate incorporates a copy of the resolution appointing the bank, and this is signed by the chairman and the clerk to the council. The names and specimen signatures of those authorized to sign on the account will also be included.

The main income flowing into local authority bank accounts comes from Government grants, rates, council house rents and trading activities such as swimming-pools and car-parks; the main expenditure consists of wages and other payments for services provided by the authority.

Local authorities finance most of their longer-term activities in other ways than from a bank loan (see Unit 19.2) and usually only temporary bank borrowing is required to cover the period before a loan is raised or revenues are received.

13.7   A Bank's Duty of Secrecy

The one duty that all customers expect from their banks is that of secrecy and any breach of this duty gives a customer a claim to damages which will be awarded by the Court in proportion to the damage done to his financial reputation. Care should be exercised in all dealings with customers' statements, requests from other banks for status reports and references, and when returning cheques for lack of funds on the account. In particular, telephone enquiries concerning the balance of an account should be handled cautiously: each bank has its own regulations but, generally speaking, the balance should be disclosed only upon the positive identification of the customer. This is difficult over the telephone but the caller could be asked to state the amounts of recent standing orders or items paid in during the past week or so, or to estimate the balance of the account. It is not very sensible to ask for the account number or for details of recent cheques; if it is a thief with your customer's cheque book at the other end of the phone, he will be able to give you this information and you will then innocently give him the balance of the account so that he knows just how much to draw out on a forged cheque!

Under certain circumstances, information about a customer's account can be disclosed. These circumstances are:

'Granted open-plan banking lacks a certain privacy, Mr Wilkins, but there are advantages in the communications field'

(i) under compulsion by law (for example, under the Bankers' Books Evidence Act 1879, the Drug Trafficking Offences Act 1986 and the Criminal Justices Act 1988);

(ii) under a public duty;

(iii) where required by the interests of the bank;

(iv) where made by the express or implied consent of the customer.

13.8   Closing an Account

From time to time a bank may wish to close an unsatisfactory bank account. Normally such action would only be taken as a last resort. However, it might be considered where a customer is constantly overdrawn without authority, perhaps caused by misuse of a cheque card or where cheques well in excess of the balance of the account are presented for payment.

When an account has a credit balance, the bank must give *reasonable* notice to allow the customer to make alternative banking arrangements. (This also has the advantage of allowing recent cheques drawn to be presented for payment.) What is considered reasonable notice will vary—a limited company customer may well need more notice than a private customer. The mechanics of closing the account are to request the customer to return unused cheques, together with the cheque card (if issued), and withdraw the balance of the account.

For an account with an unauthorized debit balance, there is no need to give notice—repayment of the debt can be demanded and the account closed. Where the customer is overdrawn, but within an agreed limit, it is more prudent to threaten closure of the account and non-renewal of the overdraft facility, with recourse to security held, if any, than to close the account without notice. With a loan account there must be a breach of the loan agreement, such as failure to make repayments, before the account can be closed.

To close a joint account a bank must follow the principles outlined above. However, further problems with joint accounts can occur, especially where the mandate is for 'either to sign'. When the bank is asked to close such an account, the best practice is to obtain the agreement of both (or all) parties, by asking them to sign the last cheque withdrawing the balance of the account. However, one party to the account can withdraw funds to leave a nil balance, thus effectively closing the account. As husband and wife joint accounts are often the subject of a matrimonial dispute, it should be noted that as soon as the bank receives notice of a dispute, the mandate is terminated and both parties must sign all future cheques. For example, if the bank received a letter from a wife stating that she is in dispute with her husband, and subsequently the husband presented a cheque to withdraw the balance of the account payment should be refused unless the cheque has been signed by both parties.

13.9 Questions

1. What are the advantages and disadvantages of being in business as a sole trader?

2. Distinguish between private and public limited companies.

3. Compare and contrast ordinary shares, preference shares, deferred ordinary shares and debentures.

4. Bankers wish to give good service to customers but must also be mindful of their duty of secrecy. How would you reconcile those two principles in the case of a telephone call from a person who says that he is your customer Albert Brown and wishes to be told, over the telephone, the balance on his current account?

    (The Institute of Bankers)

5. J. Smith & Co Ltd has an issued share capital made up as follows:

50 000 eight per cent cumulative preference	
shares of £1 each	£50 000
50 000 ten per cent non-cumulative preference	
shares of £1 each	£50 000
200 000 ordinary shares of 50p each	£100 000
	£200 000

The company also has in issue £100 000 of seven per cent debentures. Net profit, before payment of debenture interest, is as follows:

Year 1	£26 000
Year 2	£9 000
Year 3	£18 000
Year 4	£35 000

Company policy is to distribute all available profits as dividends. Calculate the dividend or interest payable on each class of shares and debentures for each year: ignore taxation.

(Answers given on p. 384.)

Bank Accounts

14.1 Types of Account

There are two main types of account offered by all the major retail banks: *current accounts* and *deposit accounts*. Other accounts offered include savings, 'cheque and save', loans, home mortgage loans, personal loans, budget and revolving credit accounts. A customer may have several different types of account and more than one account of each kind; a company customer, for example, may require several current accounts for various purposes. This Unit highlights the main features of each of these types of accounts and indicates any restrictions on the use of other bank services that may be placed on the account holder.

14.2 Current Accounts

This is the most popular kind of account. Funds are paid in by the customer, who may also ask his employer to pay his wages or salary direct into the account by means of a bank giro credit. The customer is usually issued with a cheque book although some customers use their accounts solely for the payment of standing orders or direct debits. Funds may be withdrawn on demand either by drawing cash by cheque at the branch where the account is maintained or by writing cheques in favour of another person. Current accounts should always be maintained in credit unless overdraft arrangements have been previously made: these arrangements will include an agreed 'limit' on the account beyond which the customer should not draw. Interest is calculated on the amount of the overdraft on a daily basis and charged to the account monthly or quarterly, at a rate based on a percentage over the bank's base rate. Where facilities for an overdraft are granted the bank may also make a special charge for arranging them and committing the bank's money, whether the facilities are used or not. Security might be required to back an overdrawn account (see Unit 21).

   Bank charges may be made for operating the account, based on the number of transactions passing through the current account. If any charges are to be made they are debited either monthly or quarterly and are shown on the bank statements which are regularly sent to all current account customers to show the transactions on their account. Most banks do not charge for payments into the accounts but operate an item charge for debits such as cheques paid, standing orders and direct debits. The cost of these items is calculated monthly or quarterly by the bank's computer and against this is set off a 'notional' rate of interest on the customer's average credit balance during the period. Where the notional interest exceeds the cost of the debit items no charge is made, although no interest is credited to the account. Most major banks offer 'free' banking to personal customers for accounts which remain in credit. At the time of writing (autumn 1988), some banks have announced that they will soon allow interest on current accounts (see also Unit 14.5).

Current account holders are entitled to make use of most services of the bank.

Student Accounts

Most of the major banks offer special services to students. Broadly these are packaged around a normal current (or deposit) account, but include such facilities as:

> free banking (for credit accounts);
> automatic overdrafts (often at preferential interest rates);
> cheque card (issued with few formalities)—see Unit 15.2;
> ATM card—see Unit 15.5.

In addition, most banks have student financial advisers at branches near universities, colleges and polytechnics. Such advisers are trained to help students to overcome their financial problems.

All the major banks realize that student accounts are important. While they may be unprofitable to operate in the early years, the hope is that today's students will keep their accounts with the same bank after completing their studies. In order to attract student accounts, all kinds of 'free' gifts are offered; some banks also offer interest on student current accounts with credit balances.

14.3   Deposit Accounts

These, together with savings accounts, represent the simplest form of bank account: the customer deposits funds and withdraws them as required. No cheque book is issued on this type of account and therefore the formalities of opening an account are simple: often there is no need for a reference (although this may be required if the account is opened with a cheque), the customer's name, address and occupation, together with a specimen signature and an initial deposit being all that are needed.

Payments into a deposit account, which can consist of cash, cheques, postal orders and so on, may be paid in at the branch where the account is maintained or at any other branch of the bank. Funds may be withdrawn to the amount of the credit balance on the account normally only at the branch where it is maintained, although some banks do permit limited withdrawals at other branches. Withdrawals are subject to the required period of notice—often seven days—but in practice prior notice is not always insisted upon, provided that the amounts required are not too large. No overdrafts are permitted and a customer may generally not draw cheques on a deposit account. Where a deposit account customer has a large bill to pay and does not wish to carry cash, the bank can arrange for certain payments to be made with the bank's own cheque, the customer's account being debited. Where a customer maintains both a deposit and a current account at the same branch, funds can be transferred from one to the other freely, so that if deposit account funds are required to pay a bill, the appropriate sum may be switched to the current account and a cheque issued.

Interest is calculated on a daily basis on the balance of the account. The current rate of interest allowed is displayed in all branches and changes usually follow the trend of the bank's base rate. Interest is paid net of tax to personal customers, but is paid without deduction of tax (gross) to limited companies, clubs, charities and overseas residents. The customer is sent a statement of the account at regular intervals.

A deposit account is a convenient place for funds that are surplus to immediate requirements; the attractions are that it is simple and convenient both to pay in and to make withdrawals and that the money is absolutely safe. The rate of interest paid is normally less than that paid by other investment agencies (see Table 8.3, p. 122), but reflects the degree of safety and ease of withdrawal of funds.

Most advisory services of the bank are available to deposit account holders but a range of current account services, particularly standing orders, direct debits and cheques, are not normally available. It follows that cheque cards are also unavailable to deposit account holders, although credit cards (see Unit 15.4) are not restricted to current account holders only. Deposit account holders are often issued with a card for use in the bank's automated teller machines (see Unit 15.5). The card can be used to draw cash, check the balance of the account, order a statement and to make transfers from deposit to current account.

In addition to the more straightforward deposit accounts, most banks accept larger sums of money for fixed terms at fixed rates of interest or at variable rates which reflect money market interest rates. Each deposit—generally the minimum is £500—is regarded as a separate contract and cannot be withdrawn before the end of the term. For customers with larger amounts to invest—a minimum of £50 000—and particularly companies, most banks will issue a certificate of deposit (see Units 6.5 and 19.6).

14.4   Savings Accounts

The original idea of the savings account was to appeal to the 'small saver', and to this end savings boxes were issued to customers. These were locked by the bank and the customer took the box home, put his money into it and then brought it to the bank for it to be opened and the proceeds placed to the credit of his account. The trend nowadays is to withdraw the locked boxes, which used to cause chaos at busy counters ten minutes before closing time on a Friday afternoon, and instead to issue boxes that can be opened at home so that savings can be changed into larger-denomination notes and coins for paying into the bank in the normal way.

Interest rates on savings accounts are very close to those offered on deposits and, as with deposit accounts, usual current account services are unavailable to the savings account holder.

During the 1960s and 1970s, the trend moved away from such accounts and several banks ceased to operate them. However, the 1980s have seen the revival of the words 'savings account' in schemes designed to attract investors' deposits. Bonus Savings Account schemes offer higher rates of interest than are paid on deposit accounts to those who are prepared to save a regular amount each month over a minimum term of one year.

In addition, accounts designed to appeal to younger savers have been launched by most major retail banks. The accounts offer a good rate of interest but young people are more likely to be persuaded to open an account by the advertising gimmicks such as gifts, regular newsletters and birthday cards.

14.5 'Cheque and Save' Accounts

Most banks offer a 'hybrid' account which combines the advantages of a current account *and* a deposit account. The customer has a cheque book but, at the same time, the balance of the account earns a reasonable rate of interest. However, in order to offer these benefits, some restrictions have to be placed on the operation of the account. Principally these are that a certain minimum balance is always maintained, and that only cheques of above a certain amount can be drawn (if low value cheques are drawn, fairly expensive charges may be made). The benefits to a bank of these restrictions are that they are assured of the minimum balance always being in the account, and they do not have to bear the handling costs of low value cheques. From the customer's point of view, surplus funds are earning a reasonable rate of interest instead of lying idle in a current account but, at the same time, are readily accessible and can be drawn without prior notice.

Some banks have taken this type of account a step further by linking a regular savings scheme with a cheque book and, in addition, permitting overdrafts up to a certain limit—which is usually linked to a multiple of the regular savings amount. Yet a further variation on this theme is the type of account that has an agreed overdraft limit which is charged for at the usual rates while this facility is being used but, when the account is in credit, earns an attractive rate of interest. Such accounts are usually offered to personal customers only, but one or two banks do make them available to business customers. They certainly have attractions to those business customers who need an overdraft at certain times of the year but have surplus funds available for investment at other times. As terms offered by different banks vary with these accounts, potential customers are advised to obtain leaflets about them and to make comparisons.

14.6   Loan Accounts

An overdraft on a current account represents one way of lending money to a customer; the loan account represents another way. Where this is used, a separate loan account is opened and debited with the amount of that loan, which is credited to the customer's current account. Repayments of the loan are made, usually monthly, by debiting the customer's current account and crediting the loan account. Interest is calculated on the daily balance of the loan account at a given percentage over the bank's base rate and this, together with any other charges for the loan, will be debited quarterly or half-yearly either to the loan account or to the current account. Thus the customer has two accounts: his normal current account—which, in the absence of any other borrowing arrangement, must remain in credit—and a loan account, on which the only transactions will be the amount of the original loan, repayments and, if they are to be applied to this account, interest and charges. It is not possible for a customer without a current account to borrow money by way of a loan.

A loan account, as opposed to an overdraft, is especially appropriate where a customer, particularly a business customer, wishes to buy some vehicles or plant and machinery and the bank manager wishes to see regular repayments being made. Should the manager find that the current account becomes overdrawn because of the loan account repayments, he might conclude that the cash flow benefits from purchasing the new assets were not being received; thus the danger signals would be perceived early on, and the matter taken up with the customer. Normally, security is needed to 'back' a loan account (see Unit 21).

A loan granted for more than a year or two—between three and seven years, for instance—is a medium-term loan available mainly to business customers. These facilities are considered in Unit 16.2(b).

14.7   Home Mortgage Loans

In recent years, banks have become actively involved in making mortgage loans for house purchase to private customers. Such lending, which used to be the virtual monopoly of building societies, is long term and repayment has to be made within between ten and twenty-five years. The maximum amount of the loan will range from 80 to 90 per cent of the cost or valuation of the house and a higher percentage may be lent to first-time buyers. Loans will start from as low as perhaps £5 000, while the maximum amount that a bank will lend is calculated on the gross annual income of the main earner and up to three times this amount may be loaned. Often the gross annual income of a joint borrower will be considered as well. Like a building society, the bank will take a first legal mortgage over the property (see Unit 21.4).

Borrowers are offered the option of either a repayment mortgage or one based on an endowment assurance policy. Under the former arrangement, as with a building society mortgage (see Unit 6.9), regular monthly payments are made to meet the interest and repayment of the principal. Thus in the early years of a mortgage most of the repayments are used to cover the interest. With the latter arrangement, the mortgage is linked to an endowment assurance policy which covers the amount borrowed. The borrowers make monthly payments to meet the interest on the principal and the premium on the assurance. At the end of the mortgage period the endowment policy matures and is used to repay the amount of the loan.

The total amount of money that any particular bank is prepared to allocate to home mortgage loans varies, as banks do not wish to become too dependent on long-term lending. Thus, at certain times, home mortgage loans may be readily available, while at others they may be restricted.

14.8 Personal Loans

Most banks operate personal loan schemes which are similar to loan accounts except that they are designed for personal customers only and that the regular (usually monthly) repayments incorporate the interest charges. Under a personal loan scheme, a customer borrows a sum of money for an agreed period of time and makes monthly repayments, which include interest, fixed so as to exactly extinguish the debt at the end of the time. Personal loans below £15 000 come within the scope of the Consumer Credit Act 1974 and are *regulated agreements*: consequently a considerable amount of information must be given in writing to the borrower by the lender (see Unit 21.1).

Personal loans are commonly used as finance for the purchase of consumer durables such as motor vehicles, furniture, carpets or television sets, and are sometimes thought of as being the same as hire purchase. There is, however, an important legal distinction between the two: under a hire-purchase agreement the goods remain the property of the finance company until the last payment and the hirer's option to purchase is made, whereas under a personal loan scheme the goods belong to the bank customer as though he had paid cash for them. Indeed, there is no need for the seller of the goods even to know that the purchaser has arranged a personal loan to raise the finance: once the bank has agreed the loan, the amount of money is transferred to the credit of the customer's current account and debited to a personal loan account, and so the bank customer pays for the goods by cheque.

The rate of interest charged on a personal loan is invariably fixed for the period of the loan, and is based on the capital sum (the amount originally borrowed), rather than on the amount of the loan outstanding on a daily basis. This means that the true rate of interest is considerably higher than the nominal rate (see Unit 9.3). The Consumer Credit Act 1974 requires both nominal and actual rates of interest to be advised to all borrowers under personal loan schemes (see Fig. 21.1, p. 307).

No security is required for personal loans but they are normally only granted to holders of a current account and the bank will check to ensure that the past conduct of this has been satisfactory before granting the loan. Many personal loan applications from customers are assessed by means of credit scoring (see Unit 13.2) whereby answers to questions are awarded points and if the applicant 'scores' above a certain number the loan is granted. Nowadays there is no real need to see a member of the bank's staff to arrange a personal loan: the application form is completed by the customer and handed in to the bank where it is credit scored and, if appropriate, the loan is granted.

Most bank personal loan schemes can incorporate a form of life assurance so that, in the event of the borrower's death during the period of the loan, the debt would be extinguished by payment under the assurance. There are often upper age limits on this assurance.

14.9   Budget Accounts

Most householders are only too well aware that at certain times of the year their bills all seem to arrive at once. The first three months of every year are apt to bring heavy bills, such as those for gas and electricity which are higher as a result of increased consumption during the winter; other bills too have a regular pattern—often the rates on a house are due in April and October, car tax and car insurance seem to come together, and so on. In an attempt to assist personal customers to even out their expenditure over the year, the banks introduced budget accounts, a service that is normally only available to current account customers. A separate budget account is opened, and a cheque book

specially printed for use with this account. The customer estimates his expenditure on items such as gas, electricity, car tax and insurance, season tickets, rates and so on for the forthcoming twelve months, adding a little to allow for inflation and bank charges: the annual total is then divided by twelve and a standing order is taken to transfer this amount monthly from the customer's current account to the budget account. As bills which are included in the budget fall due, the customer settles them by using the special budget account cheque book. Charges are made on the account, consisting of interest for any overdrafts incurred during the year and the costs of operating the account—these are usually stated in leaflets advertising the service. If all goes well, at the end of the twelve-month period the balance of the account should be approximately nil, standing order transfers of money into the account having been equal to payments made by cheque together with charges. The account is then reviewed and the customer asked to estimate his expenditure afresh for the next twelve months.

The budget account is only available for paying bills that do not come at regular monthly intervals and so items paid on a monthly basis, such as mortgage repayments or insurance premiums, would not be allowed to go through it, but would be debited to the customer's ordinary current account.

14.10   Revolving Credit Accounts

Some banks offer the facility whereby a customer makes agreed payments, usually from £10 upwards each month, from his current account into a special account. At any time the customer may overdraw the special revolving credit account up to (often) thirty times the agreed monthly payment: thus with regular payments of £10 he has available an overdraft of £300. He may use the full amount immediately if he likes; if he then makes regular repayments for say ten months, the balance of the account would be down to £200 and he could then draw on the account for a further £100. The advantage from the customer's point of view is that he may spend the funds available when and how he wishes without having to negotiate fresh loan arrangements every time. Interest and charges are normally debited to the revolving credit account, although they could be taken from the customer's current account on request.

14.11   Questions

1. Obtain some advertising leaflets from one of the major retail banks and contrast the different types of accounts they offer.

2. Name the type of bank account that would be appropriate for (i) a person who has difficulty in meeting large annual bills as they fall due; (ii) a person who wishes to buy a car but needs some finance; (iii) a person who has a temporary surplus of funds. Give reasons for your choice.

Multiple-choice Questions—7

Read each question carefully. Choose the *one* answer you think is correct. Answers are given on page 390.

1. The legal relationship between a bank and a customer with an overdraft is, respectively:

   A creditor; debtor   **C** debtor; creditor
   B mortgagor; mortgagee   **D** mortgagee; mortgagor

2. Mr and Mrs Smith have an account at your bank and have signed a 'joint and several' mandate. The account is £2 000 overdrawn:

   A both are liable for £2 000
   B each is liable for £1 000
   C they are liable in proportion to credit received
   D the drawer of the cheques which created the overdraft is liable

3. Which one of the following business units has unlimited liability for the owners?

   A J. Adams plc
   B J. Adams Ltd
   C John and Wendy Adams trading as J. Adams & Co
   D J. Adams (Holding Company) Ltd

4. Which is the odd one out?

   A preference shares   **C** equities
   B debentures   **D** deferred ordinary shares

5. When a person dies either *executors* or *administrators*, depending on the circumstances, will deal with the estate of the deceased. The legal authority for executors and administrators to act is, respectively:

   A grant of receivership; probate
   B probate; letters of administration
   C probate; trust deed
   D letters of administration; probate

6. Under a credit scoring system, which one of these points is likely to be weighted most favourably?

   A nature of property occupied, and whether owned or rented
   B marital status and dependants
   C age
   D occupation and length of time in present employment

7. Personal loans:

   A are another name for hire purchase
   B are charged interest on a daily basis on the amount of the loan outstanding
   C below £15 000 fall outside the scope of the Consumer Credit Act 1974
   D enable the borrower to make a purchase without disclosing to the seller that money has been borrowed

8. An account where a customer can overdraw up to a certain limit for any purpose dependent on a fixed monthly payment is:

   A   a personal loan   C   an overdraft
   B   a budget account   D   a revolving credit account

9. A budget account:

   A   is used to spread the cost of household bills throughout the year
   B   is used to make monthly standing order payments, such as mortgage, insurance and hire purchase
   C   offers high rates of interest to regular savers
   D   can be used as an alternative to a personal loan account

10. A customer wishes to borrow £4 000 from the bank to assist with the purchase of a car costing £8 000. Assuming that the bank is prepared to lend, which facility is most likely to be offered?

   A   hire purchase, through the bank's   C   revolving credit account
       finance company
   B   personal loan   D   overdraft

Banking Services: Personal Customers

15.1 Marketing of Bank Services

At the beginning of this book, in Unit 1.1, we saw that every bank performs three basic functions:

- (i) acceptance and safeguarding of deposits;
- (ii) withdrawal of deposits and the operation of money transfer systems;
- (iii) lending of surplus deposits to suitable customers who wish to borrow.

While these are the most basic functions, modern banking in the late 1980s and early 1990s offers a far wider—some would say bewildering—range of services to the customers. In fact a large retail bank often offers some 300 different services to its personal and business customers. If you are working in a bank you may have been issued with a pocket guide to services and certainly every branch will have a services manual which describes each service in detail, together with benefits to the customer, and who to contact for further information.

Until the mid-1960s the banks did very little in the way of advertising and marketing their services. During the late 1960s joint advertising campaigns were launched that aimed to promote banking itself, rather than one particular bank. It was the 1970s that saw the establishment of separate advertising campaigns for each bank and it was during this decade that active marketing of bank services began to take place. In the 1980s, marketing as a whole (advertising is only one part of the marketing process) has become more aggressive as the banks have been forced into competition with each other and with other financial institutions. The Institute of Marketing defines marketing as 'the management process responsible for identifying, anticipating and satisfying customer requirements profitably': all large retail banks have a marketing department to take overall control of this function. In the world of marketing, the subject can be broken down into the four 'Ps'—product, place, promotion and price—that is, the right product, in the right place, properly promoted, at the right price. More particularly, marketing as applied to banking can be defined as:

- (i) identifying present and future markets for services;
- (ii) selecting which markets to serve and identifying customer needs within them;
- (iii) setting long- and short-term goals for the progress of existing and new services;

(iv) managing the services so as to persuade customers to use them at a profit, and controlling the banks' success in so doing.

Successful marketing in the banking business requires a commitment from all staff; it cannot be restricted to management—all staff from the newest recruit to head office general management need to be involved in the marketing function. Broadly there are four areas that need to be particularly singled out for marketing to be successful.

(a) Strategy

An individual retail bank needs an overall strategy to create a unique personality for itself which is consistent with the bank's public image. For example, Midland Bank have had great success in promoting a friendly image with their Griffin. However, any such image is difficult to sustain in old-fashioned branches with high counter screens and, to be credible, the image must be promoted by staff at all levels so those in the public area should not appear isolated from the customers. The strategy also needs to take into account the strengths and weaknesses of competitors—both banks and other financial institutions—and the strengths and weaknesses of the bank promoting the strategy.

(b) Services: Price and Productivity

Bank services have to be profitable overall and therefore must meet the needs of customers in a cost-effective and productive manner. There has been much discussion about whether cross-subsidization of services should be permitted when pricing services. In other words, should one or more services act as loss-leaders, as in the retail trade? Traditionally in Britain, bank customers have not been used to paying the full cost of services used. Only in recent years has an attempt been made to charge the users of services directly; for example a direct charge may be made to a customer who places an item in safe custody or to a customer who has an interview with the manager, and the cost of returning an unpaid cheque may be charged to the drawer.

(c) The Selling Role

Nowadays all staff are trained in the art of selling the bank's services. This emphasis on developing the bank's business is a top priority but, at the same time, the right environment must be created. Many of the larger branches have been modified to create open-plan areas where staff can discuss services with customers and prospective customers. However, the selling role must be balanced against the operational needs of running the branch so as to provide a high standard of counter service to existing customers. All staff need to know the services that are available and, if a specialist needs to be brought in, how to make an appointment between the specialist and the customer. Banks now regard their various services as 'products' and talk of 'retailing their products' as if they are actual goods on shelves behind the counter. Thus, in the selling role, a bank service can be packaged and sold as a product.

(d) The Branch Manager

The branch manager is the pivot of the marketing and sales team within a branch and is also responsible for marketing in sub-branches and support branches which come under his control. It is for the manager to hold regular sales planning meetings which involve all members of his staff. He will see that staff receive suitable training for the selling role, and will carry through the requirements of special product promotions as required by the marketing department. There will also be occasions when specialist marketing staff will visit the branch either to help in selling services or to carry out a training workshop. Above all, the manager is concerned with selling the expertise of the bank and its staff to the customers and prospective customers that he meets.

Despite the efforts that have been made in the past to market the bank and its services, there remains a lot to be done. Most customers still do not see the bank as meeting all their financial needs: thus they continue to look elsewhere for insurance, mortgages, investment advice, tax advice and travel facilities. The recent development of *market segmentation* is therefore of particular interest: banks have realized that not every customer wants every bank service and so customers can be divided into groups—students, housewives, manual workers, the wealthy, the elderly and business customers, for instance. This notion of market segmentation is consequently being developed with each segment being offered its own particular package.

We shall now go on in this Unit to describe the services offered by the banks to their personal customers; some of these are equally applicable to business customers and a note is added where this is so. Specialist business services are discussed in Unit 16, and certain services used by exporters and importers are considered in Unit 17.

Most of the services mentioned in this Unit are available to current account holders and most, but not all, can be used by those with deposit, savings and other accounts. Whether or not any particular service is available to one type of account holder or another varies from bank to bank and reference should be made to each bank's literature to find out exactly which services are offered and any restrictions that may apply.

Fig. 15.1   A cheque card

15.2   Cheque Cards

All the major banking groups offer their personal customers a cheque card (Fig. 15.1), which is signed by the customer upon receipt. The card states the maximum amount for which it is valid (at the time of writing £50), the name of the issuing bank, the sorting code number of the issuing branch, the name of the customer, the card number and the expiry date of the card. It can be used in two ways: to draw cash at other banks and branches, and to 'back' cheques used to pay for goods and services. In either case a cheque has to be drawn and the card presented as a guarantee of payment. The amount of each cheque must not exceed the limit stated on the card, and this is also the maximum amount of cash that may be drawn at a bank on any one day—there is usually a page at the back of each cheque book for banks to record amounts cashed and the date. A charge may be made where a cheque is encashed at another bank, for instance if a customer of Midland Bank cashes a cheque at a Barclays branch. Larger amounts of cash can be withdrawn, but the encashing branch must telephone the drawee branch for authorization, and a charge may be made for this service. Naturally the withdrawal limit does not apply at the branch where the account is maintained so long as the account is in credit or an overdraft arrangement exists.

The bank issuing the card guarantees to a payee that any cheque not exceeding the limit of the card in any one transaction will be honoured subject to the following conditions:

   (i) the cheque must be signed in the presence of the payee;

   (ii) the signature on the cheque must correspond with the specimen on the card;

   (iii) the cheque must be drawn on a bank cheque form bearing the code number shown on the card (if the account is transferred to another bank or branch, a new cheque card must be obtained);

   (iv) the cheque must be drawn before the expiry date of the card;

   (v) the card number must be written on the reverse of the cheque by the payee.

Of the big four retail banks operating in England and Wales, three—Lloyds, Midland and National Westminster—use the same design of card, the only difference being in the name of the issuing bank. Barclays uses its own distinctive Barclaycard as both a cheque card and a credit card (see Unit 15.4).

Cards are normally available only to current account customers aged eighteen and over. A simple application form is completed which is then often credit scored (see Unit 13.2) by the bank to decide whether a card may be issued. A cheque card is issued to customers under eighteen years of age at the discretion of the branch manager.

Cheque cards are often combined with ATM cards (see Unit 15.5) into one card with both functions.

The domestic cheque card cannot be used to draw cash abroad and most banks offer the eurocheque service to their customers instead. This consists of

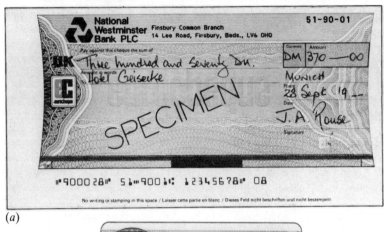

(a)

(b)

Fig. 15.2   Eurocheque documents: (a) uniform eurocheque, (b) uniform
eurocheque card

distinctive uniform eurocheques and a supporting eurocheque card (Fig. 15.2(a) and (b)) both of which are the same design for all participating banks except of course for the name of the bank. Using a eurocheque and a eurocheque card, cheques can be written in the currency of any country where they are accepted (up to a maximum of the equivalent of £100 at the time of writing, for United Kingdom bank customers). Cheques can be used for the encashment of personal cheques at banks and for the payment of goods and services in retail outlets. Besides being used abroad—and it should be noted that the service is not restricted to Europe but can be used in any country which participates in the scheme—the facility can also be used in Britain.

Eurocheque cards can also be used to draw cash from automated teller machines at participating banks in certain countries abroad.

15.3   Open Credits

Where amounts of cash beyond the cheque card limit are required to be withdrawn from another branch of the bank from that where the account is held, arrangements are made to establish an open credit. This withdrawal facility is made available by the customer's branch sending an authorization card, together with a specimen signature of the customer, to the branch concerned. If there is no convenient branch in the town where the customer wishes to cash his cheques, the arrangement can be made with a branch of some other bank. The service is particularly appropriate for business customers having factories or branches in more than one town and enables them to draw wages and petty cash locally.

The encashing branch or bank will need to know the maximum amount to be drawn under the arrangement, either per week or per cheque. Often a specimen of the signature of the person who is to receive the payments at the encashing branch—the wages clerk, for instance—will be required for identification purposes.

15.4 Credit Cards

The credit card as a method of payment has already been described in Unit 12.5. The two major bank credit cards currently available in Britain are *Access* and *Barclaycard*. The Access card (Fig. 15.3) is produced by the Joint Credit Card Co Ltd, of which the major shareholders are Lloyds, Midland, National Westminster, Royal Bank of Scotland, and Clydesdale banks. Barclaycard comes from Barclays, and TSB's *Trustcard* has links with Barclaycard and can be used at 300 000 Barclaycard retail outlets in the United Kingdom. Barclaycard and Trustcard are members of the international *Visa* group, of which the Bank of Scotland, Co-operative Bank, Girobank and Lloyds are also members. (Major retail banks in the UK are able to offer both Access and Visa cards to their customers.) Access has 310 000 United Kingdom retail outlets and, internationally, is a member of the *MasterCard* group. Thus the major credit cards can be used extensively throughout Britain and the world. By the end of 1988 Access and Visacard between them had over 28 million cards in issue.

Besides the credit cards which are issued by the banks there are also credit cards offered by the large retail groups: these are often issued and managed on their behalf by a major credit card company. Such 'in-house' credit cards have

Fig. 15.3   A credit card

the disadvantage that they can only be used at a limited number of outlets; however, some stores will only take their own credit card for purchases, not having the facilities, or perhaps the inclination, to accept other cards.

Each card carries embossed characters giving the name of the holder, his account number and its period of validity and, on the reverse, the holder's signature. The card can be used for making purchases of goods (including EFTPOS transactions—see Unit 12.6) and for obtaining a cash advance from any member bank involved in the scheme. It is also possible for cash to be drawn abroad at branches of banks particpating in the appropriate credit card scheme. Each month a cardholder who has used his card receives a statement detailing purchases and cash advances. If he wishes, he may pay only a proportion of the total amount he owes and spread the remaining payments over a number of months, for which he will be charged interest. When calculating interest charges, the credit card company charges for cash advances from the date they are taken, but it makes no charge for purchases of goods if the full amount of the account is settled within twenty-five days of the date of the statement on which they first appear. Most credit cards can also be used to draw cash at automated teller machines (see Unit 15.5).

A further service offered by most credit card companies is that of free travel accident insurance: where the fare for the journey has been paid with a credit card, cover against the injury or death of the cardholder, spouse and dependent children will be guaranteed.

Cards are issued to persons aged eighteen and over and there is no requirement that cardholders should have a current account; therefore this service could be of equal use to deposit and savings account holders. Before issuing a credit card, the company will require the applicant to complete a form which asks for personal and financial details, including details of previous credit transactions. The application will then be credit scored (see Unit 13.2) and, if satisfactory, a card will be issued and a credit limit given. Most credit card agreements fall within the scope of the Consumer Credit Act 1974 and are known as *regulated agreements* (see Unit 21.1). This means that certain information must be disclosed by the lender, in writing, to the borrower; in addition the borrower acquires certain legal rights.

Critics of credit cards believe they encourage people to overspend; nevertheless, used sensibly, the card can be of great benefit as a flexible way of spreading the cost of purchases over a period of time, and the card companies have run advertising campaigns stressing this aspect. The card companies do rely fairly heavily, however, on income from extended repayment: about three-quarters of cardholders do not settle their accounts during the nil-interest period on purchases and therefore must pay interest charges. If this kind of income were to fall drastically, card companies might well be tempted to raise their credit limits.

The companies also receive income from the retailers and other outlets that accept credit cards: they are obliged to give the company a discount on purchases, averaging between 2 and 4 per cent.

As credit cards are a means of creating money, controls on their use are

'I'm sorry, madam—Barclaycard accepts liability for faulty goods, but it doesn't exchange them'

imposed by the Treasury from time to time: these usually involve setting a maximum limit on the cash withdrawal facilities together with a minimum monthly repayment placed on all accounts, expressed as either a percentage of the balance outstanding or a fixed money amount, whichever is the greater.

Under the terms of the Consumer Credit Act 1974, when a credit card is used to buy goods and services and the goods turn out to be faulty, or the service is not provided, the purchaser has legal rights of recourse to the lender—the card company—as well as to the retailer. The Act renders credit card companies (as well as retailers) subject to claims by borrowers in respect of faulty goods and services bought on credit which have a cash price of more than £100 but not exceeding £30 000 per single item. Claims do not only cover the whole cost of the goods and services, but can also include consequential damages.

The card systems mentioned so far are 'free' in the sense that, if they are not used by the holder, there is no charge. Other cards, such as *Diners Club* and *American Express*, make an annual charge but do not have pre-set spending limits. Neither of these cards is, in fact, a credit card, and they are more correctly described as *charge cards*; cardholders are expected to pay their accounts promptly on receipt of each monthly statement and, provided they do so, there are no interest charges. The main benefit of this type of card is the convenience of being able to pay for goods and services without having to carry large amounts of cash. The differences between credit cards and charge cards are shown in Fig. 15.4.

Credit card	Charge card
e.g. Access, Visa	e.g. Diners Club, American Express
Spending limit	No spending limit
Payment may be deferred	Immediate payment after receipt of statement
No annual charge	Annual charge made

Fig. 15.4   The differences between credit cards and charge cards

A further extension of credit cards and charge cards is the *executive* card. This is only offered to people earning high salaries and carries with it a credit limit much above the 'ordinary' credit card; it also offers automatic overdrafts within certain limits and easy encashment facilities. Such cards are variously called by the issuing bank 'Goldcard', 'Premium Card' and so on.

15.5   Automated Teller Machines (ATMs)

The 1980s have seen the development of multi-function *automated teller machines*. These machines (Fig. 15.5(*a*)), which are computer-linked, provide a wide range of banking services and are operated by the latest generation of plastic cards carrying a magnetic strip recording the cardholder's personal financial details. Different banks operate different types of machines; some are located in bank branches, others are in large shops and stores, while others are in the outside walls of banks. The cardholder is given a personal identification number (PIN) to remember which, after he has inserted the card in the machine, he enters into the keyboard; this action links the machine with the bank's computer. By means of the information contained in the magnetic strip on the card, the computer can 'look up' the customer's account. The machine can then give the customer the amount of cash he wishes to withdraw—usually up to £100—tell him the balance of his account, enable him to place an order for a cheque book or a statement or carry out a transfer payment to another account, provided the payee's bank details are known. Other types of ATMs are designed to provide only encashment facilities but at high speed—often in no more than fifteen seconds—and such 'rapid cash' machines (Fig. 15.5(*b*)) are often located either inside bank branches or in separate card-access lobbies. In some cases such a degree of co-operation exists between banks that an ATM card issued by one bank will operate the machine of another—and still the right account is debited!

An ATM card can also be used when a bank customer wishes to pay in to his or her account. On presentation of the card, together with the cash or cheques to be paid in, there is no need to complete a paying-in slip.

(a)

(b)

*Fig. 15.5   Automated teller machines: (a) multi-function machine installed
outside a bank branch, (b) rapid cash machine installed inside a branch*

Most cheque cards and credit cards also incorporate the necessary magnetic
strip to enable them to be used in ATMs and similarly eurocheque cards (see
Unit 15.2) can be used to withdraw cash from the ATMs of participating banks
abroad.

ATM cards can also be used as debit cards in EFTPOS (electronic funds
transfer at point of sale) transactions—see Unit 12.6. Using the EFTPOS
system, a cardholder can pay for goods at retail outlets immediately, by giving
payment instructions to the bank's computer. After the computer has checked
that the customer has sufficient funds, the sum is transferred straight into the
beneficiary's bank account, so eliminating both the need for a cash or paper
transaction and the retailers' problem of 'bouncing cheques'. The advancement of EFTPOS will be assisted by the latest generation of cards, known as
smart cards.

Smart cards incorporate a microchip which stores information about the cardholder and his or her bank account. They also hold details of up to 200 recent transactions undertaken using the card: in effect they are an electronic cheque book and the transactions can be read on a terminal screen. A smart card can be used to draw cash from an ATM and to pay for goods and services under the EFTPOS system. It can be used both as a credit card and to debit a bank account. A credit limit can be pre-programmed into the microchip on the card and, at every transaction, the amount used is subtracted from the available purchasing power held on the card. The first use of the card in the following month will automatically reset its purchasing power at the original limit. The next few years are certain to see rapid developments in smart cards and, before too long, they may take over from magnetic strip cards currently in use.

15.6   Home Banking

While ATMs and EFTPOS offer two forms of electronic banking, home banking offers yet another. Using this system an account holder can either send information to the bank's computer by means of 'tones' down a telephone line, or can link a television and home terminal with the bank's computer by telephone. In this way banking transactions can be carried out seven days a week, twenty-four hours a day. Current accounts, deposit accounts, budget accounts and cheque-and-save accounts can usually be operated by this means. Facilities available include:

   (i) up-to-date balances;
  (ii) details of standing orders, to which amendments can be effected;
 (iii) the ability to order a cheque book and a statement;
 (iv) the ability to effect transfers between a customer's various accounts;
  (v) the ability to make payments to other account holders, such as credit card companies, the gas and electricity boards, the local council and British Telecom (the computer can also be instructed to pay a bill at a future date);
 (vi) the ability to buy and sell stocks and shares.

To prevent unauthorized use, each account holder has to key in a security code before any transactions can be made.

The system of home banking is also available to small business customers while for larger businesses, cash management systems—which operate along the same lines—are more suitable (see Unit 16.3(h)).

15.7   Travel Services

All the major banks offer a travel service consisting of the provision of eurocheques, travellers' cheques and foreign currency to customers and non-customers alike.

Eurocheques have already been mentioned in Unit 15.2. It should also be

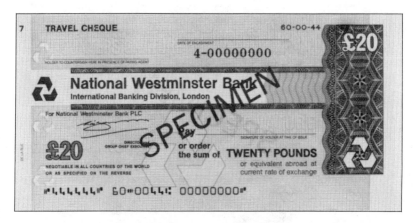

Fig. 15.6   A travellers' cheque

remembered that eurocheque cards can be used to draw cash from automated teller machines abroad.

Travellers' cheques (Fig. 15.6) provide a safe way of carrying money both in Britain and abroad. All the banks can supply travellers' cheques in sterling and other major currencies; they are also available in the common currency denomination of the European Community—the ECU (European currency units). Travellers' cheques are signed by the holder when they are issued at the bank and when they are to be cashed the holder countersigns them in the presence of the cashier who checks the signatures before making payment. If they are lost, a refund service ensures that the traveller will never be stranded without money.

Foreign currency can be obtained from all banks, but as not every branch carries a stock of currency it is wise for intending travellers to place an order a week or so before going abroad. Unused travellers' cheques and foreign bank notes (though not usually coin) can be cashed upon return to Britain. In some countries, the amount of money that can be taken out is subject to exchange control regulations, on which the banks can advise the traveller.

Most banks also sell *travel insurance* providing cover for emergency medical expenses, for accidental death or disablement, for loss of baggage, travellers' cheques, currency and money, together with personal liability cover. Application forms for *passports and visas* can also be obtained from banks and assistance given in their completion. The banks will also buy foreign currency and cash travellers' cheques for visitors to Britain.

15.8   Hire Purchase

All the major banks have links with finance houses that provide a range of hire purchase and other schemes, all of which enable the customer to pay for

*'Roughly translated it reads—Aztec Bank plc, bureau de change, travellers'
cheques welcome, closed Saturdays'*

goods by making instalments over an agreed period of time. Goods on hire
purchase remain the property of the finance company (the *owner* or *creditor*)
until the hire-purchase customer (the *hirer* or *debtor*) has made all the
payments; where other finance schemes are used the goods legally belong to
the customer from the start. However, for customers using a hire-purchase
scheme where the total hire-purchase price does not exceed £15 000, the
Consumer Credit Act 1974 prevents repossession once a certain percentage—
currently one-third—of the hire-purchase price has been paid. Hire-purchase
contracts contain an 'option to purchase' clause which permits the debtor to
purchase the item for a nominal sum at the end of the contract, thus meeting
the need for legal consideration.

The interest on hire purchase and similar contracts is usually charged at a
higher rate than on bank personal loans and is normally calculated with
reference to the capital sum borrowed: thus the true rate of interest or annual
percentage rate (APR)—see Unit 9.3—is an important factor for the debtor
to consider.

Most hire-purchase agreements for individuals, sole traders and
partnerships come within the scope of the Consumer Credit Act 1974, and are
regulated agreements (see Unit 21.1). This means that certain information
must be disclosed in writing to the debtor by the hire-purchase company, and
also gives the debtor certain legal rights.

Hire purchase and similar schemes operated by finance houses are available both to customers (with all types of accounts) and to non-customers. They are equally applicable to personal and business customers (see also Unit 16.2(*e*)).

15.9 Management of Investments

In Unit 8, we discussed the range of opportunities available to investors. One of the services provided by the banks is the management of a customer's investments: this is particularly appropriate to private customers who already have stock exchange investments or who wish to start investing in this way. To be managed properly investments need a certain amount of time and professional skill and the banks are able to provide this, for a fee. Often there is a minimum portfolio valuation that they will accept (sometimes £50 000) and for sums below this figure they frequently recommend an investment in the bank's unit trust. It is often possible to exchange existing shareholdings for units in the trust.

Investments that are taken over by the bank are usually transferred into its name so that dividends and interest received, notice of rights issues and similar matters can be attended to promptly; naturally the investments can be returned to the name of the customer upon request. In managing a customer's investments, the bank pays over dividends received to the investor at intervals, regularly reviews the make-up of the portfolio, buys and sells shares as appropriate, and sends an annual statement to the investor giving a current valuation of the investments. Some customers, particularly those uninterested in investment or those who live abroad, give the bank a complete authority to deal with the investments as they think fit; others ask the bank to refer to them before making any changes in the portfolio. When following an investment policy the bank considers the special requirements of the individual customer, such as a need for a high income or for capital growth of the portfolio. This service is available to all personal customers who are long-term investors: it is not available to speculators seeking short-term gains and wishing to make frequent changes in investments.

Specialist investment management schemes have been developed for the business customer (see Unit 16.5).

15.10 Safe Custody and Safe Deposit

Share and unit trust certificates, life assurance policies, deeds of property, wills and other valuables can be left with the bank for safe-keeping. These may be left in 'open' safe custody, in which case the receipt given for them will detail the items deposited; alternatively a locked box or a sealed envelope, parcel or suitcase may be left, the contents of which will be unknown to the bank.

Certain large city branches offer a safe-deposit service whereby a customer

'My God! Aren't they the managers of our investment portfolio?'

can rent a compartment in a specially built safe. There are usually two locks to each compartment, one key being held by the customer and the other by the bank; duplicate keys are held by the bank in case of emergency but would only be used in the presence of the customer at his request.

Unless an item is held in open safe custody the bank normally has no idea of the contents of a package or a safe-deposit compartment and care should be exercised with items that could be damaged. Where a customer deposits articles or securities with a bank for safe custody a *contract of bailment* arises (the bailee/bailor relationship mentioned in Unit 13.1) and under this contract a bank (the bailee) is bound to take reasonable care of articles left with it by the customer (the bailor). In law a distinction is made between a *gratuitous bailee* (someone who is not paid a fee), and a *bailee for reward* (someone who *is* paid a fee). The former is expected to take only the same care of the deposited goods as he would take of his own but a bailee for reward is expected to go beyond this and to use the best possible safeguards and to exercise care and skill, reflecting the fact that he is being paid for the service. Although some banks make a specific charge for safe-custody items and others do not, the distinction between gratuitous bailee and bailee for reward is largely academic because every bank takes the same care of all deposited items, including its own, and the courts seem to expect a very high standard of care from banks.

Where items in safe custody are destroyed by fire, loss or theft no liability will be attached to the bank, provided none of the events was caused by the bank's negligence: however, each case will be treated on its own merits. Nevertheless, when an item is deposited for safe-keeping, the customer should always be advised to insure the property against such risks.

The most probable liability that a bank may incur in relation to safe-keeping items is that of *conversion*. This means that if property held for safe-keeping is delivered to the wrong person, the bank will be liable for conversion. In the case of *Langtry* v. *Union Bank of London* (1896) an item was delivered by the bank on the forged signature of Miss Langtry, and the bank was held to be liable.

15.11   Status Enquiries

A customer can quote his bank as a financial reference (see Unit 16.8).

15.12   Insurance

The banks offer an insurance service to all their customers, through subsidiary companies or through their own insurance brokers. Besides the specialist insurance for businesses (see Unit 16.6), personal insurance available includes life assurance (see Unit 8.9), mortgage protection policies for those buying their home by means of a mortgage (see Unit 14.7), travel insurance (see Unit 15.7) and insurance protection of home contents, cars, caravans and boats.

15.13   Executor and Trustee Services

Specialized bank subsidiary companies offer services on all aspects of wills and trusts. The banks have the experience, impartiality and continuity to handle such tasks quickly and efficiently.

When a person dies, the estate is handled by personal representatives: if these are appointed by the deceased's will, they are known as *executors* but if a person dies intestate (that is without making a valid will) *administrators* are appointed by a court. In either case, executors and administrators have to obtain an official document from the High Court to show that they are the ones with the legal authority to deal with the deceased's property. In the case of executors this document is called a grant of *probate*; administrators, on the other hand, obtain a grant of *letters of administration*. (With some smaller estates, it is unnecessary to take out a grant of probate or letters of administration.) Before obtaining probate or letters of administration, the personal representatives must ensure that any capital transfer tax due on the estate of the deceased is paid.

Where an executor is appointed, authority over the deceased's property is vested in him from the moment of death; probate merely gives formal recognition of this. Once any capital transfer tax has been paid and grant of probate received, the executor (or executors) will collect together the estate, sell any property, pay any debts and then distribute the estate according to the wishes of the deceased.

Many people when making their wills appoint the bank to act as their executor. The bank may be sole executor or a joint executor with one or more other people being named in the will. If the bank has not been appointed as executor, it is still possible for it to act where the appointed executors find that they are unable to take on the work.

This can also be the case when a person dies intestate, or without leaving a valid will, and the estate of the deceased is handled by personal representatives who apply for a grant of letters of administration. These personal representatives are likely to be the nearest next-of-kin—surviving spouse or children of the deceased for example—but the banks' executor and trustee departments can act on their behalf and take on the task of handling the deceased's estate. When a person dies intestate, the estate is distributed according to the rules of intestacy laid down in the Administration of Estates Act 1925. These rules attempt to distribute an estate in a way in which the

'We'll arrange the insurance, of course, Mr Jonah, but I assure you the chances of being swallowed by a whale are very remote indeed'

deceased would have wished, had a will been left. Thus a part of the estate goes to a surviving spouse, while some goes to the children of the deceased. There are problems and complications in following the rules of intestacy: under some circumstances a surviving spouse can find himself/herself in difficult financial circumstances particularly where a house was in the sole name of the other partner. Therefore it is sensible to make a will.

Where a will sets up a trust for the benefit of others, such as a widow or children, the bank can administer the trust and make payments to the beneficiaries at the appropriate time.

The services of the executor and trustee company are available to all personal customers (corporate trust services for businesses are discussed in Unit 16.5).

15.14   Taxation

All the major banks offer the service of dealing with personal taxation. The service, which is often provided through a section of the executor and trustee company, provides advice on income and other personal taxes such as capital gains tax and inheritance tax. This specialist department also acts as its customer's tax agent, dealing with all the tax forms and correspondence to ensure that he gets all the allowances to which he is entitled, and where necessary handles claims for repayment of tax. The department can also provide a service to persons who are non-residents of the United Kingdom, but who have income in this country.

The tax departments are also able to advise customers how to arrange their affairs to the best advantage of themselves and their family. This involves a full consideration of the customer's will, tax position, life assurance and investment of capital, so that a suitable scheme may be worked out to reduce taxation and meet his obligations and wishes.

15.15   Indemnities

It sometimes happens that customers, both personal and business, need the indemnity of a bank before being allowed to undertake certain actions. One example of this is where a share certificate is lost: before issuing a duplicate the registrar of the company concerned will require an indemnity from a bank so that, in the event of any fraud taking place, the bank will be liable to the company for any loss. A bank is normally willing to do this but, in order to acknowledge and avoid the small risk of possible future loss, the customer will be asked to sign a counter-indemnity. In this way, if the bank does have to make a payment to the company concerned, it will itself have a claim against the customer.

15.16   Questions

1. What banking services might become useful to an accountant as he progresses from student to senior partner in a busy practice?   (*The Institute of Bankers*)

2. List and describe the main services offered by a commercial bank which are likely to be of greatest use to personal customers.   (*The Chartered Institute of Bankers*)

3. Competition for the personal customer market has increased dramatically over the past five years. Describe briefly six bank services that are likely to be of greatest use to personal customers.   (*The Chartered Institute of Bankers*)

4. You have been invited to the local college to talk to students about bank services that could be useful to them.

    What services would you talk about and what customer benefits would you mention? You have just 20 minutes for the talk and can only cover the main services.
          (*The Chartered Institute of Bankers*)

5. Your branch has recently carried out a direct-mail promotion of credit cards and one of your customers has replied that he has no need to borrow money. From an investigation of branch records, you find that the customer keeps an average balance of £550 credit on current account, but does overdraw occasionally. His account is very active and bank charges are some £25 per quarter. You are also aware that your customer travels frequently. The account has been opened for over 10 years but there is no indication that this customer has made use of any additional bank services.

    Draft a letter for your manager to sign outlining some of the relevant advantages of a credit card and persuading the customer to change his mind.
          (*The Chartered Institute of Bankers*)

6. Your manager tells you that he wishes to carry out a review of the bank's promotional activity.

    Prepare brief notes for a meeting, identifying a maximum of five products/ services which would be promoted 'in-branch'. You should indicate which times of the year you would consider most appropriate for each promotion and note your reasons for the choice.   (*The Chartered Institute of Bankers*)

7. You receive the following note from your customer, Miss Hazel Brown:

    Dear Sir,

    As you may know, I am a teacher at the local girls' Secondary School. When term ends in July, I have the opportunity of spending four weeks' holiday with a former pupil and her husband in Spain.

    I estimate that I shall need approximately £1 000 for living expenses and spending money.

    Will you please advise me of the most economical and safe way of taking money with me for this purpose.

    Yours faithfully
    H. Brown

    Required:
    Prepare brief notes outlining the alternative services you would recommend to this customer and the benefits and drawbacks of each.
          (*The Chartered Institute of Bankers*)

Banking Services: Business Customers

16.1 Introduction

Most of the major retail banks offer specialist facilities to the business customer. As we saw in Unit 10.3, a number of banks place their senior managers into 'key' branches and it may be that the business customer seeking advice or finance will need to contact such a branch. Besides the facilities available at key or larger branches, most banks have appointed a number of specialist managers (see Unit 16.8) who are concerned with the needs of the business customer, ranging from a small family business through to a large public limited company.

This Unit discusses a wide range of specialist services designed by the banks to suit the needs of different sizes of business concerns. Some of these services are also applicable to personal customers and are described elsewhere, this Unit only referring you to the relevant section.

The services that the banks offer to the business customer can be classified under seven broad headings:

   (i) financing;
  (ii) money transfer;
 (iii) foreign transactions;
  (iv) investment;
   (v) insurance;
  (vi) accounting;
 (vii) advisory service.

16.2 Financing

(a) Loans and Overdrafts

The main features of overdrafts and loans are discussed fully in Units 14.2 and 14.6, while the principles of lending are considered in Unit 21.2. However, a number of special schemes are available to encourage small businesses. Some of the schemes are backed by the Government, in that part of the bank lending is guaranteed to be repaid in the event of default by the borrower. At the same time a number of banks have developed their own small business loans. These are aimed at sole traders, partnerships and small limited companies; the loan amounts range from £1 000 up to £15 000 or more. Security for the loan is not necessarily required, although each application is considered on its merits.

Interest rates are usually variable, but are quite competitive. Life assurance for the borrower may be included in the loan package so that, in the event of early death, the amount of the loan outstanding would be cleared.

(b) Medium-term Loans

Generally loans and overdrafts are repayable on demand and are reviewed at least once a year, so that they are often regarded as relatively short-term finance. This does not suit the business that is seeking finance for an expansion and development plan lasting over several years: medium-term loans are offered by the banks to provide for this kind of borrowing requirement. The banks each offer slightly different facilities but normally such loans are made for periods of between three and seven years, although both shorter and longer periods (up to a maximum of about ten years) can be arranged. They are made available to businesses for the purchase or extension of premises, for re-equipment in plant and machinery or for other investment such as the acquisition of, or merger with, another business. The minimum amount lent on medium-term loans is about £5 000 and generally there is no maximum, each case being considered on its merits; as usual with loans and overdrafts, interest is calculated on the amount of the loan outstanding on a day-to-day basis and charged half-yearly. Repayments are fairly flexible and are agreed to suit the customer's requirements, either at an even rate during the period of the loan or to coincide with the receipt of cash benefits flowing into the business from the asset purchased with the aid of the loan. The big advantage for a business taking out such loans is that the finance will always be available over the agreed period and cannot be recalled as a result of restrictions imposed on bank lending or other intervention.

(c) Farming Advances

All the major banks have many accounts of farmers and of businesses and individuals connected with the agricultural industry. Special finance arrangements can be tailored to suit the needs of this group of customers, either directly through the bank or indirectly through subsidiary and associated companies such as the Agricultural Mortgage Corporation PLC (AMC) which is jointly owned by the clearing banks and the Bank of England. The finance provided to the agricultural industry is on either a short-, medium- or long-term basis, depending on the purpose for which it is required. Short-term finance is provided from the banks by means of an overdraft or loan to meet working capital requirements and to cover the seasonal 'swing' of most farmers' accounts, reflecting the peak in their need for borrowing during late spring and summer when money is paid out to finance crops and animals, and its reduction during the autumn and winter as sale proceeds are received. Medium-term loans for three to ten years are provided by the banks or their hire-purchase companies to finance the buying of machinery, equipment and buildings. For longer periods, AMC provides a source of finance for the purchase of land and for major long-term improvements.

(d) Leasing

This is a method by which a business can obtain items of plant, equipment and vehicles without the need for capital outlay; instead of buying them outright, it leases or rents them from the bank's leasing company, which is often associated with the finance house. A wide range of assets may be leased, from agricultural machinery to machine tools and computers, worth anything from £1 000 up to several hundred times as much. The procedure is for the business to choose the equipment it wants and this is purchased by the leasing company. An agreement is then drawn up between the leasing company and the business establishing the terms of the contract and the amount of rental payable. A fixed primary lease is established for a period of three, four or five years, at the end of which there is normally an option to renew for a further period at a much reduced rental or, sometimes, an option to purchase. Rentals may be payable monthly, quarterly or annually to suit the customer.

The advantage of leasing to a business is that, although the legal title of the asset remains with the leasing company, once the first rental has been paid the business has complete use of the asset without having to finance its acquisition out of valuable capital resources or to seek a loan to cover its cost.

(e) Hire Purchase

Hire purchase for personal customers has already been discussed in Unit 15.8. For the businessman, hire purchase provides an alternative way of obtaining a

'A word of advice. Never say "How's business?" to a farmer'

wide range of assets without the need for major capital expenditure. The advantage of hire purchase is that the cost of plant or equipment can be spread over a period of time by making regular payments; thus, apart from the deposit required, there is no need to use capital resources. In most cases the asset eventually becomes the property of the business.

(*f*) **Block Discounting**
This facility, usually provided by the bank's finance house subsidiary, is a service for retailers who provide hire purchase and other facilities for their customers. Many retailers and other businesses offer hire purchase, credit sale and rental services, particularly on the sale of consumer durables such as television sets, washing machines and cars. Most businesses do not have the necessary finance to provide these facilities for themselves, so they discount a 'block' of hire purchase, credit sale or rental agreements that they have entered into with their customers to a finance house. Thus the retailer receives immediate cash for the block of agreements sold and acts as an agent of the finance house by collecting and passing on the amounts payable from his customers; in this way he has no need to finance the agreements himself, but can nevertheless appear to be giving a personal financial service to his customers.

(*g*) **Factoring and Invoice Discounting**
Factoring companies provide their clients with a sales ledger accounting service and bad debt protection. Most companies also offer finance against the trade debtors of a firm. You will know from your accountancy studies that when a business sells goods, particularly to another business, it has to allow credit: this means that sales have been made but the payment is due to the seller. Depending on the terms that are usual within the trade concerned, it can be anything from one to three months, or even longer, before payment is received. Until then, valuable cash is tied up, restricting the growth of the business: a factoring company provides, among other things, an immediate amount of money against these debtors. Most of the large banks offer a factoring service to their business customers, usually through a subsidiary company. The services differ from one factoring company to another but most provide assistance in three main areas:

(i) As already mentioned, finance is provided by purchasing debtors and making an immediate payment. Often the payment is restricted to a certain percentage of the debt due, commonly 80 per cent, and debts must be approved by the factoring company. Naturally charges are made for this service but the increased liquidity position of a firm might nevertheless enable it to take advantage of discounts for prompt payment offered by its suppliers.

(ii) A sales ledger accounting service is also offered whereby the factoring company takes responsibility for all aspects of sales accounting within the business: this includes maintaining the sales ledger (that is, the personal accounts of all debtors), sending out regular statements of account and collecting payments as they become due. This service relieves the management of the business from the time and expense of running the sales ledger.

(iii) The factoring company provides a further service of guaranteeing full payment on approved sales to customers. The payment is made even if the customer is unable to pay as a result of insolvency.

The factoring service is only appropriate for businesses that sell to a wide range of customers at regular intervals and where the total annual sales figure is in excess of £100 000. The charges made by the factoring company vary depending on the services used: the sales ledger accounting and bad debt protection usually cost between 1 and $2\frac{1}{2}$ per cent of sales, depending on the complexity of the work involved. Where debtors are purchased and payment made by the factoring company to the business, interest is charged on the finance at rates slightly higher than current bank lending rates.

A simpler service is that of *invoice discounting*. When one business sells goods on credit to another, an invoice—a document containing details of the sale—is sent to the buyer. With invoice discounting this invoice is sold to the factoring firm which makes an immediate payment of the full amount, less discount charges, to the seller and then arranges to collect the amount due on the sale.

(h) Performance Bond
Often bank customers in the building and contracting industry are required to supply a performance bond before being permitted to tender for a contract. The bond guarantees that the company has the financial resources and expertise to see the contract through to completion, if its tender is successful. A bank is commonly asked to provide such a bond and, when giving it, usually takes a counter-indemnity so that in the event of failure to complete the contract and a requirement for payment under the terms of the bond, it will be able to make a claim against the contractor.

(i) Export Finance
See Unit 17.

(j) Merchant Bank Services
See Unit 5.3.

(k) Discounting Bills of Exchange
See Unit 6.5.

16.3 Money Transfer

(a) Cheque Clearance
See Unit 11.9

(b) Bank Giro Credits

Operation of the bank giro credit system has already been described in Unit 12.3. The business customer can use the service to make payments to suppliers and other creditors, and often finds it very useful for paying the wages and salaries of employees direct into their bank accounts. Additionally the system can operate for receiving payments: a businessman can advise his debtors of the name and address of his bank, its sorting code number and his own account number; alternatively he can include bank giro credit slips when sending out statements advising customers of the amount payable in respect of sales. For a business receiving large numbers of credits into its bank account, such as a mail-order firm or the head office of a chain of shops, special paying-in books of credits can be printed and sent to agents or customers. Banks give such firms details of all credits received into the account day by day.

Standing orders and direct debits (see Units 12.3 and 12.4) can also be of just as much benefit to business as to personal customers.

(c) Night Safes

Most bank branches have a night safe installed mainly for the use of their business customers: the entrance to the safe can be seen on the outside wall of the branch. This service is useful for business customers, particularly shops, that receive quantities of cash after the banks have closed. The bulk of their takings can be paid into the bank during mid-afternoon; any takings received after this are placed in a special lockable and numbered night-safe wallet, and at the end of the day are taken to the bank and deposited in the night safe, to which the customer is given a key when he is allocated a wallet. The entrance to the safe is unlocked, and the wallets drop down a chute into a separate safe in the bank. Next day the safe is opened by bank staff and the wallets are taken to the counter. Here they may be collected during bank opening hours by the customer or his authorized representative and the contents either paid in to the account or taken back to the business premises. Normally the bank will not unlock the wallet unless special arrangements are made for the staff to open it and pay the proceeds in to the customer's account. The charge for the night safe is usually based on the number of wallets in issue; in any case, it is a small price to pay for knowing that surplus cash is stored safely overnight. As the wallets are of limited size it is recommended that they should be used for banknotes and not coin; cheques and other valuables can also be included provided that they will not be damaged by the fall down the chute into the safe. While this service is mainly intended for business customers who will use the wallets on most working days, a group such as a church or a club organizing a fête or a fair at a weekend can also hire wallets for a few days; this avoids the risk to the organizers of having to hold large amounts of cash in their homes until the banks are open again.

Other valuables such as documents and share certificates can be deposited with the bank in safe custody or safe deposit (see Unit 15.10) in the same way as for personal customers.

(*d*) **Bank Drafts**
See Units 12.7 and 12.11.

(*e*) **Telephone and Computer Transfers**
See Unit 12.8.

(*f*) **Overseas Transfers**
See Unit 12.10.

(*g*) **Open Credits**
See Unit 15.3.

(*h*) **Cash Management Systems**
Major banks offer cash management systems to their multinational company customers, in a way similar to that in which home banking services are available to personal customers. A cash management system allows a company treasurer, using electronic banking, to look at the balances of the company's accounts held with the bank at any branch in the world. The system operates by means of a computer terminal and monitor screen in the company's office, which is linked by telephone to the bank's computer systems. The treasurer of the company is able to check balances held in different currencies, and the flow of funds can be watched as receipts and payments occur. The treasurer is able to move funds from one bank account to another by using the terminal in his or her office. In this way advantage can be taken of the best interest rates available in overseas countries and, where exchange rate fluctuations are anticipated, action can be taken to eliminate losses. By using electronic banking in this way control over funds held at banks throughout the world is as great as if the account were kept at a local branch, and the funds at the company's disposal are used to its best advantage.

16.4   Foreign Services

To a country like Britain, the import and export trade is very important. The role played by the banks in assisting foreign transactions is fully discussed in Unit 17.

16.5   Investment

From time to time businesses have surplus funds available for investment and the banks are able to provide a number of investment possibilities. Most have been described elsewhere as they are also applicable to personal customers: these include deposit accounts and money market deposits (Unit 8.2), finance house deposits (Unit 8.3), certificates of deposit, both in sterling and dollars

(Units 19.6 and 19.8), eurocurrency deposits (Unit 19.9) and stocks and shares (Unit 8.12).

Investment Management and Corporate Trust Services
The banks' executor and trustee companies are able to provide specialist services to companies. Some large businesses have considerable funds invested on behalf of pension funds or employees' savings schemes, and banks can act as trustees of such funds and administer the investments. Additionally, most banks maintain specialist companies situated on the Channel Islands and the Isle of Man where services are available to customers, both private and business, who are able to take advantage of the differing taxation structures that apply in these islands.

Where very large companies and Government agencies issue debenture trusts, loan stocks and eurocurrency issues, these invariably entail the appointment of a trustee under a trust deed to protect the interests of prospective stock or bond holders. Most major banks are able to accept appointment as trustee to such issues, adding their experience, strength and international credibility.

Trust companies are also able to undertake the trusteeship of unit trusts and insurance company funds.

16.6   Insurance

The banks provide a wide range of insurance services for personal customers (see Unit 15.12) and also offer specialist insurance for the business customer. Such insurance can be arranged through a bank's own insurance company or through insurance brokers.

Most businesses will need to take out insurance against *fire*, *theft* and perhaps *flooding*. A policy which complements these is one that covers against the *loss of profits* which would be the result of, say, a serious fire: such a policy would cover continuing overheads such as salaries and rates, loss of trading profits and the cost of temporary premises, together with expenses in connection with replacing deeds, plans, business records and documents. *Credit insurance* may be taken out by most types of business, except retail shopkeepers, to provide against the possibility of bad debts. Insurance for *motor vehicles* can be arranged to cover against the usual risks.

It is now a legal requirement that businesses should have *employers' liability insurance* to guard against their liability for accidents to employees. Most firms also take out *public liability insurance* to cover any possible claims for damages from the public—for instance, where a member of the public is injured as a result of buying faulty goods or of negligence by an employee.

Life assurance (already described in Unit 8.9) is particularly relevant for small businesses such as partnerships and private limited companies where a small number of people, perhaps only two or three, play a major part in running the business. The death of one of these key people would have a serious effect on the future of the business and it is appropriate for such a firm to take out assurance policies on the lives of its partners and directors and, similarly, *permanent health insurance* to guard against their ill-health. The banks can also advise about *pension schemes* for the self-employed, company directors and employees.

16.7   Accounting

The banks have been able to make use of the surplus capacity of their computer systems by offering their business customers a range of accounting services, including payroll, sales and purchases ledger accounting and data service.

(a) Payroll

This is a service for the calculation of weekly and monthly pay for a firm's employees and pensioners. The business customer supplies a specialist department or subsidiary company of the bank with the information required for the calculation of its employees' pay; pay advices are calculated and printed, together with a printout for the firm's own use containing details of each individual's pay and a summary of the payroll. Where employees receive their pay in cash, an analysis is printed showing the exact quantities of different denomination notes and coin that will be needed to make up the pay envelopes; where employees require cheques, these can be printed and placed with pay advices; where bank giro credits are used, the bank's payroll department is given details of each employee's bank account so that the credits can be prepared and despatched. An additional service is that of producing the required information for submission to the Inland Revenue.

The benefit to a business using the service is that its payroll staff costs and time are considerably reduced although, of course, the saving must be balanced against the charge made by the bank for its services.

(b) Sales and Purchases Ledger Accounting

Business customers can avail themselves of the banks' service of maintaining their sales and purchases ledgers: these contain the firm's own accounts recording transactions with its customers and suppliers. The *sales ledger* contains the accounts of debtors—firms and individuals that owe money to the business—and transactions record the value of goods sold on credit, cash and cheques received and allowances made for goods returned. The *purchases ledger* contains the accounts of creditors—firms and individuals that the business owes money to; transactions therein record purchases of goods on credit, payments made and allowances given for returned goods. The bank's computer services deal with keeping the accounts, recording transactions and, in the case of the sales ledger, preparing statements for sending out to customers; the business itself receives regular printouts of the balances of accounts within the ledgers. The service takes over a chore that is for any business a time- and expense-consuming necessity and gives the firm more freedom to concentrate on manufacturing and selling its products.

Factoring (see Unit 16.2(g)) could be combined with the accounting service as a means of providing a method of finance.

(c) Data Service

Where a business operates its own computer system the bank can provide details of transactions passing through its account in the form of magnetic tape rather than conventional printed statements. This cuts down on paperwork by saving the bank from having to prepare normal statements from magnetic tape and sending them to the firm, where the details would then have to be input into its own computer system.

Other data services offered by the banks to their business customers include assistance with stock control, financial assessments of company projects and the maintenance of registers of shareholders.

16.8   Advisory Services

Some of the banks have in recent years concentrated on providing an advisory service to meet the needs for financial and management advice experienced by small and medium-sized businesses. The specialist managers appointed by the bank to run this service provide advice and guidance on a range of financial planning and control systems such as budgeting, costing, pricing, capital investment appraisal, cash flow forecasting and current asset management. They also advise on business strategy such as capital raising and reorganization, takeover bids for other firms and mergers with, and acquisitions of, other companies.

With larger companies, the merchant bank subsidiary of the bank can give advice on business strategy (see Unit 5.3).

An advisory service provided mainly for businesses (but also for personal customers) is that of the *status enquiry*. This consists of a short report on a customer's financial standing and is given only to another bank. Thus if a customer is asked to supply a financial reference before being allowed to purchase goods on credit, he may give the name of his bank; the supplier will then ask his own bank to take up the reference. Similarly, a business customer allowing credit to his own clients may ask for bank references and request his bank to take them up, usually enquiring if the customer in question may be 'considered good for £ x (the amount involved)' or 'considered good for £ x per month for y months (the time period)'. The bank's reply would seem vague to someone unused to the jargon but is clear enough to the enquirer; it may say 'considered good for your figures and purpose' where the customer is considered creditworthy to the extent indicated or 'we cannot speak for your figures' where the bank does not regard the customer as satisfactory.

The range of services offered by a large bank for its business customers goes far beyond the basic banking services of paying in, drawing out and granting overdraft facilities. The owner of a business, particularly of a small business, meets many financial and management problems and the bank manager is often the only adviser to whom he can turn.

16.9   Questions

1. List and briefly describe the main services offered by the banks to business customers.

2. What forms of finance do the major banking groups in the United Kingdom provide to industry?

(The Institute of Bankers)

Multiple-choice Questions—8

Read each question carefully. Choose the *one* answer you think is correct. Answers are given on page 390.

1. A cheque card:

    A enables the holder to send guaranteed cheques through the post by writing the card number on the reverse

    B can only be used at a limited number of retail outlets to guarantee cheques up to certain limits

   C can be used to guarantee a cheque to the payee up to certain limits and for the drawer to obtain cash from banks in Britain
   D enables the holder to buy goods on credit from certain persons

2. 'This card does not have a pre-set spending limit; cardholders are expected to pay their accounts promptly on receipt of each monthly statement.' Which type of card is being described here?

   A charge card   **B** credit card   **C** cheque card   **D** smart card

3. A customer uses a card which is placed into a machine; after keying in his personal identification number a cash withdrawal is made by debit to the customer's bank account. What type of card is being used?

   A cheque card   **B** credit card   **C** ATM card   **D** charge card

4. When goods are bought using a credit card the credit card company:

   A has no liability for faulty goods
   B is liable in respect of faulty goods for any one item costing up to £30 000
   C is liable in respect of faulty goods for any one item costing between £100 and £30 000
   D is liable in respect of faulty goods only if the retailer refuses to make a refund

5. A customer leaves items in safe custody with the bank. The bank and customer are respectively:

   A bailor; bailee   **C** bailee; bailor
   B agent; principal   **D** principal; agent

6. Under a hire-purchase agreement the goods:

   A remain the property of the hire-purchase company until the agreed number of payments, including the option to purchase payment, have been made
   B legally belong to the hirer once the first payment has been made
   C legally belong to the hirer after one-third of the hire-purchase price has been paid
   D always remain the property of the hire-purchase company

7. A company that banks with you wishes to be able to draw cash for wages at a branch of the bank close to one of their factories. This is arranged by means of:

   A a bank draft   **C** a bank giro credit
   B a mail transfer   **D** an open credit

8. A company that has the use of a vehicle upon payment of a sum of money on a regular basis over a long period of time is using the finance service of:

   A factoring   **C** hire purchase
   B leasing   **D** instalment credit

9. A company customer of the bank obtains finance against its debtors, protection against bad debts and has a sales ledger accounting service. It is using:

   A invoice discounting   **C** factoring
   B leasing   **D** a discount house

10. Cash management systems provide companies with:

    A high rates of interest for large fixed-term deposits

    B the ability to monitor, using electronic banking, a number of bank accounts and to move funds between them

    C cash withdrawal facilities at all branches of the bank

    D advice on investments

Unit Seventeen

Banking Services for the Exporter and Importer

17.1 Introduction

For a nation such as Britain—a small industrialized country with a large population and few major reserves of natural resources—international trade is especially important. Many manufacturers are tempted to ignore world markets and to concentrate on selling in the domestic market: sooner or later, however, an enquiry will be received from abroad and the firm will probably go to its bank to seek advice. Whenever a business trades abroad its bank is involved at some stage: handling the documentation, making or receiving payments, granting advances—perhaps at concessionary rates of interest—or advising on trade and any exchange control regulations. In this Unit we shall discuss the role of the banks in assisting businessmen engaged in trading overseas, beginning with the services offered to exporters and the documentation and procedures involved in the export trade.

17.2 Services for the Exporter

All the major banks have overseas or international departments that are able to provide information both to established exporters and to those who are considering exporting their products for the first time.

(a) Trade Enquiries
Within an overseas department will be a specialist department in contact with bank branches established overseas and correspondent banks, which can assist customers to find potential markets for export goods and which can effect introductions to overseas buyers and agents.

(b) Credit Information
In a similar way to the operation of the bank-to-bank status enquiry service within a country (see Unit 16.8), banks are able to obtain up-to-date credit information on buyers and agents anywhere in the world.

(c) Economic and Political Reports
Most large banks prepare reports on a wide range of countries and keep them regularly updated to show the current political and economic background. Information is often included on import restrictions and other developments likely to be of interest to United Kingdom exporters. In particular, specialist

information is usually available on trading groups such as the European Community and the European Free Trade Association.

(d) Trade Regulations

Banks can advise exporters on British trade regulations. The export of goods from Britain is generally unrestricted since most goods are covered under an open general licence and there are consequently few regulations to concern exporters. However, some goods such as antiques, live animals and military equipment are restricted and an individual export licence *may* be required. The import restrictions imposed by countries abroad are more likely to concern United Kingdom exporters, and banks are able to advise on these.

(e) Travel Services

As well as providing foreign currency, travellers' cheques, eurocheques and assistance with passports and visas (see Unit 15.7), most banks can issue an exporter travelling abroad with *letters of introduction*. These are addressed to overseas correspondent banks in the countries that he plans to visit, requesting them to give assistance by way of information and advice about possible buyers of his goods and about local trading terms and conditions.

(f) Exchange Control Regulations

In some countries there are restrictions on the transfer of funds out of the country. Equally, when goods are exported, the central bank needs to ensure that payment is going to be received in a manner acceptable to it, and advice can be given by banks to exporters.

In the United Kingdom there are currently no exchange control regulations.

(g) Forward Foreign Exchange

Where payment for exported goods is made in a foreign currency rather than in sterling, there is a danger that exchange rate fluctuations occurring between the date of shipment and the date of payment may reduce the exporter's profit or even turn the transaction into a loss. This problem can be overcome by the trader entering into a *forward foreign exchange contract* with his bank. The essence of such a contract is that the bank agrees to buy the foreign currency from the exporter at the date of payment at a certain fixed exchange rate; thus whatever happens to exchange rates in the interim, he always knows how much he will receive. (Similar contracts are available for importers—see Unit 17.13.) The risk of changes in the exchange rates can thus be removed from the businessman's calculations, while the bank covers its own position by matching deals. See also Unit 19.10(*a*).

17.3   Terms of the Contract

When exporters are arranging to sell goods to a customer overseas, the terms of the contract between them must be agreed. They always specify the following:

(i) **Goods:** a full description of the items to be supplied including the quantity and quality.

(ii) **Method of payment** (see Units 17.5–17.9).

(iii) **Insurance and shipping terms:** these will establish who is to be responsible for arranging and paying for the insurance (including stating the risks to be covered) and freight charges. The more common terms are:

CIF (cost, insurance and freight): this means that the exporter's price includes the cost of the goods together with all charges incurred up to delivery of the goods at the port or airport named in the contract; thus the exporter is responsible for arranging and paying for insurance and freight to the named destination.

C & F (cost and freight): here the exporter's price includes the cost of the goods together with freight charges, but he is not responsible for insurance, this being arranged and paid for by the purchaser.

FOB (free on board): the exporter is responsible only for arranging to put the goods on board the carrying vessel at the port of loading and so his price consists of the cost of goods together with any insurance and transport costs incurred in getting them to the port and loading them on the ship. Arrangement of and payment for shipping and insurance is thereafter the responsibility of the buyer.

Other common shipping terms include *FAS* (free alongside ship) and *DDP* (delivered duty paid). With *FAS* the exporter is responsible for all charges incurred in getting the goods alongside the ship at the port of loading named in the contract. The costs of port loading and other expenses, customs formalities, freight and insurance are the responsibility of the buyer. Where a contract stipulates *DDP* the seller is responsible for delivering the goods, with all charges paid by him, to the buyer's premises.

It is important for a banker to understand these different terms of trade so that he may know what documents to expect when dealing with contracts having different terms. International rules have been established for the uniform interpretation of the principal delivery terms used in overseas trading contracts: these are known as *Incoterms* and are published by the International Chamber of Commerce.

17.4   Documents of International Trade

Documents are important in international trade because they control the movement of goods; in some cases, they are the legal title to the goods. It is important that the correct documents should be in the right place at the right time and, in order to speed delivery of the goods and subsequent payment, that they should all be correctly completed. A seemingly minor discrepancy in the documentation will almost certainly lead to a delay in receiving payment.

In the rest of this Unit we shall describe the information to be found on the basic documents of international trade and list the documents that are required when a contract specifies some of the more common terms mentioned in Unit 17.3.

(a) Invoices
An invoice (Fig. 17.1) is prepared by the seller of the goods and contains the following details:

    (i) name and address of the seller;
    (ii) name and address of the buyer;
    (iii) date of the invoice;
    (iv) a description of the goods together with the price;
    (v) details of the way in which the goods are packed—for instance, whether they are in crates, cases or drums—and shipping marks stamped or written on the packages;
    (vi) the terms of sale (CIF, C & F, FOB and so on); the charges for insurance and freight, if applicable, may also be detailed on the invoices;

INVOICE	FACTURE FACTURA	RECHNUNG FACTUUR	

Seller (Name, Address, VAT Reg. No.)
Ace Industrial Suppliers Ltd
84 Smallbrook Ringway
BIRMINGHAM B2 8AQ
England
VAT Reg No   471 4719 81

C.C.C.N No. 7301

Invoice No. and Date (Tax Point)
0871   10 Aug 19-1

Seller's Reference
342/-1

Buyer's Reference
0621

Consignee
Newtown Manufacturing Co Ltd
Unit 64   Anfield Industrial Estate
Kowloon
Hong Kong

Buyer (if not Consignee)

Country of Origin of Goods
EEC United Kingdom

Country of Destination
Hong Kong

Terms of Delivery and Payment
CIF Kowloon Hong Kong
Irrevocable Documentary Credit
FDC/3/7410

Vessel/Aircraft etc.
Seven Traveller

Port of Loading
London

Port of Discharge
Hong Kong

Marks and Numbers; Number and Kind of Packages; Description of Goods	Quantity	@	Amount (State Currency)
NMCL 0621 HONG KONG Nos 1-2 2 wooden cases containing 50 ELECTRIC MOTORS Serial No A241	50	£75	£3 750.00

TOTAL   £3 750.00 Stg

Freight £155
Insurance £48

Gross Weight (kg) 175
Cube (m³) 2.45

Name of Signatory
J.Smith   Export Clerk

Place and Date of Issue
Birmingham   10 Aug 19-1

Signature
J.Smith

It is hereby certified that this invoice shows the actual price of the goods described, that no other invoice has been or will be issued, and that all particulars are true and correct.

Fig. 17.1   An invoice

1 Consignor Ace Industrial Suppliers Ltd 84 Smallbrook Ringway BIRMINGHAM B2 8AQ England	No. 5678	COPY
		342/-1
2 Consignee Newtown Manufacturing Co Ltd Unit 64 Anfield Industrial Estate Kowloon Hong Kong	**EUROPEAN COMMUNITY** ---- **CERTIFICATE OF ORIGIN**	
	3 Country of Origin EEC United Kingdom	
4 Transport details (Optional) Seven Traveller: London to Hong Kong	**5** Remarks	

6 Item number; marks, numbers, number and kind of packages; description of goods	**7** Quantity

NMCL
0621
HONG KONG
Nos 1-2   2 wooden cases containing
           50 ELECTRIC MOTORS
           Serial No A241
	175 (gross
	weight kg)
	120 (net
	weight kg)

8 THE UNDERSIGNED AUTHORITY CERTIFIES THAT THE GOODS DESCRIBED ABOVE ORIGINATE IN THE COUNTRY SHOWN IN BOX 3

THE LONDON CHAMBER OF COMMERCE AND INDUSTRY

Place and date of issue; name, signature and stamp of competent authority

London

10 Aug   19

....
The London Chamber of Commerce and Industry

Fig. 17.2   A certificate of origin

(vii) if applicable, details of import licences and exchange permits required by the importing country;

(viii) the total amount payable.

The details of the invoice should tie up with the contract of sale; if a documentary letter of credit (see Unit 17.7) has been opened, the invoice should conform exactly with its terms. Several copies of the invoice are normally required for the use of the buyer, HM Customs and the importing authorities abroad. Some countries may require a *certified invoice* or *certificate of origin* to confirm that the goods come from a particular country; in Britain certain Chambers of Commerce are authorized by the Department of Trade and Industry to make declarations of origin (see Fig. 17.2).

(b) Bills of Lading

Where goods are transported by ship, the bill of lading (Fig. 17.3) is one of the most important documents. Depending on the terms of the contract, either the exporter or the overseas importer may arrange with a shipping company for the carriage of the goods. The bill of lading is then issued by the shipping company as a receipt for the goods and forms the evidence of a contract of carriage. It is especially important because it is also the document of title to the goods, that is, the legal holder of the bill of lading is also the legal owner of the goods, subject to the payment of any freight charges due.

Bills of lading are normally 'clean' in that they do not bear any clause declaring a defective condition of the goods; a 'foul' or 'dirty' bill may bear a clause such as 'drums leaking' or 'one case damaged'.

(c) Insurance Documents

Goods for export should always be covered by adequate insurance from the time they leave the factory to the time the buyer takes delivery. The terms of the contract establish whose is the responsibility for arranging and paying for insurance during transportation. The documents consist of either the insurance policy itself or, more likely, a certificate of insurance, and the details appearing on them include:

(i) the name and signature of the insurance company;

(ii) the name of the insured;

(iii) where applicable, the endorsement of the insured so that the right to claim under the policy may be transferred (for instance, the exporter might take out a policy but it could be the importer who makes any claim);

(iv) a description of the risks covered and the sum insured;

(v) a description of the goods together with any packing details;

(vi) the time period during which the goods are insured;

(vii) the journey covered, for instance warehouse to warehouse;

(viii) the place where claims are payable together with the name of the agent to whom claims should be directed.

| Shipper | BILL OF LADING | UK Customs Assigned No. | B/L No. 12345 |

Shipper
Ace Industrial Suppliers Ltd
84 Smallbrook Ringway
BIRMINGHAM B2 8AQ
England

Shipper's Ref. 342/-1

F/Agent's Ref.

Consignee (If 'Order' state Notify Party and Address)

To order

It is agreed that no responsibility shall attach to the Carrier or his Agents for failure to notify the Consignee of the arrival of the goods.

Notify Party and Address (leave blank if stated above)

Newtown Manufacturing Co Ltd
Unit 64 Anfield Industrial Estate
Kowloon
Hong Kong

PACIFIC

SHIPPING

COMPANY

PSC

| Local vessel* | Local port of loading* |

| Ocean vessel | Port of loading |
| Seven Traveller | London |

| Port of discharge | Final destination |
| Hong Kong | |

| Marks and Nos; Container No; | Number and kind of packages; description of goods | Gross Weight | Measurement |

NMCL
0621
HONG KONG
Nos 1-2

2 wooden cases containing
50 ELECTRIC MOTORS
Serial No A241

175 kg   2.45 m^3

Particulars of goods are those declared by Shippers

Freight details, charges, etc.

Shipped either on board the above local vessel in or off the local port named above or (if no local vessel is named above) on board the above ocean vessel in apparent good order and condition (unless otherwise stated herein) and to be carried direct or by transhipment and subject to the exceptions, terms and conditions of this bill of lading and to those of the applicable tariff conditions (copies of which are available on request) to the extent that the latter do not conflict with the exceptions, terms and conditions of this bill of lading, to the above-named port of discharge or such other alternative port or place as is provided hereunder (or as near thereto as she may safely get, lie and discharge) and there to be delivered subject as aforesaid in the like good order and condition. Delivery to be made to the consignee named above or to his or their assigns.
Weights as shown in this bill of lading as declared by Shippers, and the Master is unable to check same. In accepting this bill of lading the Shipper, Consignee and Owners of the goods, and the holder of this bill of lading, agree to be bound by all of its conditions, exceptions and provisions whether written, printed or stamped on the front or back hereof.
CONTAINER AND VEHICLE DEMURRAGE.   Attention is drawn to the Tariff Terms and Conditions for Container and Vehicle Demurrage which apply to this Contract and which may be obtained from the Carriers or their Agents.

| Ocean Freight Payable at | Place and date of issue |
| Prepaid | London 10 Aug 19-1 |

| Number of Original Bs/L | In witness whereof the Master, Owner or Agent of the ship has affirmed to the number of Bills of Lading stated above, all of this tenor and date, one of which being accomplished, the others to stand void. |
| Two (02) | |

| Number of Packages (in words) | |
| Two | |

*Applicable only when document used as a Through Bill of Lading

For the Master

CONDITIONS CONTINUED OVERLEAF

ICS
B/L
Jan.
710

Fig. 17.3   A bill of lading

The risks covered by the insurance should agree with those called for by the buyer in the contract.

(d) Air Waybill

This takes the place of the bill of lading, when goods are sent by air; but unlike most bills of lading it is not a document of title to the goods, being only an acknowledgment of goods received for dispatch. The details appearing on it are similar to those found on a bill of lading.

We can see that there are three main classifications of documents required in international trade. These are:

(i) invoices;
(ii) documents of insurance; and
(iii) documents of movement, including bills of lading, air waybills and other types of waybill for rail or road transport.

There are other documents used for international trade, particularly in connection with trade between countries of the European Community, but they are too specialized to be dealt with in this book.

In a CIF contract the exporter is responsible for providing invoices, the insurance policy or certificate, and a full set of bills of lading marked 'freight paid', the freight charge being his responsibility. A C & F contract would require the exporter to produce invoices and a full set of 'freight paid' bills of lading, insurance being the responsibility of the importer. For an FOB contract the documents required from the exporter are the invoices and a full set of bills of lading evidencing that the goods have been shipped on board the carrying vessel and stating that freight is payable at the destination.

17.5   Methods of Securing Settlement in International Trade

The methods by which settlement is to be secured are agreed between the exporter and his customer in their contract. The method of settlement required by an exporter will depend very much on the previous experience, if any, that he has of the particular market, on his knowledge of the overseas customer and on the latter's financial standing. The main methods of securing settlement (starting with the safest) are:

(i) in advance;
(ii) documentary letters of credit;
(iii) collections;
(iv) open account.

We shall discuss each of these one by one. It should be noted though that each of these is a method of securing *settlement*; the actual transfer of funds, or *payment*, between buyer and seller is effected by such methods as those discussed below (see also Units 12.10 and 12.11).

17.6   Payment in Advance

This is undoubtedly the safest way for an exporter to secure settlement but buyers are seldom prepared to pay for goods in advance of shipment, other than for small consignments. The payment is generally made by the buyer through his bank by means of a draft or by international money transfer or express international money transfer in favour of the exporter.

17.7   Documentary Letters of Credit

After payment in advance this represents the safest and fastest way of securing settlement for exports as the exporter can personally retain control of the documents of title to the goods until the moment of payment or acceptance of a bill of exchange. The parties to a credit are:

(i) the applicant (usually the buyer), who arranges to open a credit in accordance with the terms of the contract he has made with the beneficiary (usually the seller);

(ii) the beneficiary in whose favour the credit is issued;

(iii) the issuing bank which commits itself in accordance with the applicant's instructions;

(iv) the advising/confirming bank which is located in the country of the beneficiary and is usually the issuing bank's correspondent;

(v) the paying/accepting bank which makes payment to the beneficiary, or accepts his bill of exchange: the advising/confirming bank and the paying/accepting bank may be the same bank, or may be different.

Where the terms of the contract call for payment under a credit, the buyer (or *applicant*) applies to his bank (the *issuing bank*) to open a credit in favour of the exporter (the *beneficiary*). Before issuing a credit the bank must make certain of its customer's creditworthiness; if this is satisfactory, the credit is then advised to the exporter through a bank in his own country (the *advising bank*). Under the terms of the credit, the issuing bank undertakes that the seller will be paid for his goods provided he complies with certain stated conditions: these will call for certain documents, such as invoices, bills of lading and insurance documents (depending on the precise responsibility of the exporter) covering the quantity and quality of goods agreed in the contract between the exporter and the overseas buyer. Provided that the documents presented to the advising bank agree exactly with the requirements of the credit, the exporter receives the payment due to him in exchange for the documents. (The paying/accepting bank is allowed a reasonable time to examine the documents—usually 24 hours—and so the exporter could call back for payment or his accepted bill of exchange the next day.) The *paying bank* sends the documents to the issuing bank by air mail; upon receipt, they are handed to the buyer, who then awaits the arrival of the carrying vessel.

When the ship docks, the buyer presents the bills of lading to the representatives of the shipping company and, in discharge of the shipping company's responsibilities under the contract of carriage, receives the goods. Payment for the goods by the buyer to the issuing bank is a matter of arrangement between them and of no concern to the exporter. The settlement between the banks for the amount paid by the issuing bank is carried out through their *nostro* and *vostro* accounts (see Unit 12.10).

Besides the advantage of a credit to the exporter, who knows that he will receive payment provided he complies with its terms, there are benefits to the buyer. He knows that payment will only be made by the advising bank when the exact documents specified have been received—as these are the documents of title, then once they are in the hands of the paying bank, it will only be a matter of time before they are sent to him, allowing him to collect the goods. There is, however, a risk to the issuing bank because the credit only deals in documents and not in goods, so that provided the exporter complies with the terms and conditions of the credit he will be paid even though the crates supposedly containing the goods have been packed with sawdust and old newspapers. A status enquiry by the issuing bank on the exporter is therefore essential.

An example of a simplified transaction will show the sequence of events (Fig. 17.4):

(i) ABC Engineering Ltd of London have entered into a CIF contract with XYZ Import Co Ltd of New Zealand to supply certain specialized machinery. The contract stipulates that payment is to be made under the terms of a documentary letter of credit, the required documents being:
1. invoice in triplicate;
2. certificate of origin issued by a Chamber of Commerce;
3. a full set of clean, on-board bills of lading made out to order and endorsed in blank, marked 'freight paid' and 'notify XYZ Import Co Ltd';
4. insurance policy or certificate in duplicate covering marine and war risks to the buyer's warehouse for invoice value of the goods, plus 10 per cent.

(ii) The machinery is manufactured by ABC Ltd.

(iii) Meanwhile the XYZ Co Ltd have asked their bank, the North and South Bank, to open a credit in favour of ABC Ltd. As their customers are creditworthy, the bank instructs its correspondent bank in London, National Barllands, to advise a credit in favour of ABC Ltd for the invoice value (which will include insurance and freight charges).

(iv) Insurance and shipment details for the voyage are arranged by ABC Ltd; the machinery is delivered to the shipping company and the freight charges paid. Once the goods are loaded, the shipping company issues a set of shipped bills of lading marked 'freight paid' and ABC Ltd must ensure that the other details comply with the terms of the contract and the requirements of the credit.

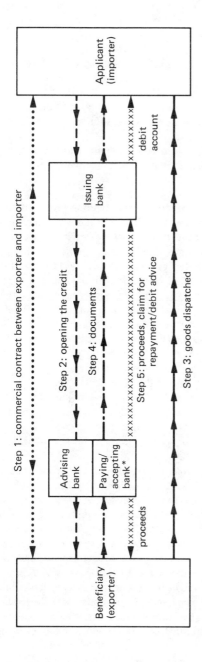

*The paying/accepting bank pays the beneficiary, or accepts a bill of exchange, if the terms of the credit have been met

Note: the advising and paying/accepting banks may be the same bank, or may be different banks

Key:

••••••••••• commercial contract   - - - - - - - credit   —·—·—·—·— documents   ××××××××× payment

——— goods

Fig. 17.4   The use of a documentary letter of credit

(v) ABC Ltd now presents the documents at the branch of National Barllands specified in the credit and, provided they agree exactly with the requirements of the credit, receives payment.

(vi) Meanwhile the goods are on their way to New Zealand by sea and the London bank sends the documents to the North and South Bank by air mail.

(vii) The North and South Bank in New Zealand releases the documents of title to their customers XYZ Ltd and, when the ship arrives, upon presentation of a signed copy of the bill of lading to the representative of the shipping company, the goods may be taken away.

(viii) The banks involved then effect book-keeping transfers between themselves to record the transaction and, at the North and South Bank, the account of XYZ Ltd is debited with the amount involved.

In this example the payment was made immediately upon presentation of the correct documents—the credit was *at sight*. It could equally well have been an *acceptance credit*: this would have meant that, instead of making an immediate payment, National Barllands Bank (the *accepting* bank) would have been authorized to accept a bill of exchange drawn by ABC Ltd for a certain *term* or time period as specified in the credit. This bill could then have been held by ABC Ltd until maturity or, if the company needed the money urgently, could have been discounted and the full value, less discount, received quickly.

Documentary letters of credit may be of two types: revocable or irrevocable. A *revocable credit* gives no undertaking to the exporter that payment will actually be made or a bill of exchange accepted because it may be cancelled or amended at any time up to presentation of the documents without the prior knowledge of the exporter. An *irrevocable credit* does not suffer from this disadvantage and consequently is almost invariably specified in contracts: under such a credit, the issuing bank gives its irrevocable undertaking to make the payment if all the terms of the credit are met, and can only amend or cancel the credit with the consent of all parties.

An irrevocable documentary letter of credit may be confirmed or unconfirmed. Where it is *confirmed*, besides having the irrevocable undertaking of the issuing bank, it also has the irrevocable undertaking of the advising bank in the exporter's country to make the payment under the terms of the credit. An *unconfirmed* credit still carries the issuing bank's irrevocable undertaking but the advising bank does not add its own, merely informing the beneficiary of the terms and conditions of the credit. From the exporter's point of view, the best payment method under a credit is by means of a confirmed, irrevocable documentary letter of credit because it contains the irrevocable undertaking of two banks, one of which is in his own country, and the terms of the credit cannot be altered without his knowledge; provided he complies with all the terms, he knows that he will either be paid or have his bill of exchange accepted.

Most documentary letters of credit are subjected to international 'rules' of

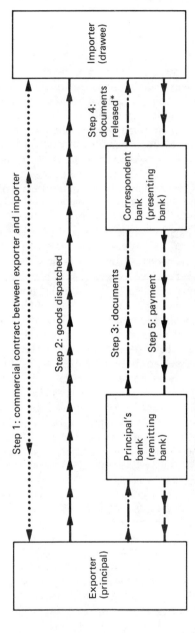

Step 1: commercial contract between exporter and importer

Step 2: goods dispatched

Step 3: documents

Step 5: payment

Step 4: documents released*

Importer (drawee)

Correspondent bank (presenting bank)

Principal's bank (remitting bank)

Exporter (principal)

* The presenting bank releases the documents either against payment or acceptance of a bill of exchange (depending on the instructions received from the remitting bank)

Key: ·········· commercial contract   ——— goods   —·—·— documents   – – – payment

Fig. 17.5   Documents against payment or acceptance of a bill of exchange

interpretation issued by the International Chamber of Commerce and known as *Uniform Customs and Practice for Documentary Credits.*

17.8   Collections

Where it is not possible in a contract between exporter and importer to agree that payment should be made under a documentary letter of credit, an alternative is to send the documents on a *collection* basis. Using this method the exporter ships the goods and arranges with his bank for the documents (invoices, bills of lading or other document of movement and, if appropriate, the insurance policy or certificate), often together with a bill of exchange, to be dispatched to an appropriate overseas correspondent bank. Depending on the instructions from the exporter and the terms of his contract with the buyer, the documents are only released upon either payment, or acceptance of the bill of exchange, by the importer (Fig. 17.5). Not all collections will include a bill of exchange.

If the documents-against-payment method is used, the exporter is able to retain a measure of control over his goods as he knows that the documents of title will not be released by the overseas bank until payment has been made. When documents are released against acceptance of a bill of exchange the exporter loses control of his goods and relies on the creditworthiness and integrity of his overseas customer to pay on the due date. Both methods have the advantage that the documents, and therefore the title to the goods, remain under the control of the banking system until either the bill is accepted or payment is made. However, if the buyer cannot pay or refuses to accept the bill, the exporter may be involved in considerable time and expense in recovering his goods; with an irrevocable documentary letter of credit, by contrast, the exporter knows that, providing he complies with the terms of the credit, he will receive his payment or have his bill accepted.

A further disadvantage of collections is that when goods are sent by air or some other form of transport where a bill of lading is not used the document of movement is an air waybill or similar which, unlike most bills of lading, is not a document of title to the goods. Thus control of the goods passes to the buyer on delivery even if payment has not taken place.

International rules also apply to documents against payment or acceptance and are known as the *Uniform Rules for Collections.*

17.9   Open Account

Where an exporter knows that he is dealing with a first-class overseas buyer he may be prepared to ship goods on an open account basis: this means that he simply sends the documents of title direct to the buyer and requests payment by a certain date. This is similar to the way in which credit sales are made between businessmen within the same country: provided their credit is considered satisfactory, goods are supplied and a regular statement of account sent out, payment being made by cheque. The only differences in international trade are that the distances involved are greater, making it more difficult to chase up any bad payers, and that an overseas buyer is more likely to settle his account by means of mail transfer or bank draft.

Very often the open account basis of international trade is forced on exporters because of short sea journeys which do not give time to process documents so as to enable more secure methods of payment to be used; bills of lading that do not constitute a transferable document of title are now being issued by shipping companies for goods on such short journeys. Similarly, with the increasing use of air and road transport (where there is no equivalent of a bill of lading to give the holder a legal title to the goods) exporting on open account is becoming more common.

Open account trading is also often used between a head office or holding company and its subsidiary companies abroad.

17.10   Financial Problems in Exporting

There are two main financial problems for the exporter: the risk of non-payment, and the provision of finance.

The problems of collecting debts in the export trade can be troublesome. It is not as easy to telephone an overseas customer about non-payment as it is a customer in the home country, it is far less easy to visit a debtor with an overdue account and, if it should come to taking a customer to court, the difficulties are very great indeed.

Exports often have to be sold on extended credit and the terms have to be better than those offered by competitors. Compared with credit transactions in inland trade, which are usually settled within one or two months, the credit offered to export customers usually needs to be between three and six months. For large-scale capital projects up to five years credit, or even longer, may need to be offered.

Solutions to both the main financial problems of the exporters are available: a Government department provides credit insurance to exporters (see Unit 17.11) and the banks offer special finance facilities, sometimes at reduced rates of interest (discussed in Units 17.12(d) and 17.12(e)).

17.11   Credit Insurance

A British Government department called the *Export Credits Guarantee Department (ECGD)* assists exporters of both goods and services by providing a special type of insurance covering two main areas of risk: the creditworthiness of overseas buyers, and the economic and political risks arising from events in overseas countries. The department does not cover risks normally dealt with by commercial insurers, such as fire and marine risks.

ECGD classifies the export trade into two broad categories:

(i) trade of a repetitive nature involving standard or near-standard goods; and

(ii) projects and large capital goods business of a non-repetitive nature, usually of high value and involving lengthy credit terms.

Cover for the first category is provided on a 'comprehensive' basis: the exporter must usually offer for cover all or most of his export business on credit terms of up to six months for at least a year in both good and bad markets. This is known as the *Comprehensive Short Term Guarantee*. Where credit terms are longer than six months but not more than five years with standard goods, the business can still be insured under a comprehensive policy but an 'extended terms' guarantee is required.

The second category of export trade is not suited to the comprehensive treatment and specific policies are negotiated for each contract. Cover for this specific insurance is given in two main ways. In the case of *Supplier Credit*, the manufacturer sells on credit (which may be long-term) and ECGD will insure him against certain risks. With *buyer credit* the exporter receives a prompt payment from his overseas customer, the cash for which is provided by a loan from a British bank; the loan is by instalments, repayment being guaranteed to the bank by ECGD.

The major risks covered under the most widely used policy, the Comprehensive Short Term Guarantee, are:

(i) 90 per cent of the loss resulting from the insolvency of the buyer or the buyer's failure to pay for goods which he has accepted within six months of the due date;

(ii) 90 per cent of the loss that remains after the policyholder has borne the first 20 per cent of the loss himself, in the event of the buyer's failure or refusal to accept goods which have been dispatched to him;

(iii) 90 per cent (if the cause of the loss occurs before shipment) and 95 per cent (if the cause of loss occurs after shipment) of losses resulting from war, political events, withdrawal of licences, export/import restrictions, etc.

Claims are payable at the following times:
For insolvency of the buyer: immediately upon proof of insolvency.
For failure to pay for accepted goods: six months after the due date of payment.
For failure or refusal to accept goods: one month after resale.
For other causes: four months after the due date of payment or date of event causing the loss.

17.12   Finance for Exporters

Several methods of finance are used by the banks to assist their exporting customers and a number of these involve ECGD giving a direct guarantee to a bank.

(a) Advances Against Shipping Documents

Most banks are prepared to grant overdraft facilities to customers who export on credit terms of up to six months. Where the bank is handling the shipping documents by passing them to a correspondent overseas bank for collection, it is usually prepared to grant an advance based on an agreed percentage of outstanding collections pending receipt of the proceeds. In some cases acceptable security for the advance would be the shipping documents which give control of the goods, together with bills of exchange in course of collection. A bank may require an exporter to insure his overseas trade with ECGD (if he does not do so already) and to assign directly to it any benefits payable under the policy.

(b) Negotiation of Bills of Exchange

Banks are usually willing to *negotiate* (purchase) sight bills of exchange or bills maturing within six months, often accompanied by shipping documents. The customer is credited with the amount, less charges, and the bank collects the proceeds of the bill when it becomes payable. The bank retains a 'right of recourse' to debit the customer's account with the full amount in the event of non-payment.

(c) Documentary Letter of Credit

Provided the exporter complies with the terms of a documentary letter of credit, he may obtain either an immediate payment or acceptance of his bill of exchange by the advising bank (see Unit 17.7). In the latter case, after acceptance of the bill, the exporter may arrange to have the bill discounted at the rate of ruling for that particular type of accepted bill, and thus he can receive cash almost immediately.

(d) Short-term Finance Linked to ECGD

A number of major banks offer special schemes to provide short-term finance for exporters, at concessionary rates of interest, linked to ECGD credit insurance. There are usually two different categories of finance schemes, 'bills or notes' and 'open account', to reflect two of the main ways of securing settlement in international trade—that is, collections of bills of exchange and promissory notes, and open account trading. The maximum export credit period to be financed under both schemes is usually six months.

Bills or notes scheme. An exporter customer must be approved by the bank and then as he ships his goods, he hands to the bank bills of exchange drawn on the buyer or the buyer's promissory notes, together with invoices, evidence of shipment, and a copy of the order from the buyer. If everything is in order the bank will credit the customer's bank account with 90 per cent (or, under some banks' schemes, 100 per cent) of the face value of the bills or notes, less the bank's charges and interest. The bank subsequently handles the bill of exchange or promissory note on a collection basis (see Unit 17.8) and receives the cash proceeds from the buyer.

Open account scheme. Here the bank makes an advance of 90 per cent (or sometimes 100 per cent), less charges and interest, against a copy of the invoice sent to the buyer, evidence of shipment, and a copy of the order from the buyer; in addition the invoice must show that settlement is to be made direct to the bank. Subsequently the bank will receive payment direct from the overseas buyer.

Under both schemes either the bank or the exporter insures the exports under ECGD's credit insurance scheme. Thus, in the event of non-payment by the overseas buyer, the bank will seek compensation for a maximum of 90–95 per cent from ECGD and there will normally be no recourse to the exporter. Banks are able to provide finance under such schemes at preferential rates of interest—1 or 1½ per cent over the individual bank's base rate—because of the low level of risk involved for them.

(e) ECGD-backed Medium-term Finance

Under a different arrangement from (d) above, ECGD is prepared to give, in approved cases, a *direct guarantee* to an exporter's bank that is providing finance for exports. The scheme only applies where export credit is given for two years or more, and is linked either to an ECGD extended-terms or specific credit insurance policy. Such finance is provided at concessionary rates of interest. Each contract is considered separately and, in approved cases, ECGD will issue a direct guarantee in favour of the exporter's bank. This covers the bank fully against non-receipt of payment three months after the due date.

An alternative arrangement to such supplier credit is buyer credit where finance is provided direct to the overseas customer. Under the scheme, he negotiates a financial agreement with the supplier's bank, so that he can borrow money to enable him to enter into a cash contract with the exporter. Payment is made to the exporter against documentation by the lending bank purchasing promissory notes made by the borrower. As these promissory notes fall due the proceeds are collected by the bank in repayment of its loan. This form of credit is only available for contracts valued at £1 million or more.

Another, more specialized, form of finance available involving the assistance of ECGD is *buyer lines of credit*. These resemble buyer credit in that they take the form of a loan made by a British bank to an overseas borrower, but instead of being linked to a single contract, they may be used to finance the supply of a variety of British goods and services falling within specified groups of industrial products.

(f) Factoring

Nearly all the major banks offer a factoring service (see Unit 16.2(g)) and some have special schemes tailored to meet the needs of exporters. The amount of finance available is normally based on a certain percentage of sales; if an overseas customer should not pay his debt, the factor usually takes steps to recover it.

17.13   Services for Importers

Most of the material we have considered so far in this Unit relates to exports. While the banks do much to assist the exporter because of the importance of exports to Britain, they also provide a range of services for importers. These can be assisted to find overseas sources of supply and the names of potential suppliers, using information gathered from overseas branches and correspondent banks. In addition the banks are able to obtain status reports on overseas suppliers: this ensures that an importer who considers entering into an overseas contract can ascertain beforehand whether the supplier is of sufficient standing and creditworthiness to carry out his side of the contract and supply the goods required.

Where importing is concerned, the banks are most likely to be involved in handling payments. The methods of securing settlement are the same for an importer as for an exporter except that the money flows are in the opposite direction for the payment. An importer may request his bank to issue a documentary letter of credit (see Unit 17.7) in favour of an overseas supplier: the bank will be particularly concerned to ensure that its customer is sufficiently creditworthy for the commitment. Where other methods of settlement are used, the bank may receive documents of titles from overseas correspondent banks relating to goods being imported, for release against payment or acceptance of a bill of exchange. Where an importer is buying goods on open account (see Unit 17.9) the bank will be involved in making international money transfers to overseas suppliers. A bank's foreign department advises its importer customers on the exchange control regulations of other countries and on United Kingdom import controls, and the requirements for import licences and documentation.

An importer is almost always required to pay his supplier in a currency other than sterling: if the exchange rates between sterling and the foreign currency alter during the period between the date of contract and the date of payment, a potentially profitable contract could turn into a loss-maker. A bank is able to provide a means of eliminating this risk by entering into a forward foreign exchange contract on behalf of its customer (see Unit 17.2(g)). Such a contract may be taken out by either an exporter or an importer wherever payment is to be received or made in a currency other than sterling, but is more likely to be used by importers. The benefits of a forward foreign exchange contract are that the trader can eliminate the risk from future exchange rates fluctuations and he can calculate the exact sterling value of an international trading transaction even though the payment will be received or made at some time in the future in a foreign currency.

17.14   Questions

1. Your customer, J. Smith (Manufacturing) Ltd, has received a first export order.

Describe to him the main methods that might be used for securing settlement from overseas.

2. What are the main financial problems facing an exporter? How are these solved in Britain?

3. What advisory services can a bank offer to its exporting and importing customers?

4. Describe the services offered by ECGD.

5. Describe the details to be found on (i) an invoice, (ii) a bill of lading, and (iii) an insurance policy or certificate.

Multiple-choice Questions—9

Read each question carefully. Choose the *one* answer you think is correct. Answers are given on page 390.

1. What is the name of the document that an exporter receives from the shipping company when goods have been placed on board the ship?

    A   invoice   C   certificate of origin
    B   bill of lading   D   bill of exchange

2. Under which one of the following circumstances would it be prudent for your United Kingdom customer to arrange a forward foreign exchange contract?

    A   export of goods priced in sterling
    B   import of goods priced in sterling
    C   import of goods priced in a foreign currency
    D   export of goods priced in a foreign currency where the rate of exchange has been agreed in the sale contract

3. The export term CIF means:

    A   carriage, insurance and freight
    B   cost, insurance and freight
    C   cost including freight
    D   charges, insurance and freight

4. An exporter sells goods to a customer abroad on FOB and on CIF terms. Who is responsible for the freight charges in each?

    A   importer; exporter   C   exporter; importer
    B   importer; importer   D   exporter; exporter

5. Under FOB terms the bill of lading would state:

    A   goods loaded on board, freight paid
    B   goods loaded on board, freight payable at destination
    C   goods received for shipment, freight paid
    D   goods received for shipment, freight payable at destination

6. There are four main methods of securing payment in international trade:
     (i) payment under documentary credit,
    (ii) open account,
    (iii) collection, that is documents against payment or acceptance of a bill of exchange,
    (iv) payment in advance.

    From an exporter's point of view, the order of preference is:

    A   (iv), (ii), (iii), (i)   C   (iv), (i), (iii), (ii)
    B   (iv), (iii), (i), (ii)   D   (ii), (iv), (i), (iii)

7. A documentary letter of credit is opened at the request of one of your customers. Is the customer:

    A   the exporter   C   the importer
    B   the beneficiary   D   the drawer

8. Under a documentary letter of credit which is:
    (i) the bank in the buyer's country, (ii) the bank in the seller's country?

    A   advising bank; issuing bank
    B   issuing bank; remitting bank
    C   issuing bank; advising bank
    D   advising bank; presenting bank

9. Your customer asks your bank to handle a collection outwards on her behalf. Are you:

    A   the presenting bank   C   the issuing bank
    B   the remitting bank   D   the advising bank

10. The Export Credits Guarantee Department (ECGD) provides:

    A   export credit insurance only
    B   direct loans to exporters
    C   export credit insurance and direct loans
    D   export credit insurance and direct guarantees to banks lending to exporters

The Money Supply, Monetary Policy and Controls

18.1 A Government's Economic Policy

The money supply has an important part to play in the overall economic policy of a government. Broadly the economic objectives of government are:

   (i) high levels of employment;
   (ii) stable prices;
   (iii) balance of payments surplus;
   (iv) economic growth.

While some of these objectives complement one another, others do not. For example, full employment will lead to a demand for consumer goods, which will in turn lead to inflation and an increase in imports leading to a balance of payments deficit. On the contrary, if a government follows policies designed to reduce inflation and the balance of payments deficit, economic growth will slow down and unemployment will rise. Thus a government has to tread warily when pursuing its economic policies while, at the same time, promoting economic growth.

Control of the money supply is important to a government because it is believed that there are links between the growth in the money supply and other economic variables (such as inflation and unemployment). If a government is able to control the rate of growth of the money supply, it may be able to control the other economic variables and thus contribute to the achievement of its economic objectives. In Britain since the mid-1970s, the Government has consistently established targets for the growth of the money stock. However, one of the problems in controlling the money supply is the definition of what this consists of.

18.2 Definitions of the Money Stock

We have already seen (in Unit 2.8) that a number of different definitions of the money stock are in use in Britain. Official statistics are published for M0, M1, M2, M3, M3c, M4 and M5. Definitions for M0, M1, M2 and M3 have already been given in Units 2.8 and 2.9; however, they are briefly defined again here for revision purposes:

M0 (narrow money) consists of notes and coin in circulation with the public, plus banks' till money, plus banks' operational balances with the Bank of England.

M1 consists of notes and coin in circulation with the public, plus sterling sight bank deposits held by the United Kingdom private sector.

M2 consists of notes and coin in circulation with the public, plus sterling retail deposits held by the United Kingdom private sector with the United Kingdom monetary sector, with building societies and in National Savings Bank ordinary accounts.

M3 (broad money) consists of notes and coin in circulation with the

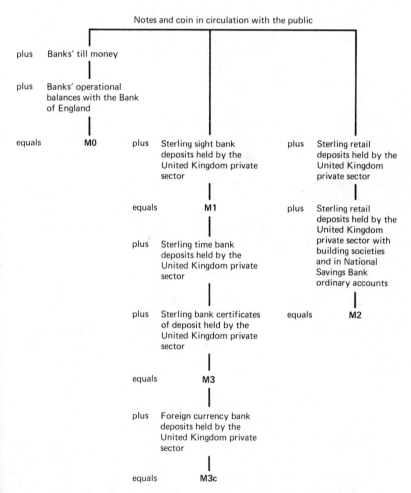

Fig. 18.1   Components of the money stock: M0, M1, M2, M3 and M3c

public together with all sterling bank deposits (including certificates of deposit) held by United Kingdom residents in the private sector.

An extension of M3 is M3c which is simply the addition of foreign currency bank deposits held by the United Kingdom private sector. (The 'c' indicates the inclusion of foreign currency items.) For M1, M3 and M3c, 60 per cent of the net value of sterling transit items—cheques and credits in course of clearance—is deducted from non interest-bearing deposits. Figure 18.1 shows the components of each of these definitions of the money stock.

M4 and M5 are both wider measures of the money stock and include many liquid assets which can be quickly turned into money, such as building society deposits and National Savings securities. Thus they give some indication of the total purchasing power in an economy—in practice it makes little difference whether a person holds funds on deposit with a bank (and thus part of M3), or in a share account with a building society (and thus not part of M3 but part of M2).

Fig. 18.2 shows the components of M4 and M5.

People hold money for different reasons but there are two major reasons: the first is in order to facilitate exchange, that is for spending purposes, and the second is to hold it as an asset, to be saved rather than spent. Since the motives for holding money vary, the stock of money is likely to change its composition in response to certain factors. For example, if interest rates rise, then we would expect more money to be held on interest-bearing deposits; if there was a fear of an increase in the rate of inflation, then we might find more money being held in current accounts for use as exchange, since people might wish to buy goods before money lost its value. As the composition of the money stock is likely to vary in this way, it is important to measure it in ways that take account of shifts which may occur in people's holding of money. For this reason there is the variety of measures of the money stock or *monetary aggregates* for which official statistics are published in the United Kingdom.

It has been argued by some economists that control of the growth of the money supply is the sole means of controlling the rate of inflation. However, problems arise immediately because of the difficulties in arriving at a clear-cut definition of 'money'. Even when it is possible to establish a statistical relationship between a particular monetary aggregate and, say, the rate of inflation, any attempt by the Government to control that particular aggregate is likely to result in banks, companies and individuals seeking ways to overcome the problems created by the controls and thus effectively frustrating them. In a highly developed financial system such evasive tactics are quite likely to succeed since there is a wide range of financial assets which can readily be substituted for one another. As a result, no single measure of the money supply can be relied upon entirely and the Government in Britain in recent years has chosen to target a number of monetary aggregates. M1 and M3 have been amongst the targets used; however, in 1984, M1 was dropped by the Government in favour of M0. In late 1985 the Chancellor of the Ex-

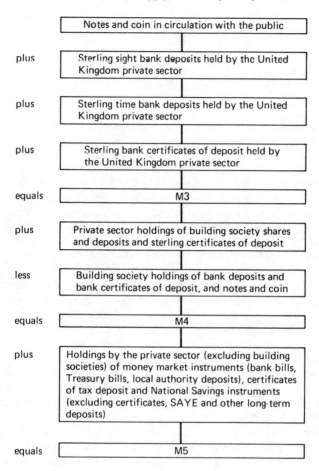

Fig. 18.2   Components of the money stock: M4 and M5

chequer announced that less emphasis would be placed on targetting the growth of M3; instead the focus of the Government's monetary policy (see Unit 18.4) was switched to the maintenance of short-term interest rates at sufficiently high levels to keep inflation under control. M3 was abandoned as a target in 1987.

Currently, therefore, the Government is targetting only M0. No formal target has been set for M3 but the Government intends to take the rate of growth of broad money, particularly M4, into account in assessing monetary conditions. Nevertheless, the other money stock figures are keenly watched by economists and the City of London as pointers to the success or otherwise of the Government's monetary policy.

18.3   Public Sector Borrowing

The monetary aggregates we have considered so far are all concerned with measuring money held by the private sector. However, in all countries, the public sector—central Government, local authorities and public corporations—has a role in the economy, to a greater or lesser extent. In particular the level of Government spending and of Government borrowing has a major impact on the banking system and the money supply.

It is important to appreciate the effect of a flow of funds between the general public and the Government. For example, payments from the public to the Government reduce the level of bank deposits held by the private sector and hence the monetary aggregates. Such payments might be in respect of taxation or might be to pay for the purchase of Government stocks and securities. At the same time, these transfers of funds from the private sector to the public sector will reduce the level of bankers' deposits held by the commercial banks at the Bank of England as the transfer of the funds from the commercial banks to the Government's account at the Bank of England is effected. The opposite effect occurs when payments are made from the Government to the general public: the money supply increases and so do bankers' deposits at the Bank of England. Such payments might be in respect of Government spending on goods and services, pensions and grants, repayment of Government stocks and securities, and interest payments on Government debt.

Although, in any one day, there will be a large number of payments in both directions between the private and the public sector it is the *net* transfer of funds, whether from the Government to the public or vice versa, that affects the banking system and the money supply. A *budget deficit* occurs if Government expenditure exceeds its revenue over a period of time; conversely, if revenue exceeds expenditure, a *budget surplus* will arise. We noted earlier that the public sector also includes local authorities and public corporations and the effects of their income and expenditure must also be taken into account as well as that of central Government. If there is a net deficit in the public sector, this is known as the *public sector borrowing requirement* (PSBR). When faced with a deficit the public sector, like any individual or private business, can finance it in one of two ways:

(i) increase its borrowing; or
(ii) realize assets.

(Conversely, the public sector faced with a surplus can either reduce its borrowing or acquire additional assets.) Governments faced with a deficit will normally finance the PSBR by means of increased borrowing. However, in recent years, some public sector assets have been sold to finance a part of PSBR and, at the same time, to pursue the Government's policy of privatization. A further way to finance a Government deficit is to cover the shortfall by the issue of additional banknotes—this method has never been used in Britain and to adopt it in such a sophisticated monetary system would only cause additional problems.

The Government of the United Kingdom has a number of different ways in which it may borrow from other sectors of the economy:

(i) the issue of gilt-edged securities;
(ii) the issue of Treasury bills;
(iii) the issue of National Savings securities and certificates of tax deposit.

The Government can also borrow from abroad.

As well as knowing the *way* in which the borrowing takes place, it is also important to identify the *source* of the money being borrowed from the point of view of the effect on the money supply. The question then is: does Government borrowing increase the money supply? The answer depends on who the lender is and this, to some extent, will be determined by the way in which the borrowing takes place—for instance by the issue of National Savings securities or of Treasury bills. Let us suppose, for example, that the following figures are known:

	£m
Government income (mainly from taxes)	9 000
Government expenditure	9 500
Deficit (PSBR)	500

Let us now look at two ways in which the Government may finance this deficit and the subsequent effect on the money supply.

(*a*) If the Government decides to finance *all* of this deficit by means of issuing National Savings securities such as Premium Savings Bonds, National Savings Certificates and National Savings Bank deposits, the most likely lenders are the non-bank private sector, that is, individuals and companies. The effects will be:

(i) the non-bank private sector will pay for the securities by drawing cheques on an account with a commercial bank;
(ii) the Government's account with the Bank of England will be credited with the amount of the cheques; and
(iii) the settlement between the commercial bank and the Bank of England will be effected by debiting bankers' deposits with the Bank of England.

Thus, from the point of view of the banking system, the effects will be:

Commercial banks

	£m		£m
Deposits	−500	Balances with Bank of England	−500

Bank of England

	£m
Public deposits	+500
Bankers' deposits	−500

As the Government has borrowed this money to finance its excess spending, the funds will be spent and will find their way into the hands of the non-bank private sector. The cheques will be banked with the commercial banks, so increasing deposits and, as the cheques are cleared, bankers' deposits at the Bank of England will increase while the balance of the Government's account will decrease. The effect on the banking system will be:

Commercial banks

	£m		£m
Deposits	+500	Balances with Bank of England	+500

Bank of England

	£m
Public deposits	−500
Bankers' deposits	+500

The end result of all this is that the initial borrowing transactions are exactly cancelled out by the subsequent spending by the Government. There is thus no change in the balance sheets of the commercial banks—no increase in deposits and no change in the money supply. The conclusion we can draw is that *borrowing from the non-bank private sector through the sale of National Savings (and other Government) securities does not increase the money supply*.

(*b*) If, however, the Government decides to finance *all* of the deficit by the sale of Treasury bills which, for the purposes of this example, we will assume are all bought by banks, the effects will be:

 (i) the banks will buy the bills, paying for them out of bankers' deposits held at the Bank of England;

 (ii) the Government's account with the Bank of England will be credited with the amount of the Treasury bill issue.

Thus, from the point of view of the banking system, the effects will be:

Commercial banks

	£m
Balances with Bank of England	−500
Treasury bills	+500

Bank of England

	£m
Public deposits	+500
Bankers' deposits	−500

The money borrowed by the Government to finance its excess spending will now be spent and will find its way into the private sector. The cheques will be banked with the commercial banks, so increasing deposits and, as the cheques are cleared, bankers' deposits at the Bank of England will increase while the balance of the Government's account will decrease. The effect on the banking system is:

Commercial banks

Deposits	£m	Balances with Bank of	£m
	+500	England	+500

Bank of England

	£m
Public deposits	−500
Bankers' deposits	+500

The net effect of this issue of Treasury bills to the banks and subsequent spending by the Government is that the Bank of England's balance sheet is unchanged, while the balance sheets of the commercial banks show an increase in deposits and an increase in holdings of Treasury bills of £500 million. Therefore, as commercial bank deposits have increased, so the money supply has increased. The conclusion we can draw is that *borrowing from the banking system through the sale of Treasury bills increases the money supply*.

As a result of considering these two different examples of financing PSBR we can see that the money supply does not necessarily increase when public sector borrowing takes place. Public sector borrowing will not increase the money supply when it is financed by the sale of Government securities to the non-bank private sector; however, it *will* increase the money supply if securities are sold to the banking sector. The link between the PSBR and M3 is broadly as follows:

Public sector borrowing requirement (PSBR)

less	Sales of Government securities to the non-bank private sector
plus	Increase in sterling lending to the private sector
equals	**Change in M3**

One reason a change in the money supply is important is because of the consequences for the Government's monetary policy.

18.4   Monetary Policy

We have already seen in Unit 18.1 that the broad objectives of Government economic policy include such things as high levels of employment, stable prices, a balance of payments surplus and economic growth. Monetary policy is concerned with the influence of money upon the behaviour of the economy —these influences include the growth of the money supply, the level of interest rates, the volume of bank lending and foreign exchange rates. Monetary policy attempts to influence the level of monetary demand, because it is considered to have a direct bearing on the economy. The policy is used to influence monetary demand by control over the following:

(i) the money supply—the monetary authorities can reduce/increase liquidity in the economy so that those seeking money to spend will find it more difficult/easier than before; and

(ii) interest rates—by altering the level of interest rates, the monetary authorities can influence investment and consumption.

18.5   Techniques of Monetary Control

We have already considered in outline (see Unit 4.9) the four ways in which the authorities carry out the Government's monetary policy. These four techniques are:

(a) directives;
(b) special deposits;
(c) interest rate policy; and
(d) open market operations.

We will now consider each one in detail.

(a) Directives

The Bank of England is in the unique position in Britain of having authority conferred on it by the Bank of England Act 1946 (see Unit 3.5) to direct a bank to take a certain course of action using, if necessary, the force of law. This legal force is rarely required, but the Bank frequently issues directives to the banks and deposit-taking institutions telling them of action they are required to take to implement the Government's policy on bank advances.

Directives used to take one of two forms: either quantitative or qualitative. *Quantitative directives* required the banks to limit the total amount of their lending to a certain figure. For example, the Bank of England might issue a directive saying that during the next six months advances must not increase by more than 5 per cent: thus a bank with advances of £5 000 million would only be able to increase its lending by a maximum of £250 million, whatever the growth of its deposits during that time. In the 1971 credit control proposals, however, the Bank agreed to abandon quantitative directives. *Qualitative directives*, which are still used, advise the banks and other institutions which types of customers they should or should not lend to, for instance, to lend to manufacturing industry but not to property companies.

(b) Special Deposits

Special deposits were first used in 1960 and are a call on all institutions within the monetary sector with eligible liabilities of £10 million or more to deposit a certain percentage of their eligible liabilities (this term is explained fully in Unit 7.6) with the Bank of England. The effect is to take money out of the banking system, which means that the banks must restrict or reduce their lending in order to maintain adequate reserves. When the authorities wish to increase bank lending, they will make a repayment of special deposits, knowing that money put back into the banking system will quickly be lent out by the banks. Interest is usually paid on special deposits at the Treasury bill rate but at certain times, when the authorities wish to penalize the banks, lower interest or even no interest at all may be allowed.

(c) Interest Rate Policy

Ever since the Bank of England developed the role of a central bank acting as lender of last resort to the discount houses, it has had the ability to influence market interest rates by changing the rate at which it is prepared to lend. In theory, interest rates affect the demand for loans and overdrafts which will have subsequent repercussions on the ability of the banks to create credit: high interest rates lead to a reduction in demand for advances, whereas low rates create a demand. This theory works well while inflation is low, but during periods of high inflation in Britain in the 1970s and 1980s, bank customers were prepared to borrow money at rates of up to 18 per cent or more.

Following the introduction of the *Monetary Control* measures in 1981 the Bank of England no longer posts a minimum lending rate. However, it may in some circumstances, announce in advance the minimum rate which, for a short period ahead, it will apply to any lending in the money market. The Bank's aim in the money markets is to keep very short-term interest rates within an unpublished band—this is achieved mainly by open-market operations (see below). Before changing the band the Bank is obliged to obtain the approval of the Chancellor of the Exchequer. While the Bank does not usually quote its dealing rates in advance, it does make public the rate at which it has dealt in the money market.

(d) Open-market Operations and Funding

Open-market operations are the buying and selling of long-term Government stocks in the gilt-edged market by the authorities in order to increase or restrict bank lending. When the authorities buy stocks on the market, the Bank of England makes payments to the individuals and institutions from whom it has purchased them. When the payment cheques are banked, additional deposits are made in the banking system and the banks are then able to 'create' more money by increasing their lending (see Unit 2.10). The reverse happens when the authorities sell Government stock in the market: the Bank of England receives payment and a transfer of money from the banking system is made when the cheques of the individuals and institutions purchasing the stock are cleared through the Bankers' Clearing House: this withdrawal of funds from the banking system reduces the ability of the banks to create credit. Open-market operations in short-term securities are also conducted in the bill markets, where the Bank buys and sells Treasury and commercial bills to influence rates and/or maintain stable conditions. In the United Kingdom dealings in long-term stock are more important from the point of view of controlling credit.

Funding refers to the translating of short-term debt, previously raised to cover Government borrowing, into longer-term debt. The Bank may reduce the issue of Treasury bills (short-term debt) and increase the issue of Government stocks and bonds with medium to long periods before repayment. These longer-dated stocks and bonds are more likely to be purchased by individuals and institutions outside the financial sector than are Treasury bills, most of which are held by banks and discount houses.

The effects of issuing more longer-term and less short-term debt are twofold. Firstly, the purchase of longer-dated stocks by non-bank holders reduces the deposits of the commercial banks in the same way as in open-market operations, causing the banks to reduce their lending. Secondly, reducing the issue of Treasury bills, which are suitable reserves for a bank, puts a 'squeeze' on the availability of these assets, and if this becomes acute the banks may have to reduce their lending by calling in overdrafts. However, there are other suitable reserves apart from Treasury bills and in practice the authorities' control of the credit base through such assets is neither precise nor reliable. In Unit 18.3 we discussed further aspects of Government financing, and the effect this may have on the money supply.

18.6   Monetary Control

We have just looked at the various techniques of monetary control used by the authorities. It is now appropriate to consider the methods by which the Bank of England controls the banking system in the United Kingdom to ensure that the confidence of depositors is maintained and that no major bank failure takes place. The techniques used have also been concerned with improving competition in the banking system.

There have been three distinct phases of monetary control during the last twenty to thirty years:

(a) the pre-1971 system
(b) 1971–1981: *Competition and Credit Control*
(c) 1981 to date: *Monetary Control*

(a) The Pre-1971 System
The 1967 report on bank charges of the National Board for Prices and Incomes

had already criticized the lack of competition amongst the banks. At the time, the major banks had a collective agreement on deposit interest rates—they all paid the same rates and there was no benefit in the customer's 'shopping around'. There was a further agreement among them that no interest should be paid on current accounts.

As far as credit control was concerned there were, prior to the 1971 arrangements, two minimum reserve ratios, applying only to the clearing banks: an 8 per cent cash ratio and a 28 per cent liquidity ratio. Both these ratios were expressed as percentages of deposits; 8 per cent of deposits had to bc held in the form of cash, either in the banks' tills or at the Bank of England, and a further 20 per cent in the form of liquid assets that could easily be turned into cash, the two amounts together making up the 28 per cent liquidity ratio.

The system was criticized for several reasons. The main problem was that the minimum reserve ratios applied only to the clearing banks and not over the whole range of banking institutions. They financially penalized the banks to which they applied, because those banks were forced to keep too high a percentage of their assets in low-yielding form. Another problem was that the quantitative and qualitative controls on bank lending and special deposit requirements similarly did not apply to the whole of the banking sector and, in times of credit squeeze, institutions outside the authorities' control were able to continue lending without restriction. It was in order to attempt to rectify these faults that the Bank of England introduced the *Competition and Credit Control* measures in 1971.

(b) 1971–1981: *Competition and Credit Control*

The major change was the scrapping of the liquidity and cash ratios and the introduction of the *reserve asset ratio*, with a minimum of 12½ per cent of eligible liabilities to be held in the form of eligible reserve assets to apply to all banks. (A list of eligible liabilities is contained in Unit 7.6.)

The special deposit requirements were extended to the whole of the banking system. Quantitative directives were ended, the authorities having decided that they would control only the total amount of credit, and individual banks should compete for shares of that total. Qualitative directives were retained and their scope was extended to cover all banks.

The banks agreed to abandon their collective policy on interest rates. Each bank established its own base rate (to which overdrafts are related) and its own deposit rate. Prior to the 1971 changes, overdraft and deposit rates had been fully linked with the Bank of England's bank rate (which became minimum lending rate in 1972) and any movement in this automatically meant changes in deposit and overdraft rates.

Problems with *Competition and Credit Control*

In their observance of the 12½ per cent reserve asset ratio, the clearing banks soon found that they were able to reduce their liquid assets from those held under the pre-1971 arrangements; they could hold less cash and fewer liquid assets and consequently more was available for lending. Thus, in the year following the introduction of the 1971 measures there was a rapid expansion of bank lending and, consequently, a rapid increase in the money stock.

Immediately after the introduction of the 1971 measures, each bank established its own deposit and base rate, although in practice all the major banks use the same (or very similar) rates. When the rates change, that for base rate usually changes by the same amount at the same time at each bank; however, there have been many occasions where deposit rates have differed slightly for quite a time. One of the principal reasons for maintaining identical base rates is that, nowadays, the larger corporate customers often have borrowing facilities with two or more banks and, if there were differences in the interest rates, these customers could undertake arbitrage operations—that is, borrow money from one source and lend it to another at a higher rate. Another reason is that all the major banks operate in similar environments under similar conditions with similar overheads.

However, with the abandonment of fixed rates for deposits, the banks were able to develop a market for larger deposits, particularly certificates of deposit, offering higher interest rates fixed for periods from three months to five years. The authorities became concerned at the ease with which banks were able to increase their deposits in this way, because of the effect this was having on the growth of advances and hence, through increased deposits, on the money supply. Consequently a scheme for supplementary special deposits was introduced in December 1973. However, the damage had been done: the considerable increase in deposits had enabled the banks to step up their lending, particularly to the 'secondary' banks and the property market. When the property market 'collapsed' in late 1973 and 1974 most banks 'got their fingers burnt'; several smaller banks and finance houses found themselves in severe financial difficulties and were only rescued with assistance organized by the Bank of England and provided by the clearing banks.

The changes introduced in 1971 certainly had a far-reaching effect on the British banking system. One of the good points was that the arrangements applied to *all* banks. However, *Competition and Credit Control* failed to produce much difference between interest rates among the banks, although it caused the abandonment of the collective agreement which existed before 1971. Its most serious fault was that it prepared the way for a considerable increase in the growth of bank lending which ultimately led to the secondary banking crisis of 1974.

(c) 1981 to date: *Monetary Control*

In the late 1960s the authorities began to pay more attention to the growth of the money stock and since the mid-1970s the targets for the growth of the money stock have been publicly announced. The main reason for announcing targets was the belief that this could have a damping effect on inflationary expectations, in particular by encouraging greater restraint in wage-bargaining behaviour. In practice it was found that the actual growth recorded was beyond the target range.

In order to increase the authorities' ability to control the growth in the money supply, the Bank of England and the Treasury began a review of their monetary control procedures. This was published in March 1980 as an official discussion paper entitled *Monetary Control* and after its publication the following changes took place:

(i) The supplementary special deposits scheme was abolished in June 1980.

(ii) The reserve asset ratio was reduced from 12½ per cent to 10 per cent in January 1981, and further reduced to 8 per cent during March and April.

(iii) In the latter part of 1980 the Bank of England began to modify its methods of operating in the short-term money markets to allow for greater flexibility in short-term interest rates. In particular the Bank began to place much more emphasis on open-market operations and less on last resort lending to the discount houses.

The Changes Introduced in August 1981

A Bank of England paper entitled *Monetary Control—Provisions* was issued at the beginning of August 1981 and set out the new monetary control arrangements which took effect later that month. The main elements of the system are:

(i) The reserve asset ratio has been abolished.

(ii) The clearing banks' agreement to hold 1½ per cent of their eligible liabilities in interest-free balances at the Bank of England (a requirement of *Competition and Credit Control*) has been replaced by an obligation on all banks in the monetary sector (see (viii) below) to hold 0.45 per cent of their eligible liabilities in interest-free non-operational accounts at the Bank of England. (This requirement does not apply to institutions with eligible liabilities below £10 million and is set at only ¼ per cent for banks in Northern Ireland.) In addition the clearing banks must keep a small proportion of their funds with the Bank interest free to enable them to settle their day-to-day clearing differences with one another.

(iii) The Bank of England has discontinued the practice of continuously posting a minimum lending rate. However, the authorities have reserved the right to announce in advance the minimum lending rate which the Bank would apply to any lending in the market.

(iv) The Bank's operational aim in the money markets is to keep very short-term interest rates within an unpublished band. This band is changed from time to time but only with the approval of the Chancellor of the Exchequer. In setting the band the authorities mainly take into account the growth of monetary aggregates and conditions in the foreign exchange market.

(v) The Bank of England's intervention in the money market continues to be conducted in the bill markets through the discount houses. To ensure that there is an adequate supply of bills for these operations, the Bank has increased considerably the number of banks 'eligible' to have their acceptances discounted with it. (In 1988 the Bank announced that it was extending the range of parties with whom it is willing to enter into a money market dealing relationship. Such new parties could include specially established subsidiary companies of banks.)

(vi) In order to ensure the efficient functioning of the bill market, 'eligible' banks are expected to maintain an average of 4 per cent and a minimum of $2\frac{1}{2}$ per cent of their eligible liabilities in the form of secured loans with the discount market. (In 1986 these requirements were formally ended, but eligible banks were asked not to make significant changes in their liquidity policies.)

(vii) The special deposits scheme has been retained and applies to all institutions in the monetary sector with eligible liabilities of £10 million or more.

(viii) A new 'monetary sector' has been defined to include: (a) all authorized institutions (under the Banking Act 1987); (b) banks in the Isle of Man and Channel Islands participating in the cash ratio scheme; (c) the Banking Department of the Bank of England.

(ix) The Bank of England has received assurances from those institutions which complied with the reserve asset ratio that they will not change the management of their liquidity, nor its composition, without prior discussion with the Bank.

The effects of the monetary control arrangements are:

(a) A greater flexibility in interest rates with more scope for market forces to influence them. However, despite the suspension of the minimum lending rate, the Bank of England is able to influence interest rates, especially the very short-term rates (up to seven days) by its operations in the money market, involving transactions in bills with the discount houses.

(b) The abolition of the $1\frac{1}{2}$ per cent cash ratio deposit, which applied to the clearing banks only, and the requirement that all institutions in the monetary sector (except for those with eligible liabilities below £10 million) are to hold 0.45 per cent of their eligible liabilities in non-operational balances at the Bank of England, has altered the asset structure of bank balance sheets and made the system fairer to the clearing banks.

(c) The abolition of the reserve asset ratio removed the formal 'asset structure' of bank balance sheets: now banks discuss with the Bank of England any changes they propose to make in their liquidity management (see below) and the composition of their liquid assets.

(d) The increase in the number of eligible banks has created a larger market in bank bills.

(e) The abolition in 1980 of the supplementary special deposits scheme has given banks greater flexibility in their lending operations, for instance in the development of mortgage loans.

In 1982 the Bank of England issued a paper entitled *The Measurement of Liquidity*. As we have already noted (see Unit 7.7) this provides for different percentages of asset cover against the different liabilities found on a bank's balance sheet. Thus a greater percentage of liquid assets is required to cover short-term liabilities, such as current account credit balances and deposit account balances, than longer-term liabilities, such as fixed-term deposits. The Bank of England's approach to bank liquidity is not to impose an across-the-board liquidity ratio, but to ensure that individual banks maintain sufficient liquidity, taking into consideration the particular circumstances of each bank. The Bank of England also concerns itself with the other companies contained within a banking group—the finance company and trust company for example. Thus a British bank has to demonstrate to the Bank of England that its subsidiaries conform to the rules on adequacy of capital, liquidity and exposure to large, individual risks.

A recent development (1988) is an agreement on common standards of capital adequacy for commercial banks in the leading industrial countries of the world. This agreement provides (*a*) a common definition of capital, (*b*) a common system of 'risk-weighting' (as outlined above) to apply to bank balance sheets, and (*c*) a standard minimum capital equal to 8 per cent of risk-weighted assets. Once this agreement is in force, it means that most world banks will operate to the same balance sheet standards.

18.7 Questions

1. Why should a Government wish to control the supply of money?

2. (i) Explain why different monetary aggregates are used in Britain, and (ii) list the main components of M0 and M3.

3. How can the Government finance its borrowing requirement? Choosing any one way, indicate by means of simple balance sheets whether or not it will increase the money supply.

4. Describe the techniques of monetary control available to the authorities in Britain.

5. What changes were introduced by the *Monetary Control* measures of 1981? Why were they introduced?

6. How does the Bank of England influence the level of interest rates? What is the effect of lowering or raising interest rates?

Parallel Money Markets and Other Financial Markets

19.1 Introduction

In Unit 6 we considered the role of money markets and, in particular, that of the discount market. However, during the last thirty years a new range of markets has developed alongside the traditional discount market, which deal in wholesale (large) amounts of funds and are known as *parallel* or *secondary money markets* (see Fig. 6.2, p. 60). They deal in sterling and other currencies and, like the discount market, they consist of specialists who bring together those who wish to borrow funds and those who have funds to lend. Also like the discount market there is no 'market place' and business is conducted by telephone and telex, but unlike the discount market there is no lender of last resort. Transactions on these markets are supervised by the Bank of England, under the terms of the Financial Services Act 1986.

The parallel money markets consist principally of:

Sterling	*Other currencies*
1. Local authority	1. Certificate of deposit
2. Inter-bank	2. Eurocurrency
3. Finance house	
4. Inter-company	
5. Sterling commercial paper	
6. Certificate of deposit	

Dealings on these markets are carried through in one of two ways: either directly between the banks, financial institutions and companies involved in the market, or indirectly using money brokers who bring lenders and borrowers together and charge a commission for their services. In the rest of this Unit we shall consider the different parallel money markets and the various functions they perform.

Two other financial markets are also considered in this Unit. These are the foreign exchange market and the financial futures market.

19.2 Local Authority Money Market

This was the first of the sterling parallel markets to come into existence, being established in 1955. As its name suggests, it is a market which brings together local authorities seeking short-term finance and institutions—not necessarily themselves local authorities—that have funds to lend. Until 1955 local authorities borrowed from the central Government almost entirely through its agency the Public Works Loan Board. During 1955, in an attempt to reduce the borrowing of local authorities, the Government limited the amount of funds that could be obtained through the Board. To get round the restrictions, local authorities borrowed increasing amounts from banks, other financial institutions and companies in the private sector and thus the market in short-term local authority finance was established. When funds are borrowed on this market a deposit receipt is issued; normally loans are repayable at either two or seven days' notice, although some are for longer periods such as three months. The smallest amount lent on this market is usually £25 000.

19.3   Sterling Inter-bank Market

This market was formed in the late 1950s, soon after the local authority market, and is a market in sterling funds in which the banks are the main participants, either lending to other banks or borrowing from them. We saw in Unit 6.5 that the banks lend part of their surplus short-term funds to the discount market; following the formation of the local authority market, the banks found that they had an alternative 'home' for short-term funds. Soon the idea of a further alternative money market came into being, and some of the non-clearing banks started to lend and borrow among themselves instead of going through the discount market; this was the beginning of the inter-bank market. Prior to the *Competition and Credit Control* measures of 1971, the clearing banks did not directly participate in the market because of the reserve ratios that they alone had to maintain at that time (see Unit 18.6); they found it more advantageous to use the discount market and other traditional categories of short-term assets. Instead, they used their money market subsidiaries to deal in this market, as these subsidiaries were not subject to requirements concerning reserve ratios and therefore could use more of their funds for lending purposes. When, in 1971, all banks became subject to the same reserve asset requirements, the clearing banks joined in the market.

It is a short-term market with most funds being lent on an overnight basis but, exceptionally, loans may go up to five years. The loans are large with a minimum of about £250 000 and lending is normally unsecured; the bank making the loan relies on the good name of the borrower, but in practice banks usually limit the maximum amount that may be lent to an individual borrower. The rates of interest on this market for money repayable at call are usually higher than those on the discount market: this is because the rates offered by the discount houses reflect the lower yields on the assets in which they invest. Despite this rate advantage of the inter-bank market, the banks still place a substantial proportion of their surplus funds with the discount market because money at call with the London money market is a highly suitable liquid asset.

Interest rates charged to company customers of the banks are increasingly being related to the rates on the inter-bank market; rates are now often linked to LIBOR (the London inter-bank offered rate) rather than to the bank's base rate. LIBOR is a more accurate indicator of the cost of money to the banks, because of the way in which interest rates on the inter-bank market are determined by the balance between supply and demand (see also Unit 9.6(*e*)).

19.4   Finance House Market

This is a small parallel market in which the borrowers are finance houses and hire-purchase companies. The lenders are banks, other financial institutions, companies and a few private individuals. Since the recognition by the Bank of England of most of the larger finance houses as banks the market has contracted considerably, and much of its business now passes through the inter-bank market.

19.5   Inter-company Market

This market has its origins in the tight restrictions imposed by the authorities on the growth of bank lending in the late 1960s. It involves a company with surplus funds lending to another company which wishes to borrow.

Business is transacted by money brokers—who act as middlemen between borrower and lender—and normally loans are only made to the top five hundred companies. The minimum loan involved is £50 000, with sums of £250 000 or larger being dealt in. Loans are generally made for any period from three months to five years and a broker will agree the terms for each individual loan to suit both the borrower and the lender. The market makes substantial use of bank guarantees in an attempt to overcome the difficulties encountered with regard to the status and creditworthiness of borrowers.

19.6   Sterling Commercial Paper Market

This market began in London in 1986. Commercial paper takes the form of unsecured promissory notes (in effect 'I.O.U.s') with a fixed maturity, usually between seven days and three months. The notes are issued as bearer securities and are sold at a discount to their face value. The issuers are industrial and commercial companies and the paper is sold either directly to institutional investors or through the intermediary of a bank or securities dealer. These intermediaries make a market in commercial paper by buying or selling at the market price.

Issuers have to be companies quoted on the Stock Exchange and must have net assets of at least £50 million. Paper must be issued in minimum denominations of £500 000, and maturities must be between seven and 364 days. The advantage of the market to issuers is that they may be able to borrow more cheaply than through other means of finance.

19.7   Sterling Certificate of Deposit Market

A certificate of deposit (Fig. 19.1) is a certificate issued by a bank or other financial institution (including building societies) acknowledging that a

Fig. 19.1   A sterling certificate of deposit

deposit has been made for a fixed period of time at a fixed rate of interest. The minimum amount accepted for sterling certificates is £50 000, larger sums being accepted in multiples of £10 000. The certificates are negotiable and payable to bearer which means that the title to them can pass freely from one person to another by *delivery* of the certificate. The rate of interest is fixed for the time period until maturity and certificates are usually issued for stated periods between three months and five years. Interest on certificates issued for a period of one year or less is paid on maturity with the capital sum; interest on certificates issued for longer periods is payable annually. The advantage to a bank of the certificate of deposit system is that it has the use of the money for the fixed time period and only has to repay on maturity of the certificate; this helps it to plan its future medium-term lending as it knows what funds are available and when they are due for repayment. For the depositor there are two advantages: firstly, the fixed rate of interest payable for the time period of the deposit and, secondly, that should the funds be needed urgently, the certificate can be sold on the certificate of deposit market. Thus, from the depositor's point of view, the certificate is more flexible than a term deposit with a bank which the bank is not obliged to repay before the due date.

As certificates are negotiable, they are an ideal way for banks and other financial institutions, companies and individuals to invest large sums of surplus money. The sterling certificate of deposit market consists of the discount houses, banks and money brokers who buy certificates from existing holders and sell to new holders. The discount houses and the banks may choose to hold certificates purchased as investments until maturity; the money brokers, by contrast, act as specialist middlemen and buy and sell only for clients.

19.8   How the Sterling Parallel Markets Intermesh

The sterling parallel markets do not work in isolation from each other—lenders to each market are often the same and an example transaction will give an idea of how the markets intermesh.

(i) Worldwide Chemicals, a large industrial company with surplus funds available, lends £250 000 to National Barllands Bank for six months, and the bank issues a sterling certificate of deposit.

(ii) The bank, considering what it may do with the funds, looks at the local authority market but decides that the rates are too low; instead, it lends the money for seven days on the inter-bank market to a bank that is short of funds.

(iii) Seven days later the loan is repaid by the bank and National Barllands looks around again: by now rates on the local authority market have improved and the money is lent to a local authority.

(iv) In the meantime, Worldwide Chemicals has brought forward an investment project and needs money quickly. It makes use of the certificate of deposit market, and sells the certificate of deposit issued by the bank to a discount house.

(v) The discount house may either hold the certificate of deposit to maturity or sell it to another holder on the market.

(vi) Upon maturity of the certificate, the holder, whether the discount house or some subsequent holder, presents it at National Barllands Bank to receive the proceeds.

19.9   Foreign Currency Certificate of Deposit Market

Certificates of deposit designated in foreign currencies are becoming more and more common. However, it was the dollar certificate of deposit that started the market and, today, this still remains the major denomination within it.

Dollar certificates of deposit were first issued in the United States during the early 1960s, and were introduced to the London market by the American banks in 1966. Since then most other banks have started to make their own issues and the American banks now account for only about half of the total amount outstanding. Like a sterling certificate of deposit, a dollar certificate is an acknowledgement by a bank of a deposit placed for an agreed period of time at a fixed rate of interest, but the currency of the deposit is dollars; again like their sterling counterparts, dollar certificates are negotiable. The dollar certificate of deposit market has developed as a secondary market where these securities may be bought and sold. The main participants in the market are discount houses, American banks and several United States and Canadian securities houses.

19.10   Eurocurrency Market

This is an international market in short- and medium-term money, of which London has become a leading world centre. The prefix *euro-* often causes confusion as it seems to suggest that the market is confined to Europe, but this is misleading; while most of the market's business is transacted in Europe, there are other centres and it has now become world-wide. For a currency to become 'euro-', it must be available for deposit or loan in a country in which it is not the domestic currency. Eurocurrency deposits are, therefore, deposits held by banks in one country in the currency of another; similarly eurocurrency loans are made by banks in one country in the currency of another. For example, eurodollars are deposits with, or loans by, banks outside the United States of US dollars; eurosterling is the deposit with, or loans by, banks outside Britain of sterling.

Any currency can become 'euro-', but the market in eurodollars was the first and remains the most important. It originated in the early 1950s when a number of eastern European banks wished to disguise their ownership of dollar deposits and placed them with correspondent banks, particularly in Britain and France. The correspondent banks began to make use of these and other dollar deposits by offering dollar loans at lower rates of interest than those ruling in the United States. Further impetus was given to the development of the market as a result of an American banking control, 'Regulation Q', which held down deposit rates in the United States but which did not apply to dollars accepted from non-residents by American banks operating outside the States. This led to the development of a series of overseas branches by American banks, particularly in London, to obtain a share of this business; European banks soon began to compete for these deposits as well. The 1958 relaxation of exchange controls in west European countries, which gave banks and businesses greater freedom of capital financing, contributed to creating the right conditions for the establishment of London as the major centre of the market. Besides the dollar, the other principal eurocurrencies are sterling, Deutschmarks, Swiss francs, Dutch guilders and Canadian dollars.

A eurocurrency transaction involves a bank outside the country of origin of a currency attracting a deposit or granting a loan in that currency. The eurocurrency market involves bringing together those who have currencies to lend and those who wish to borrow in those currencies; it is essentially a 'wholesale' market dealing with large sums of money on a short-term basis—most borrowing is for six months or less, although there is also a medium-term element in the market where borrowing can go up to five years. The market is inter-bank (or 'bank-to-bank'); a company with eurocurrency funds cannot directly place them on the market but must deposit them with a bank, and equally a company wishing to borrow must go through a bank. The lending between banks is unsecured and, as in the sterling inter-bank market, limits are set on the maximum amount to be lent to any one bank.

The market has expanded enormously since its origins in the 1950s, partly because it is free from national restrictions on the transfer of funds and from differences in interest rate structures between countries, and partly because it meets so well the needs of multinational corporations, nationalized industries and governments who need large-scale, world-wide finance at reasonable cost. As the amounts borrowed and lent are large—on the eurodollar market the minimum transaction is usually $1 million—the market can operate on smaller margins between the borrowing and lending rate than is possible in domestic banking. Since the market is free from control by national Governments there are no reserve requirements and therefore funds do not have to be tied up in low-yielding reserve assets; a greater proportion of each deposit can thus be 'lent on'. Moreover, since funds are deposited for a fixed time, lending can be matched to the maturity of deposits and so the banks operating in the market can work with very small reserves.

While the eurocurrency market is concerned with the provision of short- and medium-term loans, a market has developed in the provision of longer-term international finance—the *eurobond market*. Loans in this market are issued by consortium banks (see Unit 5.6) and issuing houses in Europe, and are designated in dollars, Deutschmarks and other continental currencies. The borrowers on this market are governments, nationalized industries, municipal authorities, building societies and multinational corporations. The method of issue is for banks in the consortium handling the loan to place the bonds with their customers and other banks in their own country. When the issue has been successfully placed, an advertisement is put in various newspapers announcing it, as required by law: this describes the issue and lists the names of the participating banks. Eurobonds can be traded in a limited secondary market that has developed in London and Luxembourg, which is run by a small group of banks and stockbrokers.

19.11   Other Financial Markets

(a) The Foreign Exchange Market

Most people are familiar with the way in which the news is reported that 'on the *foreign exchange market* the pound closed against the dollar at 1.41' (the figure changing daily of course). The foreign exchange market is a market for the purchase and sale of foreign currencies. Like the other money markets it does not have a fixed market place; instead it operates by telephone, telex and cable communications between the participants. It is not a market that deals in actual banknotes or travellers' cheques, apart from very limited transactions; instead it deals in the transfer of sums of money in different currencies from one financial centre to another. Exchange rates between one currency and another are the prices at which these sums of money change hands.

It is often necessary to make payment in a foreign currency when involved with international transactions. Thus an importer in the United Kingdom who is buying goods abroad will require foreign currency in order to make payment, that is, he requires a bank deposit in the supplier's currency and can then offer the supplier his own currency in payment for the goods. Such transactions are effected in the foreign exchange market.

The banks are the main participants in the market, operating partly on behalf of their customers and partly on their own account. There are also specialist firms of foreign exchange brokers within the market whose function is to bring buyers and sellers of foreign exchange together, for which service they charge a brokerage fee. The customers of the market include smaller United Kingdom banks, foreign banks, central banks, overseas governments and companies from all over the world.

The dealers on the foreign exchange market work in the world's major currencies. They are willing to quote their buying and selling rates for delivery now (known as a *spot* rate), for delivery at an agreed future date or for delivery within an agreed period in the future (a *forward* rate). A spot rate quoted by a dealer may be as follows:

US $1.39–1.40

The dealer will follow the 'golden rule' of foreign exchange which is to *sell low: buy high*. Thus the dealer will sell at US $1.39 and will buy at US $1.40. The difference between the two rates represents the dealer's 'turn' or profit on the transaction. Rates quoted by dealers on the foreign exchange markets are for wholesale (large) amounts of currency. A similar range of rates can be seen on display in most bank branches for retail transactions such as the buying or selling of foreign currency or travellers' cheques. However, the difference between these rates will be wider than on the foreign exchange markets because of the nature of the transaction: it is of low value and comparatively time-consuming.

There is a well-developed forward exchange market for most major currencies such as United States dollars, Deutschmarks, Swiss francs and Japanese yen, and deals can be made for delivery anything up to five years in the future. Other currencies can also be bought or sold forward, but there may be limitations both as to the amount and the time period. Forward rates are quoted either at a premium or at a discount to the spot rate or sometimes at *par* (that is, the same as the spot rate). The forward rate is calculated by either deducting a premium or adding a discount. For example:

Spot rate	US $1.39–1.40
One month forward	0.25–0.20 cents premium

Thus a dealer would quote a buying rate for delivery of the United States dollar in one month's time of:

Spot rate	1.40
Less	0.0020 pm (premium)

US $1.3980

(Note that the premium is 0.20 cents, that is, one-fifth of a cent.)

The dealer's forward selling rate is:

Spot rate	1.39
Less	0.0025 pm (premium)

US $1.3875

Thus a forward premium makes the foreign currency more expensive in the forward markets against the home currency. In a similar way a forward discount is added to spot rate, so making the foreign currency cheaper in the forward markets against the home currency. It is important to note that forward premiums and discounts are based chiefly on interest-rate differentials for the currencies concerned—forward exchange rates are *not* estimates made by dealers of spot rates in the future.

The existence of the forward market is particularly important for companies engaged in international trade because it allows them to work out in advance the cost of imports to be paid for in foreign currency in terms of their home currency; likewise, the amount of revenues to be received in foreign currency can be determined in advance.

As mentioned earlier in this section, the exchange rate between two currencies represents a price. In some economies, the exchange rate is fixed by administrative decision but the exchange rates between major world currencies, such as the United States dollar, the pound sterling and the Deutschmark are market-determined, that is, they are traded freely and find their own levels as determined by the market forces of supply and demand. The following factors will have some bearing upon these market-determined rates:

Confidence in a country's economy: economic news usually has a fairly immediate effect on rates of exchange—news about a country's money supply and the impact of oil prices are two factors which will have a particularly marked effect.

Inflation rates: these are often an indication of a country's economic well-being and a large unexpected increase in the rate of inflation would have an adverse effect on exchange rates.

Balance of payments: a balance of payments surplus will create a demand for the country's currency which will increase in value in terms of other currencies. One of the reasons for this is that there is more money flowing into the country than is coming out of it. Conversely a country suffering a balance of payments deficit will find that its currency weakens.

Interest rates: international investors are very conscious of interest-rate differentials between countries and their funds will be attracted to centres where high interest rates prevail, provided that the currency of the country is thought to be stable.

Other factors: political events within a country—civil war, civil disobedience or a failure to pay interest on international debts for example—will have a marked effect on the country's currency in the foreign exchange markets.

While the above factors help to produce a market-determined rate, support for a particular currency may be given by the central bank of the country. This would normally be carried out by the central bank entering the foreign exchange market to buy the home currency and sell foreign currency from its reserves with the objective of maintaining the value of the home currency. Such action also works in reverse when a particular currency is appreciating too rapidly: the central bank will sell the home currency and buy foreign currencies to add to the reserves. In the United Kingdom, the Bank of England occasionally intervenes in the foreign exchange market to smooth out excessive exchange rate fluctuations in sterling, and uses the Exchange Equalization Account for this purpose (see Unit 4.7).

(b) The London International Financial Futures Exchange (LIFFE)

A financial future is a contract to buy or sell certain forms of money at a specified future date, with the price agreed at the time of the deal. Under such a contract, if the market price of the financial instrument concerned should be higher on the delivery date than the price specified in the contract, or if its yield should be lower, the seller undertakes to meet the difference and, by collecting this, the buyer can obtain a price or yield which is settled at the time the contract is agreed. Conversely, if the market price of the financial instrument should be lower or its yield higher than is specified in the contract, the seller will gain and the buyer will lose the difference: but at least the buyer still has the comfort of knowing the price or yield in advance, as it was fixed at the date the contract was entered into.

The *London International Financial Futures Exchange* brings together those buyers and sellers who wish to hedge against interest rate and exchange rate fluctuations. On the exchange, 'standard' agreements (or contracts), are available for:

 (i) interest rate movements—by trading interest-bearing securities, such as bank deposit certificates in sterling or eurodollars, gilt-edged stocks and United States Treasury Bonds;

 (ii) exchange rate fluctuations—by trading a range of currencies, for example the United States dollar against the pound sterling, the United States dollar against the Swiss franc and so on.

On LIFFE, in order to make the contracts more tradable and to enable keener prices to be quoted, a limited range of standard contracts is available with fixed settlement dates. For example, the contract size for sterling bank deposit certificates is £500 000 with delivery on the second Wednesday of the delivery month which could be March, June, September or December.

With a contract covering the movement of interest rates, the market brings together those who wish to take delivery of specific financial instruments at a specified date in the future at a fixed rate of interest, with those who are prepared to supply the same financial instrument on the same terms. Similarly, with a contract covering exchange rate fluctuations, the market brings together those who wish to sell a stated amount of a certain foreign currency at an agreed future date, and those who wish to buy on the same terms. Two examples of the way in which a LIFFE contract might be of use to business are as follows:

(i) A company knows that, upon completion of a major contract, it will have a large sum of money available for short-term investment at a certain date in the future. Fearing that there will be a general fall in interest rates before the money is received, the company can use a LIFFE contract to 'lock in' to a known rate of interest by buying futures contracts in, for example, sterling bank deposit certificates for delivery in three months' time. If the general level of interest rates does fall, the investing company will be able to sell the futures contracts at a higher price than it paid. The profit made will offset the lower rates of interest now obtainable and will thus preserve the return on the short-term funds. If the general level of interest rates has increased, the investing company will sell the futures contracts at a lower price than it paid: the loss made will be offset against the higher rate of interest now payable, but will have preserved the return on the short-term funds.

(ii) A United Kingdom company knows it will have to pay an amount in United States dollars at a certain date in the future. It is concerned that, by the date of payment, sterling will buy fewer dollars. Therefore it buys sufficient futures contracts for delivery on the date of payment at an exchange rate agreed at the time of purchase.

Besides the contracts mentioned above, *currency options contracts* are available through LIFFE for a limited range of currencies. These give companies the right to buy or sell currencies at a fixed rate at a specified future date and thus provide protection for exporters and importers against volatile exchange rates. Unlike purchases of forward currency through a bank (see Unit 19.10(*a*)), they give the right, but not the obligation, to complete the deal. A further contract available is linked to the FT–SE 100 Index (Financial Times–Stock Exchange Index of 100 leading shares): this provides for a hedge against stock market movements.

Membership of LIFFE is made up of United Kingdom and overseas banks, discount houses, stockbrokers, commodity brokers and a few individuals. Only members of the exchange can deal, and so commercial companies wishing to buy or sell a futures contract must do so through LIFFE. Once a deal is made on the floor of the exchange, details are passed through the clearing house by both buyer and seller (Fig. 19.2). At the same time 'an initial margin', which represents a small proportion of the contract value, has to be paid—this is usually about £1 000–£1 500 for each contract. A buyer who does not wish to complete a buying contract before delivery may close it out by entering into an identical selling contract on the market. In practice the majority of LIFFE contracts are closed out in this way. The clearing house,

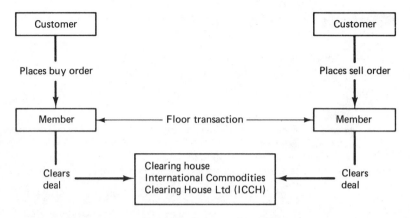

Fig. 19.2   Outline procedures for a LIFFE transaction

called International Commodities Clearing House Ltd (ICCH), is partly owned by some of the large banks, and is independent of LIFFE.

A financial futures contract is of considerable value to those who wish to hedge against future movements principally in interest rate and exchange rate fluctuations. In addition currency options contracts and the FT–SE 100 Index allow a hedge against exchange rate and stock market movements respectively. The disadvantage of LIFFE is that only a limited range of contracts is available and contracts are of fixed sizes; however, both of these points do provide tradable contracts with keen prices.

The advantage of LIFFE contracts is that they can be closed out (that is, they do not have to be completed) at any time by the buyer or the seller entering into an identical matching contract. This is in contrast to a forward exchange contract, for example, which is a legal contract between the customer and the bank which has to be completed between those two parties. However, the traditional bank forward exchange contract offers greater flexibility to exporters and importers than do LIFFE contracts. This is because, as we have seen, LIFFE contracts are for a very limited range of currencies and are for fixed contract amounts.

19.12   Questions

1. Describe the markets that make up the parallel money market.

2. Explain the main factors that affect the rate of exchange between two currencies.

3. Examine the role of the London International Financial Futures Exchange (LIFFE).

Multiple-choice Questions—10

Read each question carefully. Choose the *one* answer you think is correct. Answers are given on page 390.

1. Added to M3 to give M3c are:

   A sterling time bank deposits held by the United Kingdom private sector
   B private sector holdings of building society shares and deposits and sterling certificates of deposit
   C notes and coin in circulation with the public
   D foreign currency bank deposits held by the United Kingdom private sector

2. M4 and M5 are wider measures of the money stock. What are added to M4 to give M5?

   A private sector holdings of building society shares and deposits and sterling certificates of deposit
   B building society holdings of bank deposits and bank certificates of deposit, and notes and coin
   C foreign currency bank deposits held by the United Kingdom private sector
   D private sector holdings of money market instruments, certificates of tax deposit and national savings instruments

3. The Government decides to finance PSBR (public sector borrowing requirement) by issuing National Savings securities, such as Premium Savings Bonds and National Savings certificates. What ultimate effect will this have on the money supply?

   A it will increase
   B it will decrease
   C there will be no change
   D there will be an increase in M0, but not in M3

4. 'Banks should increase lending to manufacturing industries.' A statement such as this, issued by the Bank of England, is known as:

   A a quantitative directive   C a qualitative directive
   B the release of special deposits   D funding

5. When Government securities are sold by the monetary authorities on the open market:

   A the money supply decreases
   B the money supply increases
   C the money supply remains unchanged
   D M1 is not affected

6. The *Monetary Control* measures of 1981:

   A introduced the special deposits scheme
   B required banks to be 'recognized' by the Bank of England
   C required banks to hold 8 per cent of all deposits in the form of cash
   D abolished the reserve asset ratio

7. On the sterling inter-bank market most funds are lent:

   A overnight   C at three months' notice
   B at seven days' notice   D long-term

8. Sterling certificates of deposit:

   A are issued by Government departments
   B are negotiable instruments
   C are repayable on demand
   D have a life of 91 days

9. Eurocurrency deposits are:

   A held by banks in one country in the currency of another
   B held by banks in Europe
   C bank deposits designated in the common currency of the European
      Community
   D bank deposits in dollars

10. The spot rate of United States dollars is 1.35–1.36; the three-month premium is
    0.35–0.40 cents. What is the rate at which a bank would buy dollars under a
    three-month fixed forward contract?

    A 1.3640   B 1.3535   C 1.3560   D 1.3465

Bills of Exchange and Cheques: Further Aspects

20.1 Introduction

We have already looked at negotiable instruments, and in particular bills of exchange and cheques, in Unit 11. It would be helpful to look back at that Unit and remind yourself of some of the aspects covered. To summarize two points:

(*a*) The characteristics of a negotiable instrument are:

(i) the document must be transferable by delivery or by endorsement and delivery;

(ii) the legal title passes to the person who takes it in good faith and for value and without notice of any defect in the title of the transferor;

(iii) the legal holder for the time being can sue in his own name;

(iv) notice of transfer need not be given to the party/parties liable on the instrument;

(v) the title passes free from equities or counter-claims between previous parties of which the transferee has no notice.

(*b*) The parties to a bill of exchange and cheque are:

(i) the drawer—the person who has drawn or written out the bill or cheque;

(ii) the drawee—the person on whom it is drawn and who has to make payment (with cheques a bank is the drawee);

(iii) the payee—the person to whom the money is to be paid.

Note: Bills of exchange, except for those payable 'at sight' or 'on demand', must be presented for acceptance by the drawee who accepts the obligation of payment by signing his or her name across the face of the bill—henceforth, he or she is known as the 'acceptor'.

20.2 Types of Holder

A *holder* is defined in section 2 of the Bills of Exchange Act 1882 as 'the payee or endorsee of a bill in possession of it, or the bearer thereof'. A person cannot become the holder of a bill where there has been a forged endorsement. Holders may be classified as follows:

(*a*) Holder in Due Course
Under Section 29 of the Bills of Exchange Act a holder in due course is one who has taken a bill:

(i) which is complete and regular on the face of it ('face' includes the back!);

(ii) before it was overdue;

(iii) without notice of prior defect in title at the time the bill was negotiated to him;

(iv) without notice of previous dishonour, if such was the fact;

(v) in good faith and for value.

Every holder of a bill is deemed to be a holder in due course until the contrary is proved, but the original payee can never be a holder in due course.

The holder in due course is the person in the strongest position to enforce the bill and, therefore, if a bank can set itself up as such, it has a right of recovery from any party on the bill or cheque (or other negotiable instrument). The bank must satisfy all the conditions of a holder in due course: one of these conditions is that *value* must have been given *by the bank*. Value is given by a bank under the following circumstances:

(*a*) when the bank cashes a cheque drawn on another bank;

(*b*) when the customer is allowed, by agreement with the bank, to draw against uncleared effects;

(*c*) when the bank takes a cheque which is used specifically to reduce a loan or an overdraft;

(*d*) when the bank has a lien (see Unit 21.4) on a cheque—this arises if a cheque is returned unpaid which would create an overdraft on the customer's account if it were now debited to it.

As already mentioned, there must be no prior forgery on the bill or cheque because no one can become a holder through a forged endorsement.

(*b*) Holder for Value

Section 27 of the 1882 Act defines a holder for value as 'the holder of a bill for which value has at some time been given'. Notice that the value need not necessarily have been given by the *present* holder. For example, if a payee of a bill or a cheque received in settlement of a debt endorses it and then hands it over as a gift, the recipient is a holder for value even though he or she has given no value, because value had been given to establish the original debt.

20.3 Rights and Duties of a Holder

We have seen in the previous section that a holder in due course is the person in the strongest position to enforce the bill. Such a holder can sue on the bill in his own name, and his title will not be affected by the defects in title of earlier holders of the bill (although, of course, this does not apply if there has been a prior forgery). Where a person cannot establish himself as a holder in due course, his title will be subject to earlier defects in title.

The duties of a holder are:

(i) to present the bill for payment at the due time and place;

(ii) to present it for payment within a reasonable time where the bill is payable on demand;

(iii) to give notice of dishonour if the bill is dishonoured which, in some cases, may require the bill to be noted and protested (see Unit 11.6).

20.4   Liability of Parties

(*a*) **The Acceptor**
The primary liability on the bill rests with the drawee once he has accepted the bill, that is when the drawee becomes the acceptor. When a bill is dishonoured either by non-acceptance or non-payment, other parties to the bill become liable.

(*b*) **The Drawer**
The drawer is primarily liable on the bill until it is accepted (if it is a term bill) and the drawer is also liable to pay the holder if the bill is dishonoured. Furthermore, the drawer must compensate any endorser who has had to pay on the bill because of dishonour, provided that proper notice of dishonour was given.

(*c*) **The Endorser** (that is, any person who has endorsed the bill)
An endorser is liable to pay the holder if the bill is dishonoured, or to compensate any subsequent endorser who has had to pay on the bill, because of dishonour, provided that proper notice of dishonour was given. He then has the right to claim against any previous endorser (including the payee) and against the drawer.

20.5   Cheques

As we saw in Unit 11.7, a cheque is defined by the Bills of Exchange Act 1882 as 'a bill of exchange drawn on a banker and payable on demand'. Thus cheques are important types of bills of exchange and a holder of a cheque can be a holder in due course in exactly the same way as for a bill of exchange, and has the same rights.

A bank often acts as an agent for its customer when it collects the proceeds of cheques paid in that are drawn on other banks and branches. However, the *collecting bank* can also be a holder or a holder in due course: in the case of a holder in due course all the circumstances must be met—see Unit 20.2(*a*). In particular, value must be given and, as we have already seen, examples of this occur when the cheque paid in is used to reduce the customer's overdraft or the bank allows the customer, by agreement, to draw against uncleared effects. The collecting bank can, under these circumstances, still set itself up as a holder in due course, even though the customer has not endorsed the cheque.

If a cheque is dishonoured by non-payment, the holder has similar rights as for bills of exchange: the holder may sue the drawer of the cheque and any previous endorsers. An endorser who is forced to pay in this way may then sue the drawer and any endorser before himself. A drawer may be able to sue the drawee bank if the cheque has been wrongfully dishonoured. It is important to appreciate that the drawer of a cheque is liable to a holder in due course, even if the cheque has been stolen at some time and a 'stop payment' placed upon the cheque. The way to avoid such liability—however remote the possibility— is to cross each cheque 'not negotiable', and thus it is no longer a negotiable instrument; many cheque books are already pre-printed with such a crossing.

20.6   Protection for Banks

The danger for a bank is that if, as a result of fraud, theft or forgery, money is paid to a person who is not the true owner of the cheque, and *conversion* takes place, the true owner will look either to the paying bank or to the collecting bank for recompense.

(a) The Paying Bank

Where payment of a cheque has been made to the wrong person, the paying bank is liable to compensate the true owner and cannot debit the customer's account, unless the bank can claim certain protection against liability. Protection for the paying bank is to be found in the Bills of Exchange Act 1882 and the Cheques Act 1957, as follows:

(i) **Section 1, Cheques Act 1957.** This gives protection to a paying bank that *pays a cheque which is not properly endorsed* (that is, it has no endorsement or an irregular endorsement), provided that it has done so in good faith and in the ordinary course of business: then the bank is entitled to debit the customer's account for the amount. The payment must be in accordance with the customer's instructions and in the ordinary course of business (during normal business hours and in accordance with the crossing, if any).

(ii) **Section 60, Bills of Exchange Act 1882.** This section gives particular protection to a bank that *pays a cheque with a forged endorsement* (but not where the signature of the drawer has been forged), provided that the bank has acted in good faith, and in the ordinary course of business. This protection applies both to open and crossed cheques.

(iii) **Section 80, Bills of Exchange Act 1882.** Here protection is given to a bank that *pays a crossed cheque*, which has been received in the clearing or by special presentation, in accordance with the crossing, in good faith and without negligence. The bank is deemed to be in the same position as if it had paid the true owner.

(b) The Collecting Bank

The collecting bank may be liable for conversion if it collects money on a cheque for someone other than the true owner. Under such circumstances the bank will be liable to compensate the true owner unless it can obtain the protection of section 4 of the Cheques Act 1957, or can set itself up as a holder in due course.

(i) **Section 4, Cheques Act 1957.** This protects a bank where, in good faith *and* without negligence:

(*a*) it receives payment for a customer of a cheque, bank draft or other instrument; or

(*b*) having credited a customer's account with the amount of the instrument, the bank receives payment for itself.

If these conditions can be satisfied, the bank incurs no liability to the true owner of the cheque if the customer had no title or a defective title to the cheque. A person is a customer of the bank even if the account has only just been opened for the purpose of paying in the cheque; however, there is no protection where the person for whom the cheque is collected is *not* a customer. The bank must act both in good faith and without negligence: a bank's good faith is taken for granted but, if a cheque is crossed 'account payee', the collecting bank will be negligent if it collects the cheque for another person without making enquiries. In this circumstance the bank will lose the protection of section 4 because, although it has acted in good faith, it has also acted negligently.

(ii) **Holder in due course.** If a bank can establish itself as a holder in due course (see Unit 20.2), the general protection of the Bills of Exchange Act is available, and the bank is placed in a stronger position. Remember that, for a bank to become a holder in due course, value must be given—the customer is allowed to draw against uncleared effects or the cheques paid in are used to reduce a loan or an overdraft, for example.

Negligence and the Collecting Bank

It is difficult to define what constitutes the negligence of the collecting bank and it would be necessary to look at the facts in each case. The test then is whether a *reasonable* bank would have been put on enquiry, and whether the bank did, in fact, make such enquiries. There are two principal situations in which banks have been held to be negligent; these are:

(*a*) where the bank failed to make reasonable enquiries when opening an account—see (i)–(iii) below; and

(*b*) where the collecting bank should have been put on enquiry—see (iv)–(viii) below.

The following are examples of such negligence, together with the name of the major legal case on the particular point:

(i) A failure to obtain the name of the customer's employers—*Lloyds Bank Ltd* v. *E. B. Savory & Co* (1933); *Marfani & Co Ltd* v. *Midland Bank Ltd* (1968) (note that the bank was cleared in this case).

(ii) A failure to make reasonable enquiries about the use of a trading name.

(iii) A failure to make reasonable enquiries when opening an account and/or a failure to obtain references—*Ladbroke* v. *Todd* (1914).

(iv) Allowing cheques payable to a limited company to be credited to the private account of one of the directors—*A. L. Underwood Ltd* v. *Bank of Liverpool and Martins Bank Ltd* (1924).

(v) Crediting cheques to a customer's account when they are clearly payable to the customer as agent for someone else—*Marquess of Bute* v. *Barclays Bank Ltd* (1955).

(vi) A failure to enquire into unusual circumstances, for example a large cheque being paid into an account, inconsistent with the size of normal credits—*Motor Traders Guarantee Corporation Ltd* v. *Midland Bank Ltd* (1937).

(vii) A failure to make enquiries when a cheque crossed 'account payee' is paid in for the credit of an account other than the payee's.

(viii) A failure to make enquiries when an endorsement is clearly irregular.

20.7   Duties of Bank and Customer

We have already seen in Unit 13.1 that the basic relationship between a bank and a customer is that of debtor (the bank) and creditor (the customer); this relationship is reversed when the customer is borrowing from the bank.

In connection with cheques the bank has:

(*a*) a duty to honour cheques; and
(*b*) a duty not to pay without authority.

In addition the bank has a right to expect a customer to exercise reasonable care in drawing cheques. Let us look at each of these in more detail.

(*a*) Duty to Honour Cheques

A bank has a duty to honour its customer's cheques up to the limit of the balance of the customer's account or up to the limit of an agreed overdraft or loan, provided that the cheques are properly drawn, and that there is no other reason why the cheque should not be paid. It is worth noting that a bank must either pay the whole cheque or none of it: thus, if an account has a credit balance of £50 and a cheque is drawn by the customer for £51, the bank is legally entitled to dishonour the cheque. If a bank fails to honour cheques under circumstances when they should have been honoured, the customer can sue the bank for damages: a trader or business person has no need to prove actual loss and the bank would probably have to pay substantial damages for causing damage to the trader's reputation; a private customer, however, would have to show actual loss before being able to claim more than nominal damages.

A bank's duty to honour cheques terminates in the following circumstances:

(i) **On receipt of countermand of payment**, that is, if 'stop' instructions are received. A verbal instruction is sufficient to postpone payment pending receipt of a signed confirmation. However, a bank must normally have written instructions to countermand payment for it to be effective but this requirement is often dispensed with nowadays if a customer fails to answer a letter seeking written instructions. The cheque will be returned to the collecting bank marked 'payment countermanded by the order of the drawer' or 'awaiting confirmation' if the written instructions have not yet been received.

(ii) **On notice of the customer's death or mental disorder.** The bank must have received *notice* for it to be effective: a bank is not liable if notice has not been given.

(iii) **On notice of an act of bankruptcy committed by the customer**, or **on notice of presentation of a bankruptcy petition** against the customer or **on notice of the making of a receiving order in a bankruptcy** against the customer.

(iv) **On notice of a petition for compulsory winding up or a resolution for voluntary winding up**—both of these apply to company customers only.

(v) **On service of a garnishee order.** This may happen where a court has previously ordered the customer to make a payment to a third party and it has not been paid: the garnishee order is usually attached to the account for the amount of the debt.

(*b*) Duty Not to Pay without Authority

A bank is liable to the customer if it pays a cheque without authority—for example, one that has been 'stopped' by the customer, is out of date, is post-dated or bears a forged signature of the drawer. A list of technical irregularities which will cause a bank not to pay a cheque without authority is given in Unit 11.10.

(*c*) Duties of a Customer

A bank has the right to expect a customer to exercise reasonable care in drawing cheques. Where an alteration has been made possible through the customer's negligence, the paying bank is protected. Thus, a cheque which is drawn with the amount shown in figures but not in words and is then altered so that the alteration is *not apparent* incurs no liability for the paying bank. The major case on this point is *London Joint Stock Bank Ltd* v. *Macmillan and Arthur* (1918), the judgement being confirmed in *Joachimson* v. *Swiss Bank Corporation* (1921).

A customer also has a duty to advise the bank if he finds that his signature has been forged on a cheque. If a person knows that his signature has been forged but leads others to believe that his signature is genuine, he will be 'estopped' from denying the genuineness of the signature and will be fully liable on the cheque. The major case on this topic is *Greenwood* v. *Martins Bank Ltd* (1933).

20.8   Questions

1. Distinguish between a holder and a holder in due course of a bill of exchange or cheque.

2. Explain the liabilities of the following parties to a bill of exchange: (i) the acceptor, (ii) the drawer, and (iii) the endorser

3. Examine the statutory protections available to: (i) the paying bank, and (ii) the collecting bank. Under what circumstances would a collecting bank be held to be negligent?

4. State the main duties of: (i) a bank, and (ii) a customer.

Unit Twenty-one
Bank Lending

21.1 Introduction

In Unit 1.1 we said that one of the basic functions of a bank is the lending of surplus deposits to those who wish to borrow. For most customers, both personal and business, the banks represent one of the cheapest and most flexible sources of finance available; for the small business in particular, the bank is often the only source of advice and additional funds. The banks' lending policies have to operate in accordance with the Bank of England's qualitative directives and other controls while at the same time adequate reserves and cash in the tills must be maintained.

Regulated Agreements

A bank must also take into account the requirements of the Consumer Credit Act 1974. This Act controls *regulated agreements* (Fig. 21.1) which are any forms of credit up to £15 000 (including overdrafts and credit cards) granted to individuals and partnerships.

The Act requires the disclosure of the true cost of the credit to the customer on all regulated agreements. This is the annual percentage rate of charge (APR).

The Act prohibits canvassing for a regulated agreement outside what are called 'trade premises' without having received a prior invitation for that purpose. It is not unusual for a bank manager to visit his customer at home and chance meetings occur on many a social occasion. The Act means that the manager would commit an offence if the question of credit were discussed in these circumstances. However, the Act recognizes the continuous nature of a bank manager's relationship with his customer and no offence would be committed if the manager 'solicited' an agreement enabling his customer to overdraw on his current account.

Thus, to agree overdraft facilities on current account with an existing customer at the golf club is permissible under the Act, but to arrange a new personal loan with the same customer is not. The trade premises referred to in the Act can be either those of the banker or his customer. This means that there is no problem if the discussion with the customer takes place inside the bank, and equally there will be no difficulty if the conversation can be held in the customer's office.

For all regulated agreements—except overdrafts on current accounts—the borrower must be given written details of his or her rights and duties, the amount and rate of the total charge for credit and the protection and remedies

CREDIT AGREEMENT REGULATED BY THE CONSUMER CREDIT ACT 1974   c

PERSONAL LOAN

Customers full name(s) and address(es)

Mr John Smith
58 Lyndon Road
ANYTOWN

Midland Bank plc

Full branch address

10 High Street
ANYTOWN

PRINCIPAL LOAN

Amount of Loan   £ 1 500

Total Charge for Credit   £   360

A P R 23.8 %

Total Amount Payable
under this Agreement   £ 1 860

Repayment

Initial repayment   £ 77.50

Date of first repayment   1 November 19-5

_23_ further monthly
repayments of   £ 77.50
on the same day in each
month thereafter

I/we authorise you to pay from my/our
current account no. _01099124_

(a) an initial repayment of £ _77.50_
and _23_ further repayments of
£ _77.50_ in accordance with the
repayment schedule(s) set out above
for the total loan of £ _1 860_

*(b) the insurance premium as stated

LOAN OF INSURANCE PREMIUM

Amount of Premium   £

Amount of Loan   £

Total Charge for Credit   £

A P R _____ %

Total Amount Payable
under this Agreement   £

Repayment

Initial Repayment   £

Date of first repayment _____

_____ further monthly
repayments of   £
on the same day in each
month thereafter

IMPORTANT — YOU SHOULD READ THIS CAREFULLY

YOUR RIGHTS

The Consumer Credit Act 1974 covers this agreement and
lays down certain requirements for your protection which
must be satisfied when the agreement is made. If they are not,
the creditor cannot enforce the agreement against you without a court order.

The Act also gives you a number of rights. You have a right to
settle this agreement at any time by giving notice in writing
and paying off all amounts payable under the agreement
which may be reduced by a rebate. If you have obtained
unsatisfactory goods or services under a transaction financed
by this agreement, apart from any purchased out of a cash
loan, you may have a right to sue the supplier, the creditor or
both. Similarly, if the contract is not fulfilled, perhaps because
the supplier has gone out of business, you may still be able to
sue the creditor.

If you would like to know more about the protection and
remedies provided under the Act, you should contact either
your local Trading Standards Department or your nearest
Citizens' Advice Bureau.

N.B. The references above to unsatisfactory services apply
only to the insurance cover when taken, and cash loan
means the principal loan.

This loan is granted on the terms set out overleaf.

This is a Credit Agreement regulated by the
Consumer Credit Act 1974.
Sign it only if you want to be legally bound by its terms.
Signature(s) of
Customer(s)   _J. Smith_

Date(s) of Signature(s)   1 October 19-5

*Delete if not applicable

YOUR RIGHT TO CANCEL
Once you have signed this agreement, you will have for
a short time a right to cancel it. Exact details of how and
when you can do this will be sent to you by post by us.

For **Midland Bank plc**
A Jones _____ Manager
28 September 19-5 Date of Signature

PERSONAL LOAN ACCOUNT No. 16035282

302 4

Fig. 21.1   A cancellable personal loan agreement form

available under the Consumer Credit Act. The following information will be detailed in such regulated agreements:

(i) a statement such as 'this is a credit agreement regulated by the Consumer Credit Act 1974';

(ii) the name and address of the borrower and the lender;

(iii) the amount of the credit or the credit limit;

(iv) the timing and amount of repayments;

(v) APR (annual percentage rate of charge—see Unit 9.3);

(vi) a description of the goods or services to be financed by the agreement;

(vii) the cash price, the TCC (total charge for credit which is the interest plus the charges) and the total amount payable;

(viii) a statement covering variable interest rates (if applicable);

(ix) security requirements;

(x) a statement of the protection and remedies available to the borrower.

The agreement must be signed by both the borrower and the lender. The Act requires that much of the information contained in a regulated agreement must be in a legible size of print—that is there cannot be any 'small print' clauses. Some information has to be highlighted by bold print or capitals, while other details must be printed close to where the borrower signs so that he or she is more likely to see them.

The Act allows certain regulated agreements to be cancelled by the borrower. Broadly 'cancellable agreements' are those that are signed at a place other than on bank premises or on the trader's business premises where credit is offered by a shop. However, bridging loans for the purchase of land (see Unit 21.10(a)), loans which are secured on land and overdrafts are not cancellable. An agreement is cancellable only if it contains a cancellation notice (see Fig. 21.1): this tells the borrower of the right to cancel and the way in which this may be done. The lender must send a further copy of the agreement or a separate notice of cancellation rights within seven days of the original agreement being signed. The borrower then has five days after receipt of the cancellation notice in which to cancel. There is no right of cancellation where the agreement is signed in the bank: a copy of the agreement is handed to the borrower. It should be noted that whenever there are joint borrowers, such as husband and wife, a copy of the agreement must be given to each.

Special rules exist where the borrower offers land and buildings as security which may well be the case with a second mortgage, for example. Here the lender (the bank) has to send a copy of the agreement to the borrower for him or her to study a week before sending out the actual agreement which is to be signed. During the week the lender must not contact the borrower about the agreement unless requested to by the borrower. Once the actual agreement for signature has been received, the borrower has a further week to make up his or her mind. Once it has been signed and returned, however, the borrower cannot cancel the agreement. These rules do not apply where the loan is to finance the purchase of the land and buildings offered as security or for bridging loans to cover the purchase of land.

The Consumer Credit Act also deals with the rules for calculating the amount payable if the borrower wishes to pay off the amount outstanding on the agreement before legally bound to. Clearly, in such circumstances, it would be unfair to expect the borrower to pay the full interest and charges as if the loan had run for its full time: such amounts will be reduced by a rebate on the credit charges.

Credit Scoring

Nowadays most personal loan applications are credit scored (see Unit 13.2). It is no longer necessary to see the bank manager or other bank officer in order to arrange a personal loan. Instead, an application form is completed which can be handed in to the branch or sent by post; upon receipt by the bank the application is credit scored to assess whether or not the loan should be granted.

However, despite the use of credit scoring, much lending does still rely upon the judgement of the bank manager, or other officer, who will interview the customer and make a decision based on the interview and other information available in the branch. The manager's lending judgement is really only another type of credit scoring.

21.2   The Basic Questions

The bank manager faced with a request for loan or overdraft facilities must always remember the four basic questions:

(i) how much does the customer want to borrow?
(ii) what does he want it for?
(iii) how long does he want it for?
(iv) how is it to be repaid?

None of these questions mentions security for an advance: the question of security is a secondary one, and is discussed in detail in Units 21.4–21.9.

We shall consider each of the basic questions in turn.

(a) How Much?

Among the things the manager should bear in mind are the customer's own resources and whether the bank is being asked to lend too much in comparison with these resources: most managers agree that if the customer has a reasonable amount of his own money invested in the project he will have plenty of incentive to see it through to a profitable conclusion. Although no hard and fast rules can be laid down it is often thought that the bank should not have more invested in the business or project than the customer. This rule does not necessarily apply to personal borrowing, but some contribution from the customer is still required. When a personal loan is being granted to buy goods, the manager must bear in mind any current Government restrictions: these usually take the form of specifying a minimum deposit and a maximum repayment period.

'Jackson, could you adopt a more suitable expression?'

Above all, the manager should look at the proposition, check any figures given and attempt to see that the bank advance will fit into the scheme and that the amount being requested is sufficient to carry out the project. If the advance is inadequate the manager may later find himself in the difficult position of having to lend more money to protect previous lending.

(b) What For?
Naturally a lender of money is entitled to know the purpose for which the advance is required. A manager must bear in mind Bank of England qualitative directives and the purpose of the advance should also be within the terms of the bank's own policy. For personal advances the purpose is usually easy to understand—for example, to buy a car—but for companies the proposition may form part of a complex scheme which the manager needs to understand and assess.

(c) How Long For?
A high proportion of the deposits of a bank are repayable either on demand or at seven days' notice. It makes commercial sense that where the sources of advances are repayable at such short notice, the lending should similarly be repayable at short notice. Technically all bank overdrafts and loans, except for medium-term loans and personal loans, are repayable on demand. In practice it is not possible to call in advances at such short notice and provided a customer 'plays ball' with his bank, financing arrangements are not withdrawn without agreement.

Advances for capital expenditure, such as the purchase of a car or a piece of machinery, are usually arranged on a loan or personal loan account. Such advances are required to be repaid within an agreed period of time; a manager always expects the borrowing to be repaid well before the equipment becomes due for disposal, and on certain goods Government controls fix a maximum repayment period. Where additional machinery is being purchased for a business, the manager would expect to see increased cash flowing into the bank account. For personal borrowing, such as for the purchase of furniture or central heating or finance for a holiday, the repayment terms are agreed at the time of granting the advance.

Businesses often require working capital finance to help them over the period between commencing to manufacture their product and receiving cash from their customer. During this time they have to buy raw materials and to pay other costs involved in the manufacturing process such as wages, factory rent and rates, heating and lighting, together with the expenses involved in selling the goods; even when the goods are sold, payment is not received instantly. The length of time it takes to start with cash, go through the manufacturing and selling processes and, when payment is received, return to cash again is known as the *working capital cycle*. Banks are prepared to assist approved customers with finance for working capital and this is usually done by placing a 'limit' on the current account and permitting an overdraft up to this limit. Some businesses, such as those concerned with agriculture, are seasonal and require working capital only at certain times of the year; others require the same facilities throughout the year for a number of years.

(d) How Is It To Be Repaid?

The repayment of every advance will normally come from the customer's future earnings. Where an individual wishes to borrow by way of a personal loan, perhaps in order to buy a car, repayments must come each month from his wages or salary. In order to assess his proposition the manager asks for details of his earnings and normal outgoings, including any existing mortgage and hire-purchase repayments: this information is needed because often a customer asks for a loan without having calculated whether or not he can make the repayments. For businesses too, the advance can only be repaid from future profits (unless the business is to cease trading and sell off its assets to pay its creditors). Therefore the manager needs to ensure that lending the bank's money will increase the profits of the business, after allowing for the interest and charges to be made on the advance. Nowadays a bank manager is trained to consider the future profitability of business customers and it is usual for him to ask the customer for a cash budget and projected profit and loss account and balance sheet for the forthcoming year. A *cash budget* gives a month-by-month estimate of future cash receipts and payments and shows the estimated closing bank balance at each month-end for the period for which it is prepared and can thus provide a guide to the maximum overdraft that is likely to be needed. It relies for its accuracy on the estimates made by the business itself, however; moreover, the longer the period of the budget, the less accurate it will be in the more distant months. A manager soon comes to know those customers that stick to their forecasts and those that produce a budget simply to keep him happy. The *projected profit and loss account* and *balance sheet* for a future accounting period complement the information contained in the cash budget and also show the estimates of gross and net profits; these too may be used to assess the future profitability of the business. Unit 22 gives a detailed description of customers' accounts and their interpretation.

Where security is taken it should never be looked upon as the source of repayment, but only as something to fall back on if the expected source of repayment should fail.

21.3   The Customer

There is one highly variable factor in any lending proposition: the customer. One of the tasks of every branch manager is to get to know his customers— very often, though, he only meets those customers who wish to borrow money. To help in the task of knowing the customer all branches maintain reference sheets and files which contain details of past lending, letters received from customers and copies of letters sent out, and summaries of telephone conversations and interviews held; where business customers are concerned the file should contain copies of sets of accounts for past years. The manager refers to all this information prior to an interview with a customer. He takes into account the borrower's health and age and the value of connected family and business accounts held at the branch. With a personal customer he looks particularly to see if any past advances were repaid in accordance with the arrangements made. With a business customer, besides being concerned with the past history of the account, the manager wants to satisfy himself that the customer has experience at his job, has the necessary degree of management ability to run the business and is ploughing back profits into the business. Always, he is looking for a degree of integrity in his customer and must be constantly on the watch for the small percentage of rogues and the somewhat higher percentage of muddlers and eternal optimists that are among the customers of most branches.

21.4   Security for an Advance

Although every lending proposition should 'stand up by itself'—that is, it should be good enough not to need any security—a manager often asks for suitable security from the customer in case the advance should go wrong. There is a wide range of securities to cover a bank loan, and the main types are considered in more detail later in this Unit. There are three main requirements of any security acceptable to a bank:

(i) it should be easy to value;

(ii) it should be easy for the bank to obtain a good legal title;

(iii) it should be readily marketable or realizable.

A fourth requirement, though a less essential one, is that it is useful if the value of the security increases as time goes by.

Security may be either direct or collateral: it is *direct* when it is deposited by the customer to secure his own account; *collateral* security is deposited by another person to secure a customer's account. There are four main securities that are often taken:

(i) a mortgage of stocks and shares;

(ii) an assignment of a life policy;

(iii) a mortgage over land;

(iv) a guarantee.

The first three may be either direct or collateral security, but the fourth is always collateral because it is given by one person to secure another person's account. In each case a legal document has to be signed in the favour of the bank and the customer's or guarantor's signature witnessed. (If you work in a bank you should ask the security clerk to let you see the bank's mortgage, assignment and guarantee forms: they look very complicated, being full of legal language and have been developed over many years to cover most eventualities. These forms have to be completed and certain other procedures carried out when taking securities: the bank's regulations are taught on training courses for security clerks and are contained in bank instruction manuals.)

A *mortgage* is the conveyance or transfer of an interest in land or other assets as security for a debt. Where a bank takes a *legal mortgage* of property or shares, it has ownership of the property and can sell or do anything it likes with it; under an *equitable mortgage* the bank does not have such powers and the mortgage deed merely establishes a claim on the land or other assets. Upon repayment of the advance the mortgage is reconveyed and ownership of the land or other property reverts to the 'true' owner. A legal mortgage is taken where the bank wants to make absolutely certain that in the event of a forced sale of the security it will receive all the sale proceeds; an equitable mortgage is taken where the bank is prepared to rely less on the security concerned, because it could happen that others might have similar equitable claims on the property.

Whereas a mortgage transfers an interest in assets, an *assignment* is the transfer to another person of the right to receive a sum of money, or some other benefit. For instance, under a contract of life assurance, the beneficiary of the policy has a right to receive a sum of money when a certain event happens (after a certain number of years from the date of the policy, for example) and this is the right that is assigned or transferred to the bank by means of a legal document—that is, the life assurance company is asked to pay the benefits to another party, the bank.

The methods of taking each of the four major types of security are briefly described in turn in Units 21.5–21.8. Although these procedures may sound complicated, they are fully explained to members of the bank's staff who attend a securities course at a training branch. The details given in the remainder of this Unit are, therefore, intended only as a general introduction to taking security but before we look more closely at the methods we need to consider three other ways in which a bank acquires rights over security taken; these are *lien*, *pledge* and *hypothecation*.

(i) **Lien.** This is the right to retain the property of another until legal demands against the owner—such as settlement of a debt—have been satisfied. In law there are many types of lien: for example a hotel proprietor has a lien over a guest's luggage until the hotel bill is paid. In banking if a customer is overdrawn, a bank has a general lien over any property belonging to the customer that comes into its hands in the ordinary course of business: such property includes cheques paid in for the credit of the customer's account. Items held in safe custody are *not* covered by a bank's lien as they are considered to have been deposited by the customer for a specific purpose. A general business lien carries no right of sale, but a bank's lien does have a right of sale. However, a lien is no substitute for properly executed security. Realistically, it gives rights which amount to little more than nuisance value, that is, the owner cannot have his or her property back until the debt is repaid.

(ii) **Pledge.** This is the delivery of goods, or documents of title to goods, to the lender as security for a debt. It differs from a lien in that it is security that derives from an express agreement between the borrower and the lender whereas a lien arises independently by the operation of common law. A pledge differs from a mortgage in that the lender obtains possession while the borrower retains legal ownership; with a mortgage, possession generally remains with the mortgagor (for example, the bank's customer, the borrower), while the rights to title pass to the mortgagee (for example, the bank, the lender). It is important for the lender to keep the pledge until the debt is repaid. The lender has the right to sell the goods if the debt is not repaid.

(iii) **Hypothecation.** This is an agreement to give a charge over goods or documents of title to goods. It is used when the goods (or documents) have not yet been received by the customer, and is a legal agreement to give a pledge once the goods (or documents) are available. Unlike a mortgage the lender does not obtain ownership of the goods and unlike a pledge the lender does not obtain possession.

A *letter of hypothecation*, which is often known as a *trust letter*, is taken when a pledgor of goods or documents of title seeks the release of the goods to him so that they may be sold and the loan repaid. Thus, if the bank has the customer's goods warehoused in the bank's name, the bank will give authority for the goods to be released to the customer, so enabling them to be sold. Under the terms of the letter of hypothecation, the customer agrees to account to the bank for the proceeds of the sale of the goods. A letter of hypothecation may cover one particular transaction only or, where trading customers are concerned, may cover all future transactions in which the bank is involved in providing finance.

21.5 Stocks and Shares as Security

Stocks and shares that are quoted on a stock exchange are generally acceptable to banks as security for an advance.

(a) Valuation
They are easy to value: the *Financial Times* gives the prices of most of the well-known stocks and shares and the *Stock Exchange Daily Official List* contains an even wider range.

(b) Obtaining a Legal Title
It is usually easy to obtain a good legal title over stock exchange securities: the transfer of stocks and shares from one person to another is effected by means of a stock transfer form. The bank has the choice of taking either a legal or an equitable mortgage. In the former case, the customer deposits his share certificate with the bank and signs and has witnessed the bank's form of mortgage, together with a stock transfer form covering the shares in question. The bank then sends the share certificate and the completed stock transfer form to the registrar of the company whose shares are concerned; the registrar thereupon prepares a new share certificate in the name of the bank. Thus the bank becomes the legal owner of the shares and receives any dividends paid by the company; these are normally credited to the customer's account. When the advance is repaid and the customer wishes to receive back his security, the bank transfers the shares back into his name by completing another stock transfer form and sending it, together with the certificate in the bank's name, to the company registrar who then prepares another new share certificate.

An equitable mortgage over stocks and shares is somewhat simpler in that, while the customer still deposits his share certificate and completes the bank's form of mortgage together with a stock transfer form, the share certificate is not transferred into the name of the bank but is held in the bank's safe together with the signed mortgage and stock transfer form. If necessary, at a later date, the bank can use the transfer form to put the shares into its own name. Upon repayment of the advance, the equitable mortgage form is filed at the bank and the share certificate returned to the customer (unless he wishes it to be held in safe custody).

Equitable mortgages only may also be taken over Premium Savings Bonds, National Savings Certificates and deposits with building societies and the National Savings Bank. The bank's mortgage is executed and signed, but an uncompleted but signed withdrawal or encashment form is held also. Such items are less satisfactory as security because the terms under which they are issued do not allow a legal mortgage to be taken over them, and also because it is relatively easy to obtain duplicate bonds, certificates and pass books. It is much more difficult to obtain duplicate share certificates since a registrar will only issue these if an indemnity is signed, usually by a bank (see Unit 15.15).

Most stocks and shares require a stock transfer form to be completed to effect a change of ownership; one type of stocks and shares, however, may be transferred without completion of such a form. These are called *bearer securities* because the certificates do not name the owner but are designated in the name of 'bearer'; such certificates, like bearer cheques or bank notes, are transferred by passing them from one person to another. When a bank takes these as security, a mortgage form is signed to show the customer's intentions, but there is no need for a stock transfer form.

(c) Marketability
Stocks and shares are usually readily marketable and can be sold through a stockbroker, the proceeds being received within a week or so. Some shares, even though they are quoted on a stock exchange, are more difficult to sell: these are usually the shares of small companies for which there is a limited market. The shares of public limited companies that are not quoted on a stock exchange and those of private limited companies are especially difficult to realize, either because the market is limited or, in the case of private companies, because of restrictions placed on the transfer of shares: as security for an advance, therefore, shares in these kinds of companies are usually unsatisfactory.

Premium Savings Bonds, National Savings Certificates and so on are not marketable in the sense that they can be sold by one person to another. However, they can provide a useful form of security in that, if a signed repayment or encashment form is held, this can be completed and sent to the appropriate authority together with the certificates or other documents and the funds will be received within a few days. However, some of these investments may require a period of notice before repayment will be made.

(d) Increase in Value
Unfortunately, from the security point of view, stocks and shares fluctuate in value according to supply and demand on the stock market and other factors. This means that a bank must exercise considerable care when shares are deposited as security to ensure that, when stock market prices are falling, the value of the security does not fall below the amount of the advance. One of the tasks of the security clerk is to value shares deposited at regular intervals.

The values of National Savings Certificates and of building society and National Savings Bank deposits increase over a period of time as the benefits of interest are received. In some cases interest may not, however, be added to the value of the security but may instead be paid direct to the customer. With Premium Savings Bonds there is always the chance that the customer will win the top prize, pay off the advance from the bank and require investment advice!

21.6   Life Policies as Security

Besides being a good method of long-term saving, most endowment and whole-life policies having a surrender value can be assigned to a bank as security for an advance. Some policies, known as *industrial policies*, are unsuitable as security because they often contain a clause prohibiting assignment: these are similar to endowment and whole-life policies except that they are for much smaller amounts, perhaps £100 or so, and the premiums are collected weekly by the insurance agent.

When a life policy is taken as security it should be read very carefully and the following points noted:

(i) *The name of the assurance company issuing the policy:* banks prefer to take a policy issued by a reputable company. British banks prefer policies of companies domiciled in the United Kingdom; where a company is domiciled overseas there could be problems of obtaining payment in the event of a claim.

(ii) *The type of policy:* there are various types of life policy issued (see Unit 8.9), and the best, from a banking point of view, are endowment or whole-life policies. The former are payable at a certain time in the future or on the earlier death of the assured; the latter are payable on the death of the assured.

(iii) *The names of the life assured and the beneficiary:* with most policies these are the same person, probably the bank customer. However, a husband may take out a policy on his own life with his wife as beneficiary and in such cases the beneficiary is not the life assured. Policies of this type are written under the Married Women's Property Act 1882 whereby the proceeds of the policy are placed into a trust for the beneficiary and thus are entirely separate from the assets of the life assured. With such policies it is important that all interested parties 'join in' the bank's form of assignment.

(iv) *Restrictive clauses:* policies may contain clauses which restrict travel by air to scheduled flights only or exclude dangerous occupations and hobbies.

(v) *'Age admitted':* Before paying a claim on a policy, all assurance companies require proof of the age of the life assured. This is to avoid the assured stating to the company that he is younger than he actually is, which would result in cheaper premiums. It is quite common to find policies where the age is not admitted and this is unsatisfactory from the bank's point of view because the assurance company would not pay out on such a policy in the event of a claim. Where a bank takes a policy as security it is usual to make sure that it is 'age admitted', if necessary by obtaining the customer's birth certificate and sending this to the assurance company for its attention. (In any case, the customer would have to do this at some time before the policy was due for payment.) As this needs the customer's co-operation, it is a good idea to get it done before any borrowing is allowed: once he has taken the advance he may become distinctly less co-operative in helping the bank to complete the security satisfactorily. This also applies to anything else that the customer needs to sign: it is always advisable to get his signature before allowing the borrowing to commence.

We will now consider how well life policies meet the four basic requirements of any security.

(a) Valuation

Life policies are easy to value: most endowment and whole-life policies have a surrender value except perhaps in the first year, and occasionally in the second as well. This may be ascertained by writing to the assurance company although surrender values are stated on the policy document itself in some cases. Naturally, the longer the policy has been in force, the more premiums will have been paid, and the higher will be the surrender value relative to the sum assured. (While surrender values certainly increase over time, the surrender of a policy hardly ever makes good financial sense since surrender values, in the early years of a policy, are nearly always less than 100 per cent of premiums paid and in later years although they may be greater than 100 per cent of premiums paid, they never represent a good return on the investment.)

When a policy is used as security for an advance it is usual for the security clerk to write to the assurance company at regular intervals—perhaps every two or three years—and ask for an up-to-date surrender value (if it is not stated on the policy itself).

(b) Obtaining a Legal Title

It is a relatively simple matter to obtain a good legal title to a life policy, but it should be remembered that all interested parties must join in the assignment. If, for example, a policy is on the life of a husband and in the favour of his wife, then both should join in the assignment form and have their signatures witnessed before the policy can be taken as security for the husband's account. As a life policy is not a negotiable instrument it is necessary to give notice to the assurance company of the assignment in favour of the bank and to ask if there are any prior assignments. Suitable records must be maintained to ensure that the customer continues to pay the premiums on the policy, and from the bank's point of view it is useful if premiums are paid by standing order or direct debit. If the customer stops paying premiums before maturity of the policy the bank must consider whether to make the payments itself and debit the customer's account, thus increasing his indebtedness, or to allow the assurance company to make the policy 'paid up' on the basis of the premiums already paid. As life policies, like all insurances, are contracts of utmost good faith (*uberrimae fidei*) between the assurance company and the life assured, there is a danger that the contract could be rendered invalid, with consequences on the bank's security, if incorrect statements were made by the assured. For example, the principle of utmost good faith requires the assured to disclose material facts even though the assurance company has not asked about such facts.

When the customer repays his advance and requests the return of his policy, the bank must reassign its rights back to the original beneficiary.

(c) Marketability

A life policy can always be realized by the bank surrendering it to the assurance company and the proceeds will be received quickly, with a minimum of formality.

(d) Increase in Value

Provided the premiums continue to be paid, life policies increase in value as time goes by. In addition, every year or sometimes every two or three years, the assurance company sends out bonus notices to those policyholders who have 'with profits' policies, stating how much of the profits earned by the company in investing its surplus funds has been allocated to the policy. Such bonuses will be paid in addition to the sum assured when a claim is made on the policy or upon maturity.

21.7   Land as Security

A mortgage over land is a fairly complex affair and taking it as security for an advance may involve the bank's customer in the expense of legal fees. A person owning land, which includes anything on it such as houses and other buildings, always holds evidence of his legal title, which in Britain takes one of two forms: either a land certificate or a bundle of deeds and documents. Where a land certificate is held the land is known as *registered land* and the details of the land and its owner are kept at the Land Registry (a central register); otherwise the land is *unregistered land* and no central record is maintained. The system of registering the title to land started in 1925 and eventually the whole country will be registered. As it will be some time before the system is completed, bankers taking a mortgage over land need to know how to obtain a good legal title over both types.

Irrespective of whether the land is registered or not, there are two main classes of title: freehold and leasehold. Where the title is *freehold* there is no time limit on the owner's possession: it is his until he chooses to sell it. With a *leasehold* title, however, the leaseholder pays a sum of money (known as the ground rent) to the freehold owner of the land and holds it in return for a set period of time, often initially either 99 or 999 years but usually less in the case of older property. Apart from the ground rent and any restrictions imposed in the lease, there is little difference from the bank's point of view between a freehold property and a leasehold property with a long lease still to run.

(a) Valuation

Land is much more difficult to value than stocks and shares or life policies: it is the branch manager who usually carries out an inspection and gives an estimated valuation. The figure he decides on may be reasonably accurate if the land includes a building of a standard design, such as a semi-detached house, but his valuation could be considerably inaccurate if it consists of a farm or factory premises. It is rare for a bank to use professional valuers; minor inaccuracies are not of great importance because the security is taken as a form of insurance against possible future difficulties and, when arranging the advance, neither the customer nor the bank wishes to have to realize the security.

(b) Obtaining a Legal Title
The method of obtaining a legal title over land differs between registered and unregistered land.

(i) **Unregistered land.** The procedure is not very different from the taking of stocks and shares or life policies as security. For unregistered land, the legal title of the owner is evidenced by a bundle of deeds, which when held as security must be kept in the bank's safe. The bank prepares a mortgage form—which may be either legal or equitable (see Unit 21.4)—for signature by the customer, and the completed form is held with the deeds. Where the bank is taking a legal mortgage, the deeds are commonly sent to the branch solicitor who inspects them in order to prepare a *report on title*, stating whether the customer has a good and marketable title to his property. At the same time the solicitor may carry out various searches against the customer's name on the Land Charges Registry (nothing to do with the Land Registry) and the local planning registers. The former reveals any matters outstanding such as a bankruptcy order against the customer or claims against the property; the latter, known as *local searches*, indicate whether the property is likely to be affected by local authority developments such as the building of a new road. If the branch solicitor does not make these searches, the security clerk will carry them out. Where the property is leasehold it is necessary to check that the ground rent has been paid to date and a note made to check this annually.

When the advance is repaid the title of the legal mortgage is reconveyed to the customer and the deeds together with the bank's reconveyed mortgage are handed back; an equitable mortgage is filed at the bank among the old security papers and the deeds returned to the customer.

(ii) **Registered land.** There are two ways in which a bank may take registered land as security for an advance: either by deposit of the land certificate, protected by notice of deposit, or by registered charge. These methods are the equivalent of an equitable mortgage and a legal mortgage respectively.

When the *notice of deposit* method is used the customer deposits the land certificate and signs the bank's mortgage form. The bank then sends the certificate to the Land Registry where the details of all registered properties are maintained, requesting it to write the certificate up to date: the Registry then compares the certificate with existing records and makes any necessary alterations. At the same time the bank also encloses the special Land Registry form giving notice of deposit. This is recorded at the Registry and the bank's interest in the property noted in the charges (or mortgages) section of the certificate which is then returned to the bank. Thus the bank's interest is noted both at the Registry and on the land certificate; the bank is protected by its notice of deposit and will be immediately advised of any attempted dealings in the land. It is still necessary for local searches to be carried out and, if the property is leasehold, for ground rent receipts to be obtained.

Upon repayment of the advance the bank withdraws its notice of deposit and again has the certificate sent to the Land Registry for writing up to date. Thus the bank's interest is removed and the certificate can then be handed back to the customer.

If a *registered charge* is to be taken the customer deposits the land certificate at the bank and signs a mortgage form. The bank then sends the completed mortgage form to the Land Registry, together with the land certificate. The certificate is withdrawn and a new one, called a charge certificate, is issued: this has the bank's mortgage form stitched inside. Local searches and checks on the payment of ground rent, where appropriate, are also carried out.

When the advance is repaid the bank returns the charge certificate to the Land Registry who withdraws it and re-issues the land certificate, which can then either be kept at the bank in safe custody or handed back to the customer.

Whenever there are buildings of any value on land that has been taken as security it is essential to check that they are insured against fire risk. This is, of course, primarily the customer's responsibility, but the bank should ensure that the fire insurance is of a sufficient amount and that the premiums are paid to date; a note should also be made to check future payments.

A person will only be in possession of the deeds or land certificate relating to his land and property if it is free from mortgage. As we have seen, when the bank takes a mortgage, it takes possession of the relevant documents of title; a building society acts similarly. Most personal customers and a number of business customers have a mortgage outstanding on their property; this is the *first mortgage*. Such a customer can still use the value of his property as security for an advance but the bank, instead of being able to take a mortgage as previously described, must take a *second mortgage*. Suppose that a customer bought a house five years ago for £20 000 by paying a deposit of £2 000 and borrowing £18 000 on mortgage from a building society; if the house is now worth £28 000 and the mortgage outstanding is £17 000, then he has an *equity* of £11 000 in his house, an amount that could be used as security for an advance by giving the bank a second mortgage. A special second mortgage form is signed by the customer; the deeds, of course, remain with the first mortgagee. In the event of the customer's default it would be necessary to seek the agreement of the first mortgagee to sell the house. (It is unlikely that the first mortgagee will agree to this, unless the mortgagor is in default here too, thus casting considerable doubt on the value of a second mortgage as security.) If the house were sold for £28 000, the first mortgage would be paid off and the balance, in theory £11 000, would be paid to the second mortgagee, any surplus after that being paid to the customer. Reference should be made to a more specialist book on practice of banking for further consideration of second mortgages.

(c) Marketability

Technically, land and property is easily realized provided the bank has taken a legal mortgage over unregistered land or a registered charge over registered land. In practice, however, a bank is generally reluctant to realize such security particularly when the customer's own house is concerned, and will only sell the property as a last resort when all else has failed. Other land and property may be put up for sale very quickly; owing to the vagaries of the property market, however, it may be some time before it is sold and the proceeds received. Stocks and shares and life policies can be realized much more quickly than can land.

(d) Increase in Value
Over a period of time most land and property rises in value, especially houses of a type for which there is a steady demand, such as semi-detached and smaller detached properties. Factory premises also rise in value provided that they are well maintained and are easily converted to other uses; large, highly specialized factories that would be difficult to convert do not rise in value very much, and should their sale be forced, may be worth less on the property market than they are to the firm owning them. Farm land and buildings usually rise in value as time goes by.

21.8   Guarantees as Security

A guarantee is a collateral security involving three parties, in which the third party, the guarantor, agrees to be liable for the debts of a second party, the bank customer, if he doesn't pay the first party, the bank. Guarantees are often taken from the directors of a limited company as part security for the company bank account, thus preventing the directors from hiding behind the 'shield' of limited liability (see Unit 13.5) for at least a part of the company's debts. They may also be taken from members of a club or society to guarantee an advance to the club, and from friends and relatives to guarantee a personal account. One company from a group of companies may guarantee the bank accounts of the other companies in the group: where all group companies guarantee each others' accounts this is known as an *interlocking guarantee*.

Guarantees used to secure regulated agreements under the Consumer Credit Act 1974, must be in a prescribed form. The bank's guarantee form usually has a heading 'Guarantee and Indemnity subject to the Consumer Credit Act 1974' (the difference between a guarantee and an indemnity is explained later on in this Unit). It details the name and address of the bank, the principal debtor and the guarantor; the amount of the debt is stated. The rights of the guarantor are listed, together with the effect of the debtor's failure to fulfil his obligations. The box where the guarantor is to sign contains the warning that it should be signed only if the guarantor wants to be legally bound by the guarantee's terms. The guarantor is entitled to a copy of the guarantee and to a copy of the regulated agreement which the guarantee secures.

(a) Valuation
Most guarantees are easy to value in that the money amount is usually stated

on the guarantee form. How much a bank would actually receive from the guarantee if the security was realized is a different matter (see paragraph (*c*) below).

(*b*) Obtaining a Legal Title

The mechanics of taking a legal guarantee are very simple. When a person offers himself as a guarantor of an account the manager usually explains to him that in the event of the customer's default, he will be liable to pay up to the amount of the guarantee. The guarantor then signs the bank's form and, if he docs not maintain an account at the same bank and branch as the account being guaranteed, the bank takes steps to check his financial standing by making a status enquiry on his bank and branch; if the reply is satisfactory the advance is granted to the customer. Regular, perhaps annual, status enquiries continue to be made on the guarantor as long as there remains a liability under the guarantee, and the bank also writes at regular intervals, possibly every five years, to remind the guarantor of his liability. A bank could ask a guarantor, besides signing the bank's form, to deposit security, such as stock and share certificates, life policies or deeds of land, as support to the guarantee.

(*c*) Marketability

The major problem of guarantees is that, however hard the bank tries to explain the potential liability, the guarantor never expects to be called upon to pay. There can be serious ill-feeling between the guarantor and the bank if this should happen; it may be difficult to persuade him to pay without taking court action, something that a bank would only undertake as a last resort. Thus although the bank may hold a guarantee for, say £5 000, the manager may in his own mind consider that the bank would receive less if it asked the guarantor to pay. Where additional security has been deposited in support of the guarantee, this may be realized as part or full payment of the guarantor's liability.

(*d*) Increase in Value

Where a guarantee is for a fixed sum, as is generally the case, it does not, of course, go up in value over a period of time: in fact, with inflation, the purchasing power of the money will fall. In future years, if borrowing on the customer's account continues, it might be necessary for the guarantor to sign a guarantee for an increased amount.

There is often some confusion among banking students between a guarantee and an indemnity. With a *guarantee*, as already mentioned, there are three parties, the guarantor agreeing to pay the bank if its customer does not. With an *indemnity* there are two parties: the bank and the indemnifier who is primarily liable for the debt of the customer. Contrast the following statements: *'if Joe does not pay you, I will'* and *'lend Joe £50 and I will see that you are repaid'*. The former is a guarantee, with a secondary responsibility being taken by the guarantor if Joe does not pay; the latter is an indemnity whereby the person making the statement assumes primary responsibility for

'Very well then—two hundred and fifty *million—my coffee's getting cold!'*

the money. The distinction may seem a fine one but there are certain circumstances in which a guarantor could not be forced to pay, whereas an indemnifier could. Therefore, to be on the safe side, most banks incorporate an indemnity clause into their guarantee forms.

Besides taking guarantees and indemnities to secure the accounts of customers, the banks also join in indemnities on behalf of their customers (see Unit 15.15), the commonest example being where a customer has lost a share certificate.

21.9   Other Securities

There are other securities that may be acceptable to a bank granting an advance. These include a *letter of set-off*, which formalizes the bank's right to set off a credit balance on one account with a debit balance on another account of the same customer. Thus a customer with money on his deposit account might be permitted to overdraw his current account on the basis of the right of set-off. A similar situation might exist where a group of companies maintains accounts at the same branch: some individual company accounts might be overdrawn, while others have credit balances but by arrangement with the bank the group might be charged interest only on the 'net indebtedness'.

A security commonly taken from companies is a *fixed and floating charge* which covers all the assets of the company including stocks, debtors, machinery and plant. The floating part allows the company to buy and sell assets without restriction—the charge only 'crystallizes' when certain events take place, such as default on an advance.

It is inappropriate in this book to describe these in detail; they are covered in the more specialized books dealing with securities for advances.

21.10   Special Lending Situations

There are certain special situations in which a bank may be asked to lend, and it is appropriate to consider some of these now.

(a) Bridging Loan

This is an advance sometimes needed by customers moving from one house to another. It involves the bank advancing the deposit or the purchase price of the new house to the buyer pending receipt of the sale proceeds of the old house and/or the provision of a building society mortgage.

There are three main steps in the purchase of a house:

(i) **Date the buyer expresses interest.** In order to back up his interest the purchaser is usually asked to pay a small amount, often around £250. This is normally paid to the vendor's estate agent, who often retains it as a part of his commission fee if the sale goes through. There is no binding contract at this stage, the sale being 'subject to contract' and if the purchase does not proceed, the amount is repayable. Various steps are now taken which include a survey of the property, an application for a mortgage, a legal report on title and the preparation of the contract.

(ii) **Date the contracts are signed.** If the purchase proceeds, contracts are signed and exchanged by buyer and seller. At this stage the buyer pays ten per cent of the consideration monies, say £10 000 on a house costing £100 000, to the seller's solicitors. A legally binding contract now exists and, within the contract, a completion date is fixed.

(iii) **Date of completion.** On this date the balance of the consideration monies is paid and the buyer becomes the legal owner of the property and obtains it with vacant possession.

Normally a bank only agrees to a bridging loan for the purchase of a property when a binding contract exists for the sale of the customer's old property. If such a contract does not exist, however, the bank may be prepared to grant an advance that is 'open-ended' in the sense that the repayment date of the loan is not known and will be dependent on the sale of the customer's existing property.

In any bridging loan involving the transfer of property it is necessary for the bank to work closely with the customer's solicitor and the usual security taken is a solicitor's letter of undertaking. Before granting a bridging loan the bank must firstly look closely at the lending proposition to see if the customer has done his calculations correctly with regard to the sale and purchase prices; in particular, the bank needs to know that any building society or other mortgage that the customer plans to take out on the new property will actually be available. Secondly, the bank needs to hold a solicitor's undertaking agreeing to pay the net proceeds of sale direct to the bank. Thirdly, if the solicitor giving the undertaking is not known to the bank, an enquiry must be made as to his integrity, through his banker. Fourthly, the bank will wish to obtain control over the deeds of the property being purchased by the customer. This is achieved by the customer instructing his solicitor to give the bank an undertaking to hold the deeds of the new property to the order of the bank. The bank then allows the customer to pay over the purchase monies and, at the same time, checks that he has adequately insured his new property against the risk of fire. (Fire insurance is the responsibility of the purchaser from the date of signing the contract.) Where the customer is arranging a building society or other mortgage on his new property, the solicitor's undertaking agrees to hold the deeds to the order of the bank pending release to the building society and to pay the amount of the new mortgage, when received, direct to the bank.

While the change from one house to another is the most common occasion for bridging loan finance, other types of bridge-overs are sometimes needed to cover urgent temporary finance pending the receipt of funds from another source; for instance, the bank might grant a temporary loan which will be repaid by the receipt of funds from the sale of investments or the surrender of a life policy. A company might require temporary finance pending the receipt of the proceeds of a share or debenture issue.

The very nature of a bridging loan—temporary finance to be repaid from a known source—means that the customer's account may be overdrawn only for a short period; a house bridge-over, for example, may be for no more than two or three days. As such the interest charged by the bank for the facility will be low in comparison with the costs of setting it up. Thus it is usual for a special charge—an *arrangement fee*—to be made to cover the administrative costs of arranging a bridging loan.

(b) Produce Advances

These are advances where goods (produce) are taken as security. Such an advance is self-liquidating in that the goods which form the bank's security are sold to repay the advance. The bank must be certain of the commercial integrity of its customer, especially with regard to the quality and marketability of the goods.

The security taken by the bank consists of either obtaining the documents of title to the goods or arranging for the goods to be warehoused in the bank's name, rather than by the bank taking actual delivery of the goods—no manager wants the banking hall cluttered up with his customers' goods. The customer is required to sign a *memorandum of pledge* (see Unit 21.4). The goods are usually released to the customer by the bank against a *trust letter*, or *letter of hypothecation*, in which the customer acknowledges the bank's security rights in the goods and undertakes to hold in trust for the bank the goods and the sale proceeds and to pay the latter in to the bank.

(c) Other Types of Advance

These include probate advances to enable executors and administrators to pay inheritance tax on a deceased's estate (see Unit 13.6). More specialized advances include ships' mortgages, agricultural charges, discounting bills of exchange and the assignment of debts; further details of these would be found in any book on banking practice.

21.11   Questions

1. What are the basic requirements of any security? How are these met in the case of (i) life policies, and (ii) guarantees?

2. If you, as a lending banker, had the choice of taking either shares or land as security, which would you prefer? Give reasons for your decision.

3. You work at a small bank branch. The sub-manager is ill and you are deputizing for him. His diary shows the following:

    '2.30 J. Smith—requires loan to exchange car.'

    The manager asks you to take this interview. What information would you collect beforehand, and what questions would you ask at the interview before making your decision?

4. Describe what is meant by (i) a bridging loan, and (ii) a produce advance. Give an account of the operation of each.

5. What are the main criteria which govern a bank's decision to lend money to a prospective borrower? What part does security play in the final decision?

                                                              (*The Institute of Bankers*)

Multiple-choice Questions—11

Read each question carefully. Choose the *one* answer you think is correct. Answers are given on page 390.

1. Which of the following is in the strongest position to enforce a bill of exchange or cheque?

    A   holder
    B   holder for value who has not, himself, given value
    C   holder in due course
    D   holder for value who has, himself, given value

2. In which one of the following circumstances would a bank *not* have given value?

    A   bank cashes a cheque drawn on another bank
    B   customer is allowed to draw against uncleared effects
    C   customer is not allowed to draw against uncleared effects
    D   cheque paid in is used to reduce an overdraft

3. To whom is an endorser liable if the bill of exchange is dishonoured?

   A the payee
   B a previous endorser
   C the drawer
   D a subsequent endorser or holder

4. Section 1 of the Cheques Act 1957 gives certain protection to the paying bank that has:

   A paid a cheque—whether open or crossed—which was not properly endorsed
   B paid a cheque with a forged endorsement
   C paid a crossed cheque received from another bank
   D set itself up as holder in due course

5. Which one of the following lending questions is *least* important?

   A amount to be borrowed
   B security available
   C purpose of loan
   D how loan is to be repaid

6. The Consumer Credit Act 1974 controls *regulated agreements*; these are:

   A personal loans/overdrafts and credit card agreements up to £15 000
   B all overdrafts
   C loans to limited companies
   D any bank loan or overdraft above £15 000

7. Which one of the following bank securities is likely to alter in value from day-to-day?

   A a guarantee
   B a life policy
   C shares
   D land and buildings

8. How would a life policy be taken as security?

   A assignment
   B mortgage
   C pledge
   D letter of hypothecation

9. 'A right to retain the property of another until legal demands against the owner have been satisfied.' What type of security is this?

   A pledge
   B mortgage
   C lien
   D assignment

10. A customer offers as security freehold unregistered land. What would be the evidence of title?

   A land certificate
   B bundle of documents of title
   C lease
   D mortgage

Interpreting the Accounts of Customers

22.1 Introduction

We saw in Unit 21.2 how it was important for the bank manager to consider the future profitability of his business customers when considering any request for an advance. Banks are constantly lending money to businesses of all sizes and types and every time that a manager grants a loan or allows an overdraft facility, he takes a risk—the risk of not getting all the money back, or at least, the risk of having difficulty in recovering some of it. The main problem for the manager is in assessing the degree of risk he is taking with his depositors' funds.

How then does the manager set about assessing this risk? We have seen that the manager has his own impressions of his customer as to reputation, financial standing, business ability, prospects and so forth, and these impressions have been acquired through their past dealings together. In addition to those impressions the manager will want to study the customer's accounts in order to interpret them and draw out of them some conclusions which will aid him in assessing the risk.

22.2 What Accounts will the Bank Manager See?

Obviously the manager is less concerned with the day-to-day book-keeping transactions of his customers than with the accounts that are made up at the end of the trading year. These *final accounts*, as they are called, will consist of the following:

Trading account. This compares the purchases and sales of the business for the year, together with an adjustment for change in the stock level from the beginning to the end of the year, and shows the gross profit for the year.

Profit and loss account. This shows all the expenses of the business for the year and deducts them from the gross profit to give net profit.

Appropriation account. This is used by partnerships and limited companies to show how the net profit has been *appropriated*, or divided, among the partners or shareholders; a sole-trader business does not include this account among its final accounts as all the net profits belong to the trader himself.

Trading account of J. Smith Ltd for the year ended 31 December 19–9

	£		£
Stock at 1 Jan. 19–9	15 000	Sales	130 000
+ purchases	90 000		
	105 000		
−Stock at 31 Dec. 19–9	14 000		
Cost of goods sold	91 000		
Gross profit	39 000		
	130 000		130 000

Fig. 22.1   A trading account

Balance sheet. This shows what the business owns and owes at a certain stated time. The balance sheet is not an 'account' as it doesn't form a part of the double-entry book-keeping system, but is a statement of the assets and liabilities at a given date. It has been likened to a snap-shot taken of the business at an instant in time: next day it could look rather different.

A manufacturing business will precede the trading account with a *manufacturing account* which shows the factory cost of producing the goods that are subsequently sold. The factory cost is made up of materials, labour, direct expenses and the overheads incurred in running the factory and this total cost is brought into the trading account instead of, or in addition to, purchases of finished goods for resale.

An example of a simple set of final accounts, excluding a manufacturing account, is shown in Figs. 22.1–22.5.

Profit and loss account of J. Smith Ltd for the year ended 31 December 19–9

	£		£
The various expenses of the business, e.g. wages and salaries, rent and rates, heating and lighting, etc, together with provisions for depreciation and bad debts would be listed here, totalling for example	30 000	Gross profit	39 000
Net profit	9 000		
	39 000		39 000

Fig. 22.2   A profit and loss account

Appropriation account of J. Smith Ltd for the year ended 31 December 19–9

	£		£
Corporation tax	3 500	Balance of unappropriated	
Transfer to general		profits brought forward	
reserve	1 000	from previous year	2 000
Proposed dividend on		Net profit for year	9 000
ordinary shares	5 000		
Balance of unappropriated			
profits carried forward			
to next year	1 500		
	11 000		11 000

Fig. 22.3   An appropriation account

'He has this thing about changing his cell round so that the debit side is nearest the window'

The balance sheet in Fig. 22.4 is presented in a horizontal form with the capital and liabilities on the right and the assets on the left. It is not uncommon, however, for the assets to be presented on the right-hand side and the liabilities on the left. Alternatively, balance sheets, especially those of companies, can be presented in a vertical form as shown in Fig. 22.5.

Balance sheet of J. Smith Ltd as at 31 December 19–9

	£			£
Fixed assets		*Authorized share capital*		
Premises		100 000 £1 ordinary shares		100 000
(net of depreciation)	45 000			
Fixtures and fittings				
(net of depreciation)	4 000			
Motor vehicles				
(net of depreciation)	5 000			
	54 000			
		Issued share capital		
		50 000 £1 ordinary		
		shares, fully paid		50 000
Current assets				
Stock	14 000	*Revenue reserves*		
Debtors	22 000	General reserve	15 000	
Cash	500	+ transfer	1 000	
	36 500			
				16 000
		Profit and loss a/c*		1 500
		Ordinary shareholders'		
		interest		67 500
		Current liabilities		
		Creditors	12 000	
		Bank overdraft	2 500	
		Proposed dividend		
		on ordinary		
		shares	5 000	
		Corporation tax	3 500	
				23 000
	90 500			90 500

* Balance of appropriation a/c

Fig. 22.4   A balance sheet (horizontal presentation)

Balance sheet of J. Smith Ltd as at 31 December 19–9

	£	£	£
Fixed assets			
Premises (net of depreciation)			45 000
Fixtures and fittings (net of depreciation)			4 000
Motor vehicles (net of depreciation)			5 000
			54 000
Current assets			
Stock	14 000		
Debtors	22 000		
Cash	500		
		36 500	
Less current liabilities			
Creditors	12 000		
Bank overdraft	2 500		
Proposed dividend on ordinary shares	5 000		
Corporation tax	3 500		
		23 000	
Working capital			13 500
			67 500
Authorized share capital			
100 000 £1 ordinary shares			100 000
Issued share capital			
50 000 £1 ordinary shares, fully paid			50 000
Revenue reserves			
General reserve	15 000		
+ transfer	1 000		
		16 000	
Profit and loss a/c*		1 500	
			17 500
Ordinary shareholders' interest			67 500

* Balance of appropriation a/c

Fig. 22.5   A balance sheet (vertical presentation)

However different this presentation may look, the figures going into it are exactly the same and a banker must be able to read and find his way about differently presented sets of accounts. While all businesses produce a set of final accounts once a year it is common to find that interim accounts are prepared half-yearly, quarterly or even monthly by larger organizations.

Before we examine a set of accounts in detail a brief word of explanation about some of the items appearing on the balance sheet is appropriate.

Fixed assets. This section of the balance sheet comprises those items that do not change daily and are likely to be retained for use in the business for some time to come. They have been described as the 'means by which companies produce the goods or services they offer to customers and clients', for without premises, fixtures and fittings, motor vehicles and machinery the business would not be able to function. It is usual for fixed assets, with the exception of freehold land, to be depreciated over a period of time or with use. Thus the value of the assets is reduced and the amount of depreciation is charged as an expense of the business in the profit and loss account.

Current assets. This section of the balance sheet contains stock, debtors, bank (if the business has funds at the bank) and cash. The current assets are sometimes described as the *circulating assets* because, unlike the fixed assets, they are changing from day-to-day throughout the working capital cycle.

Stock. This item on the balance sheet represents the estimated valuation of the stock of the business. A manufacturer may well have different sorts of stock to include under this heading: raw materials, work-in-progress and finished goods, for example. A business that both buys and sells the same goods, such as a shop, does not have these different categories of stock although it may have many hundreds of different lines of goods in stock. Whatever the complexities most stock will be valued on the basis of either cost or net realizable value, whichever is the lower.

Debtors. The figure for debtors records the total amount owing to the business by its customers at the balance sheet date. A provision for bad debts is usually deducted from this figure and any bad debts written off are charged to the profit and loss account.

Capital. This is the amount that the owners of the business have invested in it. Limited companies can issue various types of shares (see Unit 13.5(*b*)) and the authorized and issued share capital of the company is normally stated on the balance sheet. The amount shown against issued share capital, for each class of share, is the *nominal* amount. If the shares were originally issued by the company at a premium, for example if a £1 share was originally issued for £1.50, the amount of the premium is credited to the *share premium account*, which is a *capital reserve*.

Revenue reserves. These are the profits of the company that over the years have been kept in the business and not distributed to the shareholders. The cash which represented them has been invested in the assets of the business. In the case of a sole trader or a partnership there would be no specific revenue reserves but the profits not withdrawn from the business would represent reserves. A limited company also often has capital reserves (see Unit 7.3(*b*)) which, unlike revenue reserves, cannot be distributed to the shareholders in the form of dividends.

Current liabilities. This section of the balance sheet contains those liabilities that are normally due to be paid within twelve months from the date of the balance sheet. It always contains creditors, the bank balance (if overdrawn) and, for companies, the amount of a dividend proposed but not yet paid, and corporation tax which will be paid during the next twelve months.

Creditors. The figure for creditors records the total amount owing by a business to its suppliers at the date of the balance sheet.

Proposed dividend. Obviously this item only appears on a company balance sheet and represents the amount of dividend that the directors propose should be paid to shareholders in the near future.

Corporation tax. Another item that is only found in company accounts (although, of course, individuals running their own businesses also have to pay tax).

22.3   Interpretation of Accounts

This involves understanding what the accounts tell us and is not, in itself, difficult. The problem is knowing where to start because we are faced with a mass of figures and information and some logical method is needed to extract the information. However, before we start, a word of warning! It is easy to think that interpretation of accounts consists solely of calculating a number of ratios, percentages, and so forth: there is more to it than this and it is a waste of time to make these calculations unless useful and significant information can be derived from the answers.

There are six main areas to consider when looking at a set of accounts: the *shareholders' stake*, any *long-term loans* made to the business, the firm's *working capital*, its *liquidity*, the *trading figures* and *other items*. We shall consider each of these in turn.

(*a*)   Ordinary Shareholders' Stake
This means the ordinary share capital and reserves of a limited company or, for sole traders and partnerships, the balance of the capital account. In the balance sheet of J. Smith Ltd referred to earlier, the ordinary shareholders'

stake amounts to £67 500. A bank is unlikely to be prepared to put more money into the business than its owners have done, without a very good reason. The accounts will show if profits are being retained in the business, which is an indication of a good policy. The profits figure for the current year can be compared with that of the previous year—most sets of accounts show, in a separate column, the previous year's figures. A banker looks to see how the figures compare and will want to know the reason for a fall in profits. He may be able to see from the profit and loss account that the reduction in profit is due to a large increase in a particular type of expense, such as administration expenses. If sales have increased by 60 per cent and administration expenses have also increased by 60 per cent then something is wrong because, although some expenses may rise as sales increase (variable expenses), few will increase exactly in proportion and many expenses remain the same (fixed expenses) and do not, in the short term, vary with sales.

The percentage return on ordinary shareholders' funds (ordinary share capital + reserves) can be calculated and the trend discovered by comparison with previous years. The calculation is made as follows:

$$\text{Percentage return on ordinary shareholders' funds} = \frac{\text{Net profit before tax}}{\text{Ordinary shareholders' funds}} \times \frac{100}{1}$$

A similar calculation which is often used when assessing balance sheets is *return on capital employed*. This compares the profit made with the long-term funds of the business, that is, all the share capital and the reserves plus long-term loans. It is calculated as follows:

$$\text{Return on capital employed} = \frac{\text{Net profit before interest and tax}}{\text{Shareholders' funds} + \text{Long-term loans}} \times \frac{100}{1}$$

With either of these calculations, a fall in the percentage from one year to the next would indicate that the business was not using its capital effectively. A bank that has several customers in similar types of business can make a direct comparison between them of their effectiveness in using the ordinary shareholders' funds and the capital employed.

(b) Long-term Loans

If a business has long-term loans (not a bank overdraft which is technically repayable on demand) they are listed after the capital and reserves. A bank needs to know when any such loans are due to be repaid and whether they are secured on the assets of the company—that is, is there any security left for the bank? If they are loans from the company's directors and they are for substantial amounts, a *letter of postponement* could be taken from the directors, whereby they postpone their own repayment in favour of the bank's.

(c) Working Capital

The amount of working capital may be calculated as follows:

$$\text{Working capital} = \text{Current assets} - \text{Current liabilities}$$

Sufficient working capital ensures that the business is able to pay its creditors without difficulty, hold adequate stocks and allow its debtors a reasonable time for payment. As a business expands it needs to carry larger stocks and increased debtors and will need an increase in the amount of its working capital rather than trying to delay payments to creditors.

The method of calculating working capital stated above gives an answer in pounds and, if calculated year by year, can show the trend of a particular company's business. The working capital requirements of a small shop are totally different from those of a large departmental store, however, and in order to make a comparison between businesses more meaningful the *working capital ratio* or *current ratio* can be calculated:

$$\text{Current ratio} = \frac{\text{Current assets}}{\text{Current liabilities}}$$

A satisfactory current ratio is usually regarded as being about 2:1, that is, for every £1 of current liabilities there should be £2 of current assets. Thus if a creditor demands immediate payment there are sufficient current assets to be realized to meet his requirements. It is also very useful for a business to calculate its current ratio and make comparisons from year to year.

When a manager lends money to a business customer he often attempts to estimate what the working capital will be if he grants the advance. The bank overdraft will form a part of the current liabilities and thus help to reduce and worsen the current ratio; the ratio will be further aggravated if the advance is used to assist with the purchase of a fixed asset. Consider the following balance sheet:

Balance sheet of ABC Co Ltd as at 31 December 19–9

	£		£
Fixed assets	23 000	*Capital*	30 000
Current assets		*Current liabilities*	
Stock 4 000		Creditors	7 000
Debtors 8 000			
Bank 2 000			
	14 000		
	37 000		37 000

The current ratio is 2:1 (£14 000 ÷ £7 000) which is satisfactory. Suppose the company now approaches the bank for overdraft facilities of £5 000 to purchase a machine (a fixed asset) costing £7 000; if the advance is granted the balance sheet will appear as follows:

Balance sheet of ABC Co Ltd as at 31 December 19–9

	£			£
Fixed assets	30 000	*Capital*		30 000
Current assets		*Current liabilities*		
Stock	4 000	Creditors	7 000	
Debtors	8 000	Bank	5 000	
	12 000			12 000
	42 000			42 000

The current ratio has thus altered to 1:1 (£12 000 ÷ £12 000) and if the overdraft limit is strictly adhered to the company could have difficulties in paying pressing creditors.

(d) Liquidity

When referring to the liquidity of an asset we mean the ease and speed with which it can be converted into cash. The balance of the bank account and cash on hand are, of course, perfectly liquid, whereas debtors are 'near-liquid'. Stock is not as liquid as debtors because it has to go through the process of being converted into debtors before it becomes cash.

In any business, certain liabilities have to be paid off in the very near future and part of the interpretation procedure must be in seeing that payments which are due can in fact be met. This is why bankers are interested in the liquidity of assets. It may be that the bulk of the current assets are in the form of stock, which means that cash cannot be forthcoming for some time, especially if the stock is turning over slowly and the business sells only on credit and has no cash customers. It should not be too difficult to determine whether the assets are sufficient and liquid enough to meet pressing liabilities. A banker must also be concerned as to future liquidity in deciding whether the repayments to the bank will be maintained as promised by the customer or in deciding how repayments are likely to be made. If he suspects that the facilities being requested are inadequate and that the customer will soon be back asking for more, it would be appropriate to ask the customer to prepare a cash budget (see Unit 22.4).

A general impression of the liquidity position can be obtained by seeing how far current assets less stocks go towards repaying the current liabilities. When expressed as a ratio this is known as the *liquid* or *quick ratio* and is calculated as follows:

$$\text{Liquid ratio} = \frac{(\text{Current assets} - \text{Stock})}{\text{Current liabilities}}$$

Thus for the ABC Co Ltd mentioned earlier the liquid ratio is 1.43:1 (£10 000 ÷ £7 000) in the first balance sheet and 0.67:1 (£8 000 ÷ £12 000) in the second.

A liquid ratio of 1:1 is quite reasonable: it means that the business, without selling its stock, could cover its current liabilities in full. A ratio of 1.5:1 is even better but a ratio any higher than this could indicate that too much is tied up in debtors and bank—idle money that is not working for the business.

(e) Trading Figures

In comparing the sets of accounts from two or three years, any large fluctuations in debtors, creditors and stocks should be noted.

A bank should find out how many debtors' accounts there are: it is better to spread the risk of bad debts widely, rather than have a few large debtors. From the year-end accounts it is possible to calculate the period of credit being allowed by the business by comparing debtors with sales. For example, suppose that debtors are £6 000 and sales for the year are £36 000: the average period of credit being allowed is 1/6 of a year (two months).

Similarly, the make-up of creditors needs to be known: are there many small creditors' accounts or one or two very large ones? If one large creditor exerts pressure for repayment this could create financial difficulties for the company. The period of credit being taken by the company can be calculated by comparing creditors with purchases. For example, if creditors are £4 000 and purchases for the year are £40 000, the average period of credit taken is 1/10 of a year (about five weeks).

The bank manager must consider if the figures for credit allowed and taken are reasonable, bearing in mind the type of business—if the customer were running a sweet and tobacco shop one would not expect to see substantial debtors on the balance sheet! If possible, the figures calculated should be compared with those of the previous year; if the period for creditors is increasing while that for debtors is decreasing this would indicate that the firm's resources were being stretched.

The banker needs to know certain points about the stock of the business. He needs to find out if the stock includes any 'dead' or unsaleable items; he needs to know how it is valued—as already mentioned, a common valuation is at the lower of cost and net realizable value. In particular the bank should find out how fast it is being 'turned over', that is, how many times the average amount of stock held is sold and replaced in a year. This may be calculated from a trading account by dividing the total cost of goods sold in a year by the average cost of stock held. Suppose we find that the average stock is sold (turned over) four times in a year, that is, stock remains in the stores, on average, for $\frac{1}{4}$ of a year (three months) before being sold and replaced. Is this a good turnover? It is for a furniture dealer but not for a fishmonger! In other words, it depends on the type of business. As stock 'turns over' profits are made, so obviously a quick turnover is very desirable.

In addition to looking at debtors, creditors and stock, the bank can calculate the *gross profit percentage* from the trading account and the *net profit percentage* from the profit and loss account as follows:

$$\text{Gross profit percentage} = \frac{\text{Gross profit}}{\text{Sales}} \times \frac{100}{1}$$

$$\text{Net profit percentage} = \frac{\text{Net profit}}{\text{Sales}} \times \frac{100}{1}$$

These figures indicate the profitability of the business for each £100 of sales both before and after deduction of expenses. Comparative figures for previous years should indicate a steady trend and any sudden fall in the percentages warrants further investigation.

(f) Other Items

When looking at a set of accounts a banker must be alert to many things. In particular he should check whether the business has any investments listed on the assets side of its balance sheet: if so, there is the possibility that they could be sold to provide additional funds or could be used as security.

Any large item in the accounts should be inspected and considered and particular attention paid to any major changes that have taken place since the previous set of accounts.

22.4   Projected Accounts

One problem with interpreting customers' year-end accounts is that such accounts look to the past, in that they record what has gone on in the previous year, whereas it is from the future trading that profits will come to repay any proposed advance. The other problem is that by the time year-end accounts are prepared and sent to the bank manager, another six months could have elapsed so that the accounts are well and truly historical. This is not to say that accounts from the past are of no value to the bank: they are of considerable value in recording the progress of the business and establishing trends for the future which are, apart from any major change in trading, likely to continue.

To assist both bank and customer in planning for the future it is common for the manager to ask for the production of a month-by-month *cash budget*. This records the anticipated monthly cash/bank receipts and payments and estimates the closing bank balance at the end of each month. An example of a cash budget is shown in Fig. 22.6.

A cash budget shows clearly the extent of the need for bank overdraft or loan facilities. In the example in Fig. 22.6 the company would realize that it needs a maximum of about £4 500 and could approach the bank manager in plenty of time to make the arrangements.

It follows that as a cash budget is a projection into the future, it is only as good as the figures going to make it up. When a bank manager asks for a cash budget some customers put down a few hastily thought-up figures to 'keep him happy', although most give the matter more thought. It is a simple matter for a manager to check the progress of the customer's forecasts by inspecting the balance of the bank account at each month-end to see if the trend anticipated by the budget is reflected in the working of the account: he thus soon gets to

Cash budget of XYZ Trading Co Ltd for the six months ending 30 June 19–0

	Jan	Feb	Mar	Apr	May	June
Cash receipts	£	£	£	£	£	£
From debtors	2 000	2 500	2 750	2 250	3 000	3 000
Cash sales	500	750	1 000	750	1 000	1 000
Sale of old machinery					250	
	2 500	3 250	3 750	3 000	4 250	4 000
Cash payments						
To creditors	1 500	2 000	2 500	2 000	1 500	1 500
Wages	1 000	1 250	1 500	1 250	1 000	1 000
General expenses	500	1 000	1 000	500	500	250
Purchase of new machinery				2 000		
	3 000	4 250	5 000	5 750	3 000	2 750
Opening bank balance	1 000	500	(500)	(1 750)	(4 500)	(3 250)
Add cash receipts	2 500	3 250	3 750	3 000	4 250	4 000
Deduct cash payments	3 000	4 250	5 000	5 750	3 000	2 750
Closing bank balance	500	(500)	(1 750)	(4 500)	(3 250)	(2 000)

Fig. 22.6   A cash budget (note: bank balance in brackets indicates an overdraft)

know those customers whose forecasts are wildly optimistic and those who are consistently nearer the mark. No cash budget can be completely accurate, however: so many variables are involved, ranging from the unknown future rate of inflation to an unexplained change in sales.

Any business that seriously attempts to produce a realistic cash budget must involve itself in estimating future sales, purchases and expenses. These can be combined to make up a set of *projected* or *budgeted accounts* which show what the trading profit and loss account should be like for the next six or twelve months, together with a balance sheet at the end of the period. These can be of great use to both bank manager and customer as an indication of future profitability and also as an early warning of impending difficulties so that corrective action can be taken well in advance. Also, as time goes by, the actual results for the accounting period can be compared with the projected figures and any major discrepancies investigated. Nearly all large companies already prepare these projected accounts and have sophisticated control systems to highlight any variances from the actual results. However, the further ahead in time the projections are made, the less accurate they usually turn out to be in practice; for example, a slight increase in the buying price of materials not anticipated by the projected accounts will scarcely affect the budgeted accounts for the forthcoming three months, but will have a greater effect on accounts for the next six months and a considerable effect on the accounts for the next year.

22.5   'Going Concern' and 'Gone Concern'

Most balance sheets are prepared on a *going concern* basis which means that the business is expected to continue to trade and, under such circumstances, the values shown in the balance sheet are those that the assets are worth to the company. No banker intentionally lends money to lose it, but sometimes a company's plans go wrong for a variety of reasons and a manager may have to look critically at a business balance sheet and estimate what the assets might realize in the event of a forced sale. Such an exercise involves going through the company's assets as shown on the balance sheet and reducing them by different amounts in an attempt to estimate their sale value. Often a bank's head office can give guidelines as to how much assets should be reduced by, if a balance sheet must be studied from the *gone concern* point of view.

Land and premises. These are assets where, despite the failure of the business, actual values may be greater than cost. Nevertheless they may be reduced by varying amounts depending on the specialized nature of the premises. It may be that the bank has taken the property as security and wishes to sell it: if the proceeds of sale do not fully repay the overdraft, the bank could claim as a general creditor of the business for the remaining indebtedness.

Motor vehicles. If these have been satisfactorily maintained they may well realize something approaching the figure shown in the balance sheet provided that suitable provision for depreciation has been made. It is inevitable that as a business gets into financial difficulties, it will reduce repairs and maintenance of vehicles (and of plant and machinery as well) to a minimum.

Plant and machinery, fixtures and fittings, office equipment. These assets usually realize no more than a very small proportion of their balance sheet valuation. As there is only a limited second-hand market for them, a banker will often consider them at scrap value.

Stock, work-in-progress, raw materials. The stock of finished goods generally has some resale value but must be considerably reduced from the balance sheet figure. Work-in-progress is usually of no use to anybody except as scrap and is valued accordingly. The stock of raw materials, provided it does not comprise highly specialized items, can be valued at nearer the balance sheet figures.

Debtors. Most should be collectable but a check should be made to ensure that the figure comprises current or 'live' debtors and is not made up of badly overdue debts that should have been written off long ago.

Bank and cash. When a company is in financial difficulties there is one thing of which you can be certain: at the end, the bank overdraft will be at its limit or beyond, and there will be no float of cash.

Creditors. As mentioned previously the bank must prove its debt along with all the other general creditors of the business where it has lent unsecured or where, after realization of its security, there remains an amount of indebtedness.

Lending money is a complex affair and the interpretation of a customer's accounts is only one of the lending banker's considerations. Above all he should remember that, while it is the depositors' funds that are being lent, behind every set of accounts showing cold facts and figures there stands a group of human beings who make up the business that seeks new or continued bank facilities.

The four questions in Unit 22.6 present the kind of problems that a bank manager meets when lending to his business customers. Outline answers to these questions are given at the back of the book. You should realize that in practice, in a bank branch, you would have far more information about these customers than it is possible to give here.

22.6   Questions

1. Johnson Brothers Ltd owns a number of do-it-yourself shops in and around the town where you work. The brothers have always followed an expansion programme, buying suitable premises and altering the layouts of their existing shops to enable a greater range of stock to be displayed. In the past they have had overdraft facilities which have been satisfactorily cleared; the company bank account is currently in credit. The latest balance sheet shows the following position:

Balance sheet of Johnson Brothers Ltd as at 31 December 19–9

	£		£
Fixed assets		*Issued share capital*	
Freehold premises (net)	90 000	100 000 £1 ordinary	
Leasehold premises (net)	55 000	shares, fully paid	100 000
Shop fixtures and		*Reserves*	
fittings (net)	5 000	Profit and Loss a/c	60 000
Delivery vans (net)	6 000		
	———		
	156 000		

			Long-term liabilities		
			Loans from directors		10 000
Current assets			Current liabilities		
Stock	23 000		Creditors	8 000	
Debtors	3 000		Corporation Tax	7 000	
Bank	2 500				
Cash	500				15 000
		29 000			
		185 000			185 000

Relevant figures from the trading and profit and loss accounts for the year:

Sales	£143 000
Purchases	£100 000
Gross profit	£46 000
Net profit	
before tax	£20 000

The brothers come to you in February 19–0 seeking an overdraft facility of £10 000 for six months to enable them to carry out extensions at one shop at a cost of £3 000, and to allow them to build up their stocks in readiness for the spring when there is always a big increase in demand for do-it-yourself products.

How would you treat their request?

2. Your customer Elizabeth Adams Designs Ltd has been trading for two years. The directors are Elizabeth Adams, who holds a majority shareholding and her husband David, who owns the remaining shares. The company sells handmade dresses to small shops and boutiques, most of the manufacturing and selling being carried out by Elizabeth herself, assisted in production by a few outworkers. The balance sheet for the second year of trading is as follows:

Balance sheet of Elizabeth Adams Designs Ltd as at 31 December 19–9

	£			£
Fixed assets			Issued share capital	
Machinery (net of			1 000 £1 ordinary shares,	
depreciation)	500		fully paid	1 000
Delivery van (net of			Long-term liabilities	
depreciation)	750		Loans from directors	1 000
Current assets			Current liabilities	
Stock:			Creditors 3 000	
raw materials	200		Bank 350	
work-in-				3 350
progress	900			
finished				
goods	500			
Debtors	1 500			
	3 100			

Profit and loss a/c	1 000	
	___	
	5 350	5 350
	≡≡	≡≡

Relevant figures from the trading and profit and loss accounts for the year:

Sales	£10 000
Purchases of raw materials	£8 000
Gross profit	£1 000
Net loss	£500

Although there is no official overdraft limit on the account, cheques have recently been paid to meet pressing creditors. Despite the loss that was made last year, Elizabeth Adams is convinced that if she can organize production properly, she can make profits and she comes to you with the following proposition: she requires an overdraft limit of £10 000 to pay a year's advance rental of £3 500 on vacant factory premises on the Industrial Estate, to buy new machinery and fixtures for £2 500, to carry out alterations to the new premises at a cost of £2 000 and to provide additional working capital of £2 000.

How would you treat this request and what suggestions would you make to the directors?

3. Your customer, Bill Harris, comes to the bank and hands you the set of accounts shown below which he has prepared himself. The bank account has only been open a matter of months and, during the course of the interview, you learn that he is self-employed and makes wooden toy cranes which sell in the shops at £15 each. He does everything from manufacturing to selling, employing no workers.

Profit and loss statement for the six months ended 31 December 19–9

	£	£
Sales		7 020
Materials purchased	3 750	
Wages	9 000	
Rent	1 200	
	___	
	13 950	
Less stock unsold 31 December 19–9	9 750	
	___	
Cost of goods sold		4 200
		___
Gross profit		2 820
Advertising and selling expenses	1 050	
Interest on loan	120	
	___	
		1 170
		___
Net profit		1 650
		≡≡

Balance sheet as at 31 December 19–9

	£	£
Assets		
Cash at bank	150	
Debtor*	300	
Stock	9 750	
		10 200
Less liabilities		
Loan from father	3 000	
Creditors	3 150	
		6 150
Net worth of Bill Harris		4 050

* Debtor was for a sale made on 15 August 19–9

He asks you for an overdraft limit of £3 000 for twelve months to help the business become better established. How would you treat this request?

4. Your customer, the Inbetween Co Ltd, sells a range of convenience foods to retail outlets in the Midlands area. The foods are Chinese meals that only need to be boiled or put in the oven for half an hour or so and are then ready to be eaten. They are very popular with busy people and sell well. The company does not make the products itself, but buys from a manufacturer at 80p per pack and sells to the shops at £1 per pack. Sales have been fairly static for the past few years and the company has made profits of between £5 000 and £10 000 each year.

   A new managing director has recently been appointed. He is determined to expand the sales of the company over a much wider area and has already taken on an extra sales representative. Sales are currently running at 20 000 packs per month but he confidently predicts a cumulative increase in sales amounting to 5 000 packs each month commencing in June. He tells you that the financial position now (1 April) is:

	£		£
Stock	16 000	Capital	50 000
Debtors	40 000	Creditors	16 000
Bank	10 000		
	66 000		66 000

He asks for an overdraft limit of £5 000 for the next six months to cover the expansion in sales—he says it won't be needed after that because the extra profits from increased sales will bring the bank balance into credit.

In conversation you learn that as the manufacturer is a large organization, the Inbetween Co Ltd has to pay for purchases in the month after purchase. On the other hand, to be competitive with other food wholesalers, it has to allow its customers two months' credit. In order to give a good service to its customers, the company maintains an anticipated month's supply of food packs in stock to cover the expected sales in the succeeding month. Operating costs are £3 000 per month and are paid as they fall due; they are not expected to increase with the expansion of business.

How would you treat this request? (A clue: try to calculate the closing bank balance at the end of each month until the end of December.)

(Answers given on pp. 384–9.)

Multiple-choice Questions—12

Read each question carefully. Choose the *one* answer you think is correct. Answers are given on page 390.

1. On a gone concern basis which one of the following assets could be expected to realize the balance sheet value?

    A land and premises **C** machinery
    B motor vehicles **D** stock

2. Interest on a bank overdraft will be charged to a firm's:

    A trading account **C** profit and loss account
    B balance sheet **D** manufacturing account

3. Which one of the following would you *not* take into account in calculating working capital?

    A cash **C** motor vehicles
    B debtors **D** bank overdraft

4. Which one of the following would you *not* take into account in calculating liquid capital?

    A cash **C** bank overdraft
    B stock **D** creditors

5. Your bank lends money to a business on an overdraft to finance the purchase of stock. This will:

    A increase working capital **C** decrease liquid capital
    B increase liquid capital **D** decrease working capital

6. In considering an overdraft for a manufacturing company, which one of the following is the most important consideration for a lending bank?

    A security available **C** borrowing power of the company
    B cash budget for the next 6–12 months **D** amount of share capital

7. In analysing a set of accounts you calculate the following:

	19–1	19–2
Gross profit percentage	35%	34%
Net profit percentage	16%	4%

Which one of the following would you investigate?

A selling prices   **C** expenses
B buying prices   **D** owner's drawings

8. The following information is available:

	£
Sales	30 000
Opening stock	5 000
Purchases	20 000
Closing stock	10 000

The rate of stock turnover for the year is:

A 4 times   **B** 2⅔ times   **C** 2 times   **D** 1½ times

9. The following information is available:

	£
Sales	100 000
Purchases	80 000
Opening stock	10 000
Closing stock	15 000
Expenses	10 000

Gross and net profit margins are respectively:

A 20% and 10%   **C** 15% and 5%
B 25% and 15%   **D** 10% and 20%

10. You are analysing the accounts of a large supermarket: which of the following sets
    of figures is the most likely?

A net profit percentage 4%;   stock turnover 12 times p.a.
B net profit percentage 5%;   stock turnover 2 times p.a.
C net profit percentage 15%; stock turnover 4 times p.a.
D net profit percentage 10%; stock turnover 6 times p.a.

The Chartered Institute of Bankers

23.1 Introduction

No book on 'Elements of Banking' would be complete without mentioning The Chartered Institute of Bankers, which is the professional body for bankers. It was founded in 1879 and has two broad aims:

(i) to provide the educational foundation on which any man or woman can build a banking career; and

(ii) to keep its members in touch with the latest developments in banking and business generally.

An elected Council, comprising senior bankers, decides the policy of the Institute, and all local centres (see Unit 23.5) are entitled to elect representatives to the Council. The headquarters of the Institute are in the heart of the City of London in Lombard Street, but membership and other records are now maintained at an administrative centre at Canterbury in Kent.

23.2 Membership

The members are men and women engaged in banking at all levels from the junior clerk working at a small branch to chief general managers and chairmen of large international banks. At present the membership stands at nearly 130 000 from 2 400 different banks in 100 countries. There are three grades of membership:

(i) *Ordinary members* are those who have not yet passed their Associateship examinations.

(ii) *Associates* are those members who have passed the Associateship examinations and have been elected by the Council. They are entitled to use the letters ACIB (Associate of The Chartered Institute of Bankers) after their names.

(iii) *Fellows* of The Chartered Institute of Bankers (FCIB) are elected by the Council from Associates who have achieved senior professional status and have performed services on behalf of the Institute.

Bank staff wishing to become members of the Institute should write for application forms to:

The Chartered Institute of Bankers,
10 Lombard Street,
London EC3V 9AS.

23.3   Examinations

The Institute's examinations structure is reviewed regularly to ensure that it continues to meet the educational requirements of modern banking. At the time of writing there are two main levels of qualification:

(i) the Banking Certificate;
(ii) the Banking Diploma.

The Banking Certificate provides a 'technician-level' qualification for supervisory staff who are not, at present, aiming at senior managerial positions. The Banking Diploma, which is regarded as the basic qualification for most career bankers, is completed in two stages and leads to Associateship of The Chartered Institute of Bankers. For those who have passed the Associateship examinations, or who have a recognized degree, there is a further, more advanced, course of study, the Financial Studies Diploma. Fig. 23.1 shows, in outline, the current examination structure.

Stage 1. The GCSE entrant (although, in fact, there are no minimum entry qualifications) will normally take the Banking Certificate:

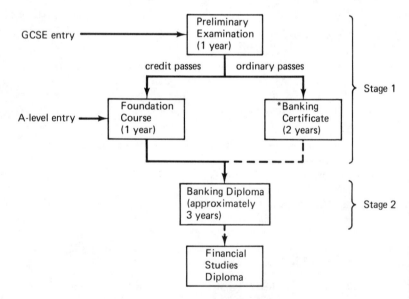

*The Banking Certificate is a qualification in its own right, but holders are entitled to enter the Stage 2 examinations.

Fig. 23.1   The Chartered Institute of Bankers: examinations flowchart

(i) Banking Certificate Preliminary, three papers (one year);
(ii) Banking Certificate Final, six papers (two years).

Successful completion leads to award of the Banking Certificate. This is a qualification in its own right, but holders are entitled to enter the Stage 2 examinations.

The A-level entrant can either take a one-year Foundation Course or can take the Banking Certificate Final examinations (two years). Both of these lead on to the Stage 2 examinations.

Whichever method is followed, broad areas of study at Stage 1 level include accountancy, economics, elements of banking, and law. The Banking Certificate course, however, includes more specialist subjects such as communications, banking law, and bank services. Stage 1 courses provide entry to the Stage 2 examinations although, as mentioned earlier, the Banking Certificate is a qualification in its own right.

Overseas, Stage 1 may be completed by taking an equivalent local qualification, approved by the Institute, or by taking single subject examinations at Royal Society of Arts Stage III or London Chamber of Commerce Third Level.

Stage 2. The entry requirements to this stage are the Stage 1 qualification or a recognized degree. Holders of degrees who are admitted directly to Stage 2 are expected to undertake a course of background study in law, economics, accounting and elements of banking.

Stage 2 consists of Parts A, B and C and is normally studied on a day-release/evenings basis. All students take The Chartered Institute of Bankers' examinations in the following subjects:

Part A
Monetary Economics
Accountancy
Law Relating to Banking

Part B
Nature of Management
Investment
Finance of International Trade

Part C
Practice of Banking 1
Practice of Banking 2

In addition there are different sets of examinations for those working in international banking, trustee and credit card departments.

Upon successful completion of Stage 2, members of the Institute qualify to be elected as Associate members and to use the letters ACIB provided that they also have at least three years' banking experience and have been members of the Institute for at least three years.

23.4   The Financial Studies Diploma

This is quite separate from the Associateship examinations; its object is to provide a degree-level qualification in banking and management subjects for those who are expected to reach senior management levels. The entry requirements are either ACIB or a recognized degree or professional qualification, and these last two must be of a standard and content acceptable to the Institute. Where a person is allowed direct entry as a result of possessing a degree or professional qualification, he or she is required to sit and pass two introductory papers before being allowed to take the Diploma course. The introductory papers, which do not have to be taken by ACIBs, are:

(i) The Monetary System, International Trade and Bank Services; and
(ii) Accountancy and the Banker.

The Diploma course, which all candidates are normally required to take, is in two sections and the subjects in each are:

Section 1
Practice of Banking 3
Human Aspects of Management
Business Planning and Control

Section 2
Marketing of Financial Services
Practice of Banking 4
Practice of Banking 5 (thesis)

All papers are examined by the Institute and tuition is available at some colleges and polytechnics, on an evening basis, or from a correspondence college. The Financial Studies Diploma is awarded to candidates who have successfully completed both sections, have at least three years' banking experience and have been members of the Institute for at least three years. Holders of the Financial Studies Diploma may use the letters Dip FS after their name.

23.5   Local Centres

The Institute has developed a number of local centres both in Britain and overseas where members can meet one another and also keep up to date in their careers. There are currently 105 local centres, of which six are overseas. Local centres run programmes of seminars, debates, group discussions, lectures and industrial visits which are open to all Institute members. These meetings are on a variety of topics, some (though not all) connected with banking, but in each programme there are some meetings chosen especially with the examination candidate in mind. Certain meetings are held jointly with the local centres of other professional organizations and thus bring bankers into social contact with other members of the local business community. Each local centre is concerned with the tuition facilities available in its area and an education officer is appointed to liaise with local colleges and to advise student members on all aspects of examination matters.

23.6   Other Services of the Institute

Each member receives a copy of the professional magazine *Banking World*. This is published monthly and contains articles on a wide range of banking and related topics and, in every issue, articles to help banking students with their examination work. The Institute publishes a range of books on banking and tuition aids, which are available from the Lombard Street headquarters either by post or by personal call.

Also in Lombard Street, the Institute maintains a specialist library consisting mainly of financial and commercial books and periodicals; this can be used by personal callers and borrowings may also be made by post within the United Kingdom. In addition, the library provides an information service for members and others who require answers to banking problems.

The Institute organizes a number of lectures and seminars on a national level. Of particular note is the regular management seminar for Associates in the 30–45 age-group at Christ's College, Cambridge. This usually lasts for one week and enables managers and potential managers from a variety of different banks to consider a specific theme and to widen their outlook on professional problems. In recent years the themes of the Cambridge seminars have included 'Bank strategies for the 1990s' (1986) and 'Banking through the looking glass' (1987).

Internationally, the Institute sponsors the International Banking Summer School which was first held in 1948 at Christ Church, Oxford. This is now held annually and cities all over the world have played host to it. It is attended by a large number of senior bankers from many different countries and a specific theme is chosen each year, as for the Cambridge seminars. These have recently included 'The Role of the Banks in International Financing' (1984), 'Competition and Co-operation in World Banking' (1985) and 'International Financial Centres' (1987).

The Institute also organizes European and American banking study tours which enable young Associates to study at first hand the banking systems of other countries.

Glossary

Acceptance Signature of the drawee of a bill of exchange, written across the face of the bill, to signify agreement to pay on the due date.

Acceptance house Specialist bank—often a merchant bank—which, by accepting bills of exchange, guarantees payment to the drawer and any other parties.

Account payee Words added to the crossing of a cheque; the collecting bank is put on enquiry, but transferability of the cheque is not affected.

Administrator Person appointed by the High Court to handle the estate of a person who has died intestate. See also **Executor**.

Annual percentage rate (APR) 'True' rate of interest which, under the provisions of the Consumer Credit Act 1974, must be quoted to most personal borrowers.

Arbitrage Act of borrowing money at one rate of interest and then lending the same money out at a higher rate of interest.

Articles of Association The regulations which govern the internal conduct of a limited company.

Assets Items owned: in connection with a business balance sheet they are divided between fixed assets—premises, machinery and so on—and current assets such as stock, debtors, bank balance and cash.

Assignment Transfer of the right to receive a sum of money or other benefit, for example a customer can assign the benefits in his life policy to a bank as security.

Authorities (the) Monetary authorities, that is, the Bank of England and the Treasury.

Automated teller machine (ATM) Computer-linked machine, operated by a plastic card, which dispenses cash and other bank services.

Bailee One to whom valuables are given for safe-keeping—a bank, for instance.

Bailment Under a contract of bailment the bailor leaves goods for safe-keeping with the bailee.

Bailor One who gives valuables for safe-keeping to another, the bailee.

Balance of payments The annual summary of the money values of the financial and economic transactions between one country and the rest of the world.

Balance sheet Statement of assets and liabilities at a certain stated time.

Bank bill Bill of exchange which has been accepted or endorsed by a bank.

Bank draft Payment instruction, similar to a cheque, drawn by a branch on the head office of the bank—as good as cash.

Bankers' Automated Clearing Services (BACS Ltd)   Computerized system of processing standing orders, bank giro credits (to pay salaries for example) and direct debits, without using paper vouchers.

Banker's lien   Right to retain and sell the property of another until legal demands against the owner have been satisfied. Unlike a general lien, a banker's lien has a right of sale. A bank does *not* have a lien over safe custody items.

Bank giro credit (BGC)   Method of transferring funds to the bank account of another, without the need to draw a cheque.

Banking Department   Functional department of the Bank of England which acts as banker to the British Government, banks, overseas central banks, some commercial companies, a few private customers and a number of international organizations.

Banking ombudsman   Independent body to whom personal customers of banks may refer disputes after banks' internal procedures have been exhausted; has power to make settlements of up to £100 000.

Bankrupt   A person who is insolvent and who has been adjudicated bankrupt by the Court.

Base rate   Rate of interest advertised by each bank to which most lending is linked.

Bill of exchange   Method of payment which can also allow a measure of credit. Defined as 'an unconditional order in writing, addressed by one person to another, signed by the person giving it, requiring the person to whom it is addressed to pay, on demand or at a fixed or determinable future time, a sum certain in money to, or to the order of, a specified person, or to bearer.' (Bills of Exchange Act 1882).

Bill of lading   Receipt for goods and contract of carriage issued by a shipping company for goods sent by sea; a negotiable instrument which may be transferred by endorsement and delivery.

Blank endorsement   An endorsement that consists only of the signature of the payee or endorser.

Bonus issue   A 'free' issue of shares made by a company to existing shareholders in proportion to their holdings: reserves are capitalized, so no new money comes into the company. Also known as a scrip issue.

Bridging loan   Short-term finance to cover a temporary shortfall: often used to enable a customer to buy a new house before receiving the proceeds of the sale of his old house.

Cable transfer   International method of payment for urgent transfers of funds. See **Express international money transfer**.

Call money   Deposits placed by banks with discount houses which can be withdrawn on demand.

Capital   Amount invested in a business by its owner(s).

Cash budget   Record of anticipated cash/bank receipts and payments, usually on a monthly basis, for some future period: helps a business anticipate the need for a bank overdraft.

Central bank   The bank of a country charged with the task of carrying out the Government's monetary policy; often Government owned. In Britain the central bank is the Bank of England.

Certificate of deposit   Bearer certificate issued by a bank stating that a certain sum of money has been placed with that bank for a given period, and at a particular rate of interest.

Certificate of Incorporation   Document issued by the Registrar of Companies which formally 'brings to life' a limited company.

Charge card   A plastic card which can be used to charge expenses, such as travel and entertainment costs, to an account. Operates in a similar way to a credit card account except that there is no pre-set spending limit and no credit facilities are offered—account holders are expected to settle monthly statements in full.

Cheque   'A bill of exchange, drawn on a banker, payable on demand.' (Bills of Exchange Act 1882.)

Cheque card   Plastic card which guarantees to a payee payment of a cheque up to a certain amount, provided that certain terms and conditions are met.

Clearing bank   Bank which is a member of the Bankers' Clearing House, or which participates in the clearing system.

Clearing House Automated Payments System (CHAPS)   Computerized payments system which provides for same day settlement, without the use of cheques or vouchers.

Collateral   Security deposited by a third party to secure a customer's account.

Collecting bank   Bank which collects payment of a cheque or bill of exchange from another bank on behalf of a customer.

Commercial bill   Bill of exchange drawn by a commercial firm, which has *not* been accepted by a bank or discount house.

Competition and Credit Control   System of monetary control in use from 1971 to 1981.

Composite rate tax (CRT)   Rate of tax deducted by banks and building societies from interest paid on personal customers' accounts. The tax is paid to the Government.

Consortium bank   A bank which is owned by other banks but in which no one bank has a direct shareholding of more than 50 per cent and in which at least one shareholder is an overseas bank.

Conversion   Converting the goods of one person for the use of another.

Corporation tax   Tax paid on profits by limited companies.

Credit card   Plastic card which enables the holder to obtain goods on credit without formality.

Credit controls   System of controls operated by the authorities in order to restrict the lending capability of banks.

Credit scoring   Method of assessing loan and other applications by awarding points to answers given.

Crossed cheque   Cheque bearing across its face two parallel transverse lines and/or the name of a bank. See also **General crossing** and **Special crossing**.

Current assets   Stock, debtors and cash/bank balances of a business: sometimes known as circulating assets because they change from day-to-day as trading takes place.

Current liabilities   Liabilities which are currently due and which will normally be settled within the next twelve months, such as trade creditors and bank overdraft.

Debenture   Sealed acknowledgement of a debt issued by a company; often certain assets are used to secure the debt.

Deposit bank   Bank that accepts deposits from customers on current, deposit and other accounts; generally deposits are repayable on demand and there are no minimum and maximum amounts.

Deposit protection fund   Fund contributed to by recognized banks and licensed deposit-taking institutions to provide some measure of protection to depositors in the event of the failure of the deposit-taker.

Deposit rate   Rate of interest paid by a bank to customers with deposit accounts.

Depreciation   Estimated fall in the value of fixed assets held by a business for an accounting period; amount of depreciation is charged to the profit and loss account.

Direct debit   Method of payment through the banking system, whereby the beneficiary originates, by prior agreement, a debit to the payer's account and passes this through the clearing system.

Discount house   Specialist institution which acts as a financial intermediary between the Bank of England and the other banks; the Bank of England acts as a lender of last resort to discount houses.

Discounting   Purchase or sale of a bill of exchange or other instrument at less than face value.

Draft   Written order relating to the payment of money, for example a bank draft.

Drawee   One on whom a bill of exchange or cheque is drawn—the payer of a bill or cheque.

Drawer   One who writes out (draws) a bill of exchange or cheque.

Electronic funds transfer at point of sale (EFTPOS)   Method by which customers pay for goods in a retail outlet: using the appropriate card, the customer's bank account or credit card account is debited while, at the same time, the bank account of the retailer is credited, all without using a cheque or paper voucher.

Eligible banks   Those banks whose acceptance on a bill of exchange makes the bill suitable security to deposit with the Bank of England when discount houses seek loans.

Eligible liabilities   Sterling deposit liabilities of the monetary sector *less*:
   (i) deposits with an original maturity of more than two years;
   (ii) deposits with other institutions in the monetary sector;
   (iii) secured call money placed with money brokers and gilt-edged jobbers on the Stock Exchange.

Endorsement   Signature of payee or holder on a bill of exchange or cheque, for the purpose of transferring it to another person.

Endowment assurance   Life assurance which provides a lump sum payable either at the end of a specified time or on the prior death of the assured.

Equitable mortgage   A mortgage where both possession and ownership of the security remain with the borrower.

Equity shares   See **Ordinary shares**.

Eurobond   Long-term funds raised against the issue of bonds on the international capital markets in different currencies.

Eurocheque   An agreed system of cheques issued by European banks to be used in conjunction with a eurocheque card. Despite the name the use of the system is not solely restricted to Europe.

Eurocurrency   Any currency held by banks, companies or individuals outside its country of origin, for example, eurodollars.

Exchange control   Restrictions imposed by a government on the movement abroad of the country's currency; intended to protect the balance of payments and/or exchange rates.

Exchange Equalization Account   Account, managed by the Bank of England on behalf of the Treasury, which holds Britain's official reserves of gold, foreign exchange and Special Drawing Rights. It is through this account that the Bank intervenes in the foreign exchange market to smooth out any undue fluctuations.

Executor   Person appointed by a will to handle the deceased's estate. See also **Administrator**.

Export Credits Guarantee Department (ECGD)   Government department which provides insurance facilities and bank guarantees for exporters.

Express international money transfer (EIMT)   International method of payment for urgent transfers of funds: the payment instructions are sent by cable or by telegraphic transfer or through the SWIFT network as an 'urgent SWIFT message'. See also **International money transfer**.

Factoring   Service provided by specialist companies against a firm's debtors—services include sales ledger accounting, credit insurance and finance.

Fiduciary issue   A fiduciary issue of banknotes is one which is backed only by Government securities and other securities.

Finance house   Financial intermediary specializing in the provision of finance for hire purchase, leasing and factoring.

Financial futures contract   Agreement to buy or sell certain forms of money at a specified future date, with the price agreed at the time of the deal. See also **London International Financial Futures Exchange**.

Financial intermediary   Any institution which provides a service of bringing together lenders and borrowers such as banks and building societies and their customers.

Fixed assets   Long-term assets of a business; the means of production—premises, machinery and vehicles, for example.

Floating exchange rates   Exchange rates between currencies that are not fixed by administrative action but which fluctuate instead, largely according to supply and demand.

Foreign exchange market   A market for the purchase and sale of foreign currencies, now and in the the future. See also **Spot rate** and **Forward exchange contract**.

Forward exchange contract   An immediately firm and binding contract between a bank and its customer for the purchase, or sale, of a specified quantity of a stated foreign currency at a rate of exchange fixed at the time that the forward contract is made, for performance by delivery of and payment for the stated foreign currency at an agreed future time, or between two agreed future dates.

Forward rate   A rate of exchange which is agreed in the present but which states how much two currencies will be bought and sold for at some time in the future.

Freehold   A title to land under which the owner has possession without any time limit. See also **Leasehold**.

General crossing   Two parallel lines across the face of a cheque, with or without the words 'and company' and 'not negotiable'. See also **Special crossing**.

Gilt-edged securities   Securities of the highest class: the term usually refers to securities issued by the British Government.

Grant of probate   See **Probate**.

Guarantee   Collateral security involving three parties in which a guarantor (the third party) makes himself secondarily liable for the debts of the second party if he doesn't pay the first party.

Hire purchase   A form of personal or business credit under which ownership of goods or equipment passes to the hirer or debtor after payment of an agreed number of instalments, and after exercise of the hirer's option to purchase.

Hirer   Hire-purchase customer, or debtor, of the hire-purchase company.

Holder   Person in legal possession of a bill of exchange or cheque.

Holder for value   Person in possession of a bill of exchange or cheque where value has been given, at some time.

Holder in due course   A holder in possession of a bill of exchange or cheque who has taken it:
 (i)   complete and regular on the face of it;
 (ii) before it was overdue;
 (iii) without notice of prior defect in title at the time the bill was negotiated;
 (iv) without notice of previous dishonour, if such was the fact;
 (v)   in good faith and for value.

Home banking   Banking service operated through a home television set and linked to the bank's computer system by telephone; service handles account balances, statements, standing order details and allows transfers to be made between accounts.

Hypothecation   An agreement to give a charge over goods or documents of title to goods.

Indemnity   A security involving two parties in which the indemnifier (the second party) is primarily liable to the lender (the first party) for the debts of another.

Inflation   A fall in the value of money: too much money chasing too few goods with the result that prices of goods and services rise.

Inheritance tax   Tax which may be due on the estate of a deceased person, depending on its size.

Instalment credit   See **Hire purchase**.

Inter-bank market   Wholesale/parallel money market in bank deposits where the dealing is mainly between banks.

Interest   Price paid for borrowing money.

International money transfer (IMT)   International method of payment for non-urgent transfers of funds: the payment instructions are sent by airmail, or through the SWIFT network as 'SWIFT messages'. See also **Express international money transfers**.

Intestate   Person who has died without making a valid will.

Investment trust   A company which buys shares in other companies to hold for investment purposes.

Issue Department   Functional department of the Bank of England concerned with issuing banknotes: note issue is backed by Government and other securities.

Joint and several liability   Term usually found on joint account and partnership mandates: each party is jointly liable for any monies owing to the bank, and also liable for the full amount as individuals.

Leasehold   Title to land under which the leaseholder pays rent to the freeholder in return for which the freeholder grants occupation and use for a set period of time. See also **Freehold**.

Leasing   Form of business finance under which the ownership of equipment remains with the lessor but the lessee has use of the item, provided that regular leasing payments are made.

Legal mortgage   Mortgage where ownership of the security is transferred to the lender.

Legal tender   Notes and coin which must, by law, be accepted when offered in payment.

Lender of last resort   Function of a central bank whereby it undertakes, if necessary, to lend funds to certain financial intermediaries. In Britain the Bank of England is a lender of last resort to the discount houses and, indirectly, to the banks.

Lessee   One who is granted use of an asset by a lessor for a set period of time against rental payments.

Lessor   One who owns an asset and rents it to a lessee for a set period of time against rental payments.

Letters of administration   Legal authority granted by the High Court to administrator(s) to deal with the property of a deceased who died intestate. See also **Probate**.

Liabilities   Items owed: in connection with a business balance sheet, they are divided between long-term liabilities such as debentures and mortgage loans, and current liabilities such as creditors and bank overdraft.

Lien   A right to retain the property of another until legal demands against the owner (for example the settlement of a debt) have been satisfied. See also **Banker's lien**.

Limited company   See **Private limited company** and **Public limited company**.

Limited liability   Limitation on liability for debts: with companies, shareholders are only liable for the nominal amount of their shares or the amount they have guaranteed.

Liquid assets   Those assets which are either cash itself or can easily be turned into cash.

Liquidation   Winding up, or closing of a business—surplus funds (if any) are returned to the owners after all the debts are paid.

London inter-bank offered rate (LIBOR)   Rate of interest on the inter-bank market to which borrowing by banks' company customers is often linked.

London International Financial Futures Exchange (LIFFE)   Provides a market in financial futures, that is, currency and interest-rate contracts. See **Financial futures contract**.

Mail transfer   International method of payment for non-urgent transfers of funds. See **International money transfers**.

Mandate   Written instructions given by account holders to a bank on the conduct of the bank account: for example on joint accounts, whether the bank may debit cheques to the account against the signature of one party only.

Memorandum of Association   The document of a limited company which sets out the rules for the external conduct of the company; the memorandum states, among other things, the objects of the company.

Merchant bank   Specialist bank mainly involved in corporate finance: services include the acceptance of bills of exchange, the financing of foreign trade, the underwriting of new issues, the management of investments and the advising of companies.

Minimum lending rate (MLR)   An interest rate which used to be formally announced and was quoted by the Bank of England for its lending to the discount market. The *Monetary Control* measures of 1981 put MLR out of regular use but it has been reintroduced from time to time.

Minor   One who has not attained the age of majority (which is eighteen in Britain).

Monetary aggregates   Measures of the money stock: measures used in Britain are M0, M1, M2, M3, M3, M3c, M4 and M5.

Monetary Control   Title of the Bank of England document which introduced a system of amended monetary controls in 1981.

Monetary sector   Authorized institutions (under the Banking Act 1987), the Banking Department of the Bank of England and certain banks in the Channel Islands and the Isle of Man.

Money at call   Deposits placed by banks with discount houses which can be withdrawn on demand.

Mortgage   Transfer of an interest in land or property to a lender as security for a debt.

Near money   Types of financial assets which function more as a store of value than as a medium of exchange, for example bank deposits subject to notice of withdrawal, balances of building society and National Savings Bank accounts.

Negotiable instrument   Instrument representing money which can be transferred to another person by delivery, or by endorsement and delivery.

Negotiate   Transfer of legal rights in a bill, cheque or other document to another.

Nostro account   'Our account with you.' A currency account held abroad in the name of a bank which is used to settle international payments. See also **Vostro account**.

Note issue   Amount of banknotes in circulation; in the United Kingdom they are mainly issued by the Bank of England, but it also includes issues by Scottish and Northern Ireland banks: note issue is backed by Government and other securities.

Not negotiable   Words added to the crossing of a cheque which prevent negotiation but not transfer.

Offer of sale   Method of launching a new issue of shares whereby an Issuing House, having bought or underwritten the shares of the company concerned, offers them to the public.

Ombudsman   See **Banking ombudsman**.

Open cheque   A cheque not bearing a crossing.

Open market operations   The buying and selling of Government stocks and Treasury and commercial bills by the Bank of England in order to increase or decrease bank lending, or to affect interest rates.

Operational balances   Funds deposited by the clearing banks with the Bank of England for clearing purposes, within the banking system and between the banking system and the Bank of England.

Ordinary shares   The 'risk-taking' shares in a limited company: they take a share of any profits available for distribution after all other expenses, including loan interest, corporation tax and preference dividends, have been provided for. In the event of the company going into liquidation, the ordinary shareholders are the last to be repaid. Also known as *equity shares*.

Parallel money markets   The secondary money markets which deal in wholesale amounts of funds; examples are local authority, inter-bank and certificate of deposit markets. Unlike on the discount market, the Bank of England does not intervene and is not a lender of last resort.

Partnership   'The relation which subsists between persons carrying on a business in common with a view of profit' (Partnership Act 1890).

Payee   Person named on a cheque or bill of exchange to whom, or to whose order, payment is to be made.

Paying bank   Bank which pays customer's cheques drawn on it.

Pledge   Delivery of goods, or documents of title to goods, to a lender as security for debt.

Preference shares   Shares which usually receive a fixed rate of dividend paid in preference (before) to the ordinary shares. In the event of liquidation of the company, preference shareholders would rank before ordinary shareholders in repayment of capital.

Private limited company   Any company which does not meet the requirements of a **Public limited company** (see below).

Probate   Legal authority granted by the High Court to an executor(s) to deal with the property of a deceased. See also **Letters of administration**.

Promissory note   An unconditional promise in writing, signed by the promisor, to pay a certain sum of money to another at a fixed or determinable future time.

Public limited company   Company limited by shares:
   (i) the Memorandum of Association of which states that it is to be a public company;
   (ii) which has been registered as such;
   (iii) the name of which ends with the words, 'public limited company' (or its Welsh equivalent) or with the letters 'plc';
   (iv) which has not less than two members;
   (v) which has a minimum issued share capital of £50 000.
See also **Private limited company**.

Public sector   Central Government, local authorities and public corporations.

Public sector borrowing requirement (PSBR)   Borrowing by the public sector which is necessary to finance its activities.

Qualitative credit controls   Instructions issued by the central bank advising banks and other financial institutions which type of customer they should and should not lend to.

Quantitative credit controls   Instructions which were issued by the central bank advising banks and other financial institutions to limit the total amount of their lending to a certain figure. (In 1971 the Bank of England agreed to abandon quantitative controls.)

Restrictive endorsement   An endorsement that restricts further negotiation of a bill of exchange or cheque.

Retail banks   Banks which have extensive branch networks and/or are the main participants in the clearing system.

Retail deposits   Smaller deposits on current and deposit accounts, usually contributed by the public.

Revolving credit account   Type of account where customers are permitted to overdraw up to a certain limit at any time; repayments are made on a monthly continuing basis. Maximum overdraft is usually linked to a certain multiple of the monthly payments.

Rights issue   Offer by a company to existing shareholders of additional new shares in proportion to their holding. To make the issue attractive, it is usually made at below market price; a shareholder who does not wish to take up the rights can usually sell them on the Stock Exchange.

Safe custody   When a bank customer (the bailor) leaves items for safe-keeping with the bank (the bailee), a contract of bailment arises.

Safe deposit   Special type of safe in which a customer may rent a compartment to keep items of value.

Savings   That part of a person's income not spent on immediate consumption.

Scrip issue   See **Bonus issue**.

Secondary money markets   See **Parallel money markets**.

Security   Documents of value deposited as security for a bank overdraft or loan—share certificates, a life policy, title deeds, a land certificate or a guarantee are all acceptable.

Set-off   Merging of a customer's debit and credit balances to ascertain the net amount of indebtedness.

Sight bill   Bill of exchange payable by the drawee on sight, that is, immediately.

Sight deposits   Deposits with banks and other financial intermediaries that are repayable on demand.

Smart card   Latest generation of cheque and credit cards, which incorporate a microchip containing information such as a person's account balance and which can be used for EFTPOS transactions. See **Electronic funds transfer at point of sale (EFTPOS)**.

Society for Worldwide Interbank Financial Telecommunication (SWIFT)   International computer-operated communications network between banks to handle transfers of international payments and other messages between member banks.

Special crossing   Cheque which bears across its face the addition of a banker's name, with or without a general crossing. See **General crossing**.

Special deposits   An instrument of monetary control which is a call by the Bank of England on all institutions in the monetary sector with eligible liabilities of £10 million or more to deposit a percentage of their eligible liabilities with the Bank.

Special presentation   Direct presentation of a cheque to the drawee bank, without using the bulk clearing system.

Spot rate   Rate of exchange for an immediate foreign currency transaction.

Standing order   A method of payment by which a customer can instruct the bank to debit his/her account by fixed amounts at regular intervals: credits are passed to the beneficiary through the clearing system.

Tap issue   Sale of Government stock which is always available for purchase, at an appropriate price.

Telegraphic transfer   International method of payment for urgent transfers of funds. See **Express international money transfers.**

Tender issue   Issue of shares or Government stock where the selling price is not fixed in advance: subscribers are invited to state the price at which they will tender. All the shares or stock are then issued at the same price, that at which the issue is fully subscribed. Often a minimum tender price is stated.

Term assurance   Life assurance which covers a fixed term, rather than whole-life.

Term bill   Bill of exchange payable by the drawee at a fixed or determinable future date.

Term deposits   Deposits with banks and other financial intermediaries repayable after a pre-determined time.

Trade bill   Commercial bill of exchange which has *not* been accepted by a bank or discount house.

Treasury bill   A promissory note, usually for 91 days, issued by the Treasury to finance the Government's short-term borrowing requirements.

Truncation   The technique of stopping the flow of paper as it enters the banking system by 'capturing' the information from cheques and credits and transmitting it by electronic means to other branches and other banks.

Trustee   Person who holds an estate in trust for another.

Unit trust   Trust which collects savings from the public, pools the funds and makes investments in accordance with the trust deed. Trustees safeguard the interests of the investors, while managers manage the funds and make the investments.

Vostro account   'Your account with us.' A home currency bank account held in the name of a foreign bank which is used to settle international payments. See also **Nostro account**.

Whole-life assurance   Life assurance which covers whole-life rather than a fixed term.

Wholesale deposits   Large deposits placed with banks by companies and financial institutions; the interest rates are linked to money market rates.

Wholesale money markets   See **Parallel money markets**.

Working capital   Current assets minus current liabilities: sufficient working capital ensures that a business can hold adequate stocks, pay creditors within a reasonable time and allow a measure of credit to debtors.

Yield   Translates into terms of a share's market price the dividend paid: shows the amount of gross income which an investor could expect to receive if £100 were invested now.

Assignments

Introduction

These assignments are intended to be of use to all teachers and students of elements of banking. While the assignments can be used as given, many teachers will wish to use the ideas which they generate to create their own assignments which reflect the emphasis of their own courses and the particular needs of their students.

List of Assignments
1. Money
2. Banks in the United Kingdom
3. (*a*) The branch where I work; (*b*) Visit to a bank branch
4. Bank balance sheets
5. Savings and investment
6. Interest rates
7. Cheques and the clearing system
8. In-tray exercise
9. The money supply and monetary policy
10. Money markets
11. Bank services
12. Bills of exchange and cheques
13. Personal lending
14. Securities for bank advances
15. Office Supplies (Rowcester) Ltd
16. In-tray exercise

(Further questions on lending propositions and interpretation of accounts will be found in Unit 22.6.)

Assignment One—Money
Activity. Extraction of money stock information from statistical data and preparation of a graph. Consideration of some of the functions of money. Legal tender.

Situation. As a student of banking, you are required to extract information about the money stock, and to present and explain it. You will also consider some of the functions, and other aspects, of money.

Materials required. The *Bank of England Quarterly Bulletin* or the *Annual Abstract of Statistics*. Graph paper.

1. Using a source such as the *Bank of England Quarterly Bulletin* or the *Annual Abstract*

of Statistics, find out the most recent figures for M0 and M3 and indicate the individual items that make up each total.

2. Draw a graph showing the growth of M0 and M3 over the last two years. Comment on two aspects revealed by the graph.

3. An elderly customer of the bank branch at which you work approaches the enquiry desk and presses heavily on the bell push. To stop the noise you go quickly to the desk. The conversation goes like this:

You: Good morning, sir. Can I help you?

Customer: Yes, you certainly can. I've just read this in the paper. (*You are handed a crumpled piece of paper which has been hastily torn from today's newspaper. The paragraph reads: '£1 COINS—WHAT A SWINDLE!' and then goes on to say that the Royal Mint has disclosed that the metal content of a £1 coin is worth only 10p.*)

Customer: (*interrupting before you can finish reading*): I've always thought these coins were a fiddle. And the same goes for those bits of paper you call banknotes—they're never worth £5 or £10. It's not like when I was a youngster—we had proper gold and silver coins. (*Pause*) Well, don't just stand there . . . what have you got to say?

Write (or role play) your reply to this customer.

4. Give appropriate advice, with reasons, in the following circumstances:

(i) A friend complains that she was not allowed on board a bus because she only had bronze coins for the fare of 50p.

(ii) Your father is selling his car and a buyer wants to pay him in full in banknotes. However, your father is concerned about having a large sum of money in the house, even for a short time, and comments to you that he might refuse to accept the cash, preferring a cheque and only releasing the car after the cheque has been cleared.

Assignment Two—Banks in the United Kingdom

Activity. Preparing a summary of the different types of banks that operate in the United Kingdom today.

Situation. The manager of the branch at which you work calls you into his office one day and explains that he is giving a talk on banking to fifth-formers at a local school. Knowing that you are studying elements of banking he asks you to prepare the guidelines for his talk which is to be entitled 'Banks in the United Kingdom today'. He explains that the talk is to help the students with their studies in economics and commerce by considering the different types of banks operating in Britain, and briefly outlining their functions. Your manager is particularly keen that his talk should be supported by at least one diagram and a handout. He also asks you to look out for cuttings and advertisements from newspapers or magazines so that he can make the talk particularly up to date and relevant to the needs of his teenage audience.

1. Prepare guidelines for the manager to follow in his talk.

2. Prepare one diagram and one handout that could be used to support the talk.

3. Supply two or three newspaper/magazine cuttings relevant to the proposed talk.

Assignment Three—(*a*) The Branch where I Work
(*This assignment is designed for part-time students who work in a bank; for full-time students, see Assignment 3(b).*)

Activity. Consideration of how a bank branch works.

Situation. You are to consider the branch where you work and to prepare a report on various aspects of the activity of the branch. (Do not disclose anything in your assignment that is confidential to the bank.)

1. Each member of staff has a job title—manager, cashier, standing order clerk and so on. Take each of the main job titles at the branch and list the areas of responsibility that are undertaken by the job-holder.

2. List the different points of contact between customers and staff at the branch. What aspects of the bank's business are conducted at each contact point?

3. What uses of computerization and modern technology are made at the branch: (i) on the public side; (ii) on the staff side?

4. Walk into the branch looking at it as if you were a customer and comment on your impressions. Consider how attractively the branch is designed and set out. Are plenty of leaflets available and are they neatly displayed? Is the atmosphere one of friendly business efficiency? What changes could be made to improve the overall 'image'? Explain your views either orally or in writing.

Assignment Three—(*b*) Visit to a Bank Branch
(*This assignment is designed for full-time students; for part-time students who work in a bank, see Assignment 3(a).*)

Activity. Consideration of how a bank branch works.

Situation. You are to visit a nearby branch of a bank, to take notes during your visit and to prepare a report on various aspects of the activity of the branch.

1. Describe your visit in terms of what you are shown, and to whom you speak.

2. How many different points of contact are there between customers and staff? What aspects of the bank's business are conducted at each contact point?

3. What evidence can you see of the use of computerization and modern technology in the branch: (i) on the public side; (ii) on the staff side?

4. Comment on your overall impressions of the visit. For example, consider how attractively the branch is designed and set out. Are there plenty of leaflets available and are they neatly displayed? Is there a branch receptionist in the public area? How does the bank promote its 'image'?

Assignment Four—Bank Balance Sheets
Activity. Consideration of assets and liabilities of banks, balance sheets of banks and relevant bank balance sheet ratios.

Situation. You work as a clerical member of staff for National Barllands Bank at a large city centre branch which acts as a training branch for new entrants. The trainees are based at the branch for six months while they learn the routine of large branch banking. During this six-month period they undertake a specified training programme under the control of an assistant manager. They also attend an induction course at the bank's training centre in London. After the six-month period is over, the trainees are assessed and allocated to branches in the area, including the one at which you work (and where they have been trained) on a permanent basis.

There are twelve new recruits this summer and, about a month into the programme, the assistant manager responsible for training asks to see you. He hands you a copy of the latest bank balance sheet (see below) and asks you to give a talk to the trainees entitled 'A retail bank's balance sheet'. He feels that such a talk would be better coming from a younger member of the staff because the trainees will be more likely to ask questions and discuss points arising from it. He also considers it will be good for you from a personal development viewpoint.

1. You are required to draft your talk along the lines of the assistant manager's notes which take the following form:

Suggested title: 'A retail bank's balance sheet.' (All trainees have a copy of the bank's balance sheet.)
Suggested topics:

(i) Explain the structure of our balance sheet and look at the main assets and liabilities: share capital and reserves, current, deposit and other accounts, liquid assets, money at call and short notice, certificates of deposit, investments and advances. Explain each one.

(ii) Ask the trainees to indicate our main sources of funds and what we do with them.

(iii) On the assets side, consider the liquid assets saying why they are liquid and the

NATIONAL BARLLANDS BANK PLC
Balance sheet as at 31 December 19–5

19—4 £m		19—5 £m	19—4 £m		19—5 £m
	Liquid assets			*Share capital and reserves*	
	Cash in tills and balances		195	Issued share capital	210
303	with the Bank of England	305	604	Reserves	625
3 124	Money at call and short notice	3 081	799	Shareholders' funds	835
426	Bills discounted	394	198	*Loan capital*	217
253	Certificates of deposit	284			
4 106		4 064		*Other liabilities*	
				Current, deposit and	
489	*Cheques in course of collection*	510	22 643	other accounts	24 881
			48	Sundry creditors	52
793	*Investments*	810	7	Taxation	8
17 202	*Advances*	19 396	29	Dividends	31
30	*Trade investments*	31			
610	*Investments in subsidiaries*	703			
494	*Fixed assets*	510			
23 724		26 024	23 724		26 024

other assets less liquid. Also mention the 'safety' of the assets and the return that the bank gets—don't forget to quote up-to-date interest rates (the *Financial Times* is a useful source).

(iv) Work out three ratios from the balance sheet, remembering to explain the significance of each. Include reference to protecting the interests of the depositors.

Assignment Five—Savings and Investment

Activity. Obtaining leaflets from organizations which provide savings and investment facilities, preparing a chart to compare different rates of interest offered by various institutions, noting any restrictions which apply and giving investment advice in particular circumstances.

Situation. You are required to be aware of savings and investment facilities suitable for members of the public.

1. Collect leaflets from major savings institutions such as banks, building societies, National Savings Bank and unit trusts. Also collect newspaper cuttings of advertisements, press comments and so on about these institutions, together with any information you can find about life assurance and pension funds.

2. Prepare a savings and investment file containing:
   (i) a chart which compares the current interest rates on offer, together with a note of any restrictions which apply, for instance, minimum or maximum amounts of deposit and notice of withdrawal. (Make sure that your chart shows the rates available, gross *and* net of tax);
   (ii) leaflets, arranged in a logical order.

3. Using the information produced for 2, give advice on savings to the following people, making any reasonable assumptions about financial status that are necessary.
   (i) Jean Adams, a 17-year-old bank clerk, has £30 per week to save. She hopes to use part, but not all, of her savings to buy a car in two years' time.
   (ii) Matthew, aged thirteen, is saving pocket money and his earnings from a paper round. In about a year he hopes to buy a racing bike.
   (iii) Mr Edwards, a married man, is about to retire. He considers that his pension will be inadequate for his wife and himself to live on. However, he will receive a lump sum of £20 000 and wonders how best to invest it.
   (iv) John Clark is a teacher, aged twenty-eight, married with two children both under the age of five. His wife does not go out to work. John is worried about the well-being of his family if anything should happen to him. His budget is very tight: he tells you that after mortgage, hire-purchase commitments and day-to-day living expenses, the most he can set aside is £25 per month.
   (v) Mr and Mrs Roberts are a middle-aged couple whose children have married and left home. The Roberts both go out to work and find that they have about £150 per month to invest. They pay income tax at the basic rate and have £3 000 outstanding on a mortgage with five years to run.
   (vi) Mr Smith has £5 000. He would like to buy stocks and shares and/or Government stocks to obtain a regular income. He doesn't want to approach a stockbroker and is hesitant about asking his bank to buy for him: the reason he gives is that he doesn't know much about investment.

Assignment Six—Interest Rates

Activity. Examination of the structure of interest rates.

Situation. You are required to find out the current structure of interest rates and to draw conclusions.

Materials required. A 'quality' newspaper, personal loan form and other bank leaflets.

1. In your own words define the concept of 'interest' and explain the factors which influence interest rates.

2. Find out the current interest rates for:
   (i) the base rate of a major retail bank;
   (ii) the overdraft rate charged for 'good' customers;
   (iii) the overdraft rate charged for unauthorized overdrafts;
   (iv) the flat rate and APR for personal loans;
   (v) the APR for credit card accounts;
   (vi) the APR charged by shops and hire-purchase companies (price tags in shops and advertisements in local papers are two sources which will give you this information).

What conclusions can be drawn about the structure of interest rates?

3. What does LIBOR stand for? Find out the current rate for LIBOR using a suitable newspaper. Why are larger company customers often quoted overdraft and loan rates linked to LIBOR?

4. Nowadays companies (and individuals) are able to borrow money abroad fairly easily. Find out, again using an appropriate newspaper, the bank base rates (or equivalent) which apply in the following countries: (i) America; (ii) Switzerland; (iii) Germany; (iv) Japan.

Briefly, what conclusions can you draw?

Assignment Seven—Cheques and the Clearing System

Activity. A case study in the encashment of cheques, use of crossings and the method of cheque clearing.

Situation. You are a cashier at Midland Bank plc, Linton Bridge Branch. Your customer, Susan Smith, hands you the two cheques shown in Fig. 1(a) and (b). She wishes to cash one and pay the other into her account.

1. Explain which cheque, if either, you would cash and give your reasons.

2. With respect to Fig. 1(a):
   (i) identify and categorize the various parties;
   (ii) explain the meaning of the items marked 1, 2 and 3.

3. With respect to Fig. 1(b):
   (i) identify the type of crossing and explain its significance;
   (ii) explain how your answer to (i) would differ if the cheque had been crossed:
      (a) not negotiable;
      (b) account payee;
      (c) Barclays Bank PLC, Worcester.

4. Which cheque will need to be passed through the clearing system? Explain how this particular cheque will be cleared.

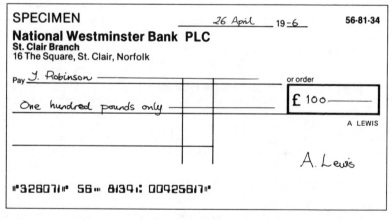

Midland Bank plc

SPECIMEN   10 May 19-6   ❶
40-51-20

21 North Street
Linton Bridge North Yorkshire

Pay __S. Smith__ _____ or order

___Fifty pounds only___

£ 50 —

S SMITH

⑂573059⑂ 90⑂ 5120: 00693912⑂
❷   ❸

S. Smith

(a)

Signature on reverse side of (a):

S. Smith

SPECIMEN   26 April 19-6   56-81-34

National Westminster Bank PLC
St. Clair Branch
16 The Square, St. Clair, Norfolk

Pay J. Robinson _____ or order

One hundred pounds only

£ 100—

A LEWIS

A. Lewis

⑂326071⑂ 56⑂ 8134: 00925817⑂

(b)

Signature on reverse side of (b):

J. Robinson

Fig. 1   Cheques for use with Assignment Seven

Assignment Eight—In-tray Exercise

Activity. Dealing with a number of problems that might arise on a day-to-day basis in a busy town centre branch.

Situation. You are employed by National Barllands Bank, a major United Kingdom retail bank. The local branch at which you work has a staff of nineteen and you have worked there since leaving school just over eighteen months ago. During the last year you have attended a nearby college each week, studying for your Stage 1 qualification of The Chartered Institute of Bankers and you have also been on bank training courses. You feel that you know thoroughly all the routine accounting procedures of banking and that you can handle most general enquiries. In recent months you have spent most of your time as a cashier and dealing with routine enquiries.

Today the bank is short-staffed: one colleague is away on a training course, a second is on day-release at the local technical college, a third is on holiday and another is off sick! You have been asked by the sub-manager to assist him in running the activities of the branch. In particular, he wants you to deal with a number of letters, telephone enquiries and other queries in the in-tray.

1. The following letter has been received:

> Walter Wall Carpets
> Park Street
> Yourtown YO1 4YZ
>
> The Manager
> National Barllands Bank
> High Street
> Yourtown
>
> Dear Sir
>
> I note that interest charges have been debited to my business account at the end of last quarter. I was concerned to see that, on looking back through past statements, the amount of interest charged has varied quite considerably. This is despite the fact that, according to my calculations, the average overdrawn balance on the account has been approximately the same for the last 12 months. I really can't see why a major bank such as yours has to alter rates so frequently. Why can't you charge me a fixed interest rate on my overdraft? To keep changing the rates plays havoc with the estimates of costs for small businesses such as mine.
>
> Yours faithfully
>
> Walter Wall

Your investigations reveal that the average balance and interest charged on the account for each quarter of last year were:

Quarter	Average balance	Interest charged
1	£9 975 o/d	£1 220
2	£9 630 o/d	£1 564
3	£10 205 o/d	£1 893
4	£9 812 o/d	£1 638

Draft a letter of reply to Mr Wall.

2. The following letter has been received:

> High Bridge House
> Lower Snodsbury
> Your County
>
> The Manager
> National Barllands Bank
>
> Dear Mr Palmer
>
> I am concerned about the regular payments made by the bank in respect of my National Brittanic accident policy. Until recently the payments were made by standing order and I had to come in each year to increase the monthly payment, as the amount covered by the policy increases in accordance with the rate of inflation. Now the company has asked me to sign a 'direct debit' authority and they say they will increase the amounts automatically. I am particularly concerned because the form they gave me to sign didn't have a money amount indicated. I really don't understand, but I'm sure you could explain it all to me very simply.
>
> Yours sincerely
>
> Ethel Everard (Miss)

The Manager asks you to draft a letter of reply for his approval.

3. You are asked to deal with the following problems:

(i) Mrs Smith is on the telephone demanding to know the balance of her current account. State how you would reply to your customer and explain the reasons for your answer.

(ii) Mr and Mrs Lewis are at the enquiry counter. They are not customers of the bank and tell you that they wish to open a current account at your branch. To open the account they want to pay in a cheque for £500 drawn by a customer of the Eastern Bank, Notyourtown branch. Detail the procedures you would follow before opening the account.

(iii) Explain to a customer, Mrs Fleming, why she cannot immediately receive cash for the £950 cheque she has just paid into her account.

(iv) A cashier asks if she may accept for the credit of J. Brown's account three cheques payable to W. Deacon. Looking at the cheques you see that all are crossed: one has '& Co' written in the crossing, the second is crossed 'not negotiable', while the third is crossed 'account payee'. Each cheque is endorsed 'W. Deacon'.

(v) Tracy Barlow, who has had a current account with your branch for twelve months, explains that next year, when she is eighteen, she will be going to college in a nearby town. She asks for a cheque card to draw cash at the branch near the college. Her account has been conducted satisfactorily and her parents have banked with you for many years. Explain to her the uses of a cheque card and advise her whether or not a card can be issued to her.

4. You remember that you promised to find out information for a friend on the different savings schemes offered by the bank. You are not sure whether a lump sum is involved or regular savings. Prepare a short summary for your friend of the schemes offered by your bank, finding out current rates if possible, and attach notes indicating the advantages and disadvantages of each scheme. The tax position will also need to be clarified.

5. The foreign clerk is very busy and you are asked to give him some assistance. Although your knowledge of foreign business is, as yet, fairly limited he thinks you should be able to draft a reply to the following letter:

Smith Brothers Engineers
Unit 10, Factory Estate
Yourtown

The Manager
National Barllands Bank

Dear Sir

We wish to purchase a new machine from Switzerland. The price quoted to us is 15 000 Swiss francs. As we have never had to make payments abroad before, we are unsure of the best method of doing this. We are wondering if we can send a cheque for the sterling equivalent, using our normal cheque book or if there are alternative ways? Your guidance would be much appreciated.

Yours faithfully

J. Smith
For Smith Bros

Draft a reply for approval by the foreign clerk.

Assignment Nine—The Money Supply and Monetary Policy
Activity. Defining the money supply, and explaining methods of control and techniques of monetary policy.

Situation. A recent newspaper article carried the headline, 'Money supply off target'. You are required to define and explain certain aspects of the money supply, together with techniques of monetary policy.

1. There are several definitions of the money supply but, in recent years, the United Kingdom Government has chosen to target M0. You are required to define M0 and to explain, in broad terms, what happens if the set target is overshot.

2. The borrowing requirement of the Government and other public sector bodies may have an influence on the growth of the money supply. List the various ways in which the Government may finance a budget deficit. Choosing one specific method, demonstrate whether it will affect the money supply—use diagrams or simple balance sheets to illustrate your answer.

3. There is a strong link between the money supply and the level of bank and economic activity. Explain the measures available to the authorities to enable them to implement monetary policy over the banking system.

Assignment Ten—Money Markets
Activity. A study of the money market interest rates and their use to a major retail bank.

Situation. As a student of banking, you are to write a report on the participants and features of both the primary and the secondary (or parallel) money markets, to consider the role of banks in these markets and to explain certain money market terms.

1. Describe the features and functions of the primary and secondary (or parallel) money markets.

2. From the *Financial Times* (or other 'quality' newspaper) ascertain the current interest rates in the primary and parallel money markets.

3. A major retail bank has just issued a certificate of deposit against a deposit of £500 000 repayable in two years' time. Prepare five extracts from the bank's balance sheet to show how, using the money markets, these funds can be put to work in five different ways. Indicate the likely return on each investment, using current rates.

4. Explain clearly the terms italicized in the following passage, which is an example of the sort of extract seen on a newspaper's money market page:

> Day-to-day credit was in short supply in the market yesterday, and the *authorities* gave assistance on a large scale. This comprised small purchases of *Treasury bills* and *local authority bills*, as well as large purchases of *bank bills*, from the *discount market*. The cost of *wholesale money* edged up in London following fears that there can be little scope for *base rate* cuts until the *money supply* figures improve. The key three-month *inter-bank rate* rose $\frac{3}{16}$ of 1 per cent.

Assignment Eleven—Bank Services
Activity. Obtaining leaflets and other information on bank services.

Situation. As a student of banking you are asked to prepare a folder of the main bank services offered to personal and business customers.

1. Obtain a range of leaflets from banks covering the main services offered to customers (to include services offered through banks' subsidiary companies).

2. Prepare a summary of the main services available to:
    (i) personal customers;
    (ii) business customers.
Indicate any restrictions which apply to particular services.

3. Prepare an advertising leaflet, suitable for issue by a major retail bank, to promote their services to students. You may make assumptions as necessary, but the leaflet should include details of:
    (i) type(s) of account offered;
    (ii) account charges (if any);
    (iii) loan/overdraft facilities;
    (iv) free/promotional offers;
    (v) other benefits and assistance.

Assignment Twelve—Bills of Exchange and Cheques
Activity. Explaining rights and obligations of parties to bills of exchange and cheques.

Situation. As a member of the staff of a bank, you are required to give advice under a number of different circumstances.

1. A customer, aged seventeen, uses his cheque card to support payment by cheque of the purchase of beer and wine for a party. As he has insufficient funds in his account to meet the cheque, what is the paying bank's position?

2. A crossed cheque was endorsed by the payee who then lost it. The finder endorsed it in favour of your customer who paid it into the bank. Your customer is now being sued by the true owner of the cheque. In course of conversation it transpires that your customer cashed the cheque for the finder, and took it in good faith, being unaware of any doubt affecting his title to it. Advise him of the legal position. Explain also if it would have made any difference in the same circumstances if the cheque had been crossed 'not negotiable'.

3. A customer wishes to pay in for the credit of his account a cheque crossed 'account payee' and drawn by a well-known insurance company for £1 000 in favour of Mrs Jane Symonds. Your customer explains that the payee is an elderly relative, who does not have a bank account of her own. Are there any risks involved if the bank collects this cheque?

4. Consider the legal implications for your bank in each of the following situations:
    (i) It has inadvertently paid a stopped cheque.
    (ii) It has paid a crossed cheque on which the payee's endorsement has been forged.
    (iii) It has paid a cheque on which the drawer's signature has been forged.
    (iv) A cashier, without asking for proof of identity, encashes an open cheque drawn by a customer of your bank for £10 payable to, and endorsed by, John Smith. It transpires that the cheque was stolen and that the thief had forged the payee's endorsement.
    (v) David Williams, managing director of David Williams Ltd, pays in for the credit of his personal account with you, a cheque for £1 000 payable to David Williams Ltd.

5. Your customer, Rowcester Machinery Co, is importing a machine from America and the suppliers require a bill of exchange to be accepted. Explain the various parties to the bill and their rights and obligations.

Assignment Thirteen—Personal Lending
Activity. Analysis of a personal lending proposition.

Situation. You are the manager's clerk at a medium-sized bank branch. The manager asks you to conduct a loan interview with Miss Georgina Smith who has made an appointment for later today. The diary entry reads '2.30 Miss G. Smith requires loan of £2 000.'

Before the interview you obtain the following background information about Miss Smith:

She is 29 years of age and has been a good customer of the bank for eleven years. She is an accounts clerk with the local council and has worked there since leaving school. Her salary is credited direct to her current account by her employer: recent salary credits to the account have been between £600 and £650 per month. Her present financial position at the bank is £610 credit in her current account (salary recently received) and £800 credit in her deposit account.

1. State any other information you would seek prior to the interview. Set out the basic questions you would ask during the interview.

During the interview you gain the following additional information:

She lives with her widowed mother in a house which, since the death of her father four years ago, is owned jointly by herself and her mother: there is no mortgage. She has £850 in a building society share account. Her monthly expenditure is:

Housekeeping	£150
Motoring	£80
Clothes	£50
Heat, light, rates and other bills	£130
Insurance	£55
Holidays and savings	£75

The proposed loan of £2 000 is to enable her to buy a more modern car at a cost of £5 500. Her present car has a trade-in value of £2 250 and she is prepared to find the balance from her own money.

2. Assume that you have discussed the proposition and concluded the interview. Prepare a report for the manager giving your recommendations for either granting or declining the loan application. In your report you should include the way in which the loan should be offered (if at all) and the method and costs of repayment.

Assignment Fourteen—Securities for Bank Advances
Activity. Examining the forms of property ownership and the types of security commonly accepted by banks.

Situation. As part of your career development, the manager of the branch at which you work shows you an interview note for one of your customers, Titanic Building Services Ltd. It has been recorded that Fred Titanic, the managing director, called to request a £10 000 overdraft facility to cover the company's working capital requirements. The facility is requested for a period of six months. Mr Titanic offers one of two security packages:

(i) a legal mortgage over the company's freehold factory premises valued at £100 000, together with a life policy taken out by the company on the life of Mr Titanic; or

(ii) a guarantee from Mr Titanic in the sum of £10 000 supported by stocks and shares in his name with a current market value of £16 000.

1. The manager asks you what points should be considered when evaluating any lending proposition.

2. The manager notes that both offers of security are acceptable. However, he seeks your view on which one might be preferable. Give reasons for your views.

3. Distinguish between:
   (i) freehold and leasehold;
   (ii) registered and unregistered land;
   (iii) mortgage and assignment;
   (iv) hypothecation and pledge.

Assignment Fifteen—Office Supplies (Rowcester) Ltd

Activity. Analysis of a company lending proposition.

Situation. You are the manager's clerk at a medium-sized bank branch and, using the information given, are required to present your decision to the manager.

Office Supplies (Rowcester) Ltd are a local company retailing office supplies and equipment. They propose to expand their business by operating a mail-order warehouse. This will take pressure off their shops which already have an annual turnover of £175 000 from orders received through the post although the facility is not promoted at all.

Balance sheet as at 31 December 19–1

	£		£
Fixed assets		*Issued share capital*	
Freehold premises at cost	250 000	100 000 £1 ordinary shares	100 000
Fixtures and fittings (net)	70 000		
Motor vehicles (net)	30 000		
	———	*Reserves*	
	350 000	Profit and loss account	160 000
			———
			260 000
Current assets		*Long-term liabilities*	
Stock	250 000	10% debentures	150 000
Debtors	50 000		———
			410 000
		Current liabilities	
		Creditors	140 000
		Bank	50 000
		Corporation tax	50 000
	———		———
	650 000		650 000
	═══		═══

Note: the debentures are secured on the freehold premises.

Other relevant figures from the trading and profit and loss accounts are:

Sales	£1 540 000
Gross profit	£430 000
Net profit before tax	£135 000

The managing director has supplied the latest figures for:

Stock	£210 000
Debtors	£40 000
Creditors	£110 000
Bank overdraft	£12 000

The company wishes to rent a warehouse for its new operation on the outskirts of town. Rent will be £12 500 p.a. and the property is ideal for the purpose. The company seeks an overdraft limit of £250 000 to enable it to equip and stock the warehouse.

From the branch records you note that the company has banked with you for a number of years and the current overdraft limit is £50 000. The account has been conducted most satisfactorily in the past.

1. Analyse the information given in the accounts, drawing attention to good or bad aspects as appropriate.

2. Indicate your view of the lending. What factors would influence the rate of interest to be charged, what security would you want, and what further information would you require?

Assignment Sixteen—In-tray Exercise

Activity. Dealing with a number of problems that might arise on a day-to-day basis in a busy town centre branch.

Situation. You are employed by National Barllands Bank, a major United Kingdom retail bank. The local branch where you now work has a staff of eighteen and you have recently been transferred there as a junior securities clerk. By this stage in your banking career you are making good progress with your examinations. At work you have been on a number of specialist bank training courses and, at one time or another, have done all the main clerical jobs in the branch. You are now moving on to securities and foreign work and are sometimes required to assist the branch accountant by preparing replies to correspondence and general enquiries—either at the enquiry desk or on the telephone. From time to time, in order to help you with your career development, the branch accountant asks you to conduct smaller-lending interviews.

Today there are several letters and other enquiries for you to deal with in the in-tray.

1. You are asked to see Miss Sanderson at the enquiry counter. You ascertain that she has called in in response to a letter written by you regarding her recurring overdrafts over several months.

From discussions with Miss Sanderson it transpires that she had to have repairs carried out to her house about six months ago at a cost of £500. Apart from this, the last few months have been difficult for her, with bills for day-to-day living, which always all seem to arrive at the same time.

Suggest ways in which the services of the bank can be of assistance to Miss Sanderson with her financial problems. What are the main points which you would bring to this customer's attention?

2. Draft a reply to the following letter:

> Acme Manufacturing Co Ltd
> Unit 27, Industrial Estate
> Yourtown
>
> The Manager
> National Barllands Bank
> High Street
> Yourtown
>
> Dear Sir
>
> We have just received an order for our products from Taiwan. As this is our first export order, there are several points on which we would like to seek your advice. In particular, we need guidance on the following:
>
> (i) The buyer wishes to pay in United States dollars, but the news is always mentioning fluctuations in the pound against the dollar.

(ii) The buyer talks of accepting a bill of exchange and mentions that we should send this, together with the documents, through the bank on a 'collection' basis. Could you please explain how this works, including an explanation of our liability on the bill of exchange, and whether there are any safer methods of collecting our money?

(iii) Is there any way in which we can insure against the possible default of the buyer and are there any other risks we should be insured against?

(iv) Are there any other services of the bank available to us in these circumstances?

Many thanks for your assistance.

Yours faithfully

J. Smith
Managing Director

3. In the lunch-break you meet a friend, who works for a firm of accountants. In the course of conversation your friend makes the following criticisms of banks:
  (i) they only lend to those who have a lot of money already;
  (ii) they are never open at times when most people can visit them;
  (iii) they always make large profits, particularly when the economy of the country is doing badly.
Give your answers, suggesting reasons for the criticisms and whether the banks can do anything, or have done something about each one.

4. You return from lunch to allow the chief securities clerk to take her lunch-break. A few minutes later a customer, Mr Wilson, rings the bell of the securities enquiry desk. He places a locked box on the desk and tells you that he wishes to place it in safe custody. He asks you to explain the following points:
  (i) the legal position between the bank and himself in respect of safe-custody items;
  (ii) he presumes that there is no need for him to insure the contents as it will be covered by the bank's general insurance;
  (iii) he asks what would be the legal position if the bank handed out his box to another customer in error;
  (iv) he says that there are some share certificates in his name included in the box: as he is currently overdrawn, he wonders if the bank has the right to open the box and take the certificates as security for the debt. If this is the case he says that he might as well leave the certificates in open safe-custody to save the bank the trouble of opening the box.
Write your answer to each point.

5. The bank manager shows you the latest balance sheet of AR Consultants Ltd, a firm of interior design consultants:

	£		£
Fixtures and fittings	10 500	Capital	24 000
Stock	52 500		
Debtors	37 500	Trade creditors	80 250
Cash	250		
Profit and loss account	5 000	Bank	1 500
	105 750		105 750

The company is run by Richard Andrews and Tony Russell who hold all the shares. They wish to open a branch of their company in a nearby town and ask the bank to provide overdraft facilities of £20 000 for fitting out the rented premises and the purchase of additional stock.

Comment on what you deduce from these figures and whether you think the bank would lend the sum required.

Further Reading

British Banking and other Financial Institutions. Central Office of Information (London, 1987).

Committee of London Clearing Banks: *The London Clearing Banks: Evidence to the* [Wilson] *Committee to Review the Functioning of Financial Institutions*. Longman (Harlow, 1978).

Crockett, A.: *Money: Theory, Policy and Institutions*. Van Nostrand Reinhold (Sunbury-on-Thames, 2nd edn. 1979).

Dyer, L. S.: *A Practical Approach to Bank Lending*. The Chartered Institute of Bankers (London, 3rd edn. 1987).

Hanson, D. G.: *Service Banking: The All-purpose Bank*. The Chartered Institute of Bankers (London, 3rd edn. 1987).

Hutchinson, H. H. and Dyer, L. S.: *Interpretation of Balance Sheets*. The Chartered Institute of Bankers (London, 6th edn. 1987).

McRae, H. and Cairncross, F.: *Capital City: London as a Financial Centre*. Methuen (London, 2nd edn. 1984).

National Consumer Council: *Banking Services and the Consumer*. Methuen (London, 1983).

Reeday, T. G.: *Law Relating to Banking*. Butterworths (London, 5th edn. 1985).

Shaw, E. R.: *The London Money Market*. Heinemann (London, 3rd edn. 1984).

Watson, A. J. W.: *Finance of International Trade*. The Chartered Institute of Bankers (London, 4th edn. 1988).

Weisweiller, R.: *Introduction to Foreign Exchange*. Woodhead-Faulkner (Cambridge, 2nd edn. 1984).

Winfield, R. G. and Curry, S. J.: *Success in Investment*. John Murray (London, 3rd edn. 1987).

Articles of interest to the student are regularly published in the *Bank of England Quarterly Bulletin, Banking World, The Economist* and in bank reviews and leading newspapers.

Answers to Questions

Unit 13

	Debentures	Cumulative preference	Non-cumulative preference	Ordinary
5. Year 1	£7 000	£4 000	£5 000	£10 000
Year 2	£7 000	£2 000	nil	nil
Year 3	£7 000	£6 000	£5 000	nil
Year 4	£7 000	£4 000	£5 000	£19 000

Unit 22

1. This seems to be a highly successful and profitable business. As overdraft facilities have been granted in the past, it is likely that the bank has copies of earlier sets of accounts so that comparisons may be made.

(a) **Shareholders' Stake.** The balance of the profit and loss account tells us that profits are being retained in the business. The shareholders' stake is £160 000 out of total assets of £185 000; the shareholders are thus financing 86 per cent of the total assets—a very healthy position from the point of view of the lending bank. The return on ordinary shareholders' funds is:

$$\frac{£20\,000}{£160\,000 \text{ (ordinary shares + profit and loss a/c)}} \times \frac{100}{1} = 12.5 \text{ per cent}$$

This seems generally perfectly satisfactory and could be compared with the return calculated from previous sets of accounts.

(b) **Long-term Loans.** These are from directors and, as liabilities are low in comparison with assets, it hardly seems appropriate to ask for Letters of Postponement.

(c) **Working Capital.** The working capital is £14 000 (£29 000–£15 000) and, as a ratio, is 1.93:1 which seems satisfactory. If the overdraft facility of £10 000 was granted the total of current liabilities would increase but, equally, there would be an increase in stocks to compensate although £3 000 of the advance would be spent on extensions to one shop and this will be reflected in an increase in the fixed assets. Overall there would be a reduction in the current ratio but it would not be too severe.

(d) **Liquidity.** The liquid capital (working capital less stocks), is *minus* £9 000 or (£9 000); as a ratio, this is 0.4:1. This is not such a good position and could indicate that the company would have difficulty in paying its way if a major creditor demanded repayment. The corporation tax is payable in one lump sum, and, depending on the date of the formation of the company, this will be due either at the end of September or at the end of December in 19–0. A low current ratio is not unusual for the retail trade where most sales are made on a cash basis (confirmed by the low figure for debtors) and with sales of £143 000 per year or £2 750 each week it would not take long to raise the money through sales to pay creditors.

(e) **Trading Figures.** The credit period being taken by the company is just over four weeks [(£8 000 ÷ £100 000) × 52]. This seems quite a short period of time and indicates that the business pays its bills promptly.

Without knowing the amount of credit sales made by the company during the year the period of credit being allowed to debtors cannot be calculated.

To calculate the stock turnover requires the figure for cost of goods sold, which may be found by deducting the gross profit from sales; this gives £97 000. The closing stock is £23 000 and the opening stock for the year is £20 000 (found by constructing a trading account). Thus the average stock is £21 500 and therefore the stock turnover is approximately 4.5 times per year, which means that the stock remains in the shops for just over eleven weeks before being sold and replaced. For the type of business that Johnson Brothers Ltd run, this seems to be perfectly satisfactory.

The gross profit percentage is 32 per cent which seems satisfactory for the trade. The net profit percentage is 14 per cent.

The figures calculated in this section can be compared with those for previous years and any major changes could be taken up with the directors.

(f) **Other Items.** Inevitably, before making the decision about granting the facilities, the manager will consider the previous conduct of the account (we are told that previous overdrafts have been satisfactorily cleared) and the ability of the directors—from the information given, they seem to be hard-working and prepared to plough profits back into the business.

A further point is the consideration of security (if required) by the bank: the shop premises appear to provide an ideal form of security.

This would seem to be a good lending proposition and the facilities should be granted.

2. The company so far has been unprofitable in both years of trading. There is a net loss of £500 in the second year and, as the balance of the profit and loss account of £1 000 is shown as a debit balance, there must also have been a net loss of £500 in year 1. (Contrast the position of the profit and loss account on this balance sheet with that of Johnson Brothers Ltd—the difference between losses in past years and profits, respectively.)

(a) **Shareholders' Stake.** Although there is the issued share capital of £1 000, this is cancelled out by the debit balance on the profit and loss account. Therefore the shareholders' stake is nil. As the company has made a loss for the year there is no return on capital employed.

(b) **Long-term Loans.** The assets of the business are partly financed by loans from directors. If any lending is to be considered Letters of Postponement would be essential.

(c) **Working Capital.** There is a deficit of working capital of £250 and the current ratio is 0.92:1—hardly a satisfactory position. Granting the proposed overdraft would make the matter even worse.

(d) **Liquidity.** If there is a lack of working capital, there is an even greater lack of liquid capital—a deficit of £1 850—and a liquid ratio of 0.45. The ratio might not be too bad if there was a substantial element of cash sales but, in selling to shops and boutiques, the company has to allow credit and there will be a time lag between making the sale and receiving the cash.

(e) **Trading Figures.** The credit period being taken by the company is nearly twenty weeks—little wonder that the bank had to pay the account overdrawn without facilities to meet pressing creditors.

Debtors, on the other hand, pay their accounts in just under eight weeks; this seems to be a satisfactory figure.

As this is a manufacturing business stock turnover is difficult to calculate on the information given; in order to reach a figure you would need to know the details of the costs of manufacture, such as the wages paid to outworkers.

The gross profit percentage is 10 per cent and there is a net loss of 5 per cent of sales. The percentage gross profit figure is rather low and a suggestion might be made that the selling prices could be increased without jeopardizing sales.

(f) **Other Items.** If the bank lent the money as proposed, the company's balance sheet would be in an even worse state than it is now. There would also be the additional costs of bank interest which, depending on interest rates and the amount the facility is used, would probably amount to approximately £1 000 per year. There is no source of repayment apart from possible future trading profits; there is no security, apart from the possibility of taking directors' personal guarantees.

This is probably the type of business that could be made profitable if it operates in a small way and puts up its selling prices, but to consider expanding by renting a factory would seem to be foolhardy. The request should be turned down and steps taken to get the bank account into credit as soon as possible.

3.   The set of accounts needs careful interpretation because they have been prepared by the customer himself and are, presumably, unaudited. The following points should be queried:

(i) As he employs no one, the wages at £9 000 for a half-year must be Bill's own drawings and seem somewhat excessive!

(ii) The closing stock figure is high in terms of both money and number of cranes, especially as this is the stock at 31 December (a toy manufacturer's stock would be at its lowest just after Christmas).

(iii) The method of valuing the stock should be ascertained.

(iv) The debtor can, presumably, be written off.

(v) The terms of the loan from his father need to be known: is the bank going to grant an overdraft limit of £3 000 so that his father can be repaid?

(a) **Shareholder's Stake.** If the stock valuation is correct, total assets are £9 900 (ignoring the debtor—see (iv) above) and Bill's stake in this is 41 per cent which is rather on the low side.

The return on the owner's funds is:

$$\frac{£1\,650}{£4\,050} \times \frac{100}{1} = 40.7 \text{ per cent}$$

The return on capital employed is:

$$\frac{£1\,650 + £120}{£4\,050 + £3\,000 \text{ (loan)}} \times \frac{100}{1} = 25.1 \text{ per cent}$$

Both of these seem to be very healthy figures.

(*b*) **Long-term Loans.** As mentioned in (v), the terms of the loan need to be known.

(*c*) **Working Capital.** Ignoring the debtor and treating the loan as a long-term one, the working capital is £6 750 which seems satisfactory. However, all but £150 of the current assets is stocks—see 'liquidity'. The current ratio is 3.14:1.

(*d*) **Liquidity.** Liquid capital is (£3 000) and, as a ratio, is 0.05. This is disastrous and probably one reason why he needs an overdraft—the creditors are pressing for payment.

(*e*) **Trading Figures.** The accounts show that the credit being taken by Bill's business is no less than 22 weeks! No wonder he needs an overdraft. In fact, things may not be as bad as they seem because of the seasonal nature of his business: the majority of purchases on credit may have been made in the month or two leading up to Christmas which should have been a busy period for him.

Stockturn is very low at 0.86 times (£4 200 ÷ £4 875) for the six months, even allowing a 'nil' figure for opening stock and thus calculating average stock at £4 875. This indicates that Bill has concentrated too much on production and not enough on selling the toys.

The gross and net profit percentages are 40 per cent and 23.5 per cent respectively. These seem to indicate that he has a good product provided he can sell the cranes. The danger with these two figures on this set of accounts, however, is that they are reliant on the closing stock value. If this has been calculated incorrectly these percentages could be totally misleading. (Try re-working them with the stock valued at £7 500!)

(*f*) **Other Items.** The whole credibility of this set of unaudited accounts relies on the stock figure. Enquiries must be made to find out more about the method of valuation and the reason why there should be so much stock left after Christmas: the stock could be valued at cost and Bill could have concentrated too much on production. It might well be that he has a good marketable product and only needs some basic financial guidance to put him on the road to good profits. His main task is to concentrate on selling for the next few months, even though the period just after Christmas is not the best time for a toy manufacturer. He could consider taking on a partner to take over the selling side of the business and to inject some extra capital. Bank assistance could be made available provided it is not used to repay the loan from his father and provided Bill returns some of his wages for the last half-year and reduces substantially the amount he pays himself in the next half-year. Security is non-existent: the only possibility, unless he has other assets, is a guarantee from his father.

4. This question is different from the preceding ones, in that the company operates to fixed standards and, if these standards continue to apply, it is possible to anticipate the future profitability of the business. Thus we are told that the creditor (manufacturer) is paid one month after purchase and that the shops are allowed two months' credit. The Inbetween Co makes a gross profit of 20p per pack and once it has paid the monthly operating costs of £3 000, the rest is net profit. Therefore, on the figures given, it will take sales of 15 000 packs to cover operating costs and at present sales levels there will be a profit of £1 000 per month. It is quite likely that an increase in sales will have little or no effect on the operating costs: there may be extra transport costs or salesman's commissions but there is no direct comparison between sales and operating costs. In such circumstances it is a temptation to expand the business as much as possible.

At present the gross profit margin is 20 per cent and the net profit margin is 5 per cent. With an increase in sales the net profit margin will increase because the operating costs are, in the short term, fixed. There is working capital of £50 000 with a current ratio of 4.125:1; liquid capital is £34 000 (liquid ratio 3.125:1): these are very good figures. The shareholder's stake is over 75 per cent of total assets—again very good.

Thus far, the company looks an excellent lending proposition, although there is no obvious security to take (if it is even necessary). Presumably the company rents offices and a warehouse and the costs of these are included in the operating costs. We, as bankers, are in a position to check the future financial position of the company because we have the facts and figures available (we shall have to take the managing director's word for the increased sales figures). We need to prepare a cash budget for the company until, say, the end of December. This will appear as follows:

	April	May	June	July	Aug	Sept	Oct	Nov	Dec
	£	£	£	£	£	£	£	£	£
Cash receipts									
From debtors	20 000	20 000	20 000	20 000	25 000	30 000	35 000	40 000	45 000
	20 000	20 000	20 000	20 000	25 000	30 000	35 000	40 000	45 000
Cash payments									
To creditor (manufacturer)	16 000	16 000	20 000	24 000	28 000	32 000	36 000	40 000	44 000
Operating expenses	3 000	3 000	3 000	3 000	3 000	3 000	3 000	3 000	3 000
	19 000	19 000	23 000	27 000	31 000	35 000	39 000	43 000	47 000
Opening bank balance	10 000	11 000	12 000	9 000	2 000	(4 000)	(9 000)	(13 000)	(16 000)
Add cash receipts	20 000	20 000	20 000	20 000	25 000	30 000	35 000	40 000	45 000
Deduct cash payments	19 000	19 000	23 000	27 000	31 000	35 000	39 000	43 000	47 000
Closing bank balance	11 000	12 000	9 000	2 000	(4 000)	(9 000)	(13 000)	(16 000)	(18 000)

Pity the manager who granted the company an overdraft limit of £5 000 until the end of October! He might not have started to get worried until the end of September, but by the beginning of January he would have some explaining to do to head office. The balance sheet of the company as at 31 December is as follows:

	£			£
		Capital		50 000
		+ Net profit (for		
		the nine months)		37 000
Current assets		*Current liabilities*		
Stock	48 000	Creditors	48 000	
Debtors	105 000	Bank	18 000	
				66 000
	153 000			153 000

The company has vastly improved its profits: £37 000 for nine months instead of £5 000–£10 000 per year. Working capital is now £87 000 with a current ratio of 2.3:1 and liquid capital is £39 000 with a liquid ratio of 1.59:1. Both of these figures are still perfectly satisfactory. Credit allowed and credit taken remain at two months and one month respectively. The shareholder's stake in the business is reduced to 57 per cent but this is still quite a good figure. So what has happened? The company has *over-traded*—it has tried to expand too quickly with insufficient capital. It is 'caught' between its credit-taken and credit-allowed terms neither of which, presumably, it can do anything about because of the size of its supplier and the need to remain competitive with other wholesalers. The way out of the problem for the bank manager is to insist that the present high rate of expansion is levelled off (as surely it must anyway with this type of product). If this happens the backlog of debtors will soon put cash into the bank account. An alternative would be for the company to seek extra capital or a long-term loan.

The answer is, of course, to check the financial data given by the company and anticipate what the overdraft will be. If you wished to lend to this company it would need a maximum overdraft of £19 000 in January and, after this, even if the expansion continued, the end-of-month overdraft would start to fall and the balance would be in credit by the end of July in the following year.

Answers to Multiple-choice Questions

Question number:	1	2	3	4	5	6	7	8	9	10
Set number 1:	B	C	C	C	A	B	D	D	A	C
2:	B	A	D	D	B	A	B	B	C	A
3:	C	A	B	A	A	D	D	B	A	B
4:	A	C	D	B	D	B	A	B	C	A
5:	D	A	B	C	C	A	B	C	C	B
6:	D	B	C	D	A	C	B	D	A	B
7:	A	A	C	B	B	D	D	D	A	B
8:	C	A	C	C	C	A	D	B	C	B
9:	B	C	B	A	B	C	C	C	B	D
10:	D	D	C	C	A	D	A	B	A	C
11:	C	C	D	A	B	A	C	A	C	B
12:	A	C	C	B	C	B	C	C	B	A

Index